LESSONS FROM THE LEGENDS

BASKETBALL OFFENSE SOURCEBOOK

FEATURING
COACHING INSIGHTS
FROM
34
NAISMITH
HALL OF FAME COACHES

JERRY KRAUSE AND RALPH PIM

TRIUMPH
BOOKS
CHICAGO

The *Naismith Lessons from the Legends* series is dedicated to:

The Zag players, coaches, and fans, who have made
this part of my basketball life so very special.

—JERRY KRAUSE

My parents, Lorin and Alice Pim.
Thank you for instilling in me the
principles that I try to live by every day.

My wife, Linda. You have brought peace and
happiness into my life. I love you with all my heart.

—RALPH PIM

Coaches Choice
P.O. Box 1828
Monterey, CA 93942
www.coacheschoice.com

Library of Congress Control Number: 2004104663

Book Design:	Diana Michelotti, Artistic Enterprises, Cary, North Carolina
Diagrams and Production:	Artistic Enterprises, Cary, North Carolina
Cover Design:	Preston Pisellini

All logos contained herein are the trademarks and copyrights of the school or organization represented.

Cover photo of Judy Conradt: Elsa/Getty Images. Cover photo of Larry Brown: Tom Pidgeon/Getty Images. Cover photo of Pete Newell: Pete Newell Challenge. Cover photo of John Wooden: Ken Levine/Getty Images. Photos of coaches Barry, Brown, Case, Condradt, Daly, Gardner, Hannum, Hickey, Hinkle, Holman, Keaney, Kundla, Lambert, McGuire, McLendon, Meanwell, Moore, Naismith, Newell, Sharman, Shelton, Taylor, Wilkens, and Yow, courtesy of the Naismith Memorial Basketball Hall of Fame. All other photographs provided by the Sports Information Departments of the College or University of the particular coach in the image.

This book is available in quantity at special discounts for your group or organization. For further information, contact:

Triumph Books
542 S. Dearborn St.
Suite 750
Chicago, IL 60605

Printed in U.S.A.
ISBN-13: 978-1-57243-718-0
ISBN-10: 1-57243-718-9

TABLE OF CONTENTS

FOREWORD

In my career in and around the game of basketball, I have been truly fortunate to have spent time with and learned from some of the true giants of the game. Mike Krzyzewski, Bob Knight, and Pete Newell are not only among the finest coaches in the game, but are also among its greatest teachers and guardians. I have witnessed their respect and admiration for the coaches who were the innovators and strategists of their day. To be a truly great teacher of the game, one must have an understanding of its evolutio, and an appreciation for its history and those who advanced it to where it is today. To best grasp where basketball is and should be going, it is vital to understand where it has been, and how it got to this point.

The future of the game lies with its teachers, the bona fide guardians of the game's history and its future. Two fine basketball minds and outstanding coaches, Jerry Krause and Ralph Pim, have provided us with a wonderful and comprehensive reference book full of lessons from these Hall of Fame coaches, who are distinguished teachers. This book should serve as a useful guide and fascinating retrospective on the thoughts and ideas of the game's finest minds. Jerry and Ralph have done the game a fine service with this work; basketball coaches and fans alike will enjoy and benefit from the *Legends* series.

—Jay Bilas
ESPN College Basketball Analyst

DR. JAMES NAISMITH
INVENTOR OF BASKETBALL

PREFACE

The information contained in this book is the authors' best attempt to preserve the legacy of the game's greatest coaches. We spent over three years researching the material that is included in the first edition of the *Naismith Lessons from the Legends*. We utilized many resources, including the archives at the Naismith Basketball Hall of Fame in Springfield, Massachusetts. We studied technical books written by Hall of Fame coaches, as well as articles that were published in professional journals. We read newspaper accounts describing their coaching exploits. In addition, we interviewed Hall of Fame coaches, players, assistant coaches, family members, and school administrators in order to capture the essence of each coach's personal and professional legacy.

Every attempt was made to sort through all the material and present the most accurate description of each coach. We may not have succeeded in every case, but we are confidant that you will enjoy reading this one-of-a-kind book featuring the coaches who have made basketball the world's greatest game. We believe it truly is a close look at the "best from the best"—the best ideas about basketball and life from the best people in this area, the Naismith Basketball Hall of Fame inductees.

Now it is your turn to help the authors improve and "make the next game" better in our second edition. If you have additional information, articles/clinics (technical basketball or just human interest), stories, or pictures that could be included in this book, we encourage you to contact the authors so we can share it with our readers in future editions. Please send materials or contact the authors/publisher at:

The Basketball Legends Series
Attn: Krause/Pim
Coaches Choice Publishing
P.O. Box 1828
Monterey, CA 93942
1-888-229-5745
www.coacheschoice.com

ACKNOWLEDGMENTS

From start to finish, this book has been a team effort. Our deepest thanks go to:

Robin Jonathan Deutsch, director of New Media and Library Services at the Naismith Basketball Hall of Fame, for his tremendous support of our project and his assistance in making the Hall of Fame library materials available to us.

John L. Doleva, president and CEO, Michael W. Brooslin, curator, and Jim Mullins, operations manager, of the Naismith Hall of Fame for their warm hospitality on our many trips to Springfield, Massachusetts.

The following Naismith Basketball Hall of Famers who were kind enough to speak with us on selected subjects over the years: Leon Barmore, Larry Brown, John Bunn, Lou Carnesecca, Ben Carnevale, John Chaney, Clarence Gaines, Cliff Hagen, Marv Harshman, Bailey Howell, Bob Kurland, Earl Lloyd, Ed Macauley, Arad McCutchan, Ray Meyer, Ralph Miller, Pete Newell, C. M. Newton, Lute Olson, Arnie Risen, Bob Pettit, Adolph Rupp, Dolph Schayes, Bill Sharman, Dean Smith, Bob Wanzer, Stan Watts, John Wooden, Morgan Wootten, James Worthy, George Yardley, and Kay Yow.

Hank Raymonds, Les Robinson, Ellen Anderson, Tom Crean, and Jay Carter Biggs for providing valuable information that helped in our research.

Artistic Enterprises for their hard work and attention to detail creating the diagrams and laying out the book. Penny Rose, our patient administrative assistant and word processor.

Finally, sincere appreciation goes to Diana Michelotti of Artistic Enterprises and Jim Peterson of Coaches Choice for their belief in and vision for the *Legends Series*—to provide basketball fans and coaches with these valuable lessons about life and basketball.

DIAGRAM LEGEND

PLAYERS	① ② ③ 4 5
MOVE DIRECTION	——————→
MOVE to SCREEN	——————⊢
DRIBBLE	⌇⌇⌇⌇⌇⌇→
PASS DIRECTION	- - - - - - ▶
PASS SEQUENCE	**1st, 2nd, 3rd Pass**
COACH	**C**
DEFENDER POSITION	X_1
DEFENSIVE PLAYERS	X_1, X_2, X_3, X_4, X_5

To create consistency throughout the book, the diagrams illustrating the Lessons from the Legends by the Hall of Fame Coaches have been redrawn using the diagram legend above.

LEGACY OF
Harold "Andy" Anderson

- Pioneered the run-and-shoot, fast-break style of play in the Midwest.

- Was the first coach in basketball history to take two different universities to the NIT tournament.

- Established records for the most victories in a single season at Toledo and Bowling Green.

- Emphasized sportsmanship and fair play.

- Selected as one of the 50 greatest sports figures in the state of Ohio.

- Led Bowling Green to a second-place finish in the 1945 NIT tournament.

- Is the namesake of Anderson Arena at Bowling Green State University.

Harold "Andy" Anderson

"A good fast-breaking attack must be as well-organized as any set offense."
—Harold "Andy" Anderson

BIOGRAPHY

Born: September 11, 1902 in Akron, OH

Died: June 13, 1967

Inducted into Naismith Basketball Hall of Fame in 1985

Harold "Andy" Anderson coached at Toledo and Bowling Green and compiled a collegiate coaching record of 504-226. He was the first coach in basketball history to take two different colleges to the NIT. During his eight seasons at Toledo (1934-1942), Anderson led the Rockets to a 142-41 record and a third-place finish in the 1942 NIT. Anderson became basketball coach and athletic director at Bowling Green in 1942 and held those positions until 1963 and 1965, respectively. His Falcon teams ranked among the best in the nation during the 1940s and secured five NIT bids in six years (1944, 1945, 1946, 1948, 1949). Anderson led Bowling Green to a 362-185 record and directed the Falcons to six NIT and three NCAA tournaments. Anderson was selected as one of the 50 greatest sports figures in the state of Ohio. He was elected to the Helms Athletic Federation Hall of Fame in 1963. Anderson was the NABC president in 1962-63 and was instrumental in forming the East-West All-Star Game. The basketball arena at Bowling Green was renamed the Harold Anderson Memorial Arena.

Harold "Andy" Anderson...

Harold Anderson was born in Akron, Ohio in 1902. Even though many individuals thought he was too small to compete in athletics, Anderson excelled in football, basketball, and track at Central (OH) High School from 1917-1920. He made All-City in football and basketball, and set a state record in the 220-yard low hurdles. Central reached the finals of the State basketball tournament, and Anderson was named to the All-State team. Anderson attended Otterbein College (OH), where he won eleven athletic letters participating in football, basketball, baseball, and track. He was an All-Ohio Conference performer in both football and basketball. In addition to being a star running back in football, Anderson averaged 45 yards as a punter. Anderson also led the baseball team in hitting for three consecutive seasons. Anderson was president of the junior and senior classes and graduated in 1924 with a degree in French.

After graduation, Anderson turned down a professional baseball contract with the St. Louis Cardinals because of his less-than-perfect vision and his concern that he couldn't make it in the major leagues wearing glasses. Instead, he spent one year teaching in the Akron public school system and playing semi-pro football and basketball. The following year, Anderson received his first basketball coaching position at Wauseon (OH) High School, which he led to the state semi-finals and a 24-5 record. He coached at Toledo (OH) Waite High School from 1926 to1934, recorded three city championships, and compiled a record of 100-33. The University of Toledo was so impressed with Anderson's coaching ability that the Rockets hired him as their head coach in 1934. During his eight years at Toledo, Anderson brought the school from basketball obscurity to national prominence. During this period, his teams had a 142-41 record. His efforts with the Rockets climaxed with a third place finish in the 1942 NIT.

At Toledo, since no position existed on the university's faculty for Anderson, he taught in the public school system. In 1942, Bowling Green offered Anderson a position as a teacher, basketball coach, and athletic director.

Anderson continued his magic at Bowling Green, where he led the Falcons to six NIT tournaments and three NCAA tournaments. In 1945, Bowling Green finished second in the NIT to powerful DePaul University, which was led by future Hall of Famer George Mikan. His overall record at Bowling Green was 362-185. Anderson's fondest memory during his tenure at Bowling green occurred during his final season when the Falcons defeated Loyola of Illinois 92-75. This victory was called the greatest triumph in

Bowling Green basketball history. Loyola entered the game with a record of 21-0 and was ranked second in the nation. Howard Komives' 32 points and Nate Thurmond's 24 points and 12 rebounds propelled Bowling Green to the upset victory. Loyola rebounded from the loss and won the 1963 NCAA national championship. Anderson said, "I thought we had the best team in the country that year, and maybe we did." (Heeren, 1966). Unfortunately, Komives was slowed by a leg injury, and the Falcons were beaten in the regional finals of the NCAA tournament by Illinois.

Another landmark game occurred in 1946 when Bowling Green won the Chicago Stadium Round-Robin Tournament by defeating Oklahoma A&M in the finals. Oklahoma A&M, led by All-American Bob Kurland, went on to win the NCAA tournament that year. Anderson said, "We weren't given a chance to win that one, but our big boy (6-foot 11-inches Don Otten) did a great job, and we held Oklahoma A&M to one field goal in the first 14 minutes of the game." (Welty, 1964)

Anderson always thought of himself as an educator first, and a basketball coach second. He advocated sportsmanship and fair play, and his teams had a reputation for playing hard, clean basketball. In a game played in 1947, a player from Xavier faked a Bowling Green defender out of position and drove to the basket. Without any chance to stop the score, another Bowling Green player threw a block into the Xavier player and sent him flying into the basketball uprights. Almost before the official had called the foul, Anderson yanked his player from the game and censured him quite severely when he reached the bench. The player, who was one of the leading players on the team, sat out the rest of the first half before returning to play.

Anderson's ultimate mission was to prepare his players for life. He constantly reminded them that they were in college for an education, and basketball was merely a means by which this objective would be obtained. Of Anderson's 229 letter winners, 222 received their college degree.

The young men that played for Anderson were referred to as "Andy's boys." He helped them during their college years and remained in contact with them after graduation.

All-American Charlie Share definitely agreed that "Andy" touched many people's lives, including his own. Share arrived on the Bowling Green campus in 1946 as an awkward 6-foot 11-inch youngster who had played just one year of high school basketball. Andy patiently worked and developed Share into one of the best big men in the country who later played ten seasons in the NBA. Share recalled, "Andy did so much for me, not only as a basketball player but as a person. He knew my poor background, and he did so much to straighten me out."

Crystal Ellis, one of the first African-Americans on the Bowling Green campus, credits "Andy" for helping him endure difficult times. Ellis had a part-time job sweeping the floor at a local campus hangout, and one day the racial taunts became too much for him. He packed his bags and took a bus home. Later that day, Ellis was enjoying the comforts of home and saying that he would never return to Bowling Green. Suddenly, there was a knock on the back door, and it was "Andy." Crystal and his family invited Anderson in, and soon they were sitting around the table eating homemade pie. They talked for a while, and then Crystal said he was ready to go back to Bowling Green and continue his education and basketball career. The mutual respect and trust between Anderson and the Ellis family helped Crystal earn a college degree and prepared him for a distinguished career as an educator and superintendent of schools in Toledo (OH).

Howard Komives was a roughneck high-school player from the slums of Toledo when Anderson recruited him. "Howie could have been the biggest juvenile delinquent in Toledo," recalled Anderson. "But instead of going out on the prowl, he played basketball three hours a day." Komives was a natural hard worker on the basketball court, but it took some prodding by Anderson to get him to concentrate on his academics. Komives, who earned All-American honors and later starred in the NBA with the New York Knicks, told Anderson, "I could never have gotten a college education without your help." (Heeren, 1966)

The most prominent of Anderson's players at Bowling Green was All-American center Nate Thurmond. The versatile Thurmond went on to a 14-year NBA career and was selected as one of the NBA's "All-Time Top 50 Players." Thurmond broke the NBA record for the most rebounds in a quarter with 18 and recorded the first quadruple-double in NBA history (22 points, 14 rebounds, 13 assists, and 12 blocked shots). Anderson and Thurmond were inducted into the Naismith Basketball Hall of Fame in the same year. "Coach Anderson was one of the big reasons I went to Bowling Green," Thurmond said. "Coach Anderson and his wife, Colinne, were just good people. She used to help us with our studies, and we got to know the family very well. It was like leaving one family and coming to another family." Ellen Anderson, the youngest daughter of "Andy," fondly remembers Thurmond sitting in their living room while her mother tutored him in a Shakespeare class.

Colinne Anderson was the chief tutor, adviser, and sometimes cook and landlady for her husband's team. One of Anderson's greatest stars, Chuck Chuckovits, who later married Colinne's sister, recalled his association: "She tutored me through the University of Toledo. I was satisfied just getting by, but that wasn't enough for her. She wouldn't let me go until I had the work down cold, even if it meant working until one in the morning. She was a tremendous influence in making me finally appreciate education and seeing that I went on and received a degree."

After Chuckovits scored 41 points and broke the national collegiate scoring record, the modest Anderson told reporters, "He'll make a great coach out of me yet." Anderson always gave credit for the success of his teams to the players. He believed the key to winning was having talented players who were fundamentally sound.

Anderson set a pair of records that have remained intact for more than 50 years. He holds the record for most victories in a single season at both Toledo and Bowling Green. "Andy" believed desire and determination were prerequisites for a successful team. "A player must love the game and have a desire to play that is so strong that he is willing to spend hours practicing in order to perfect his skills," stated Anderson. "He must also have a strong desire to win."

One of Anderson's coaching rivals was Hall of Famer Ed Diddle from Western Kentucky. Over the years, Bowling Green and Western Kentucky engaged in several highly contested battles, and during one of the games, Diddle gave Anderson one of his famous red towels. Diddle had the highest respect for Anderson, both as a coach and as a friend. The Commonwealth of Kentucky named Anderson a Kentucky Colonel in 1962. Diddle said, "During the many years of my coaching career, my teams played against many outstanding coaches. At the very top of distinguished coaches and personalities, I place Harold Anderson. He was not only one of the most outstanding students and leaders of the game of basketball—he was a gentleman and a friend." (Diddle, 1967)

SOURCE

Anderson, Ellen, Ph.D., LPCC. Interview with Ralph Pim, March 5, 2003.

Anderson, Harold. Vertical Files, Archives. Naismith Memorial Basketball Hall of Fame Library. Springfield, MA.

Diddle, E.A. (1967, December 1). Letter to Mrs. Harold Anderson.

Heeren, Dave. (1966, February). Anderson's Story No Movie Plot. *Ft. Lauderdale News.*

Welty, Gene. (1964, December 17). BG Won't Be The Same Without Andy Anderson. *BG Sentinel-Tribune.*

LESSONS FROM THIS LEGEND...

FIVE SCORING OPTIONS IN OUR TEAM OFFENSE

By Harold "Andy" Anderson

Authors' Note: Harold Anderson brought basketball into national prominence at both the University of Toledo and Bowling Green University with his fast-break style of play. He was one of the pioneers of the run-and-shoot, fast-break attack. Anderson believed that basketball should be an interesting, crowd-pleasing game, and he helped make basketball a major sports spectacle in the post World War II era. He developed his fast-break philosophy, using a five-step system that allowed his players to exploit an opponent's weakness on every possession.

The unprecedented growth of basketball is due to the game's increase in speed, action, and scoring. My offensive philosophy is based on a five-step theory. I believe that team offense is predicated on a series of steps, one following the other in a logical sequence. We explore these steps every time we gain possession of the ball. If one step is unavailable, we move on to the next step.

FIVE SCORING OPTIONS

The five steps, or options, in our offense at Bowling Green include:

1. Long pass
2. Two-man triangle or return pass
3. Fast break
4. Set offense
5. Continuity offense

LONG PASS

When a defensive player obtains possession of the ball, his first thought is to look for an open teammate near the basket. If the player is open, we pass the ball ahead. While this scenario will usually occur on interceptions in the backcourt, occasionally it will be available after a defensive rebound. (See **Diagram 1.0**)

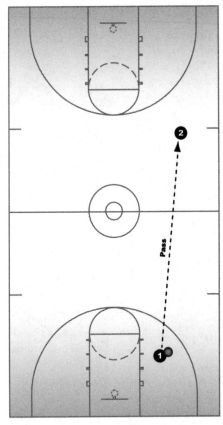

Anderson 1.0

TWO-MAN TRIANGLE OR RETURN PASS

This step occurs most often on interceptions or steals near mid-court. The interceptor may not be open for a drive into the basket but can pass to a teammate, cut for the basket, and receive a return pass. (See **Diagram 1.1**)

FAST BREAK

The fast break is an important part of our offensive system. We use it at every possible opportunity and believe it is the quickest, easiest, and most efficient way of scoring. A good fast-breaking attack must be as well organized as any set offense. In fact, we spend more time working on it than we do on our set offense.

Our fast break is the lane type. We try to break three players down the floor in straight lines in order to keep the defense spread as much as possible. We attempt to get the ball in the hands of our best ball-handler in the center of the court. He will dribble the ball down the middle of the court as far as possible. If no one stops him, he will drive to the basket and score. If a

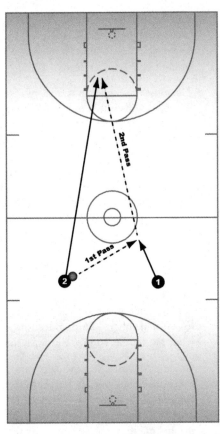

Anderson 1.1

defender is in his path, the dribbler will pass to a teammate who has filled one of the two outside lanes.

The player in the center is the key to the fast break. He must combine good dribbling, clever ballhandling, good passing, and good shooting with an uncanny ability to see the floor and make the correct decision.

Quite often, the situation calls for a two-on-one fast break. We use the straight-line attack and try to keep the defender in the middle between the two offensive players. The ballhandler will either dribble all the way to the basket and score, or he will pass to a teammate when the defender stops him. The reason why so many shots are missed on this type of fast break is because the player with the ball leaves the floor undecided whether to shoot or pass. We want the ballhandler to concentrate on the shot. If at the last second he is unable to shoot, we have a teammate move to a floor position where he can receive a perfect pass. Our rule for the player without the ball is the following: If you have not received the pass by the time you are ten feet from the basket, cut to the middle of the free-throw lane and be a safety release for the ballhandler. There is very little chance of the pass being intercepted because this player is no longer in line with the defensive player and the dribbler. (See **Diagram 1.2**)

CARDINAL PRINCIPLES FOR OUR FAST BREAK

1. No fast break is effective unless the defense is outnumbered. Sprint down the floor, and always try to be a few steps ahead of the player with the ball.
2. Keep the defense spread as much as possible.
3. The ballhandler should always take the ball to the basket and make the defender commit himself.
4. After securing a rebound, never dribble to the side or corner. Bring the ball straight up the middle, and look for an open player.

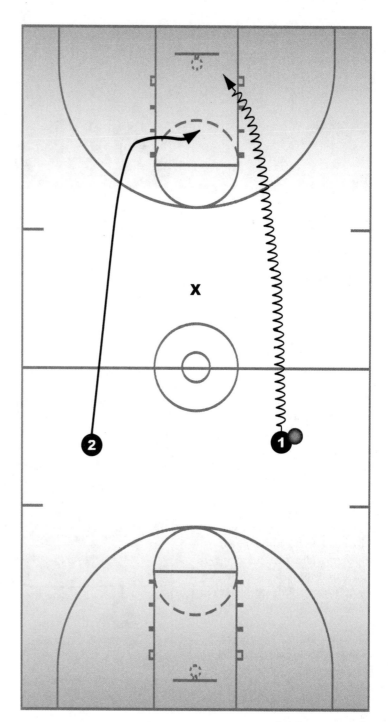

Anderson 1.2

5. Dribble as little as possible in the backcourt. Always look to pass ahead to an open teammate. Passing is always faster than dribbling.

6. On a two-man break, the player without the ball swings back to the middle of the lane.
7. Never take a bad shot. If you can't get a good shot, hold up and start our set offense.

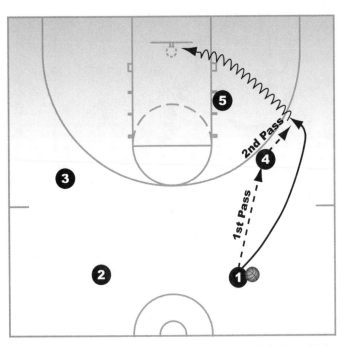

Anderson 1.3

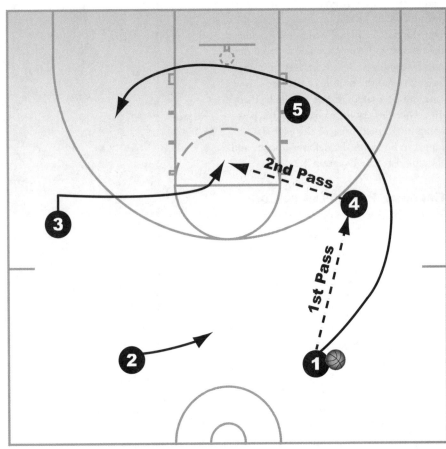

Anderson 1.4

SET OFFENSE

Every team needs some form of a set offense. The initial alignment of the players is designed to create the proper spacing. Our system is based upon execution and timing, and involves a series of options. If one does not work, we move on to the next option. The key player is the pivot man on the side of the ball. I don't want the ball to be thrown back out and the play started again. Our players realize that our set offense is made to be broken at any time an opportunity presents itself. If any player can free himself, we want him to do it.

The first option is shown in **Diagram 1.3.** O1 passes to O4, cuts around the ballhandler, receives a return pass, and dribbles to the basket for a score.

If O1 is not open for the return pass, we move to our second option, and O4 looks to pass to O5 in the pivot area (see **Diagram 1.4**). Upon receiving the pass, O5 has the following choices: make a return pass to O4; pass to O3 who is cutting across the lane; pass to O1 stepping back toward the ball; take the shot; or pass the ball to O2.

Anderson 1.5

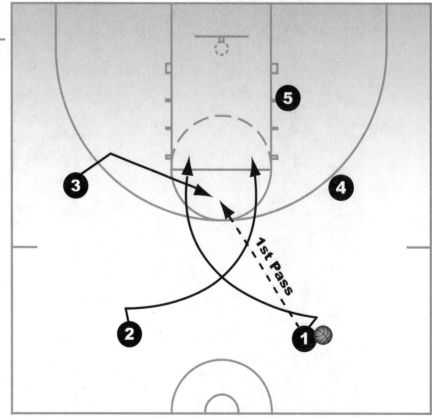

Anderson 1.6

CONTINUITY

As I mentioned earlier, we do not throw the ball back out and start our offense again. If for any reason we do not get a shot from our set offense, we swing into a figure-eight weave. We use both the three-man continuity and the four-man criss-cross. We make our players pass the ball rather than dribble over to a teammate. We also try to keep our players moving at a moderate pace, just enough to keep the defense moving. Many scoring opportunities are lost if the ball is passed too quickly. We insist that our players look for the cutters. Remember there are no secrets in basketball. It is the execution that makes plays work.

SOURCE

Anderson, W. Harold. (1945). Offensive Basketball at Bowling Green. *1944-1945 Converse Basketball Yearbook.*

If neither of the first two options is open, O3 cuts across the floor, looking for the pass from O4 (see **Diagram 1.5**). Upon receiving the ball, O3 looks to score or pass to an open teammate.

If none of the aforementioned options is available, O4 passes to O2 (see **Diagram 1.6**). O2 looks for the following scoring opportunities: pass to O4 who is cutting toward the basket; pass to O5 in the pivot area; or pass to O3 who has moved to the spot vacated by O4.

We will also use the old-style pivot play (scissors cut). As shown in **Diagram 1.7**, O3 breaks to the top of the circle and receives the pass from O1. O1 and O2 make a scissors cut and look for a return pass.

Anderson 1.7

LEGACY OF
Justin "Sam" Barry

- Led the movement to abolish the center jump after each basket.

- Advocated the establishment of the midcourt 10-second line to reduce stalling tactics.

- Did more to speed up the game of basketball than any other coach in America.

- Called the "Grandfather of the Triangle Offense."

- Led USC to the Final Four in 1940 and eight Pacific Coast Conference championships.

- Coached baseball at USC and directed the Trojans to the NCAA national championship in 1948.

- Holds the longest winning streak by a coach against a single opponent (40 consecutive games against UCLA).

Justin "Sam" Barry

"The elimination of the center jump after every basket is the greatest equalizer ever made in the game of basketball."
—Justin "Sam" Barry

BIOGRAPHY

Born: December 17, 1892 in Aberdeen, SD

Died: September 25, 1950

Inducted into the Naismith Basketball Hall of Fame in 1978

Justin "Sam" Barry starred in basketball, baseball, and football at Madison (WI) High School. He continued his athletic career at Lawrence (WI) College and later completed his degree at the University of Wisconsin. Barry returned to Madison High School to begin his coaching career in 1916 and was strongly influenced by the coaching strategies of Wisconsin coach Walter "Doc" Meanwell. From 1918 through 1922, he compiled a 36-19 record at Knox College and won the Illinois Intercollegiate Conference title in 1919 and 1920. Barry coached at the University of Iowa for seven seasons and led the Hawkeyes to the Big Ten championship in both 1923 and 1926. In 1930, Barry moved to the University of Southern California (USC). At USC, Barry coached basketball for 18 years and baseball for 11 seasons. He led teams to both the Final Four and the College World Series. His 1940 basketball squad participated in the Final Four and his Trojan baseball team won the NCAA national championship in 1948. The Trojans won or tied for the Pacific Coast Conference basketball championship on eight occasions and compiled an overall record of 260-138. Barry was influential in the development of the game and advocated both the elimination of the center jump after every basket and the adoption of the ten-second rule.

Justin "Sam" Barry...

Justin "Sam" Barry was a three-sport standout at Madison (WI) High School and was selected to the All-State team in basketball. He attended Lawrence College and competed in football, basketball, and baseball. Barry was captain of the basketball team and received All-State honors in 1913. Upon graduation from college, Barry was an accountant for the state of Wisconsin for two years before going into coaching. Barry's passion for athletics fueled his desire to become a teacher and a coach.

Barry did more to speed up the game of basketball than any other coach in America. He originated the idea of eliminating the center jump after each basket and began experimenting with this drastic rule change while coaching at the University of Iowa. "As a member of his Iowa teams from 1925 to 1929," said Forrest Twogood, "I vividly remember early fall scrimmages without the center jump."

Authors' Note: During its first fifty years, basketball was a slow-paced game with little action and minimal scoring. After every score, the ball was brought to mid-court for a center jump and the game clock continued to run during the process.

Barry continued to experiment with the elimination of the center jump when he moved to the University of Southern California. He began campaigning for a new rule that allowed the team that had been scored against to take possession of the ball at the baseline under its own basket. Other coaches joined the campaign, but many of them, including Nat Holman, felt that the team that scored should be rewarded with the possession of the ball. Others argued that the ball should be put in play by the team that had been scored against at mid-court.

In a landmark decision in 1937, the Basketball Rules Committee eliminated the center jump, and Barry's view prevailed. Once the new rule was in place, games became more action-packed, offenses opened up their attack, and game scores more than doubled.

Barry was a master of half-court offensive schemes. He was the grandfather of today's popular triangle offense. Barry called his attack the center opposite offense, which he based on concepts from Hall of Fame coach "Doc" Meanwell at Wisconsin. Three of Barry's players on the 1946 USC team, Tex Winter, Alex Hannum, and Bill

Sharman, became outstanding coaches and used many of the principles of the center opposite offense throughout their careers. Hannum and Sharman were inducted into the Naismith Memorial Basketball Hall of Fame.

Tex Winter emphasized the triangular formation of the players and called the offense the triple post offense. Winter later shortened the name to the triangle offense. He implemented his system in the NBA as an assistant for Phil Jackson. Subsequently, it served as the offensive cornerstone for the NBA championships won by the Chicago Bulls and the Los Angeles Lakers.

Alex Hannum used Barry's center opposite offense during his career as a head coach in the NBA and led the Philadelphia 76ers to a record 68 wins during the 1966-67 regular season. Bill Sharman's Los Angeles Lakers won 69 games five years later using the same principles from Barry's USC offense. That record stood until Tex Winter and the Bulls won 72 games in 1999 using the triangle offense. Hall of Fame coach Pete Newell called the triangle offense the best offense in the NBA.

Barry believed that proper execution of the fundamentals was the key to success. Barry described it in these words, "To develop the best team, a coach depends on floor plays that are fundamentally sound and that bear relation to one another. Many teams are ruined by too many plays. A few flexible plays well learned that may be used against most any style of defense will get the best results." (Barry, 1926, p. 12)

Barry insisted that his players not only work hard in practice and in games but also demonstrate sportsmanship. "Try to develop determination of spirit and a desire to win," stated Barry. "Point out to the men that if they still lose after playing their best, there is no disgrace. This of course requires hard work, fair play, and individual sacrifice, which are all part of the fundamentals of the game." (Barry, 1926, p. 13)

"The point uppermost in the coach's mind as well as that of the team is the championship," exclaimed Barry. "Instill in the team the fact that in order to win a championship, they must have confidence, determination, coolness, and the proper attitude at all times." (Barry, 1926, p. 16)

Barry also served as an assistant football coach for Howard Jones and played a key role in the program's success. Barry was Jones' top assistant from 1929 to 1940 and helped the USC football team compile a 25-game winning streak and win national championships in 1931 and 1932. He was regarded as one of the best football scouts in the country. After Jones' sudden death in 1941, Barry took over the reins of the football team, thus becoming head coach of basketball, football, and baseball simultaneously.

In 1942, Sam entered the Navy for service during World War II. As a lieutenant commander, Barry was in charge of physical and military training of Navy personnel in the South Pacific and received a Naval Commendation for his work.

As the years passed, Barry suffered physically from the stress of his various coaching responsibilities. Despite medical warnings, he agreed only to give up his daily football responsibilities. He continued as head basketball and baseball coach, chief football scout, and sideline assistant in football. Tragically, Barry collapsed and died in 1950 while climbing the hill to Memorial Stadium in Berkeley to scout a football game. At USC's next home football game, the student body paid tribute to Barry during halftime, taking the field in a block "SC" formation and, after the Coliseum lights were turned out, lighting candles for a minute of silence in memory of the coach.

Pete Newell remembered Sam Barry as an outstanding man who always shared information with young coaches. Newell's first game as a collegiate head coach was against Barry's USC team. Newell's team struggled offensively and had trouble creating open shots. After the game, Barry shared some of his strategies with Newell. "I loved Sam Barry," said Newell. "This is the type of guy he was. He knows that I'm really down, and we happen to walk out of the building around the same time. He had this terrific double-screen play that we just couldn't handle. He'd pop Alex Hannum behind the double-screen and get an open shot all night. I was curious on how they ran that play, so he starts taking me through it, right there in the parking lot. He's got his wife out there, and she's part of the double-screen with an old buddy of mine who was leaving with me. I'm the passer; Sam's coming off the screen. We're using his car as the fifth player. Here is this great coach showing me one of his best plays. I couldn't wait for the next practice day. And you know, I used that play the rest of my career." (Jenkins, 1999, p. 40)

Barry's colorful and pleasing personality made him one of the most popular coaches of his era. He was affectionately known as "Elevator Sam" because he was up off the bench every time the ball bounced. Legendary coach Clair Bee called Barry "one of the finest men I ever met," and Hank Iba believed Barry was "one of the greatest all-around athletic figures of his time." (Deutsch, 1996, p. 56)

Hall of Fame coach Nat Holman coached against USC and remembered Sam Barry in these words, "Sam was a gentleman of exemplary behavior" (Holman, 1970). "He possessed qualities that made him stand out above the crowd. His teams were always well coached and tough to beat. Sam was the architect who put the parts together and made his teams colorful. His greatest single influence was his dedication—not only to the job of coaching but what he did for people. He had a strong heart —no tears —and lots of guts. He put his heart into coaching, and he gave it all he had."

SOURCE

Barry, Justin. Vertical Files, Archives. Naismith Memorial Basketball Hall of Fame. Springfield, MA

Barry, J.M. (Sam). (1926). *Basketball: Individual Play and Team Play.* Iowa City, Iowa: The Clio Press.

Deutsch, Robin Jonathan, (Ed). *Basketball Hall of Fame Class of 1996 Yearbook.* Springfield, MA: Naismith Basketball Hall of Fame.

Holman, Nat. (1970, May 25). Letter to Forrest F. Twogood.

Jenkins, Bruce. (1999). *A Good Man: The Pete Newell Story.* Berkeley, CA: Frog, Ltd.

THE USC OFFENSE

By Justin "Sam" Barry

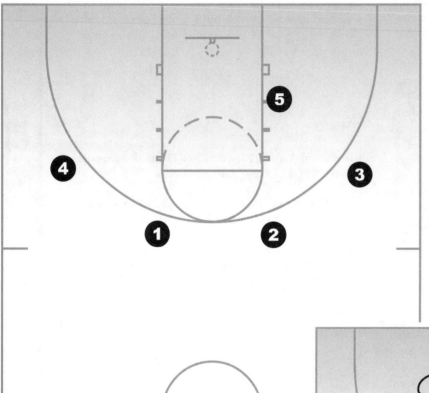

Barry 1.0

The University of Southern California offense stresses ball control and features a set style of attack. The guards control and advance the ball, while the front line players cut or screen to create high-percentage shots. The offense is predicated upon proper spacing between players, excellent passing, and screening.

The front line consists of the center and the two wing men (forwards). The wing men originate each play by moving to designated floor positions. Screens and cuts are utilized to free teammates for scoring opportunities.

The center plays a vital part in this attack. He should be an excellent screener and an aggressive rebounder. He must also be able to post-up and take the ball strong to the basket.

Variations in the basic plan of attack allow the guards to originate plays by passing and cutting. Both inside and outside screens, as well as the scissors cut, are used.

BASIC FORMATION

The initial alignment is shown in **Diagram 1.0**. O1 and O2 are the backcourt players in charge of the ball. O3 and O4 are the wing men in the second line. O5 is the center and occupies the front-line position.

PLAY 1

Play 1 is designed to set up a scoring opportunity for O4. The sequence of events is shown in **Diagram 1.1**.

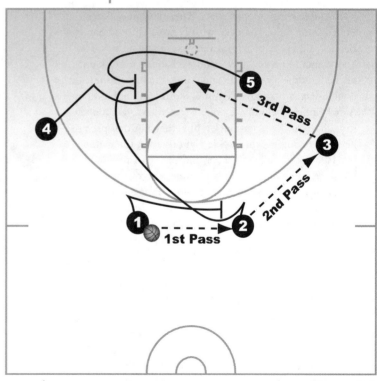

Barry 1.1

LESSONS FROM THIS LEGEND...

1. O1 passes to O2, follows his pass, and sets a screen.

2. O2 passes to O3 and breaks off the screen set by O1.

3. O2 sets up on the weakside free-throw lane block.

4. O5 cuts across the lane and sets a double-screen with O2.

5. O4 times his cut to take advantage of the double screen by O2 and O5 and looks for the pass from O3.

PLAY 1A

Play 1A is designed to free O5 if his defender switches to stop O4 in Play #1. The sequence of events is shown in **Diagram 1.2**.

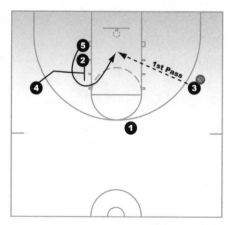

Barry 1.2

1. All moves follow the pattern in Play #1, until O4 starts his cut off the double-screen.

2. When O4 sees O5's defender start to switch, he stops behind O2.

3. O5 cuts around the double screen set up by O2 and O4 and looks for the pass from O3.

PLAY 2

Play 2 is designed to provide a driving

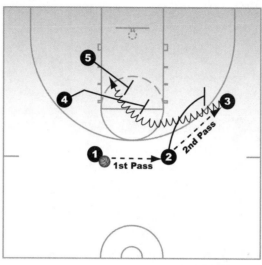

Barry 1.3

opportunity for the wing man. This play can be very advantageous for a left-handed player. The sequence of events is shown in **Diagram 1.3**.

1. O1 passes to O2.

2. O2 passes to O3 and sets a ball-screen.

3. O4 and O5 set a doubled-staggered screen in the lane.

4. O3 drives his defender into the three-man staggered screen and looks for scoring opportunities.

PLAY 2A

Play 2A provides a scoring opportunity for O1 (see **Diagram 1.4**).

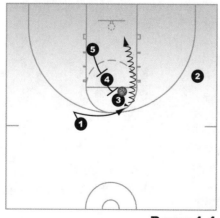

Barry 1.4

1. All moves follow the pattern in Play #2, until O3 picks up his dribble.

2. At this point, O1 cuts hard to the outside of O3, receives a hand-off, and looks to drive to the basket.

PLAY 3

Play 3 employs a scissors cut by the guards and sets up a scoring option for the center. The sequence of events is shown in **Diagram 1.5**.

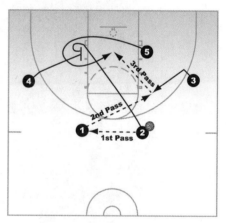

Barry 1.5

1. O2 passes to O1 and breaks to the opposite free-throw lane block.

2. O1 passes to O3.

3. O4 and O2 form a double-screen.

4. O5 breaks across the lane and makes a curl-cut off the double-screen, looking for a pass from O3.

LEGACY OF
Larry Brown

- Became the first coach in basketball history to win both an NCAA championship (1988) and an NBA championship (2004).

- Is respected by his peers for his exceptional teaching ability and his meticulous attention to detail.

- Emphasizes aggressive defense, rebounding, running the floor, and always giving the maximum effort.

- Has earned a reputation for quickly transforming losing teams into winners.

- Is only coach in NBA history to lead seven different teams to the playoffs.

- Is only U.S. male to both play and coach in the Olympics.

- Holds the ABA single-game record for assists with 23.

Larry Brown

*"All the successful teams I've ever seen
have three characteristics.
They play unselfish, they play together,
and they play hard."*
—Larry Brown

BIOGRAPHY

Born: September 14, 1940 in Brooklyn, NY

Inducted into the Naismith Basketball Hall of Fame in 2002.

Larry Brown is the only coach in basketball history to win both an NCAA championship and an NBA championship. He has posted a winning record in 28 of his 32 seasons as a head coach on the professional and collegiate levels. His overall coaching record at the end of the 2004 season was 1,339-881. In 21 seasons as an NBA head coach, Brown has won 933 games and ranks seventh all-time among NBA coaches. He is the only coach in NBA history to lead seven different teams to the playoffs. In 2004, Brown directed the Detroit Pistons to the NBA title. Brown also coached four years in the ABA, earning Coach of the Year honors three times. On the collegiate level, Brown led the University of Kansas to the NCAA national championship in 1988. He also directed the UCLA Bruins to the NCAA title game in 1980. Brown was selected Naismith Coach of the Year in 1988, USA National Coach of the Year in 1999, and NBA Coach of the Year in 2001. Brown is the only U.S. male to both play and coach in the Olympics. He was a player on the 1964 Gold Medal team and an assistant coach on the 2000 Gold Medal team. In the 2004 Olympic games, Brown led the USA men's basketball team to a bronze medal. As a player at North Carolina, Brown played for future Hall of Fame coaches Frank McGuire and Dean Smith. He was also a three-time ABA All-Star and holds the ABA record with 23 assists in one game.

Larry Brown...

Larry Brown believes in getting his teams to play "the right way," which means players must be disciplined, unselfish, aggressive, and committed. Brown learned the importance of unselfish play and teamwork more than 50 years ago. As a youngster growing up in Long Beach, New York, Brown used to carry water and Cokes to the players at the Central School basketball court across the street from his home. There, Rochester Royals guard Red Holzman, along with New York Knicks players from the early 1950s, would practice during the summer months.

"Coach Holzman taught me how to play," Brown said. "He was the one who showed me the importance of finding the open man, moving without the ball, and the concept of playing team defense. That's why every time when I walk into Madison Square Garden, I always look up to see where his banner is. It's my way of thanking him." (Lawrence, 2004)

Brown has had other mentors, too, from Frank McGuire, to Dean Smith, the man he still refers to as "Coach Smith." Brown began his coaching career in 1965 as freshman coach at the University of North Carolina. More than 100 players participated in the opening try-outs. "I didn't know how to cut down the squad, so I just ran them the entire first practice without ever picking up a basketball," remembered Brown.

The next day Dean Smith, the head coach at North Carolina, came in and said, "I've got good news and bad news. The good news is you've got the roster cut down as I asked. The bad news is, all the scholarship kids want to quit." This marked the humble beginning of a coaching career that has spanned more than three decades and has earned Brown a spot as the seventh all-time winningest coach in the NBA.

Brown played at the University of North Carolina and led the Tar Heels in scoring as a junior with 16.2 points per game. After completing his playing career in 1963 at North Carolina, Brown was drafted by the NBA, but was told that he was too small to guard players like Jerry West, Oscar Robertson, or John Havlicek. Instead, Brown joined the Akron Goodyear Wingfoots, an AAU team in Akron, Ohio. At night, Brown made his mark in the National Industrial League as a skilled 5-9 point guard, while during the day, he was a mill worker.

"They called it an executive training program," Brown recalled. "They let you play ball, and then coach kids on the weekends. We got paid by the hour, then got overtime for basketball. They told me to wear a tie and jacket, but, by the way, bring overalls and work boots with a hard toe."

The hard-nosed Brown refused to let his tough surroundings diffuse his basketball dream. After playing one season with the Goodyear Wingfoots, Brown earned a position on the U.S. Olympic team and won a gold medal in the 1964 Olympic games.

Brown went on to play five years in the ABA and led the league in assists three times. He won a championship with Oakland in 1969, appeared in three All-Star Games, and set the ABA record for assists in one game with 23. Along the way, Brown earned the reputation as a "traveling man," as he played for five different teams during his five-year ABA career.

Brown began his professional coaching career with the Carolina Cougars in the ABA and then directed the Denver Nuggets during their transition from the ABA to the NBA. He has also coached New Jersey, San Antonio, Los Angeles (Clippers), Indiana, Philadelphia, and Detroit in the NBA. In the college ranks, Brown coached two years at UCLA and led the Bruins to the NCAA championship game in 1980. He also coached at the University of Kansas for five seasons, where he directed the Jayhawks to the 1986 Final Four and the 1988 NCAA national championship.

Brown earned a reputation for quickly transforming losing teams into winners. "People recognize his ability to take a group of guys who have always had naysayers and prove they can do what it takes to win," said NBA player Aaron McKie. "He has consistently been able to take bottom-feeders and win." (Kahn, 2002)

His first team at San Antonio won 21 games, then won 56 games the next season. He took the lowly Clippers from a 31-51 mark to 45-37 in one year. At Indiana, Brown took a .500 Pacers team into the Eastern Conference finals two years in a row. He led Philadelphia to five straight NBA play-offs and a trip to the NBA Finals in 2001. It marked the first time that Philadelphia had been in the Finals since 1983. On the collegiate level, Brown joined the University of Kansas in 1983, after the Jayhawks had suffered back-to-back losing seasons. Brown immediately put Kansas back on the college basketball map with a 22-10 record in his first season.

The crowning point at Kansas was the NCAA national championship in 1988. Kansas entered the NCAA tournament with eleven loses, and few people thought they would survive past the first or second round of the tournament. Brown wouldn't let his team think they didn't belong. He designed the perfect game plan for Kansas to upset Oklahoma in the championship game. Oklahoma had beaten the Jayhawks twice during the regular season, and the prevailing opinion was that the Sooners won the national title by beating Arizona in the semi-final game. After a high scoring first half, Kansas slowed down the pace and outscored Oklahoma 12-8 during the final six minutes to capture an 83-79 victory.

When it was over, Brown referred to some of the coaches that he deeply admired, "Coach Smith has done this, Coach Iba, Coach McGuire. It's a phenomenal feeling. I've had some great moments, but nothing tops this." (Bedore, 1988)

Authors' Note: Brown played for coaches Frank McGuire and Dean Smith at North Carolina and Hank Iba on the 1964 Olympic team.

Brown was named ABA Coach of the Year three times, NBA Coach of the Year in 2001, USA National Coach of the Year in 1999, and the Naismith Coach of the Year in 1988.

Indiana Pacer president Donnie Walsh called Brown the "last of a dying breed of coaches who are teachers" (Kahn, 2002). Brown believes basketball should be "played the right way," which consists of aggressive defense, rebounding, running the floor, and always giving your best effort.

Unselfishness and strong defense have been trademarks of a Larry Brown-coached team. He encourages players to take open shots, but wants them to be aware of the score, situation, shot clock, and most critically, open teammates who might have a higher-percentage shot. He constantly fine-tunes his offensive sets to maximize the strengths of his players.

Doc Rivers, former NBA star and coach, recalls that Brown's methods require patience and concentration from the players. During any given practice, Brown can spend 20 to 30 minutes on a particular fundamental, such as the proper angle at which to set a screen.

"It's his attention to detail," said former assistant coach Randy Ayers. "He wants everybody on the team to be better, even if you don't play. He wants the 10th, 11th, 12th guys to improve by the end of the year, so that if they're called on, or if they go to another team, they're ready. That's what sets him apart. He's about all the right things in basketball." (Jasner, 2002)

Eric Snow played for Brown at Philadelphia and said, "Coach Brown breaks it down and goes through it with you over and over again. I haven't been around anyone who takes the time with you like that to get it right. Most coaches just don't look at it that way anymore. You can tell how much he loves and respects the game." (Kahn, 2002)

In his first year with Detroit, Brown led the Pistons to the 2004 NBA Championship. He took the team to the highest level by pushing them physically and mentally, but he also listened to his players. "He didn't just come in and change everything," said Ben Wallace. "He asked for our input, and asked if we felt comfortable with some of what he wanted to run. Any time you have a coach asking you what you think and what you want to do, it makes it easy for you to go out there and do your thing." (Neel, 2004)

Herb Brown, Detroit Piston's assistant coach and Larry's brother, probably described Brown best when he said, "Larry loves teaching. It's part of his mission in life to be the best coach he can possible be. And he'll never stop. He'd have to be comatose to give it up." (Neel, 2004)

SOURCE

Brown, Larry. Vertical Files, Archives. Naismith Memorial Basketball Hall of Fame. Springfield, MA.

Bedore, Gary. (1988, April 5). Kansas is NCAA Champion. *The Lawrence Journal World.*

Jasner, Phil. (2002). Born to Coach. 2002 Commemorative Enshrinement & Grand Opening Program. Naismith Memorial Basketball Hall of Fame.

Kahn, Mike. (2002, October 4). Sixer's Brown Last of a Dying Breed of Coaches. CBS SportsLine.com.

Lawrence, Mitch. (2004, June 14). *Brown Chasing His Own Hoops History.* Web Site: <http://www.ESPN.com>.

Neel, Eric. (2004, June 14). *Brothers In Arms.* Web Site: http://www.ESPN.com>.

LESSONS FROM THIS LEGEND...

DRILLS FOR THE TRANSITION GAME

By Larry Brown

I've probably been the most fortunate person in the world, because I think I've had the greatest background in terms of being around great coaches. My high school coach was an amazing coach who developed an outstanding program. I played for Frank McGuire at North Carolina for two years, and he was inducted into the Hall of Fame. I was on Dean Smith's first two teams at North Carolina, and of course, he's in the Hall of Fame. I played for Coach Henry Iba on the Olympic Team.

When I was a young coach, I used to go to the NCAA tournaments with Frank McGuire and Dean Smith. I remember how all the veteran coaches used to share ideas; never fearing that any knowledge that they may pass on to the other person would ever hurt them. Their only aim was to improve the game. This is something that we do not have enough of now. Legendary coaches like Hank Iba, Adolph Rupp, and Ray Meyer not only loved the game but the fellowship that they had with one another was very important to them.

I am not an innovator. I come to clinics and see so many people that get awestruck and sometimes doubt themselves when they can't figure out brilliant things. I heard "Bear" Bryant speak one day, and he said, 'You are not going to find any new things down here at the University of Alabama, but if there is something good and you see it, come down here, and we will do it better.' I think that is a great point. We have over-coached and have probably under-taught. If you learn a couple of things from these clinics and plan to implement them in your program, make sure you know how to teach them.

ADVANTAGES OF THE TRANSITION GAME

I want my teams to play an up-tempo game. Some coaches don't allow their players to run because they are afraid that they will relinquish some of their control, but I don't believe that. Here are some reasons why I think you should incorporate the transition game into your philosophy:

- Players like to run and prefer the up-tempo style of play.
- It creates opportunities for lay-ups and high-percentage shots.
- It is more difficult for your opponent to apply defensive pressure.
- It keeps teams honest and makes them not crash the boards as hard.
- It wears down your opponent, both physically and mentally.
- It is a great conditioner.
- It allows you to play a lot of people.

PRACTICE PLANNING

We try to design all our drills so our players are in position to fast break. We rarely practice half-court. We always want to advance the ball to the baseline as quickly as possible and then get the ball from one side of the court to the other. This creates open shots, and we work on this every day in practice. We start practice by stretching for 15 to 18 minutes and then do a series of transition drills that provide good conditioning, as well as pressure, for our players. These drills stress execution and concentration and are good for developing mental toughness.

PEER PRESSURE

We have basic rules that remain consistent throughout the drills. We also incorporate peer pressure by setting team goals. It is effective and comes from within the team concept. We do not move on to the next drill until our goal is reached.

Now, here is where the peer pressure comes into effect. We select a "magic number" each day that represents the number of consecutive shots that must be made before we go on to another drill. There is no yelling from coaches, encouragement is minimal, and time is not a factor. If it takes three minutes or thirty minutes, we will not move on until it is done correctly. The first time I committed to the peer pressure system, we used a certain drill, and it took 27 minutes to get it right. The good news is that ten days later it took two minutes, and the players were united and off to the next drill.

FAST BREAK DRILLS

We have five drills we do every day from the start of practice through the NCAA tournament. Let me emphasize, we do the same five drills every day, day in and day out. The only change is the "magic number." It ranges from 12 to 30, depending on your intuitive feelings on what they can handle. I am convinced these drills carry-over to game success and that daily peer pressure situations are healthy and will help create winners.

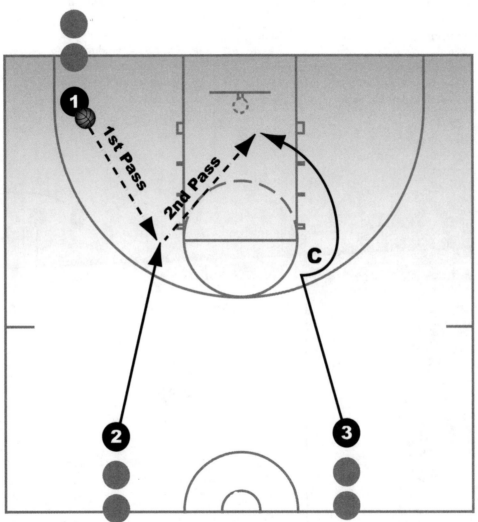

Brown 1.0

TWO-MAN LAY-UPS

See **Diagram 1.0**.

a. O1 passes to O2, who makes a jump stop.

b. O3 runs his imaginary defender into a screen set by the coach and receives a pass from O2 for a lay-up shot.

c. O2 rebounds the ball and outlets to O3, who has replaced O1 to start the next rotation.

d. Set team goals.

e. No bounce passes.

f. Add another ball when players are proficient with the drill.

LESSONS FROM THIS LEGEND...

THREE-LANE FLY DRILL

See **Diagram 1.1** and **Diagram 1.2**.

a. O1, O2, and O3 spread out across the baseline.
b. O1 rebounds the ball and outlets to O2. O3 is sprinting up the floor.
c. O1 sprints up the middle and receives a pass back from O2.
d. O1 makes a running pass to O3, who is sprinting down the court for a lay-up. After O1 makes the pass to O3, he cuts around the coach and breaks back down the court.

e. O3 makes the lay-up and sprints wide to become the next outlet man.
f. O2 sprints to rebound, outlets to O3, and goes back down the middle of the court.
g. O3 passes back to O2.
h. O2 passes ahead to O1 for a lay-up.
i. The drill can be run either one or two trips.
j. Rules: no dribbles; no fumbles; no bounce passes.
k. Set team goals.

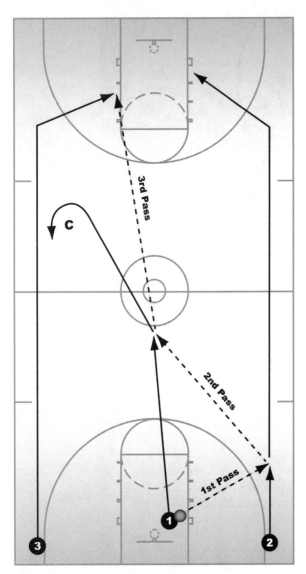

Brown 1.1

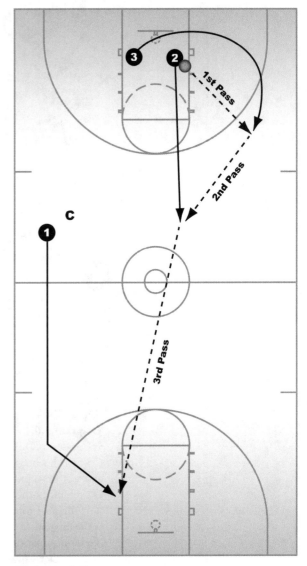

Brown 1.2

LESSONS FROM THIS LEGEND...

THREE-MAN WEAVE

a. The weave is run the same as any other three-man weave with basic rules.
b. The drill is run as one round trip.
c. We have three different sets of rules: five passes; four passes; and three passes.
d. Rules: no dribbles and no fumbles.
e. Set team goals.

FOUR-MAN DRILL

See **Diagram 1.3**.

a. O4 rebounds the ball and outlets to O1, O2, or O3.
b. O1 runs in the middle; O2 and O3 run in the lanes.
c. O1, O2, and O3 pass back and forth.
d. At the free-throw line, O2 and O3 angle to the basket, looking for the lay-up.
e. O4 trails the play and rebounds the ball without letting it hit the floor.
f. O2 and O3 cross and run the lanes back.
g. Repeat the action for two round trips.
h. On the last trip, hit the trailer for the lay-up.
i. Rules: no dribbles and no fumbles.
j. Set team goals.

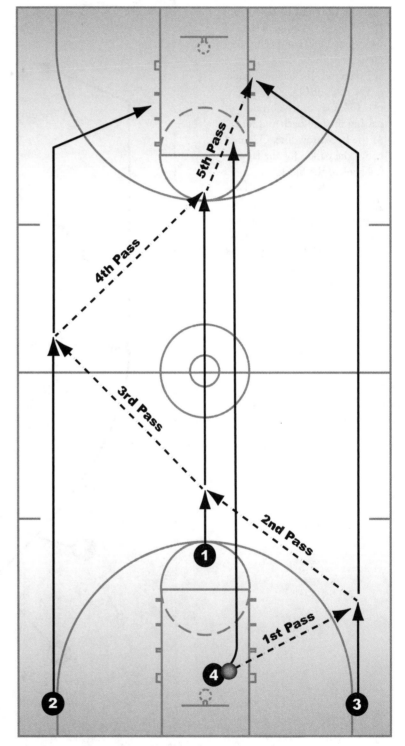

Brown 1.3

LESSONS FROM THIS LEGEND...

FIVE-MAN DRILL

See **Diagram 1.4**.

a. O1 runs the middle of the floor; O2 runs the right lane; O3 runs the left lane; O4 runs to the strongside block; and O5 trails the play.

b. O5 rebounds the ball and outlets to O1, O2, or O3.

c. O1, O2, O3 run the break, passing the ball back and forth.

d. At the free-throw line, O2 and O3 cut to the basket for the lay-up.

e. O4 runs to the block.

f. O5 rebounds the ball and starts the break in the other direction.

g. Two round trips are run, and on the last trip, the pass is made to the trailer, O5, for the lay-up.

h. Rules: no dribbles, no fumbles, and no bounce passes.

i. Set team goals.

SOURCE

Brown, Larry. (1986). Transition Basketball. *MacGregor Flashback Notebook.*

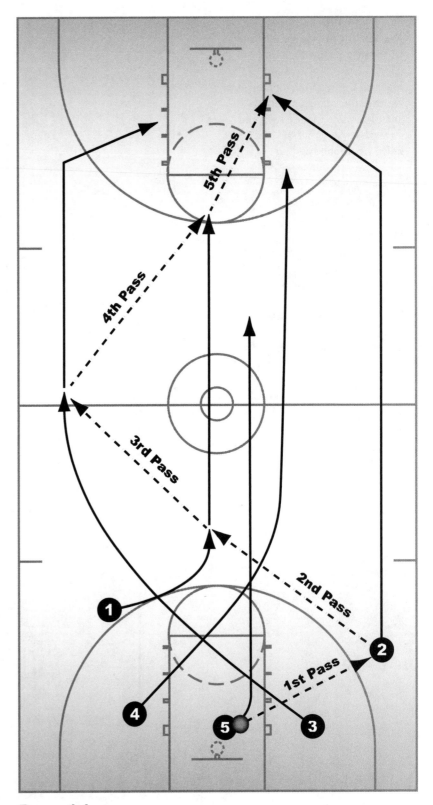

Brown 1.4

LESSONS FROM THIS LEGEND...

EARLY OFFENSE

By Larry Brown

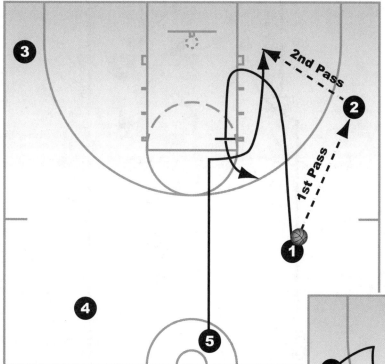

Brown 2.0

If the pass into the post is denied, (see **Diagram 2.1**) then O1 pops out to the top after setting the screen. O2 passes to O1. O1 looks for a possible high-low pass inside to O5 or to the weakside for a pass to O3 who is cutting off the screen from O4. O3 looks for a shot, drive, or pass into the post to O4. Another option is for O3 to set a back screen for O4 on the weakside.

The first option in our early offense is designed to get the ball inside to our center. In **Diagram 2.0**, O1 passes to O2 and begins the give-and-go cut to the basket. O1 stops and moves up the lane to set a back screen for O5. O2 looks to make the pass to O5 in the post after the cut off the back screen.

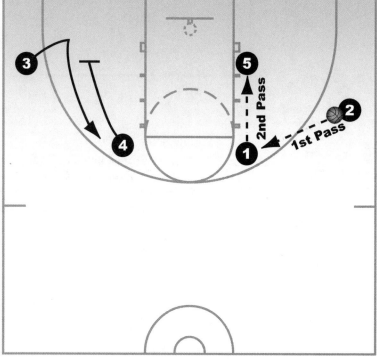

Brown 2.1

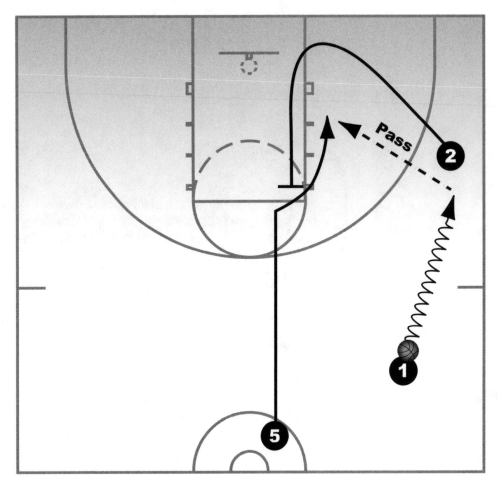

Brown 2.2

Another variation in our early offense is to use our big guard and center. Instead of passing to O2, O1 dribbles to the right wing (see **Diagram 2.2**). O2 starts toward the basket and cuts up the lane to set a back screen for O5. O1 looks to pass to O5 in the post.

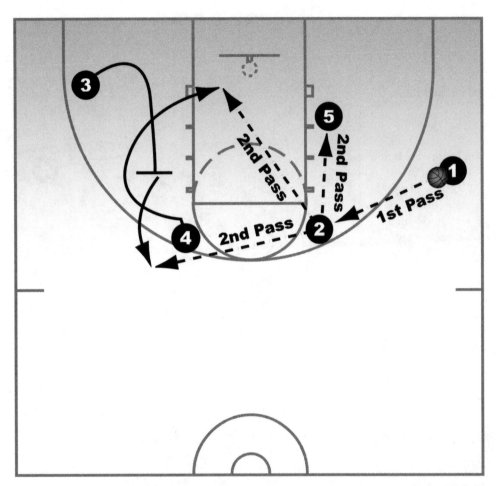

Brown 2.3

If the post pass is denied, O1 passes to O2 at the top after he has set his back screen (see **Diagram 2.3**). O2 either looks for a high-low pass to O5, the shot or drive, or passes to O4, who is cutting off O3's back screen on the weakside. If those options are denied, O2 looks either to O3, who has popped out to the wing for a shot, or to O4 for a post feed.

SOURCE

Brown, Larry. (1995). Indiana's Early Offense. *Spalding Basketball Playbook: Plays from the Pros.* Indianapolis: Masters Press.

GAME-WINNING PLAYS

By Larry Brown

THE MOVING CROSS SCREEN

This play involves movement and mis-direction and is designed to get O4 an open shot. As shown in **Diagram 3.0**, O1 begins the play by passing to O5 at the top of the circle. O2 makes a base-line flex cut off O4 into the lane to give the impression that he is the focal point of the play. O2 quickly cuts back and sets a cross screen for O4.

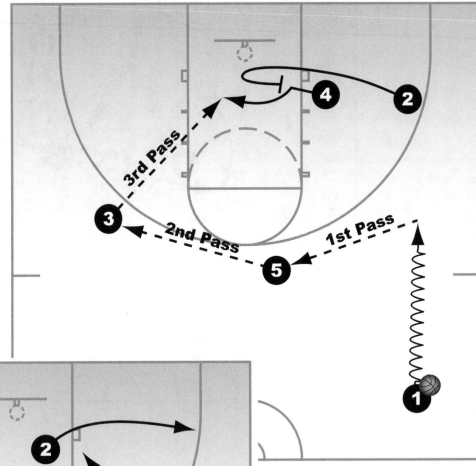

Brown 3.0

In **Diagram 3.1**, O5 passes to O3, screens for O1, and then moves to the weakside board. O2 pops out to the corner. O3 looks for the post-feed to O4. The secondary option is for O3 to pass to O1.

Brown 3.1

LESSONS FROM THIS LEGEND...

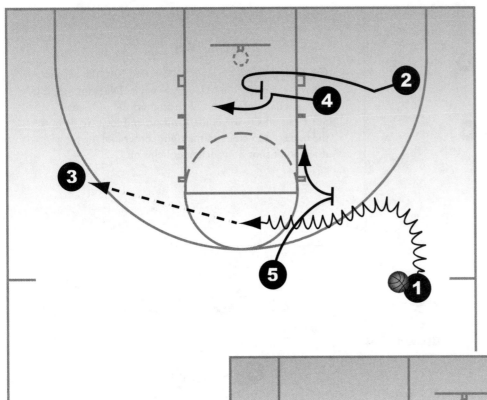

Player O1 spots up at the top of the circle, O5 rolls to the weakside rebounding position, as O2 breaks out to the corner. O3 feeds O4 in the post and screens for O1. This provides O4 with either scoring or passing options (see **Diagram 3.3**).

Brown 3.2

THE MOVING CROSS SCREEN WITH PICK-AND-ROLL

The same action can develop with O1 and O5 beginning the play with a pick-and-roll. O1 dribbles off O5's screen (see **Diagram 3.2**). At the same time, O2 makes the baseline flex cut. O1 passes to O3. O2 cuts back to set the cross screen for O4.

Brown 3.3

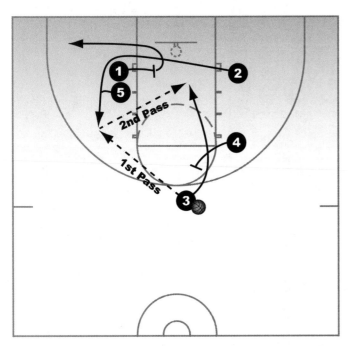

Brown 3.4

BASELINE SCREEN PLAY

This play involves movement off a baseline-staggered screen. In **Diagram 3.4**, O3 initiates the offense. O2 cuts off staggered screens set by O1 and O5. O1 pops back to the left corner after setting the screen, and O5 stays on the left block. O3 passes to O2 and cuts off the back screen set by O4. O2 looks to throw the lob pass to O3.

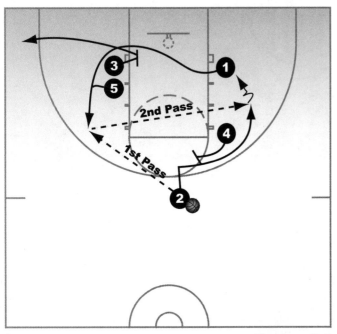

Brown 3.6

If the lob pass to O3 is denied, O4 flashes to the ball and receives the pass from O2. As shown in **Diagram 3.5**, this sets up a hand-off, with O2 cutting off O4. O2 makes a quick cut off O4 to get the hand-off and looks to drive to the basket. O3 clears to the right corner looking for a three-point shot if his defender helps on O2.

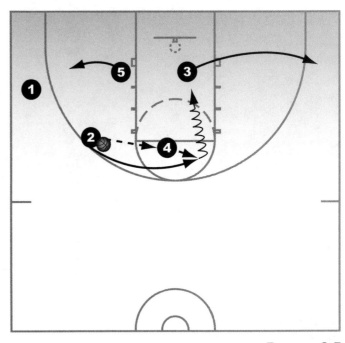

Brown 3.5

FLARE-AND-ISOLATION PLAY

In **Diagram 3.6**, O2 initiates the offense. O1 cuts off the staggered screens set by O3 and O5. After setting the screen, O3 pops back to the left corner, while O5 stays on the left block. O2 passes to O1 and flares off the back screen set by O4. O1 throws a skip pass to O2 for the shot or a drive to the basket.

LESSONS FROM THIS LEGEND...

Brown 3.7

If O4's defender attempts to step out and help on the flare for O2, O4 cuts to the basket for the pass from O1 (see **Diagram 3.7**).

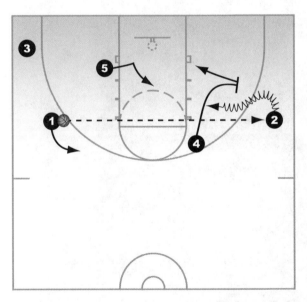

Brown 3.8

FLARE TO PICK-AND-ROLL

Diagram 3.8 demonstrates the flare option with a pick-and-roll action. If O2 does not have a shot or a drive to the basket after receiving the skip pass, O4 can set a wing pick-and-roll. O1 and O3 spot-up on the perimeter as the pick-and-roll takes place. O4 rolls to the basket after setting the screen, and O5 flashes into the lane. O2 looks for the jump shot or an open teammate

SIDE OUT-OF-BOUNDS PLAY —STAGGERED SCREENS

This side out-of-bounds play is designed to get your best shooter a scoring opportunity. In **Diagram 3.9**, O2 has the opportunity to use two sets of staggered screens.

O2 sets up at the three-point line above the right elbow. He begins the play by breaking off a high double-stack screen of O4 and O5. Standing shoulder-to-shoulder, O4 and O5 and are positioned at the left elbow.

If O2 does not receive the pass, he cuts to the left corner. O4 and O5 break down to set a staggered screen for O1. O1 cuts to the top of the circle and receives the pass. O4 and O5 now set a second set of staggered screens for O2, who cuts back to the right wing for the pass from O1.

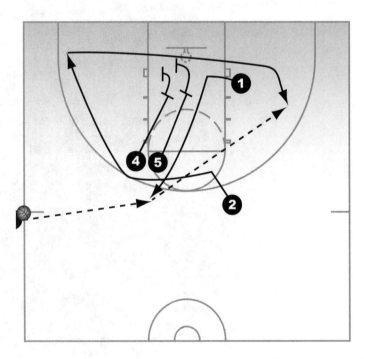

Brown 3.9

SOURCE

Ociepka, Bob and Raterman, Dale (2001) *Basketball Playbook 2.* Contemporary Books. Chicago, IL.

LEGACY OF
H.C. "Doc" Carlson

- Designed the figure 8 continuity offense.

- Practiced medicine as a registered physician, as well as coached basketball.

- Led Pittsburgh to the Helms Foundation national championship in 1928 and 1930.

- Produced teams that were highly conditioned.

- Conducted landmark research in the area of fatigue and basketball.

- Was the first coach to take an eastern collegiate team across the country to play western universities.

- Was the originator of the first college basketball clinic in 1930.

H. C. "Doc" Carlson

"Learning the value of team play
is to learn one of life's lessons."
—H.C. "Doc" Carlson

BIOGRAPHY

Born: July 4, 1894 in Murray City, OH

Died: November 1, 1964

Inducted into the Naismith Basketball Hall of Fame in 1959

H.C. "Doc" Carlson was the basketball coach at the University of Pittsburgh from 1922 through 1953 where

he and compiled a record of 369-247. The charismatic Carlson also doubled as a practicing physician. Known

for his invention of the figure 8 offense, Carlson led Pittsburgh to Helms Foundation national championship

in both 1928 (with a record of 21-0) and 1930. The figure 8 offense was a continuity offense that broke down

an opponent's defense and created lay-up opportunities. In 1931, Carlson was the first coach to take an east-

ern collegiate team across the country to play western universities. He served as president of the NABC

Coaches Association in 1937 and was elected to the Helms Foundation Basketball Hall of Fame. Carlson was

the main speaker for the dedication of the Basketball Hall of Fame in 1961.

H.C. "Doc" Carlson...

H.C. Carlson spent his boyhood years in Pennsylvania and graduated from Fayette City H.S. (PA) in 1912. Both his father and stepfather died in mining accidents, and his family could not afford to provide him with a college education. Carlson attended the University of Pittsburgh on an athletic scholarship. During his collegiate years, Carlson was much better known as a football star than as a basketball player. During his football career, Pittsburgh lost only one game. Carlson was captain of the undefeated 1917 team and earned All-American honors. He also starred in basketball and baseball. While attending medical school, Carlson financed his education by playing professional football for Cleveland.

In 1920, the University of Pittsburgh Medical School granted Carlson his M.D. degree. As a young doctor, Carlson found it difficult to face the potential death of a patient nearly everyday. To take his mind off the problems of his vocation, Carlson turned to coaching. In 1923, he became the head basketball coach at Pittsburgh. During sleepless nights, he diagramed plays in his prescription book and tried to create new plans of attack. It was from this setting that Carlson designed what many basketball historians called the first true continuity offense, a system that he called the figure 8 offense. (Bjarkman, 1996, p. 12)

Carlson's continuity offense revolutionized offensive thinking because the initial pass was made to a player moving away from the basket, rather than toward the basket. The passer then cut toward the basket looking for a return pass. The figure 8 offense originally had three players moving and two players stationary. Carlson eventually developed a four-player and a five-player continuity. Joe Lapchick, legendary Hall of Fame coach, claimed that every modern offensive scheme evolved from the innovations of "Doc" Carlson.

Carlson believed basketball was an important endeavor because of its carryover into life. He regarded it as a lesson in discipline, sportsmanship, honesty, cooperation, companionship, and, most of all, a lesson in the competitive democratic system. Basketball was never an end in itself, but was the means for building upon the formal education of the classroom, with the practical experiences of life. Carlson emphasized that it was impossible to always score more points than your opponent, but "everybody can win all the time in the synthesis of enduring healthy and happy patterns of life." (Carlson, 1962, p. 19)

Carlson wanted his students and players to see the good in everyone. He was a special person who generated sunshine and made life pleasant for everyone around him. Carlson was called a healer. "He could seize your heart without a scalpel and sutures,... and he could ease your pain. His smile was more quieting than a sedative. 'Doc' gave out gaiety and he felt it coming back at him. It was like a boomerang—a blessed boomerang." (O'Brien, 1982, p. 11)

Students remembered how Carlson wrote encouraging notes and urged them to be more compassionate and focus on the good, rather than the bad. "Doc" felt his daily duty was doling out happiness. He loved to buy students ice cream cones, and his office was always well stocked with candy and chocolate bars. (O'Brien, 1982, p. 11)

Carlson believed "offense is the highlight in any sport" and that a good offense was the best defense (Carlson, 1928, p. 75). He always wanted his team to control possession of the ball, because it eliminated scoring opportunities for the opposition. At the end of games in which his Pittsburgh team had a big lead, they would put on a passing exhibition. Spectators counted every pass and watched the clock to see if they could really make 70 passes in one minute as Carlson claimed they could. This group came to be known as the "runners" and did nothing but move the ball without any intention of taking a shot.

Carlson was a strict man-to-man defensive strategist. He despised zone defenses and thought they ruined the action of the game. He often instructed his team to hold the ball for much of the game in order to counter "tactless" zone play. When his team stalled on the road, Carlson was known to throw candy and peanuts into the stands to the hostile home crowds. (Bjarkman, 2000, p. 7)

Carlson was a colorful showman on the sidelines and often received the wrath of opposing fans. A fan at Washington and Jefferson hit Carlson on the head with an umbrella. West Virginia fans tried to cool him off by pouring a bucket of ice water on his head after Carlson continually complained of bad officiating by saying, "This burns me up." (Bjarkman, 1996, p. 14)

During Carlson's long and distinguished career, he was one of the most outspoken critics of officiating that basketball has ever known. He was very disturbed over what he considered were "home calls" and advocated officiating that was consistent and fair to both teams. On one occasion, Carlson offered his glasses to the referee. Another time, he took the water bucket and other supplies from the bench and set them at the referee's feet announcing, "You might as well have these, you've taken everything else from us!"

"Doc" Carlson was the originator of the college basketball clinic, the first being held at the University of Pittsburgh in 1930. Originally, he devoted most of his effort to teaching his system of offense, but as the clinic developed over the years, he included coaches from all of the local colleges as clinicians.

Many critics said the removal of the center jump after each basket would make the game so fast that it would kill or seriously injure many players. To counter such criticism, Carlson undertook extensive research in fatigue. Carlson's "Basketball Research in Fatigue" provided concrete evidence that the new faster version of basketball did not have any adverse side effects on the players. Carlson's research was one of the greatest contributions to this phase of basketball coaching.

A Carlson-coached team was always in superb physical condition. Hall of Fame coach "Phog" Allen said that he had never seen better trained teams than Pittsburgh.

Carlson died at the age of seventy, just two months after retiring as director of the student health services at Pittsburgh. The famed and beloved Carlson had been associated with the University for half a century.

SOURCE

Bjarkman, Peter C. (1996). *Hoopla: A Century of College Basketball.* Indianapolis: Masters Press.

Bjarkman, Peter C. (2000). *The Biographical History of Basketball.* Chicago: Masters Press.

Carlson, H.C. (1928). *You and Basketball.* Braddock, PA: Brown Publishing.

Jones, Tommy Ray. (1964). *Henry Clifford Carlson M.D.: His Contributions to Intercollegiate Basketball Coaching.* Unpublished Master's Thesis. University of Pittsburgh.

O'Brien, Jim. (1982). *Hail to Pitt: A Sports History of the University of Pittsburgh.* Pittsburgh: Wolfson Publishing.

THE FIGURE 8 OFFENSE

By H.C. "Doc" Carlson

The figure 8 offense received that name because the descriptive lines resemble a figure eight. These lines represent the pathways traveled by the players, and these pathways of travel give continuity to the action. Scoring opportunities come as a result of certain plays set up as breaks in the continuity. Three players or five players may establish the figure eight pattern. The course of action may be lengthwise or crosswise of the floor. The action may be confined to quadrants, or the entire offensive half of the floor. A third course of action may be diagonal, by travelling between diagonal corners of the offensive half of the floor. Many teams that have tried this system of play overemphasize continuity and do not develop sufficient breaks or scoring opportunities.

Three men in the backcourt may establish continuity, with or without the use of the dribble. A player is stationed at each side of the court near the mid line, and a third man is in between them, close to the basket. The first player passes to the second player across the court, and runs between the receiver and the basket. The third player, who was closest to the basket, replaces the first player. The new set-up almost exactly duplicates the first set-up, except that the ball is on the opposite side of the floor, with a change of position for two players. Some teams employ the dribble, with the dribbler going very close to his receiver. The purpose is very apparent, which is to separate a teammate from his opponent. The figure eight pattern may be either spread out or be very compact to suit the desires of the coach. With three players involved, the passer passes and advances diagonally up the floor in front of the receiver. His next thought is to replace his receiver after a pass.

The three-man continuity has received widespread attention and application. It is easily taught and assimilated. With three players in combination, the passer passes and goes in front of only one player, the receiver. It is best to learn the three man maneuvers before going on to teach a five-man combination.

If five players are to be employed in the continuity, the passer advances diagonally in front of two teammates. He does not replace his receiver in this set-up. The five-man combination obviously gives greater distance for the passer to cut. The figure eight pattern may be spread out, or it may be flattened by having the players go close to their receivers. The first step in teaching this type of action should be to establish continuity. The breaks or scoring opportunities may be developed later.

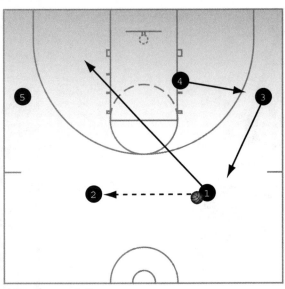

Carlson 1.0

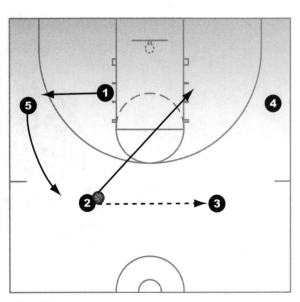

Carlson 1.1

LESSONS FROM THIS LEGEND...

CROSSWISE CONTINUITY

In **Diagram 1.0**, O1 passes to O2 and goes in front of two players, O2 and O5. O1 is replaced by O3, and O3 is replaced by O4.

In **Diagram 1.1**, O2 passes to O3 and goes in front of two players, O3 and O4. O2 cuts diagonally forward to the pivot position. O2 is replaced by O5, and O5 is replaced by O1.

In **Diagram 1.2**, O3 passes to O5 and goes in front of two players, O5 and O1. O3 cuts diagonally forward to the pivot position. O3 is replaced by O4, and O4 is replaced by O2.

In **Diagram 1.3**, O5 passes to O4 and goes in front of two players, O4 and O2. O5 cuts diagonally forward to the pivot position. O5 is replaced by O1, and O1 is replaced by O3.

Diagram 1.4 shows the figure eight appearance of the players' lines of travel in this continuity. The dotted line shows the passage of the ball. Ten passes across court with accompanying cuts by the players will give the original set-up. The foregoing continuity, with only return passes as breaks for scoring opportunities, will be sufficient for many teams. For other teams, mastery of the crosswise continuity will only be the beginning. Competition will demand the development of other continuities with scoring opportunities.

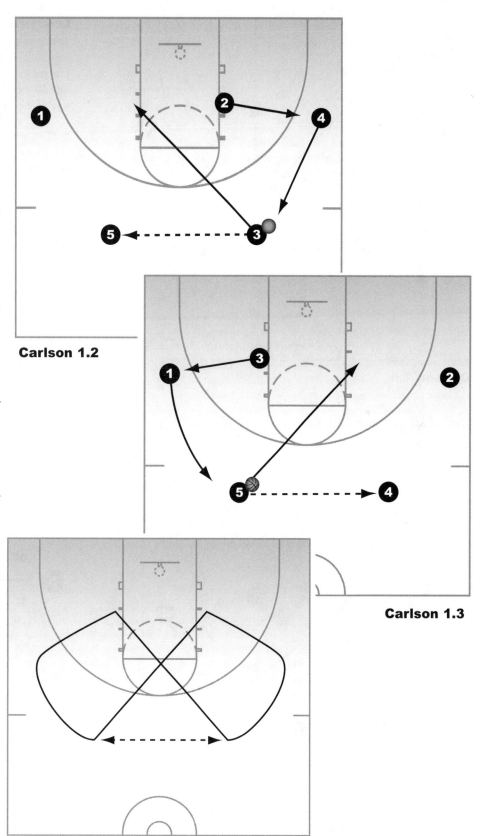

Carlson 1.2

Carlson 1.3

Carlson 1.4

LESSONS FROM THIS LEGEND...

LENGTHWISE CONTINUITY

The continuity with the ball passing lengthwise of the floor follows the regular rule of the five-men continuity. The passer passes and goes in front of two players. He cuts diagonally in the general direction of the straight passage of the ball.

In **Diagram 1.5**, O1 passes straight up the floor to O3 and goes in front of two players, O3 and O4. He cuts diagonally toward the basket-end of the floor. O1 is replaced by O2, and O2 is replaced by O5. This results in three players near the ball and two away from the ball.

In **Diagram 1.6**, O3 passes out to O2 and goes in front of two players, O2 and O5. He cuts toward the midline to the side of the floor opposite the ball. O3 is replaced by O4, and O4 is replaced by O1. Again, we have three players in close proximity to the ball.

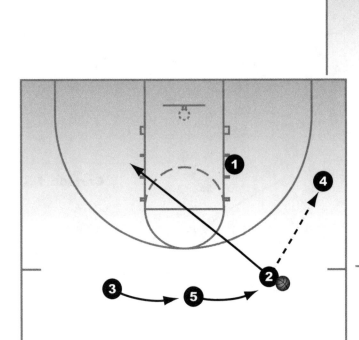

Carlson 1.5

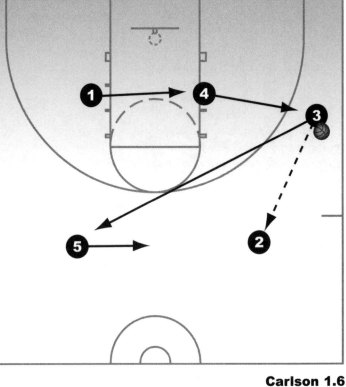

Carlson 1.6

In **Diagram 1.7**, O2 passes ahead to O4 and goes in front of two players, O4 and O1. He cuts diagonally toward the basket end of the floor. O2 is replaced by O5, and O5 is replaced by O3.

Carlson 1.7

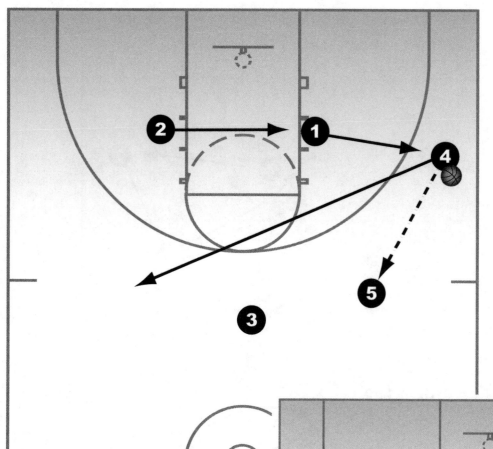

Carlson 1.8

In **Diagram 1.8**, O4 passes out to O5 and goes in front of O5 and O3. He cuts diagonally toward the midline to the side of the floor opposite the ball. O4 is replaced by O1, and O1 is replaced by O2.

In **Diagram 1.9**, the figure eight is seen in a different direction from that in the crosswise continuity. The dotted lines show the passage of the ball as being parallel with the sidelines. The lengthwise continuity must be practiced on both sides of the floor.

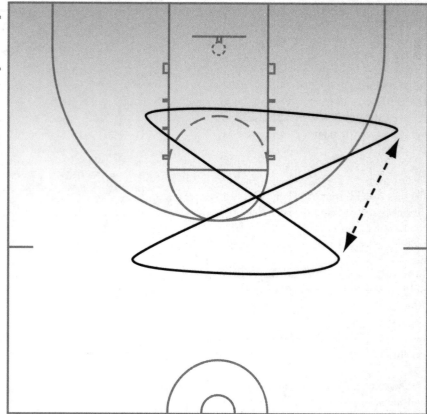

Carlson 1.9

LESSONS FROM THIS LEGEND...

TEACHING PROGRESSION

In our early stages of teaching, we separate each continuity. Once our players understand the pattern, we interchange the continuities. Our rule is to develop the continuity first and then incorporate the plays or scoring opportunities. It is best to set up the plays in outline form and establish their execution as a matter of habit. In this way, the breaks in the continuity come as a natural sequence when an opportunity for a scoring play presents itself. Again, it is well to remember that, though the continuity is taught first, the scoring opportunities are really more important.

DIAGONAL CONTINUITY

The next continuity presents the diagonal passage of the ball and follows the rule of the passer going in front of two players. In this continuity, the fifth player rests until there is a change to another continuity.

In **Diagram 1.10**, O1 passes diagonally to O5 and cuts in front of O2 and O5. He cuts diagonally toward the basket end of the floor. O2 is replaced by O3, and O3 is replaced by O4.

In **Diagram 1.11**, O5 passes diagonally out to O3 and cuts in front of O3 and O4 to replace O1. He cuts diagonally toward the basket end of the floor. O5 is replaced by O1.

In **Diagram 1.12**, O3 passes diagonally to O1 and cuts in front of O2 and O1. He cuts diagonally toward the basket end of the floor and replaced O5. O3 is replaced by O4, and O4 is replaced by O5.

In **Diagram 1.13**, O1 passes diagonally out to O4 and cuts in front of O4 and O5. He cuts, as shown in the diagram, and replaces O3. O1 is replaced by O3, and the formation of three players in and two players out is continued.

In **Diagram 1.14**, we have the figure eight and the passage of the ball for the continuity diagonally across the floor. As with the lengthwise continuity, the diagonal conti-

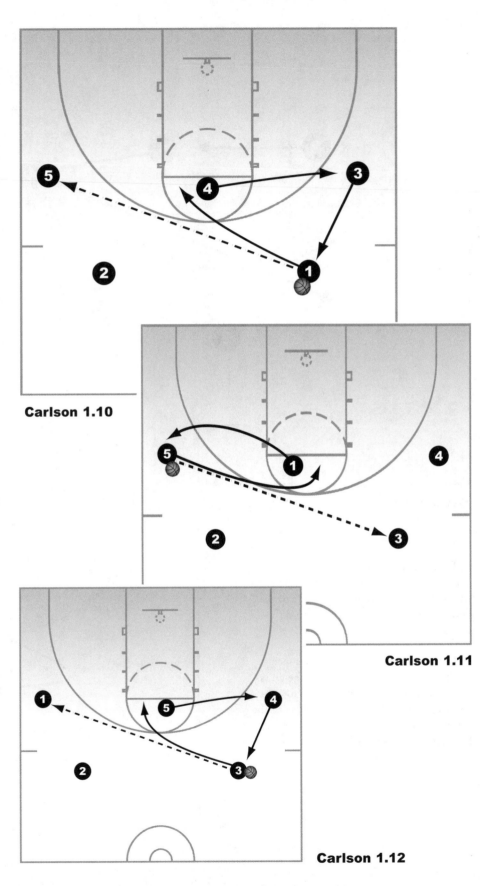

Carlson 1.10

Carlson 1.11

Carlson 1.12

LESSONS FROM THIS LEGEND...

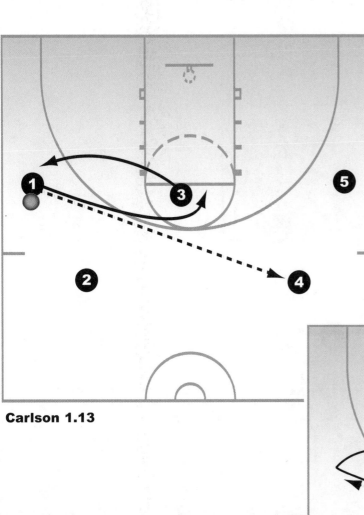

Carlson 1.13

nuity must be practiced on both sides of the floor.

So far, three different continuities and their variations that the coach and players should practice and master separately, before they try to interchange them or insert breaks or scoring plays, have been discussed.

PIVOT-MAN CONTINUITY

The last continuity to be reviewed here is the pivot-man continuity. It portrays a possible break in the continuity, as one part of pivot play. Only the continuity will be shown, the return pass or scoring break being apparent. The passer goes in front of two players. This continuity may be a

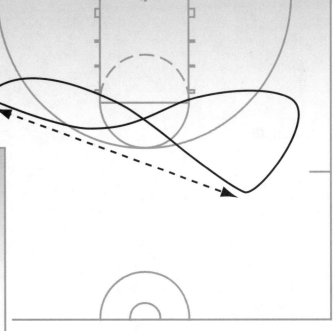

Carlson 1.14

three-man continuity by keeping the ball on one side of the court. It may be a five-man continuity by using both sides. The following description uses five players.

In **Diagram 1.15**, O1 passes to O4 and cuts in front of O3 and O4. He cuts past the pivot man, O4, as shown in the dia-

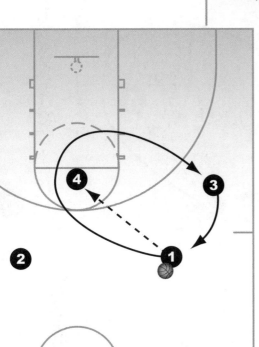

Carlson 1.15

41

Carlson 1.16

gram. O1 is replaced by O3. Since O1 does not get a return pass, he fills in the place vacated by O3.

In **Diagram 1.16**, O4 passes out to O2. He then moves in front of O2 and O5 and cuts back toward the basket. The set-up is practically the same in **Diagram 1.17**, except that the ball is in the back-court.

In **Diagram 1.17**, O2 passes to O4 and cuts in front of O5 and O4. He then cuts past the pivot man O4. O2 is replaced by O5. Since O2 does not get a return pass, he fills in the place vacated by O5, and is cheated the set-up shown in **Diagram 1.18**

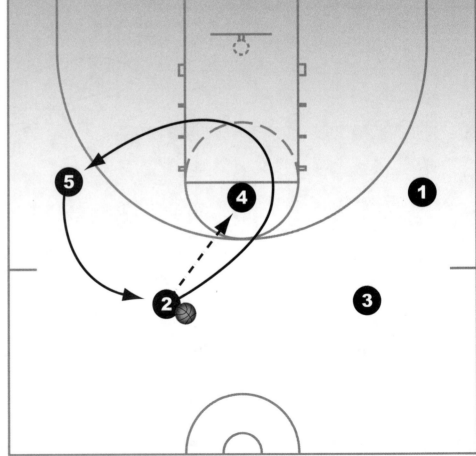

Carlson 1.17

LESSONS FROM THIS LEGEND...

Diagram 1.18 illustrates the pass out by the pivot man and the maintenance of the formation with three players in and two players out.

Diagram 1.19 shows the double continuity forming a figure eight line of travel. The broken lines portray the passage of the ball.

CLOSING POINTS

These continuities are presented in the order of difficulty and in the best order of learning. These set-ups may come from either a slow-break or a fast break. The practice of these continuities gives enough fundamental training to justify them, even if they are never used in game tactics.

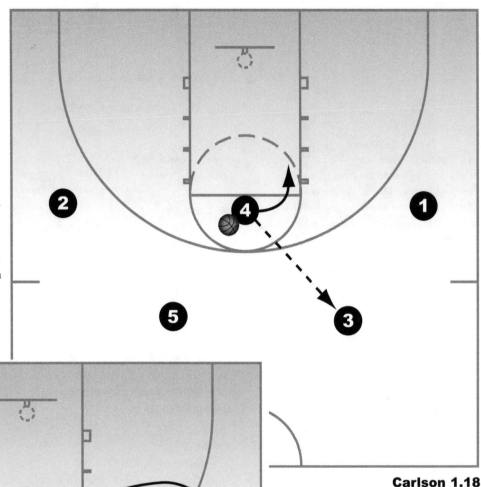

Carlson 1.18

SOURCE

Carlson, H.C. (1934, November). Five-Man Figure 8 Continuities. *The Athletic Journal.*

Carlson 1.19

LESSONS FROM THIS LEGEND...

BASKETBALL FUNDAMENTALS

By H.C. "Doc" Carlson

In every occupation, there are certain fundamentals—the sum total of which, is that occupation. The fundamentals in themselves are for the most part uninteresting, but in order to become proficient, we must know and concentrate on them individually. Fundamentals are those integral parts on which the degree of perfection determines the quality or limits of success in any occupation.

ATTRIBUTES OF A WINNING PLAYER

- Desire
- Self-confidence
- Effort
- Enthusiasm
- Preparedness
- Perseverance
- Honesty
- Courage
- Willingness to improve

THE ABILITY TO VISUALIZE AND DREAM

Before going into the most important basketball fundamentals, it is appropriate to realize that the ability to visualize the fundamentals is of the utmost importance. The player, who thinks and dreams and lives the idea of doing the fundamentals correctly, has a greater chance of coming through than the player who does not know the fundamentals and thinks of them only when performing them on the gymnasium floor. A lot of clever things seem to be done unconsciously which really are the results of previous sustained thoughts and the visualization of them, for the mind must first direct before the body can execute.

Authors' Note: Readers should remember that visualization, as a common tool from sport

psychology in modern basketball, was recommended by Carlson in 1928.

THE LAW OF LIFE

The law of life is growth, and the law of growth is activity. In other words, we either grow or die figuratively; if we are to grow, we must be active physically and mentally. We must know the fundamentals in order to visualize them. Image yourself executing the fundamentals properly under different circumstance—practice them physically, persevere, and then success will come.

MOST IMPORTANT BASKETBALL FUNDAMENTALS

SHOOTING

- Shooting is the most important fundamental. The team that scores the most points wins the game, and points are made only by shooting baskets. Better passing and handling of the ball make for easier shots, but the final test is in getting the ball in the basket.

  Authors' Note: Carlson was able to emphasize the importance of shooting to success, even in the earliest times in basketball history. Today it is widely recognized as the most important factor related to winning. (Krause J.V. [April 2003], NABC Research Committee Report, Unpublished document).

- Shoot with care and confidence. Practice with the idea of making every shot. You cannot shoot with the feeling that the shot is going to miss, nor can you shoot carelessly and expect to improve.

- Shoot and feel that the goal is as big as a tub. Learn the short shots first. For the greatest accuracy, use the backboard when shooting close to the basket.

- Do not take bad shots. The ball is your most precious possession when you are playing basketball. When you have it, you are in a position to score, and the opposition is not. Rather than take a poor shot, pass the ball to a teammate.

- The most common and sensible shots are the two-handed push shots from the level of the chest in shooting from a distance, and the shot with either hand under the basket.

- In shooting foul goals, our formula is to have all muscles relaxed, so that they are receptive to the message, "This is one more point." *Authors' Note: Carlson is referring to free throws*

PASSING AND RECEIVING

- Passing and receiving represent cooperation. It is the same cooperation evident in the banding of individuals in society to overcome the common enemy. The welfare of the individual must be the welfare of the team.

- The fundamentals of good passing include accuracy, speed, and mechanical deception. Another important feature is to have confidence in your teammate's ability to handle the pass.

LESSONS FROM THIS LEGEND...

- Just as in shooting, practice is the basis for improvement. You must try to make every pass accurately. Get in the habit of doing things right all the time.

- There are many types of passes. Any pass that includes the fundamentals of accuracy and timing with speed or deception may be considered efficient in the present development of the game.

- For general purposes, passes can be categorized in two classes: a baseball pass in the backcourt for a long pass, and a push pass inside the offensive territory where short passes are more successful. Each of these types includes aerial and bounce passes. The delivery must be adapted to the type of pressure from the opposition.

DRIBBLING

- Next in importance is the dribble, both as a matter of individual effort or as a part of teamwork.

- The dribbler must utilize deception and includes feints, stops, pivots, and handling the ball at the same time.

CUTTING

- Cutting is the eluding of your opponent and getting in a more advantageous position to receive the ball.

- To cut and receive a pass is beautiful to behold.

- To cut and be missed is depressing to the cutter. One of the ways of smoothing over this situation and strengthening the morale of the team is to have the player who missed the cutter speak first and apologize for missing. Another morale builder is for the player who cuts and fumbles a pass to communicate to and reassure the passer that the next pass will be caught.

- To cut properly, you must judge the right time to break, because to get to the proper spot too quickly enables your opponent to catch up with you. Another factor is change of pace. If you have started too soon, you can go slowly for a short distance, and then pick up the pace to reach the necessary speed.

- Another method of cutting is to out-speed your opponent. Being unable to do this, you can feint in one direction and go another. Sudden stops and pivots may also be applied in cutting.

- In addition to practicing cuts on the gymnasium floor, interested players will visualize their cutting at home or on the streets. A player can approach a chair and swerve to either side; chasing a dog is good practice. Get the idea implanted and then let speed develop in the gym.

Authors' Note: Many of these critical coaching cues advocated by Carlson on fundamental skills are taught by coaches today.

SOURCE

Carlson, H.C. (1928, September). Basketball Fundamentals. *The Athletic Journal.*

LEGACY OF
Lou Carnesecca

- Coached 24 years at St. John's and led every one of his teams into postseason tournament play (18 NCAA tournaments and 6 NITs).

- Directed St. John's to the NIT championship in 1989.

- Demonstrated enthusiasm, passion, and respect for the basketball profession.

- Maximized the talents of gifted players within a team concept.

- Became the 30th coach in NCAA history to reach the 500-victory mark.

- Led the New York Nets to the 1972 ABA Finals

Lou Carnesecca

We emphasize our fast break game and try to score before our opponents have the chance to set up their halfcourt offense.
—Lou Carnesecca

BIOGRAPHY

Born: January 5, 1925 in New York, New York

Inducted into the Naismith Basketball Hall of Fame in 1992

Lou Carnesecca was the head coach at St. John's University for 24 years and led every one of his teams to postseason play (18 NCAA tournaments and 6 NITs). He compiled a 526-200 record during his head coaching tenure at St. John's. Carnesecca was an assistant to future Hall of Fame coach Joe Lapchick for seven years, before becoming the Red Storm's head coach in 1965. He left the college game to coach the New York Nets from 1970 to 1973 and led New York to the ABA Finals in 1972. Carnesecca returned as head coach to St. John's in 1973 and stayed until he retired in 1992. The highly energetic Carnesecca directed St. John's to an NIT championship in 1989 and a Final Four appearance in 1985. He was selected National Coach of the Year by the NABC and USBWA in 1983 and 1985. He was named Big East Conference Coach of the Year on three occasions. Carnesecca served in the Coast Guard during World War II and then attended St. John's University. He played baseball for legendary coach Frank McGuire and helped lead his team to the 1949 College World Series. After graduation, Carnesecca's first coaching position was on the high-school ranks at his alma mater, St. Ann's Academy. Carnesecca is a member of the New York City Sports Hall of Fame.

Lou Carnesecca...

Lou Carnesecca is affectionately called "Looie" by sports fans everywhere. "Looie" developed a passion for sports at an early age and played whichever sport was in season, every available moment. Carnesecca did this against the wishes of his father who thought that sports were a waste of time. His parents came to New York City from Italy, and Italian was the only language spoken in the home. Carnesecca did not start speaking English until he was six years old.

Carnesecca attended St. Ann's Academy and knew even then that he wanted to become a basketball coach. He was highly influenced by future Hall of Fame official Dave Tobey. Tobey had an illustrious career, both as a coach and as an official, and authored one of the first books on basketball officiating. Carnesecca played both basketball and baseball at St. Ann's, but admitted that he was not a very good athlete. "I was a lousy basketball player," stated Carnesecca. "It took me three years to make the junior varsity, and when I finally made it, I think it was because the coach, Brother James, realized I loved the game so much that he put me on the team. I didn't play very much. Instead, I learned the game from the seat of my pants, which, looking back, may have been a blessing in disguise." (Carnesecca, 1988, p. 25)

When Carnesecca graduated from St. Ann's in 1943, the United States was embroiled in World War II. Carnesecca joined the Coast Guard and traveled to Okinawa, Guam, Yokohama, and Tokyo. He was discharged at the end of World War II and enrolled at St. John's University. Carnesecca was a second baseman on the baseball team and played in the 1949 College World Series. St. John's legendary basketball coach Frank McGuire also coached the baseball team. McGuire recognized Carnesecca's love for the game of basketball and put him to work refereeing scrimmages, scouting players, and scouting opponents. "It was Frank who gave me my chance," said Carnesecca. "I've never forgotten that. Thanks to him, I always saw the game from a coach's point of view." (Carnesecca, 1988, p. 34)

Carnesecca's first job was at his alma mater, St. Ann's Academy. He worked around the clock to become the best coach possible. "Once I had the job at St. Ann's, it was total immersion in basketball," stated Carnesecca. "It became a passion with me, a fixation, a mania. I don't think I spent one day, or part of a day, when I wasn't thinking about basketball. If there ever was a fanatic, I was it. Basketball was something I loved and couldn't get enough of." (Carnesecca, 1988, p. 40)

Carnesecca worked for Hall of Fame coach Joe Lapchick at St. John's for seven years before becoming the head coach in 1965. Carnesecca gave credit to St. John's coaches Lapchick, Buck Freeman, and Frank McGuire for establishing his coaching philosophy. They taught Carnesecca that talented players win games and that coaches should never think that they are geniuses. Freeman believed that 65-75 percent of a team's success was determined by the talent of its players, 15-20 percent was coaching, and the remaining 5-20 percent was luck. Lapchick was a low-key, humble man and despised the so-called geniuses of the game, the coaches who thought they were so smart and better than everybody else. Lapchick was a brilliant strategist and a master psychologist who got the maximum out of his players. Carnesecca called Lapchick, Freeman, and McGuire "three of basketball's greatest minds." (Carnesecca, 1988, p. 7)

Carnesecca always believed that players win, not the coach. He never criticized his players in the press because that destroyed confidence and team unity. Carnesecca was a master at building the confidence of his team members. "My way of trying to motivate my players is to tell them how good they can be; to build them up, instead of tearing them down," said Carnesecca. "Tearing them down can be counterproductive. I try to put myself in their place. Nobody likes to hear about his faults, especially in public. I can always do that in private. I'm a believer in the old adage that you can attract more bees with honey than you can with vinegar." (Carnesecca, 1988, p. 206)

The first quality that Carnesecca looked for in a recruit was talent. "There's no substitute for talent," stated Carnesecca. "After that, I'm interested in his attitude. Is he coachable? Will he get along with the other players on the team? Is he selfish or unselfish? I want to know what his work habits are. I want to know about his character, his family background, and what kind of person he is." (Carnesecca, 1988, p. 123)

On game night, the animated and energetic Carnesecca often wore brown pants, a blue button-down shirt, and a tie. Spectators could watch Carnesecca's tie and know how the game was going. Most of the time, he loosened the knot, and it was hanging around his chest. The tougher the game, the lower the knot. Later in his coaching career, Carnesecca's colorful sweaters became his trademark.

The biggest change in basketball during Carnesecca's career was the size, strength, and skill of the players. Carnesecca said, "When I first started in the game, the "big man" on a team was maybe 6 foot 7 inches or 6 foot 8 inches. Joe Lapchick was the big man of his day at 6 foot 5 inches." (Carnesecca, 1988, p. 207)

With so many more bigger, taller, and faster players, Carnesecca recommended increasing the size of the court. He was not in favor of raising the height of the basket, because no matter how high you raise it, the rules will always favor the taller player. Carnesecca campaigned for years for a red, white, and blue basketball, similar to the ball used in the American Basketball Association. He thought it would be so much easier for the fans in the cheap seats to see the ball, and it would make the game more interesting and appealing to the spectators.

Few coaches have ever been as happy in their jobs as Carnesecca was. He had a passion for the game and a deep respect for the coaching profession. Carnesecca was a man of great depth, compassion, and warmth.

SOURCE

Carnesecca, Lou. Vertical Files, Archives. Naismith Memorial Basketball Hall of Fame. Springfield, MA.

Carnesecca, Lou and Phil Pepe. (1988) *Louie In Season.* New York: McGraw-Hill.

LESSONS FROM THIS LEGEND...

ATTACKING THE BOX-AND-ONE DEFENSE

By Lou Carnesecca

It is very rare when a coach has four or five great players in his starting lineup. Many of us have been fortunate to have two or three outstanding players on their squad at the same time, and almost all coaches have had one outstanding player. My topic today is attacking the box-and-one defense. It is a vital part of our offense, and unfortunately, it is an area that most coaches are unprepared.

PREPARING YOUR TEAM

There must be great mental and physical preparation for this offense. Your attack must be well organized. The first thing we must determine is to recognize what type of special defense our opponent is playing. When are they playing it, and which players are doing it? Are they doing it to your high scorer? If it is your high scorer, is he an inside or outside player?

You must also prepare your high scorer, psychologically. He must move without the ball and not get frustrated due to the lack of open space. By the mere fact that our opponent's defense is being geared to stop his scoring, some of our other people will get good open shots. Your star player must be reminded that he will not be forgotten and that he will receive multiple screens so that he will get good open looks at the basket.

You must also prepare your other players. When they see their star player being double-teamed, they must know that they will be getting their shots. You must develop confidence in them. And you must prove to them that by the fact that the defense is geared to stop that one player, that a lot of shots will be coming to them.

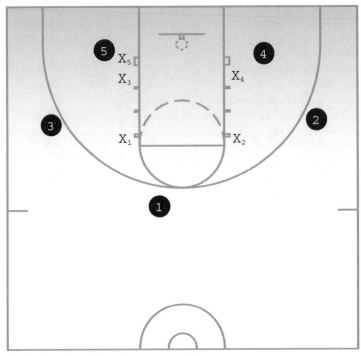

Carnesecca 1.0

BASIC PRINCIPLES

The following principles apply in any attack against a zone:

SPLIT THE DEFENSE

The first thing we do is to position our players in the seams of the defense. By splitting the defenders, we immediately cause a problem for the defense. Our objective is to get two defenders guarding one offensive player.

ATTACK FROM THE REAR

It is very important to place one player on the baseline behind the defense, because sooner or later he is going to break into an open area and become a post.

THINK ONE PLAY AHEAD

Spend time on passing. Make sure the pass is accurate and delivered at the right time. If the pass is not good, it causes the offense to be standing a little bit, and allows the defenders the chance to catch up. Offensive players cannot wait until they catch the ball to look for the next play. They must see the whole floor and think one play ahead.

STEP IN AND TOWARD THE DIRECTION OF YOUR PASS

It is very important that after a pass is made, to step in and toward the direction of the pass. Now, when that player receives a return pass, he is closer to the basket and has a higher-percentage shot. It is also important to be positioned so that the player has a good passing angle.

LESSONS FROM THIS LEGEND...

GET THE BALL INSIDE

Post play is essential to your success. The cardinal rule is to attack from the rear and the blind side. This principle hasn't changed since the 1930's. It is important that as the post comes up, he makes himself available. He comes up with his hands extended; he gives a good target, not with one hand, but with two. And as he receives the ball, he is not only ready for the shot, but also sees the next logical pass. The post player must be aggressive.

OFFENSIVE REBOUND

It is important that every player has specific offensive rebounding responsibilities, including defensive balance. It cannot be helter-skelter.

BASIC ATTACK

In **Diagram 1.0,** O5 is going to be the player being "boxed". It is very important that we are organized and everyone knows when a certain play is being run to free O5.

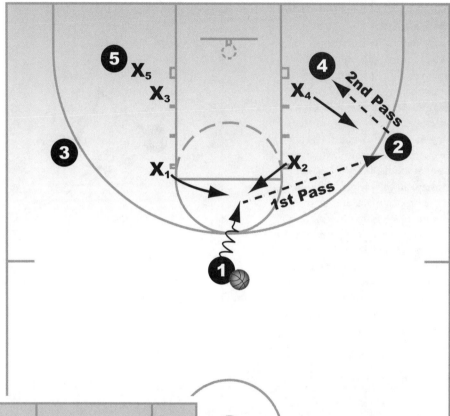

Carnesecca 1.1

As shown in **Diagram 1.1** , the first thing we are going to do is to have O1 split the two front defensive players. By positioning O2 on the wing, we have placed a tremendous strain on the defensive man on the baseline. If he comes out, we dump the ball inside to O4. Or O2 can dribble in several directions for a short jump shot. Notice we haven't involved our great player, O5, yet. We will get him involved later. We have prepared our other players to play without him. We have them ready and you can see that we can get some pretty good shots.

When O1 is advancing the ball, there is no reason that O4 cannot come up and attack from the rear (See **Diagram 1.2**). This may free O4 for a short jumper or a scoring pass to another teammate. Another option is that O3 can attack from the other wing.

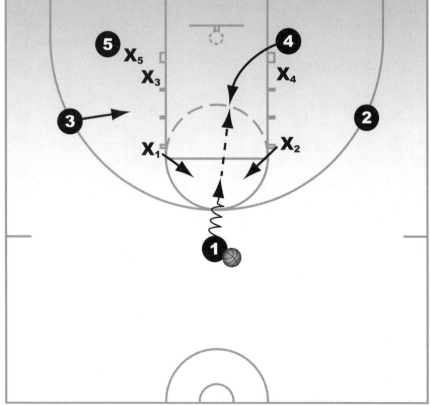

Carnesecca 1.2

51

LESSONS FROM THIS LEGEND...

DOUBLE SCREEN FOR YOUR STAR PLAYER

If your star player hasn't touched the ball for five minutes and it is time to get him a scoring opportunity, we call a special play (see **Diagram 1.3**). This is a set play, and everyone knows that we are going to run it. O1 gets the defensive guards to commit themselves to stop the middle drive. O1 passes to O3, steps in the proper direction to get the proper angle, and then gets the return pass from O3. O3 then goes and puts a good screen on O5's defender. O5 looks for the short jumper. If the defense switches, as shown in **Diagram 1.4**, the player who sets the screen pins the defender on his back and comes to meet the pass from the O1.

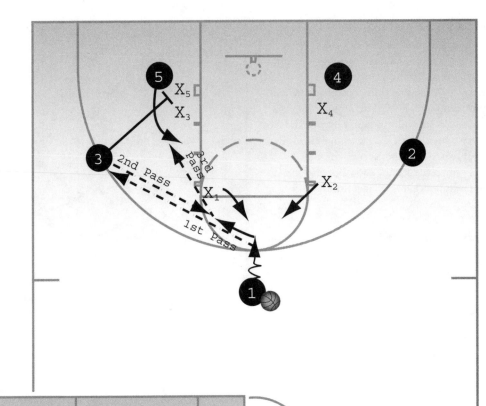

Carnesecca 1.3

Carnesecca 1.4

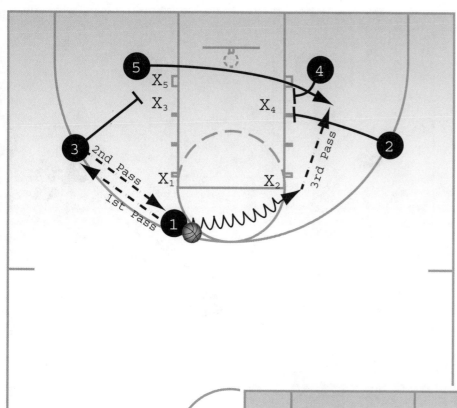

Carnesecca 1.5

From the same formation, we can give our star player a double screen (see **Diagram 1.5**). The play starts the same way, with O1 passing to O3. O3 returns the pass to O1. O3 goes down as before to set a screen. The defensive player thinks that the screen is coming again. After the return pass, O1 starts to dribble, and O2 and O4 give our star player a double screen. As soon as O5 comes around the double screen, O2 takes a step up the lane (see **Diagram 1.6**). O5 can either take the jump shot or pass to O4 or O2.

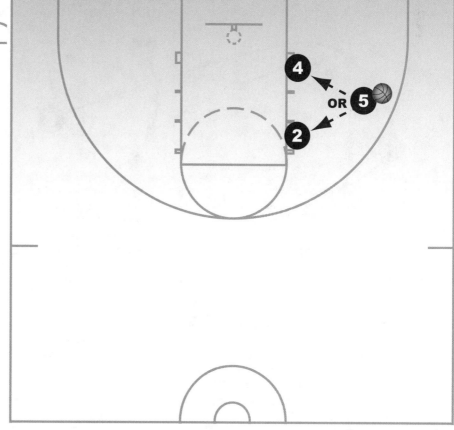

Carnesecca 1.6

LESSONS FROM THIS LEGEND...

1-3-1 ATTACK

I have been using this formation for almost 30 years, and it is a simple 1-3-1 attack. Assume that O2 is our best player and is positioned as shown in **Diagram 1.7**. We can pass the ball and go behind for a hand-off, or if O2 is being overplayed, we call "clear" and take it on the dribble. Now we have our set offense in motion. The basic principle is that our star player will receive two screens in an attempt to get him a good look at the basket.

O2 is the first cutter (see **Diagram 1.8**). O4 is the second cutter, and after making the screen, O5 is the third cutter.

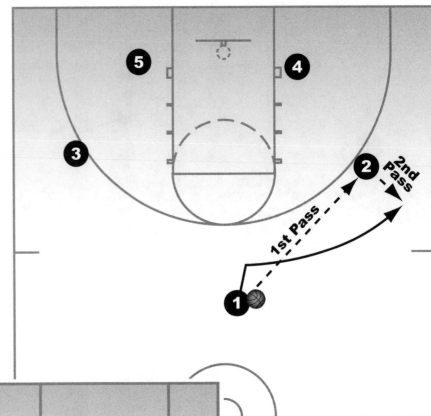

Carnesecca 1.7

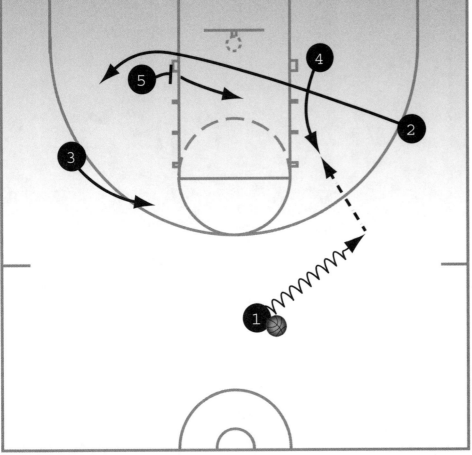

Carnesecca 1.8

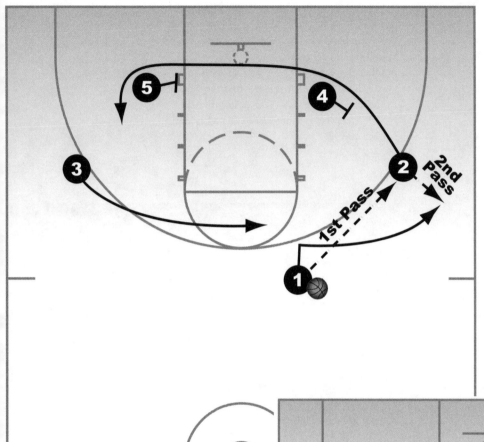

Carnesecca 1.9

Diagram 1.9 shows similar options, but begins with O1 passing to O2 and going outside of O2 for the return handoff. Then, the rest is the same. The ball is reversed first to O3 and then to the star player, O2 (see **Diagram 1.10**.).

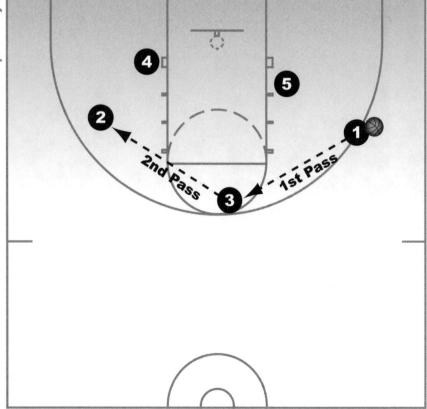

Carnesecca 1.10

LESSONS FROM THIS LEGEND...

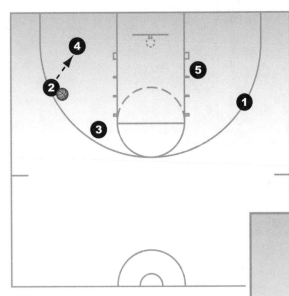

Carnesecca 1.11

If O2 doesn't have the shot (see **Diagram 1.11**), pass it to the baseline. If O4 who is on the baseline doesn't have the shot, the ball should be passed back to O2 (see **Diagram 1.12**), O2 reverses the ball to O3, makes a diagonal cut across the lane, and uses the screen by O5 to get the ball as it is reversed from O2 to O3 to O1 and back to O2.

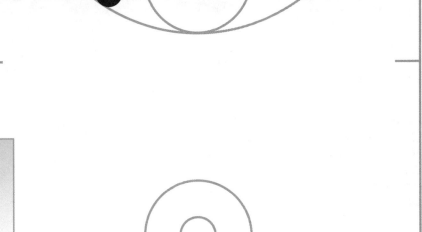

Carnesecca 1.12

The following point is important. The timing on the original cut by O2 is vital to the success of the play. O2 must hesitate in the lane on the screen by O5. Don't be in a hurry. Notice that we have an overload after the first movement with O2, O4, and O3 all on the same side. You must have the proper spacing and the proper timing. On the cut back by O2 (see **Diagram 1.12**), O4 must move up a little to keep the defense busy. Now, as shown in **Diagram 1.13**, O2 has three options besides the shot. He can dump the ball to O5, O4 can flash to the middle, or O3 can come to the foul line for a short jumper.

Carnesecca 1.13

"COME-BACK" OPTION

The next set play off the 1-3-1 attack is called the "come-back" option. It starts the same way. But, don't forget, the player on defense is getting screened all night, and he's getting tired. As shown in **Diagram 1.14**, O1 passes to O2 and gets the pass back. O2 goes as before but stops in the lane after rubbing off the screen set by O4. The ball is reversed to O3, who has split the defense in the top of the key. O4 turns and again screens for O2, who pops out along the baseline

We can also run the "come-back" option on the opposite side (See **Diagram 1.15**). In this case, O2 has already made his cut to the opposite side. O2 has passed to O4, and the ball has been returned to O2. Now this diagram shows what happens next. O2 reverses the ball to O3 and starts off the screen by O4. However, instead of going all the way through, O2 reverses and comes back again using the screen of O4.

KEY POINTS

You can never tell where the defense is going to be. We teach our players how to read the defense and explore all available

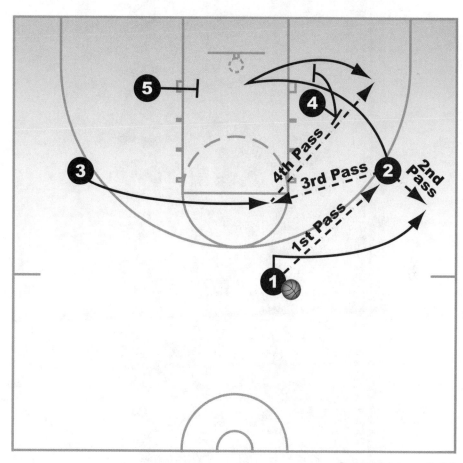

Carnesecca 1.14

options. We give them organization in our offensive attack. Our players know that we have something specific that we are trying to run. We just don't let things happen by accident.

We begin our preparation during the very first week of practice. We normally work on this type of offense once or twice a week for 10 to 15 minutes.

We emphasize our fast break game and try to score before our opponents have the chance to set up their half-court defense. We also position our players in key offensive rebounding positions so that we can have two and three scoring opportunities on the same possession. We also want to get the ball inside and draw fouls. By drawing fouls, not only do we score points, but we also get that good player sitting next to their coach.

SOURCE

Carnesecca, Lou. (1984). The Box and One Attack. *Medalist Flashback Notebook (Vol. 10).*

Carnesecca 1.15

LEGACY OF
Everett Case

- Promoted the growth of basketball in the Southeast; called the "Father of ACC Basketball."

- Led North Carolina State to a third-place finish in the 1950 Final Four.

- Popularized fast-break basketball in the South.

- Turned games into gala events with his spotlight introductions and pep bands.

- Known by his admirers as the "Old Gray Fox," because of his gray hair and his chess player's mind.

- Created the Dixie Classic, the premier holiday tournament of its day.

- Led the Frankfort (IN) High School Hot Dogs to four state championships.

Everett Case

"One of the best ways to improve offensive footwork and balance is to practice without permitting even a single dribble."
—Everett Case

BIOGRAPHY

Born: June 21, 1900 in Anderson, IN

Died: April 30, 1966

Inducted into the Naismith Basketball Hall of Fame in 1982

Everett Case coached North Carolina State University from 1946 to 1964 and compiled a 376-133 record. He was named ACC Coach of the Year in 1954, 1955, and 1958. During Case's first ten years at North Carolina State, the Wolfpack won six consecutive Southern Conference tournaments, three straight Atlantic Coast Conference tournaments, and six of seven Dixie Classics. Case's teams dominated the Southern Conference and won 108 of 119 league games. North Carolina State finished third in the NIT in 1947. In 1950, Case took the Wolfpack to the NCAA Final Four for the first time in school history and finished third. Prior to Case's arrival at North Carolina State, he carved a niche as a future Indiana Basketball High School Hall of Fame coach by leading the Frankfort Hot Dogs to four state championships. In twenty-one seasons at four different high schools, Case registered a 467-124 record.

Everett Case...

Throughout basketball's history, few individuals have devoted more to the game than Everett Case. A lifelong bachelor, Case's passion for the sport was ignited during his formative years in Indiana when he experienced the excitement of "Hoosier Hysteria." He never played the sport in high school, yet Case's 1919 Anderson High School yearbook stated his future goal was to become a basketball coach. He was to realize his dream at age eighteen and continued coaching for forty-seven years. The young coach with the engaging smile and dynamic personality immediately proved that he was in the right profession. In 1922, Case arrived in Frankfort, Indiana and changed the way the game of basketball was played.

His 17 year-career as the Frankfort Hot Dog coach resulted in a 385-99-1 record. Case ranks second to Bill Green in Indiana high school state championships with four. The man with an astounding record and innovative coaching tactics is credited with starting such traditions as the announcing of starting lineups before the game, using game films to scout opponents, and cutting down nets after a championship win. *ESPN The Magazine* recently highlighted the fact that most of his money came from owning a small hot dog stand just blocks from the high school. Frankfurters forever.

The Hot Dogs put it all together in the 1925 season to finish 27-2 and win the state championship. The final game saw Frankfort run past the upstart Kokomo Wildcats 34-20. That year was the first time radio broadcasts were heard, and sixty-four sectionals were used. To top off the magical season, Dr. James Naismith watched the game from press row at the State Fair Grounds and presented the victors their medals. The 15,000 spectators were the largest crowd ever to witness a basketball game.

Current New Castle resident and former Frankfort forward Buck Plunkett still remembers the celebration after the game. "On our way back home, cars lined up along the side of the road to greet us at Lebanon. They lined up for over fifteen miles, until we arrived at the courthouse for a celebration."

A classic contest between Frankfort and Logansport in 1927 created much controversy. The Berries were stranded by snowdrifts on their way to the game, had to get picked up by Frankfort officials, and started the varsity game shortly before midnight. At the time, there was no ten-second rule in high school basketball, and Case held the ball the final eleven minutes of the first half with Logansport leading 7-6. By holding the ball at the opposite end of the court, the Hot Dogs stalled the entire second half, until just under four minutes remained. They rallied for a controversial 10-7 victory, and another chapter was written in the Everett Case file. The game caused post-game fights, cancellation of a rematch, and the creation of a ten-second line.

After collecting another championship in 1929 and dealing with accusations of illegal recruiting, Case left Frankfort to coach at Anderson for the 1932-33 season. He left the state to coach at the University of Southern California during the 1934 season, while he earned his master's degree and worked under Coach Sam Barry. One year in the sun led Case to return to the state where basketball is king and the city he loved, Frankfort. One mediocre season was followed by another state championship.

The 1936 team produced two college All-Americans, a high school coach, and two college coaches. They compiled a record of 29-1-1. According to the *Times* weekend edition, March 6, 1986, "It was and is generally considered the finest basketball team in Indiana history, until the Oscar Robertson led Crispus Attucks champs of 1955-1956."

The tie came from two overtime grudge matches between the Hot Dogs and Indianapolis Tech. After nine ties, and fifty-one field goal attempts from each team, Case and Tech coach Bayne Freeman agreed to end the game.

Ansel Street commented in the *Times* article, "Nobody knows quite why they decided to leave it at a tie. I guess the coaches just decided that was enough." The IHSAA ruled after the season to prohibit ties, hence that is the only tie in Indiana high school history.

Ralph Montgomery is one of just two members of that team still alive. He still resides in Frankfort, and has fond memories of playing under Coach Case. "He had a lot of confidence in us and used much psychology in his coaching methods. We had confidence in him, and played the way he taught us. We played as a team, not as individuals like many teams today."

Case was one of the first basketball coaches known to film games. He meticulously studied every play and looked for options to maximize the strengths of his team. While pursuing his master's degree and working for Hall of Fame coach Sam Barry at the University of Southern California, Case analyzed various methods for shooting free throws. His results supported the use of the underhand shot.

At the conclusion of World War II, Case was selected head coach at North Carolina State University. The selection of Case forever changed the game of basketball in the South. A brilliant coach, promoter, and motivator, he became the catalyst that made basketball the number one sport on "Tobacco Road." Jim Weaver, the first commissioner of the Atlantic Coast Conference, believed that Everett Case meant more to basketball in the South Atlantic region of the country than any other person. Case started the tradition carried on by Hall of Fame coaching legends Frank McGuire, Dean Smith, and Mike Krzyzewski.

"Coach Case was a visionary," said Les Robinson, who played for Case and later coached the Wolfpack. "He was a great coach, yes, but he was also a great promoter. Coach was a Madison Avenue type of businessman. He was years ahead of his time. He was marketing the game in an era when 'market,' meant where you go to get groceries." (Robinson, 2002)

Case directed his attention to promoting his team and his sport throughout North Carolina. He crusaded for every youngster to have a basketball hoop in his backyard. He often used his own money to purchase basketball equipment for playgrounds and boys clubs. Case dreamt of creating in North Carolina the same "basketball fever" found in his native state of Indiana.

Case established a tournament called the Dixie Classic. He knew it was the perfect way to bring national attention to basketball in North Carolina. The eight-team, three-day tournament matched the "Big Four" of the area (North Carolina State, North Carolina, Duke, and Wake Forest) against four of the nation's top teams. The Classic became a fixture on the holiday social calendar for North Carolinians, and its reputation quickly spread throughout the United States. It became the premier sporting event in the South Atlantic region and was the forerunner of the many popular holiday tournaments that make up basketball today.

Known by his admirers as the "Old Gray Fox," Case was a magnificent showman and turned game night at Reynolds Coliseum into a gala event. By darkening the Coliseum, he heightened the crowd's anticipation and introduced the Wolfpack under a spotlight to the cheers of the fans. This type of pregame ritual had never been seen before in the South. Case also installed a sound meter to supposedly measure the noise level in the Coliseum. In reality, the sound meter was not functional and was controlled with a switch by a man standing courtside. Nevertheless, it was a great way of building excitement and increasing State's

home-court advantage. Case was the first coach to authorize a pep band to play at home games. Opposing coaches accused Case of hiring the organist that played "Dixie" and sent the crowd into a frenzy. Cutting down the nets after winning a championship was also brought by Case to North Carolina, a tradition from his days as a high school coach in Indiana.

Another great highlight on game night was watching the silver-haired Case. It appeared that Case spent as much energy on the sidelines as his players did on the court. "I shoot for every one of my boys," stated Case. "If it looks like they're going to miss, I try to lean, or twist or scrooch'em in." (Lowery, 1951)

Case was one of the true innovators during his era. His racehorse style of basketball spread like wildfire across the state of North Carolina. The up-tempo, run-and-shoot game created excitement for both the players and the fans.

Case and his teams were so dominant that it forced other schools in the conference to revamp and update their basketball programs. North Carolina hired Frank McGuire, Duke brought in Vic Bubas, and Wake Forest chose Bones McKinney in an attempt to catch the Wolfpack. And in the process, the Atlantic Coast Conference (ACC) became one of the most respected leagues in college basketball.

Eight years after Case's death, North Carolina State defeated Marquette to win the 1974 NCAA championship. The Final Four that year was held in Greensboro, North Carolina. On the triumphant trip back to Raleigh, Wolfpack coach Norm Sloan ordered the team bus to stop at the cemetery where Everett Case was buried. It was in the early hours of the morning when Sloan led his players to the gravesite to honor the man who made the NCAA title a possibility. It was a fitting tribute to the "Father of ACC Basketball."

SOURCE

Case, Everett. Vertical Files, Archives. Naismith Memorial Basketball Hall of Fame. Springfield, MA.

Lowery, Raymond. (1951, February 25). Tar Heel of the Week: Everett N. Case. *The News & Observer.*

Morris, Ron. (1988). *ACC Basketball: An Illustrated History.* Chapel Hill, NC: Four Corners Press

Robinson, Les. Interview with Ralph Pim, May 22, 2002.

LESSONS FROM THIS LEGEND...

NORTH CAROLINA STATE'S CHANGE-OF-PACE ATTACK

By Everett Case

One of the most difficult phases of offensive basketball to teach is what I call "the change-of-pace attack." Players must learn when to fast break, when to employ a semi-fast break, and when to bring the ball up slowly.

Too many teams employ just one tempo for the entire game. They play either a "race-horse" game or a slow deliberate style with no fast breaking. Either style, when used continually, becomes stereotyped and easier for the defense to solve.

Since the majority of breaks (fast, semi-fast, or slow) germinate from recoveries off the defensive board, much of the responsibility for the tempo of the break rests with the defensive rebounders. They must size up the position of the opponents, and then decide whether to strike quickly or slowly.

ALWAYS LOOK DOWNCOURT FOR OPEN PLAYERS

The defensive retrievers, who are usually the guards or the center, must work continually on the outlet pass to the forwards. They should position themselves soundly after the rebound, look downcourt, and get a fairly long pass out to the forwards, if possible.

Quite often, however, the forwards are covered, or there is danger of an interception. In this contingency, the guards must play together, crossing on every pass to safeguard against interceptions and lend deception to the break.

SEMI-FAST BREAK

The center goes downcourt, always watching to see if the guards are successful in hitting one of the forwards with a pass. If

this pass is consummated, we then have a situation that I call the semi-fast break.

Authors' Note: Today, we call this situation the secondary fast break.

SLOW-BREAK

If the semi-fast break does not develop, the guards must bear the brunt of advancing the ball. They bring the ball upcourt between themselves, always looking for an outlet pass to the forwards. If they advance to the frontcourt without being able to pass to the forwards, we have a slow-break situation. We then rely on a series of set plays and fast handling of the ball for our scoring opportunities.

THE GUARDS ARE THE QUARTERBACKS OF THE OFFENSE

You need a good floor general to change the mode of attack and to make the quick decisions on whether to go in with a fast, organized break, a semi-fast thrust, or a slow break. I call my guards the quarterbacks of the offense. Since they normally can look downcourt and see the positions of both their teammates and the opponents, they are the players who are given the responsibility of determining the offensive pattern. Many times they will yell, "Set it up!" This means that the ball must be passed back to them, and that the break opportunity has failed to materialize and a more deliberate style is called for.

THE FAST BREAK MUST BE ORGANIZED

I definitely favor and use an organized fast break in which every player maneuvers in various patterns. I use a cross in the ball-handling with emphasis on rolls and turns

when defensive opposition is encountered. Each player is thoroughly schooled on the stops, three-quarter inside turns, and pivots which fit into this type of offense. This greatly facilitates the smoothness and speed of the offense.

I permit traveling in straight lanes, but only until defensive opposition is met. Then, we start our cross-passing, pivoting, and turning. The players are warned never to pass through a guard or give him a chance for an interception, especially in 2-on-1 or 3-on-2 situations.

The cross-over game produces fewer interceptions and lends a great deal of deception to the attack, enabling us to get in for good short shots.

Diagram 1.0 outlines a situation for the fast break after an interception by one of our forwards. We assume that O1 has intercepted a pass from X1. The interceptor, O1, starts in with a fast dribble, but X2 slides back to keep him from going all the way in. O1 is forced to stop and make a three-quarter inside turn. O2, seeing O1 dribbling in, continues down the opposite side of the court.

If X2 is guarding O1 on the side, O2 slides in behind and receives a bounce pass from O1. However, if X2, after forcing O1 to stop, slides back and attempts to intercept O1's pass to O2, the latter (O2) cuts to the foul-line area in front of X2 for a pass from O1.

O1 follows the pass for a possible return from O2 and a good shot in front of the basket, or he may be able to drive in on the right side for a lay-up.

LESSONS FROM THIS LEGEND...

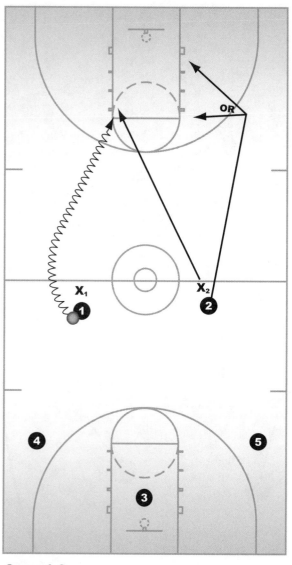

Case 1.0

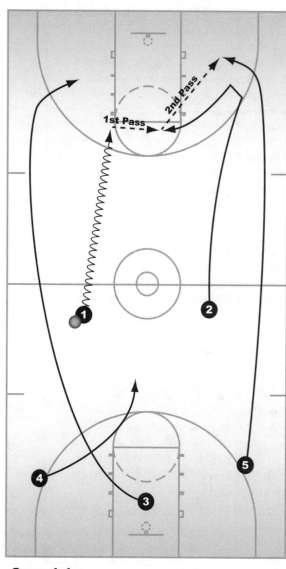

Case 1.1

The basic requisite for this type of offense is timing. The players must synchronize their moves with the man who has the ball. When a defensive man stops the ballhandler, the other front-line offensive player much change speed or direction. He must cut in sharply as soon as his teammate executes the three-quarter inside pivot. The key to the cut is the inside pivot. The cut must not be too soon or too late.

Diagram 1.1 shows the moves of the back-line players, who will normally be the center and the guards. As soon as the back-

board men perceive O1's interception, the center (O3) cuts down the side of the floor on which the pass was intercepted, while the guard (O5) breaks down the opposite side.

When O1 is forced to stop and turn, he has the option of passing to O2, who has cut to the free-throw area, or he may pass to O3 coming around on the outside. If O1 passes to O2, O2 has the option of shooting, passing back to O1, or passing to guard O5 who is coming around on the outside. O4 is the safetyman.

Most players, after an opposing shot, have a habit of turning and following the flight of the ball. This is bad. I teach my players not to follow the flight of the ball but to watch their man until he commits himself. This takes an instant. If the opponent makes a move to go in, the guard steps in front of him to cut off the direct route to the basket, and then plays for the rebound.

Since the majority of fast-break opportunities develop from missed shots, rebounding is of vital importance, and a great deal of practice time must be devoted to it. We

LESSONS FROM THIS LEGEND...

normally have our three taller players (center and guards) on the defensive boards, which gives us a triangular deployment for short rebounds and an assigned responsibility for each player. *Authors' Note: In the early days of basketball (unlike today), the two players nearest the defensive basket were called guards, while the two who played closest to the offensive basket were termed forwards.*

If the rebound falls beyond the foul circle, over the heads of the center and guards, our forwards become responsible for the rebound. Good body position is very important in keeping your opponent from securing the rebound.

Diagram 1.2 outlines an organized fast-break pattern after a rebound is secured close to the basket. X4 has taken the shot, and O3 has retrieved the rebound. The rebounder looks downcourt and passes out to O2. O1 breaks across for the pass from O2, while O3 cuts around on one side, and O4 cuts down the opposite side.

O1 has the option of either dribbling and then passing to O3 or O4, or he may stop, roll, and pass to O2. O2 has the option of passing to O4 or O3 on the outside. O5 trails as the safetyman. Whenever our organized fast break is stopped or the semi-fast break does not materialize, we go into our set plays.

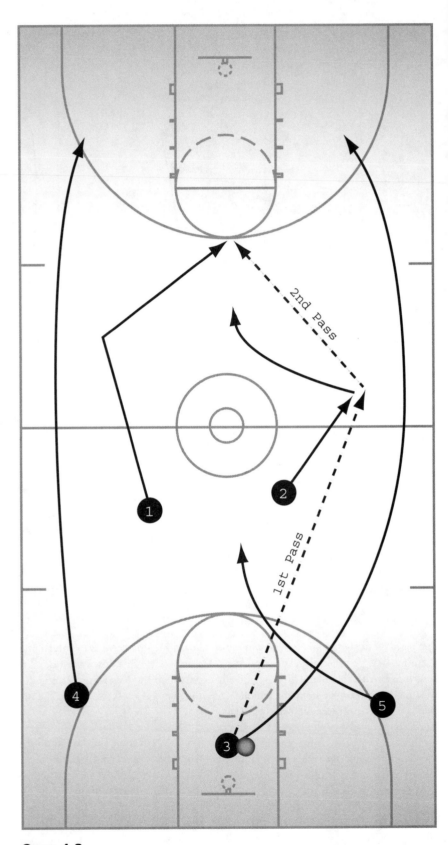

Case 1.2

LESSONS FROM THIS LEGEND...

OUR BASIC SET PLAY

Diagram 1.3 illustrates our basic set play. Guards O4 and O5 manipulate the ball between themselves, always crossing on every pass and always meeting the ball. O4 passes to O2 and goes around him, while O5 comes over and takes O4's place. O3 moves out to the side opposite the pass and screens for O1.

O2, receiving the initial pass, looks for his first option, which is a pass to O1, who is cutting off the screen to the foul line. If O2 passes to O1, he goes around him. O4, timing himself with O2, breaks around for a pass from O2 (if O1 cannot break loose).

If O4 is covered, O2 may pass back to O1 for a shot or may pass to O3, who is breaking back towards the basket after his screen.

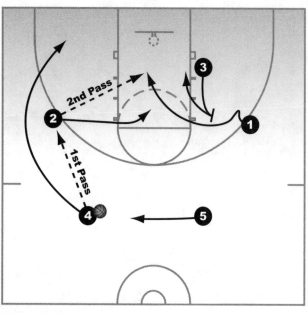

Case 1.3

MASTERY OF THE FUNDAMENTALS

A mastery of the fundamentals is essential in this type of offense, and many tedious hours must be devoted to the teaching of the basic skills, with particular emphasis on clever footwork, stops, turns, rolls, pivots, dribbling, change of pace, and passing.

AVOID OVER-DRIBBLING

A word of caution in regard to dribbling: I believe there is entirely too much of it in basketball. Far too many players have formed the bad habit of bouncing the ball one or more times before looking for a teammate to whom to pass.

Indiscriminate dribbling breaks up team play, gives the defense time to cover, and temporarily immobilizes the four other players. The opponents, on the other hand, can concentrate on the player driving with the ball.

One-man dribbling exhibitions may be pretty to watch, but they are neither as pretty nor as useful as a fast, snappy passing game with everybody moving and cutting. A team that moves quickly and makes sharp cuts forces the defense to react, thus opening up many more scoring opportunities.

There is a definite place for the dribble, but I restrict its use to certain sections of the

court and then under varying conditions. One of the best ways of discouraging the dribble is to practice floor play for several days in succession without permitting even a single dribble. You will be amazed at the improvement in footwork and balance.

After permitting no dribbles or bounces for several days, we permit only the player who intercepts a pass to dribble, provided no teammate is in front of him to pass to. We then permit the forwards to dribble-drive to the basket after outfacing or out-maneuvering their guards.

I do not permit my guards to take many dribbles unless they are out in the open or have faked their opponents out of position. I continually stress, "Don't dribble if you can pass, because the pass is so much easier than the dribble."

CLEVER FOOTWORK

Another important fundamental is clever footwork. The first requisite of a good player is "clever feet," and we spend hours developing the ability to shift quickly.

In the drill we use for this purpose, the entire squad spreads out over the court, assuming the basic defensive stance with knees flexed, upper trunk bent over low,

weight forward on the balls of the feet, and arms at the side.

I then move my arms in the direction that I want them to move: either right, left, forward, or backward.

We also employ rope skipping and shadow boxing drills to develop footwork. These drills represent an important part of our practice agenda. I often tell my players, "Your bodies can only move where your feet take them." Slow, cumbersome shifts on defense and slow-motion fakes on offense are invariably the product of insufficient practice.

In this article, I have attempted to explain exactly what I stress in my floor offense, as well as some of the fundamentals that are vitally connected with the execution of this offense.

SOURCE

Case, Everett. (1948, December). North Carolina State's Change of Pace Attack. *Scholastic Coach*.

LEGACY OF
Jody Conradt

- Helped propel women's basketball into the national limelight during the 1980s.

- Is an exemplary role model, known for her organization and meticulous attention to detail.

- Demanded the maximum effort from her players both athletically and academically.

- Directed Texas to the 1986 NCAA National Championship and the first unbeaten season in NCAA women's history.

- Has compiled 847 wins and is fourth on the list of all-time winningest Division I men's and women's coaches.

- Led Texas to a 183-game winning streak against Southwest Conference opponents.

- Selected National Coach of the Year seven times.

Jody Conradt

*"Disorganization really distresses me.
I want to feel like I've completed a task.
I don't want anything left undone."*
—Jody Conradt

BIOGRAPHY

Born: May 13, 1941 in Goldthwaite, TX

Inducted into the Naismith Basketball Hall of Fame in 1998

Jody Conradt reached the 800-win club on January 22, 2003, joining Pat Head Summit as the only women's coaches in history to win 800 games. At the conclusion of the 2004 season, Conradt's overall record was 847-269, which placed her fourth on the list of all-time winningest Division I men's and women's basketball coaches. She began her coaching career at Sam Houston State in 1969 and compiled a 74-23 record over a four-year span. She coached three seasons at the University of Texas-Arlington before accepting the position at the University of Texas in 1976. During Conradt's tenure, Texas emerged as a national basketball power. In her 28 years at Texas, Conradt has led the Lady Longhorns to 26 postseason tournaments. Her teams dominated Southwest Conference play and compiled a 183-game winning streak against conference opponents from 1978-1990. Conradt led Texas to the 1986 NCAA title with a 34-0 record. Conradt's peers and the media selected her National Coach of the Year on seven occasions. In 1987, she received the Carol Eckman Award, the highest honor given by the Women's Basketball Coaches Association.

Jody Conradt...

In the first grade, Jody Conradt's dream was to play high school basketball. Her parents gave her the belief that every young woman had the chance to be what she wanted to be and supported her desire to be a basketball star.

Girls' basketball was a big sport in her hometown of Goldthwaite, Texas and often drew larger crowds than the boys' games. The girls played six-player basketball, which was the standard style of play for decades. Her dream of becoming a basketball star came true, as Conradt averaged forty points a game during her four-year high school career.

Conradt attended Baylor University, played on the inaugural varsity team, and averaged twenty points per game. She earned a degree in physical education in 1963 and then accepted a teaching and coaching position at Waco Midway High School (TX), where she taught her players the traditional six-player girls' game.

She began her college coaching career in 1969 at Sam Houston State, where she coached three women's sports—basketball, volleyball, and track and field—on a $600 annual budget. Four years later, Conradt accepted the job as coordinator of women's athletics at the University of Texas-Arlington. There was no women's basketball program when she arrived, so Conradt's first squad consisted of volleyball players that she recruited for the basketball team. During her tenure, she won state college championships in basketball, volleyball, and softball, including a stunning upset over nationally ranked Stephen F. Austin in basketball.

In 1976, the University of Texas hired Conradt to take over the fledgling programs in basketball and volleyball. She wasted no time in beginning to chart a path that would lead Texas to unprecedented heights. Conradt knew that Texas high schools produced some of the best players in the nation, and she was one of the first coaches to recruit the state from corner to corner. Conradt also revamped the Longhorn's schedule to include Top Ten teams and prestigious tournaments, because she believed to be the best, you must play the best.

By the end of her second year, Conradt's team was ranked 15th in the final polls. Her success on the court, visibility in the community, and her charismatic nature attracted a major fan base in a football-crazed market. From 1984 to 1987, Texas finished the season ranked number one in the AP ranking. In 1986, Texas won the NCAA championship with a 34-0 record, one of only three teams in NCAA Division I history to go undefeated.

Conradt's willingness to change with the times helped her reach the pinnacle of her profession. Six-girl high school basketball in Texas was replaced by the full-court game, and the new wide-open style of play sometimes clashed with Conradt's traditional coaching background. Gradually, Conradt began experimenting with new strategies and recruited athletes to play a full-court, up-tempo style of basketball.

Under the direction of Conradt, the Lady Longhorns became recognized as one of a select few programs, where the overall marketing, public relations, media efforts, and winning ways showed the world what women's basketball could be.

"Coach Conradt has one philosophy," said former Longhorn's star Kamie Etheridge. "You focus your entire life on doing your best in everything you do, and that attitude will start showing up on the basketball court." (Hollandsworth, 1987)

Conradt molds a team in her image and expects her players to be punctual, well mannered, and classy. She won't tolerate talking back or making excuses. She is straightforward, sometimes brutally. "She knows when to push the right button," said Etheridge. "She can completely destroy you with her comments in practice, but she knows when to stop, and then she builds you up to where you feel like a world beater again."

Conradt is legendary among her players for her strict rules about academics. She expects her players to attend every class, and if they cut one, they have to swim laps the next day at 6 a.m. She once dismissed a player from the team for missing a postseason meeting on academic progress, and has been known to allow a player to miss a game to prepare for an exam.

Conradt is modest about her accomplishments, and although she is adamant about striving to win, she doesn't let the game overwhelm her. She maintains her sense of humor even on the court. During one game, she noticed one referee allowing a lot of contact under the basket. "Get them off our backs," she kept yelling, to no avail. Finally, she went up to the referee and remarked, "If I had known you were going to let the other team jump all over us, we would have brought our saddles." (Hollandsworth, 1987)

When recruiting student-athletes, Conradt looks for certain "intangible qualities" that indicate a player will be a good team member and leader. Such qualities include work ethic, commitment, passion, focus, intensity, and personal responsibility. "A good team member must have extraordinary communication skills," Conradt said. "Not just speaking, but listening and sensing." (Conradt, 2001)

"Our style of play demands intensity," explained Conradt, "and we push a player's work habits. If she's willing to work, then she knows she can be successful. I want my players to come out of here with something meaningful. They're going to graduate. I'm not going to cut corners on that at all." (Hollandsworth, 1987)

Team problems are handled quickly. "I don't like conflict," Conradt said. "When there's a conflict, I want it resolved as quickly as possible."

Conradt's organizational skills are legendary. If you check Conradt's desk, you'll find all the paper clips pointed in the same direction. Her office files are alphabetized and color-coded by year. At home, every hanger in her bedroom closet is color-coded. All cans and bottles in her cupboard must have the label facing out. Even as a young child, Conradt made sure that every stuffed animal was always lined up in exactly the same place. "Everything for her must be in perfect order," said Donna Lopiano, women's athletic director at Texas. "She is the ultimate example of a compulsive-obsessive personality, and I say that with the deepest respect." (Hollandsworth, 1987)

Conradt recognizes that her meticulous attention to detail makes her an exceptional coach. "Disorganization really distresses me," Conradt said. "That's probably the overriding thing in my life. I want to feel like I've completed a task. I don't want anything left undone." (Hollandsworth, 1987)

Jody Conradt is what sports purists appreciate in a competitor—a combination of skill, intelligence, grace and wit, coupled with a burning desire to win. She is renowned as one of the game's most respected names. Her efforts have helped lay the path for the popularity of the collegiate women's game today.

SOURCE

Conradt, Jody. Vertical Files, Archives. Naismith Memorial Basketball Hall of Fame. Springfield, MA.

Conradt, Jody. (2001, November 2). Teambuilding and Leadership. Lecture to the Lyndon B. Johnson School of Public Affairs. University of Texas at Austin.

Deutsch, Robin Jonathan. (1999, Spring). Enshrinement '98. *In the Paint.*

Hollandsworth, Skip. (1987, February). She's Stealing The Heart of Texas. *Women's Sports & Fitness.*

FAST-BREAK OFFENSE

By Jody Conradt

Our offensive philosophy has two components. The first component is a running game, which utilizes our strengths—speed and quickness, and offsets our weaknesses— lack of size and board strength. The second component is a set offense that enables us to take a high percentage shot by capitalizing on the specialized skills of our players.

SIMPLICITY AND EXECUTION

While we certainly advocate using one's personnel to the fullest, we do not believe that a coach can successfully change offenses from game to game, week to week, or even season to season. With each season, our coaching staff learns more about our offense and changes evolve. We try to always keep in mind that simplicity and execution are the most important factors in success. We want our players to know what is expected of our offense and how they can capitalize on each player's individual strengths. Just as we try to recruit players who can fit into our scheme, we also believe that it is possible to teach players to fit into a system.

PRIMARY PURPOSE OF A FAST BREAK

The primary purpose of a fast break is to keep pressure on the defense. An effective break should create numerous 3-on-2, 2-on-1, and 1-on-0 situations. A good running team utilizes the fast break from the following situations:

1. A rebounded field goal or free throw
2. A made field goal or free throw
3. An inbounds play
4. A loose ball
5. An interception

Situations 4 and 5 (loose ball and interception) are the most easily converted situations because of the surprise element. However, most fast breaks will come from a rebound situation, and the majority of practice time should be spent accordingly.

COMPONENTS OF THE FAST BREAK

To begin the fast break, the defense must first get the rebound, and the rebounder should pivot to the outside, away from the opposition, to make a quick outlet pass. The outlet person, who is usually a guard, should break to the sideline, no further downcourt than the free-throw line extended and call for the ball. Upon receiving the pass, she should take the ball down the side of the court toward the centerline to avoid the congestion in the middle of the floor.

The outlet person should pass the ball to the middle person in the center lane as she approaches mid-court. At this point, the following three lanes should be filled: 1) the middle lane by the dribbler; 2) one outside lane by the outlet person who continues downcourt; and 3) the other outside lane by whoever can get there first (probably the player who did not get the rebound). The fourth person should become the trailer, and the rebounder should remain at mid-court to act as a safety.

The middle person then dribbles downcourt until the defense commits itself. If no one guards her, the middle player should drive in for a lay-up. The players in each lane should be slightly ahead of the ball as the middle player dribbles downcourt. Requiring the players to call out their positions as they advance downcourt aids in making sure that all lanes are filled. The

middle girl should stop at the free-throw line if she cannot get a lay-up. The two wings should stay well spread so that the defense is forced to cover a greater area in the 3-on-2 situation.

If the three women leading the fast break cannot score quickly, the trailer can break down the free-throw lane line to the basket for a return pass from one of the wings.

KEYS TO A SUCCESSFUL FAST BREAK

1. Make as few passes as possible.
2. Lead the receiver with the pass.
3. Maintain proper spacing.
4. Give up the break if the defense is not outnumbered.
5. Have the wings ahead of the middle player who has the ball.
6. Make sure that he middle player is prepared to hold up the play when necessary.
7. Keep the ball in the middle whenever possible. Don't cross-court pass.
8. Don't always work for the lay-up. A high-percentage shot from short range is acceptable and occasionally even desirable if rebound strength is evident.
9. Talk. Let your teammates know where you are and what you are doing.
10. Don't force the break.
11. Always move forward.
12. Use trailers.
13. Always maintain control.

LESSONS FROM THIS LEGEND...

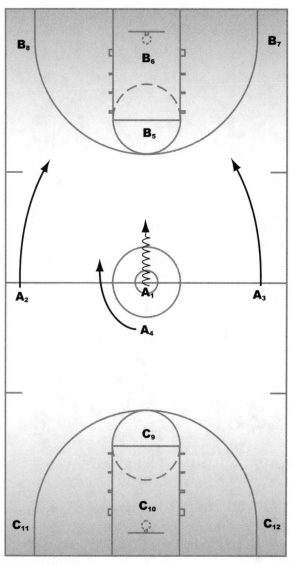

Conradt 1.0

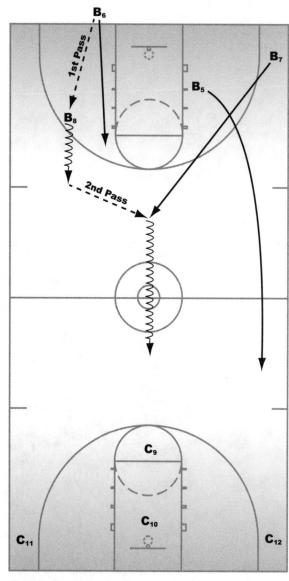

Conradt 1.1

FOUR-ON-TWO DRILL

Twelve is the ideal number of players for this drill. If less than 12 are to be used, one or more groups may have three players and will work 3-on-2. If you have more than twelve players, allow more than four in a group, and have players in the group alternate.

As shown in **Diagram 1.0**, the drill begins with group A moving the ball downcourt in an effort to score against B5 and B6. B7

and B8 are not involved until group A either scores or loses possession to B5 or B6.

If group A scores, B6 inbounds the ball to B8. B8 passes to B7, who is cutting to the middle of the floor. B8 promptly fills the right lane. B5 sprints to fill the left lane, and B6 moves in as the trailer. group B drives down the floor and attempts to score against C9 and C10 (see **Diagram 1.1**).

SOURCE

Conradt, Jody. (1986). Fast Break Offense. *MacGregor Flashback Notebook Vol. XII.*

LEGACY OF
Charles "Chuck" Daly

- Excelled at uniting players with diverse personalities into championship teams.

- Led the Detroit Pistons to back-to-back NBA championships in 1989 and 1990.

- Believed defense and aggressive rebounding were the keys to winning.

- Became the first Hall of Fame coach to win both an NBA championship and an Olympic Gold Medal.

- Received worldwide notoriety as coach of the Olympic Dream Team in 1992.

- Regarded as one of the best-dressed coaches in the game of basketball.

Charles "Chuck" Daly

"A pessimist is an optimist with experience."
—Chuck Daly

BIOGRAPHY

Born: July 20, 1930 in St. Mary's, PA

Inducted into the Naismith Basketball Hall of Fame in 1994

Charles "Chuck" Daly began his coaching career at Punxsutawney High School (PA), where he coached from 1955 to 1963. He was an assistant at Duke University from 1963 to 1969 and then became the head coach at Boston College in 1970. In 1971, Daly became the head coach at the University of Pennsylvania. He led Penn to four straight Ivy League championships and NCAA tournament appearances from 1972 to 1975. In the NBA, Daly coached at Philadelphia, Cleveland, Detroit, New Jersey, and Orlando. He was the first Hall of Fame coach to win both an NBA championship and an Olympic gold medal. Daly coached the Detroit Pistons to back-to-back world championships in 1989 and 1990. He led Detroit to three Central Division titles, five 50-plus win seasons, and nine straight winning seasons. He gained worldwide notoriety as the coach of the Olympic gold medal Dream Team in 1992.

Charles "Chuck" Daly...

Chuck Daly calls himself a basketball "lifer." His passion for the game began as a youth growing up in Kane, Pennsylvania. Daly spent hours in the gymnasium improving his basketball skills. He also discovered the school library had a subscription to *Scholastic Coach* and he anxiously awaited each issue so he could learn more about the game he loved. When Daly was in the tenth grade, he told his mother that he was going to be a college basketball coach.

Daly's coaching career started in Punxsutawney, Pennsylvania, a town made famous by its legendary groundhog. Daly nurtured his coaching skills by reading, attending clinics, and visiting with legendary coaches. One of the best clinics that he attended was at Kutsher's Country Club in the Catskill Mountains that featured speakers like Clair Bee, Pete Newell, and Frank McGuire. In the summers, Daly attended basketball camps all over the country, including the Everett Case Camp at North Carolina State.

During his high school career, Daly learned what might have been the most important lesson in his life. After seven successful years, Daly suffered through a disastrous losing season. During the course of that year, Daly discovered that you couldn't win without good players. Daly described the impact of the losing season in these words, "It gave me a deeper understanding of what coaching is all about, of what is possible and what isn't. How much I knew was not all that mattered. I could know every way to throw a bounce pass, every man-to-man defense, and everything about attacking a zone, but if my players couldn't execute it, the team wasn't going to win."

In 1963, Daly traveled to Louisville to see the NCAA semi-final and championship games. It was the first time that he had attended the Final Four, and he anxiously bought a ticket from a scalper and sat in the last seat of the last row of Freedom Hall. After the game, Daly read in the newspaper that Fred Shabel, an assistant coach, was leaving Duke University. He decided that he would write Duke's head coach, Vic Bubas, concerning the opening on his staff. Daly explained it in these words, "Talk about chutzpah! He (Bubas) was one of the most famous coaches in the country, just back from taking his team to the Final Four, and he gets a letter from an unknown high

school coach in Punxsutawney, Pennsylvania, who wants to be his assistant. Well, I'm here to tell you that miracles do happen" (Daly, 1990, p. 47). Daly interviewed for the position and was given the job. Ironically, one year after attending the Final Four with a ticket bought from a scalper, Daly was on the bench as an assistant, coaching the Blue Devils in the NCAA semi-final game against UCLA.

Daly accepted his first head coaching collegiate position at Boston College. He then coached six seasons at the University of Pennsylvania and led his teams to four Ivy League championships and four NCAA tournament appearances. Daly left the Quakers for an assistant's position in the NBA with the Philadelphia 76ers.

In December of 1981, Daly accepted the head coaching position with the Cleveland Cavaliers. After just ninety-three days, Daly was fired. It was the most difficult time in his career. Daly described it this way, "I was nearly fifty-two, didn't have a job, and didn't know where I could go. Once you've been in the pros, you become a little tainted, and there's no going back to the college ranks. I was feeling pretty low, and a lot of people were asking pointed questions about whether my career was over. None of the people I used to know were calling anymore. It was a disaster. My phone never rang, and nobody came around. It was as if I had died." (Daly, 1990, p. 81)

Daly finally received another chance in the NBA and accepted the head coaching position at Detroit in 1983. Jack McCloskey, the Piston's general manager, had watched Daly's teams at Penn and knew that he was an outstanding coach who stressed defense.

Over nine seasons, Daly molded Isiah Thomas, Joe Dumars, Bill Lambeer, Dennis Rodman, John Salley, and Rick Mahorn into one of the toughest and most intimidating defensive units in NBA history. They were called the "Bad Boys" and won back-to-back NBA championships in 1989 and 1990.

The stylish Daly was selected coach of the year by *Gentleman's Quarterly*, and was also called "The Rock Hudson of Coaching" for his beautiful head of hair. His success was built upon his ability to unite diverse personalities into a smooth functioning team. A prime example was Dennis Rodman. Daly saw the potential in Rodman to be an outstanding player because of Rodman's desire to run the floor, rebound, and play defense. Daly described it in these words, "I saw in him a mustang out on the range—a wild colt who wanted to run loose, to be free. He didn't want any restraints on him, so I knew handling him would be a touch-and-go matter. But he loved to play, and he loved to win." (Daly, 1990, p. 152)

Daly was highly competitive and described himself as being on edge all the time. "It's the fear of losing, that's what it is. I've had to live with it my entire life. I am a competitive person, and the fear of failure, the fear of losing, overwhelms me at times." (Daly, 1990, p. 184)

Daly's fear of losing even surfaced when he coached the star-studded Dream Team in the 1992 Olympics. Lenny Wilkens, an assistant coach for the Dream Team, said, "Chuck worries about everything. He worries when he can't find anything to worry about—because he figures he missed something, and something had to be going wrong if only he could find it. No wonder the Boston Globe's Bob Ryan nicknamed him 'The Prince of Pessimism.'" (Wilkens, 2000, p.221)

Daly knew that he was described as a pessimist, but responded in these words, "A pessimist is an optimist with experience." (Daly, 1990, p. 192)

Daly believed the most important assets for a coach were "a lot of experience, bad hearing, and a small ego."

Daly stressed to his players that teams win championships, not individuals. "The players must have ability," said Daly, "but it is essential that they perform as a team. They have to be unselfish, and it's hard to find unselfish players."

Daly built his championship teams on defense. "The big step was to get our players to believe in playing defense, which is nothing but hard work," said Daly. "But how do you do it? How do you get guys to play defense when all the glory is on offense?"

Daly (1990) answered those questions with the following answer. "If you study the game by reading, listening, watching, and learning from others, you realize that defense is the only common denominator to winning. I've read a lot about successful basketball coaches, and I've learned that if a team's defense is consistent, the team will win more than it loses, even if it has only average players. I believe that 90 percent of the coaches in our profession want to be known as defensive-minded coaches. The problem is convincing the players. A player's mentality is always geared toward scoring. That's what the game is all about. Scoring produces victories and makes the crowd cheer. When the ball goes through the hoop, the player is the hero. Every eye is on him, and every cheer is for him. It can be a hard sell."

Daly continued his emphasis on defense by stating, "Probably the most important factor in playing defense is defensive rebounding. There's a basic philosophy that goes back to the invention of the game that all coaches spout but don't necessarily believe. I probably say it a thousand times a year. 'If you don't give them a second shot, you'll never lose a game.' Boxing out and not letting your man get a second shot is the single most difficult thing to sell to your players. Defense isn't very entertaining, but if you want to succeed, it is the only way to go. If I have any phrase that sums it all up, it is 'Defense wins championships.' It's not very colorful, but it works for us."

A key component in Daly's coaching style was his communication with his players. He involved them in the decision-making process and listened to their opinions. He also tried to keep them fresh throughout the season. Daly cautioned coaches not to take the fun out of the game for players. "Be careful not to make the game too complex," Daly said. "Players love to play this game, and we shouldn't take that joy away from them."

SOURCE

Daly, Chuck and Joe Falls. (1990). *Daly Life*. Grand Rapids, MI: Masters Press

Daly, Chuck. Vertical Files, Archives. Naismith Memorial Basketball Hall of Fame. Springfield, MA.

Wilkens, Lenny and Terry Pluto. (2000). *Unguarded*. New York: Simon and Schuster.

ATTACKING ZONE DEFENSES

By Chuck Daly

Your zone attack can be very simple if you can get consistent good outside shooting and second shots. However, it is my contention that the only way to really defeat a defense is to understand it as fully as possible. The premise of every good zone defensive team is that they only give one shot. The nights that you miss your outside shots and do not get second shots, you will definitely lose.

ZONE OFFENSIVE CONCEPTS

I initially will talk about our zone offensive concepts rather than specific attacks, and the reason being that these might prove to be more helpful to you because of the differences in your personnel and ours. Along this line, might I suggest that you evaluate your own thinking and come up with an offense designed for your personnel rather than mine or someone else.

TWO PLAYERS IN THE LANE

Because of the importance of getting second shots, we try to utilize two players in the area of the lane at all times. We insist on getting two people inside of the triangles of their zone defense (see **Diagram 1.0**). Basically, what I am talking about is that in any zone defense, the players will end up in the shape of a triangle. If you don't put two people inside this triangle, you can't win because you won't get second shots.

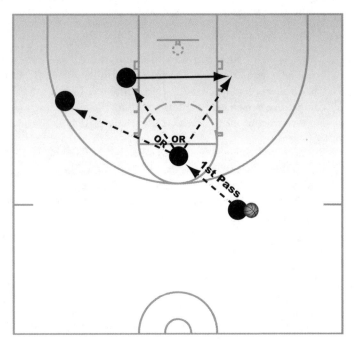

Daly 1.1

INSIDE-WEAKSIDE-LOW EXCHANGE

On any entry of the ball from the perimeter to the post area, we immediately want our high post to look to the weakside and low post where we want an automatic slide across the lane (see **Diagram 1.1**).

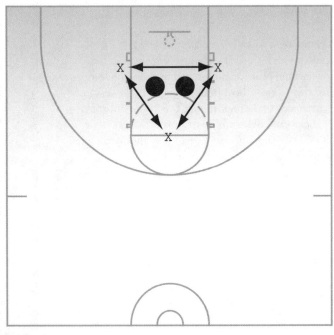

Daly 1.0

LESSONS FROM THIS LEGEND...

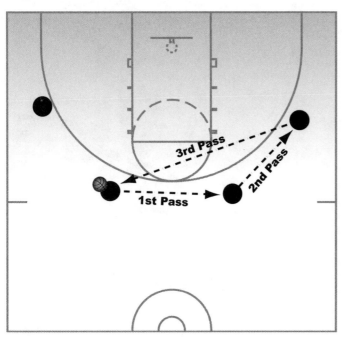

Daly 1.2

SKIP PASSING

The third concept is skip passing, which I think of not only as a play in attacking zones, but also in attacking man-to-man defenses because of the emphasis on helpside positioning. **Diagram 1.2** illustrates a simple skip pass.

BASELINE ATTACK

The final concept is one we are particularly enamored with over the past several years. Presently, most zone attacks are from the midcourt line toward the baseline. We believe that the attack can come from the baseline, which makes your back player your feeder, and the zone defense becomes much more vulnerable. We position the baseline player midway between the corner and the foul-lane line, with his heel almost touching the baseline. This is what we call the gray area, which is very difficult for the zone to cover because of the down and out slides taught by most coaches. The player in this position should be able to 1) receive the overhead pass, 2) pass to open teammates, and 3) shoot a high percentage from this area. In **Diagram 1.3**, you can see his position and his angle of passing. Surprisingly, he does have a passing lane along the baseline that allows him to get the ball to the weakside of the basket, which in many instances results in easy baskets.

Daly 1.3

OUR ZONE ATTACK

We have a normal 1-2-2 set with our big people on the lane. We want our big guard in position O2 and our big forward in position O3. Our ball handler is in position O1 (see **Diagram 1.5**).

There are a couple of ways that we will attack. When the entry pass is to the wing, we can have the weakside forward come from behind the defense looking for an opening (see **Diagram 1.6**). When the ball is thrown to the high-post area, the receiver immediately turns and looks inside to the low-post players.

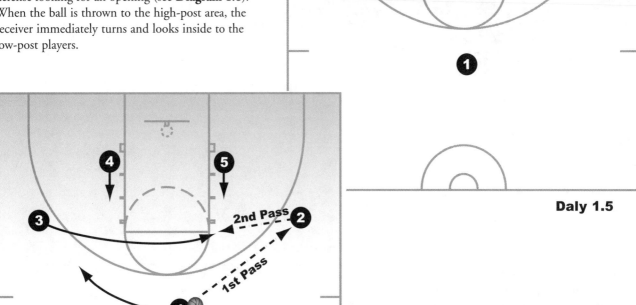

Daly 1.5

Daly 1.6

Another way that we will attack a zone is with the skip pass. I honestly believe that it is the coming thing. Princeton uses an attack where skip passes are used exclusively, and they spread the floor and pass better than any team in America. **Diagram 1.7** shows the Princeton attack. The post man cuts inside, while the perimeter players maintain perfect spacing on the perimeter. They make skip passes and look inside until they get the shot that they want.

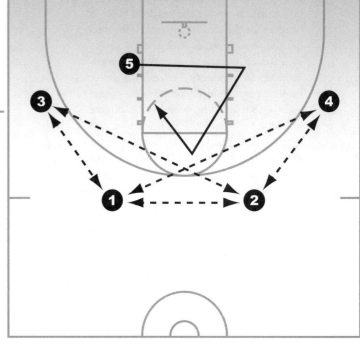

Daly 1.7

LESSONS FROM THIS LEGEND...

Another thing that the skip pass creates is a way to get the ball inside. It is amazing how the skip pass allows the middle to open and the ball to penetrate (see **Diagram 1.8**). This pass creates problems for zone defenses because if you penetrate the defense, you can break the zone down.

The next thing we look at is the baseline attack. We put O5 back there almost with his heels on the line. **Diagram 1.9** shows the pass to O5. O3 breaks across the lane looking for the pass. If he cannot get the pass, he makes what we call a "slice move" down the lane. We score a lot of lay-ups off this move. At the same time, O2 flares to the baseline, and O1 flares to the offside. The pass from O5 can go either to O3, O2, or O1.

To defend against the "slice move," most zone defenders drop to the level of the ball, which makes O1 open for the skip pass.

BE CREATIVE

I believe you should listen to everyone you can and then decide in your own mind what is good for your team. I think that too many times in our profession, we have people who are followers. We need leaders and creative thinkers in basketball. Do what you feel is best for you and your situation.

SOURCE

Daly, Chuck. (1975, September). Attacking Zone Defenses. *The Basketball Bulletin*.

Daly, Chuck. (1976). Zone Offensive Concepts. *Medalist Flashback Notebook*.

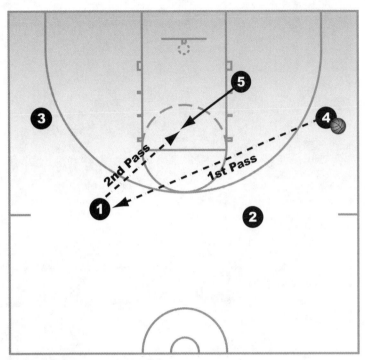

Daly 1.8

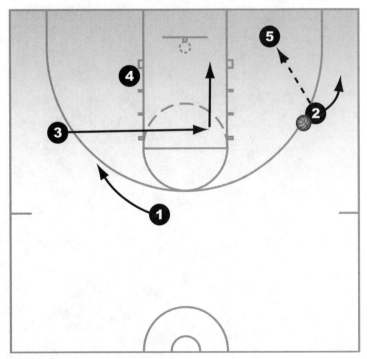

Daly 1.9

LEGACY OF
Edgar " Ed" Diddle

- Pioneered the fast break and brought national prominence to Western Kentucky University.

- Won 759 games and 32 conference championships during his 42-year career.

- Led Western Kentucky to three NCAA tournaments and eight NIT tournaments.

- Was the first coach in basketball history to coach 1000 games at one school.

- Regarded as one of the most colorful coaches of all time.

- Had a trademark red towel that he would wave, chew, or toss along the sidelines.

- Is the namesake of the E.A. Diddle Arena at Western Kentucky.

Edgar "Ed" Diddle

"Sometimes, psychology will work as good as a sixth man on the floor."
—Edgar "Ed" Diddle

BIOGRAPHY

Born: March 12 1895 in Gradyville, KY

Died: January 2, 1970

Inducted into the Naismith Basketball Hall of Fame in 1971

Edgar "Ed" Diddle was the head basketball coach at Western Kentucky University from 1922 to 1964, where he compiled a record of 759-302. He was the first coach in basketball history to coach 1,000 games at one school. Diddle led Western Kentucky to three NCAA tournaments, eight NIT tournaments, and 32 conference championships. The Hilltoppers finished second in the NIT in 1942 and fourth in 1954. Diddle pioneered the fast break, and his teams were always among the leaders in points scored. Western Kentucky's best record under Diddle came in 1938 when they were 30-3. Prior to coaching at Western Kentucky, Diddle coached at Monticello (KY) High School and Greenville (KY) High School. He directed Monticello to the state finals in 1921. Diddle was inducted into the Kentucky Athletic Hall of Fame and the Helms Athletic Foundation Hall of Fame. In 1961, Western Kentucky named their new basketball facility the E.A. Diddle Arena.

Edgar "Ed" Diddle...

Most people addressed the legendary coach as "Mister Diddle." He was beloved throughout Kentucky for his coaching talents and his wholesome, fun-loving attitude toward life. At the time of Diddle's retirement, Governor Louie B. Nunn declared that Diddle "built a proud national reputation for the school he so dearly loved and for himself in the world of sports. His greatest contribution, however, was to send young men of high character, morality, and a competitive spirit into all walks of life beyond the field of athletics." (Gardiner, 1984, p. 247)

Diddle created a family environment for his players and proudly assumed the role of "father" while "his boys" were away from home. "I feel responsible for the boys on my squad. If their parents feel safe in sending their seventeen- and eighteen-year old boys to me to play ball at Western, then I feel obligated to improve them morally, as well as mentally." (Gardiner, 1984, p.71)

Mr. Diddle always expected the best from his "boys," and he usually got it. His influence on his players was remarkable, both during their playing days and as alumni. Almost to a man, his former players credited the principles instilled in them by Diddle as a large part of their success.

All-American Bob Lavoy said, "I learned through Coach Diddle that there was no other way but to give it your best— if you wanted to keep your self-rerspect. He was truly an out- standing and unique person, and I am a better man for having been associated with him." (Gardiner, 1984. p. 252)

Paul Walker, who became an Ohio High School Hall of Fame coach and coached future Hall of Famer Jerry Lucas at Middletown High School, credits Ed Diddle for his coaching foundation. "In my coaching,"

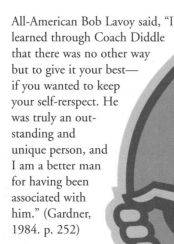

said Walker, "I tried to use the same strategies he taught me: strong discipline, psychology, repetitive drilling of the fundamentals, and rapport and respect of my players. I respected and admired him for his love and interest in his players, for his coaching ability, and for the many young men that he helped to become useful citizens." (Gardner, 1984. p. 250)

Diddle always demonstrated the highest integrity and advocated fair play and sportsmanship. He expected his players and Western Kentucky fans to treat their oppo- nent with respect. On many occasions, Diddle stood in front of his home crowd to quell the booing of the oppo- nent. He also insisted that his players never embarrass themselves or Western Kentucky. On a road trip during the 1935-36 season, Diddle learned that a team member had appropriated a hotel towel. Immediately, Diddle ordered the driver of the bus to turnaround and drive back to the hotel so the player could return the towel with an apology.

Diddle never claimed to be a basketball technician, but he was a master psychologist. He believed that psychology worked similar to that of having six players on the court. Max Reed, a player during the mid 1930s stated, "Mr. Diddle was a great psychologist. None was greater at motivating players" (Gardiner, 1984, p. 250). Former player Bob Lavoy expressed his thoughts concerning Diddle's motivational skills in these words, "I honestly do not know how much basket- ball knowledge Coach Diddle possessed, but I'm inclined to believe he had more knowledge of how to motivate people to reach their true potential. The acceptance of mediocrity was not in his vocabulary or his mannerisms. I believe he could have been the Chief of Psychology at Johns Hopkins, the Mayo Clinic, and all points in between." (Gardiner, 1984, p. 133)

Diddle's emotional, nervous nature, coupled with soaring gymnasium temperatures, led Diddle to have a towel available on the bench which he used to cool his forehead or dry his hands. Through the years, Diddle's red towel became his emotional release and the badge of Western Kentucky basketball. Sportswriters and fans loved to watch Diddle wave, toss, and chew his red towel. George Barker wrote in *The Nashville Tennessean Magazine*, "A fan can watch the towel and know how the game is going. It goes something like this:" (Gardiner, 1984, p. 196)

1. Tossed high into the air: pure climatic joy
2. Whirled overhead: satisfaction and gay expectation
3. Slapped violently on the floor: extreme disappointment with players or referee
4. Twisted or braided: Outcome doubtful
5. Chewed: outcome very doubtful
6. Used to shield the eyes: horror or dismay

The hard-driving Diddle was a true showman on the court and he viewed the basketball court as a stage for his theatrics. During one game against rival Murray State, a fan ran by the Western Kentucky bench and grabbed his red towel. Diddle charged after the thief before being restrained by his assistant coach.

Diddle's tactical legacy in college basketball was the fast break. Frank Keaney at Rhode Island and "Piggy" Lambert at Purdue preceded Diddle in introducing "race-horse basketball," but he was one of the earliest coaches to adopt it. Diddle explained his philosophy in these terms, "Attack is our stock in trade. You don't need a play if you get a half-step start on the opposing team" (Gardiner, 1984, p. 138). Diddle built his teams on the three S's: size, speed, and stamina.

One of the cornerstones of Diddle's coaching philosophy was actually learned on a football field. "When I first started coaching at Western," explained Diddle, I coached football and baseball, as well as basketball. Our football team went down to play Centenary College in Louisiana, where a former college teammate of mine, Bo McMillan, was coaching. He beat our brains out, 75-6. When we met at the center of the field at the end of the game, I asked Bo, 'What did I do so wrong that we lost by that much?' He said, 'Eddie, you can't win if you don't have the players!' I realized right then how important recruiting was to successful coaching, and I tried never to forget it." (Given, 2001)

Diddle had a habit of scrambling words or using the wrong word. When Western Kentucky joined the National Collegiate Athletic Association (NCAA) in 1939, its name often baffled Diddle. He frequently referred to it as the "N double CA." Then, conscious of his mistake, Diddle's correction would come out "NCA double A." Words such as kleptomaniac and hypochondriac or ambidextrous and amphibious often led to confusion. When told by an assistant coach that one of his players might be a hypochondriac, Diddle exclaimed, "Oh my gosh! What did he steal?"

Ill health plagued Diddle and forced him to retire. As his career wound down, a series of heart attacks, kidney problems, recurring gout, and other ailments kept him in constant pain.

The legendary Mr. Diddle is probably best described by Hall of Fame coach Ray Meyer when he stated, "I believe Ed Diddle was one of the most colorful coaches of all time. He was a fierce competitor. His teams reflected him. They were great competitors on the court, and gentlemen off the court." (Gardiner, 1984, p. 248)

SOURCE

Diddle, Ed. Vertical Files, Archives. Naismith Memorial Basketball Hall of Fame. Springfield, MA.

Gardiner, Harvey C. (1984). *Mr. Diddle: Motivator of Men*. Nashville: Parthenon Press.

Given, Ed. (2001). The One and Only Mr. Diddle. *Naismith Memorial Basketball Hall of Fame Enshrinement Program*.

SHOOTING DRILLS

By Ed Diddle

Authors' Note: Coach Diddle designed charts that recorded every shot taken during a game. He believed it was important to know the exact floor location where shots were attempted and the percentage made.

Fundamentals are basketball. It is only through the mastery of shooting, passing, jumping, pivoting, running, dribbling, body balance, feinting, and faking that one can have a good basketball team. We are not doing our job properly as coaches unless we spend a great deal of time on these major aspects of the game.

If a player is a good fundamentalist and he has the desire and the physical equipment with which to play, he should be a good ballplayer. Knowledge of the fundamentals will lead a player to poise, relaxation, and confidence. You must work on all fundamentals. If a player can do only one thing well, he is only part of a basketball player.

Fundamental drills should be related to the types of offense and defense used. For instance, if you are using a fast-break offense, your fundamental drills should be geared to that type of offense. If you use a pressing defense, your drills should be selected to improve that facet of the game. But no matter what drills you chose, spend a great deal of time on them.

The majority of our fundamental drills are performed on a competitive basis. There is nothing that can take the place of the kind of competition that occurs when two players get together and try to execute their fundamentals and see which one can do the job better.

SHOOTERS ARE DEVELOPED THROUGH HARD WORK

The good shooters are those players who have started early, have a good eye for the basket, have good hands, and have worked at it so much that it becomes easy for them. I don't think everyone can learn to be a great shooter, but I do think that if a player has a large amount of desire for the game, and if he has all the other attributes of a good basketball player, he can become a good shooter by working at it diligently.

I am sure you will find that all the outstanding shooters spend long hours shooting at the basket and analyze their own shortcomings and correct them. I don't think shooters are born; they are made through great desire and hard work. A player must develop confidence in his shooting ability. He must believe that his shot will go into the basket. If he should happen to miss, he must feel sure that he will make his next attempt.

LENGTH OF SHOOTING DRILLS

We spend about thirty minutes each day in shooting practice. Each player has his own ball, and he practices shooting from the place on the floor where he shoots the most during a game. We let him do this for fifteen or twenty minutes and begin our formal shooting drills. We use several different drills and rotate them from day to day to keep the practice from becoming dull.

Repetition is one of the most important aspects of learning, and we carry this principle into all our drills. One of the most important things for a new basketball coach to remember is that doing things over and over again plays a major role in any success he might have.

Impress upon your players that they must give their best each day in practice; for as they practice, so will they play. If they try hard in practice, they will automatically play hard in the game.

WHAT TO SHOOT AT

Not many players know what they are shooting at. They do not know whether they should be shooting at the back of the rim, just over the nearest rim, or at the backboard. We teach our players to shoot the ball rather softly and just get the ball to the basket. We want the players to shoot just over the nearest rim and just get the ball to the basket. We also want players to have a little backspin on the ball, because this means they have good control and that the ball is just coming off the tips of their fingers.

We want players to use the backboard on the lay-up shot or the short angle shot. At this angle and distance, we feel that using the backboard greatly improves the chances of making the shot.

LESSONS FROM THIS LEGEND...

SHOOTING DRILLS

AROUND THE WORLD

Divide the team into two groups with one group on each end of the floor. The better shooters should be on one end, and the poorer shooters on the other end to make competition even. The first shooter starts under the basket and keeps shooting until he misses, and then the rest of the shooters follow in turn. If a player misses, he may stay at his present position or "take a chance" and shoot a second shot from that position. If he hits the second shot, he continues to the next position. If he misses his chance, he goes back to the starting point. The first player to go all the way "around the world" and make the shot from the right corner is the winner (see **Diagram 1.0**).

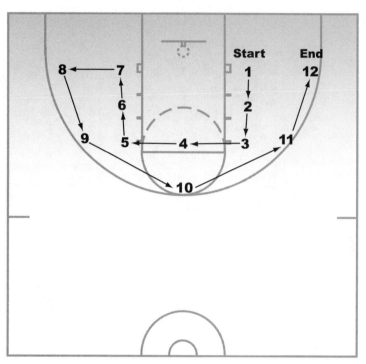

Diddle 1.0

TEAM 21

Divide the squad into teams, with each team having a ball. Team A1 competes against A2; Team B1 competes against B2; and Team C1 competes against C2. On the command "start" from the coach, the front player in each line starts shooting. A long shot counts two points, and a short shot is one point. Players must shoot short shots from the spot where they rebound the long shot. After shooting long and short shots, the shooter passes to the next player in line and goes to the rear of the line. The coach keeps score, and the first team to reach 21 points wins. Play two out of three games in all three positions. (A, B, and C) (see **Diagram 1.1**).

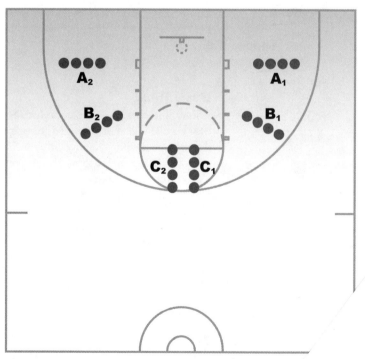

Diddle 1.1

LESSONS FROM THIS LEGEND...

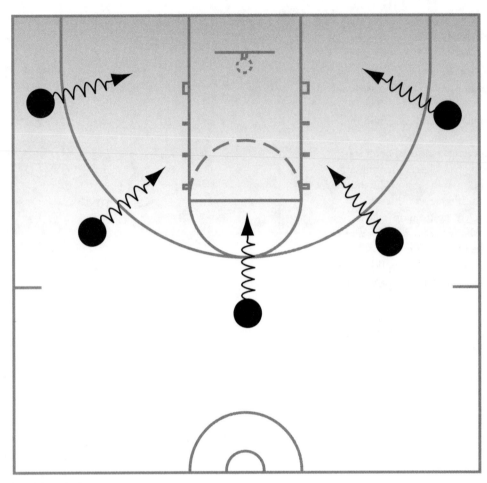

Diddle 1.2

BUMP DRILL

This drill teaches players to concentrate on the shot, even though they may be fouled or "bumped" during the act of shooting. This drill may be used in shooting either inside or outside shots. The arrows in **Diagram 1.2** show various approaches to the basket. The coach stands near the spot from which the player will shoot the ball. Shooters dribble by the coach one at a time and go up for their shots. The coach slightly pushes the shooters' hips or shoulder as they shoot. Players soon learn to disregard the "bump" and concentrate on making the shot.

LESSONS FROM THIS LEGEND...

SHOOTING OVER THE SCREEN DRILL

This drill provides good experience for players in learning to shoot over a teammate's screen. Forwards can screen for guards' shots, or guards can screen for forwards' shots (see **Diagram 1.3**).

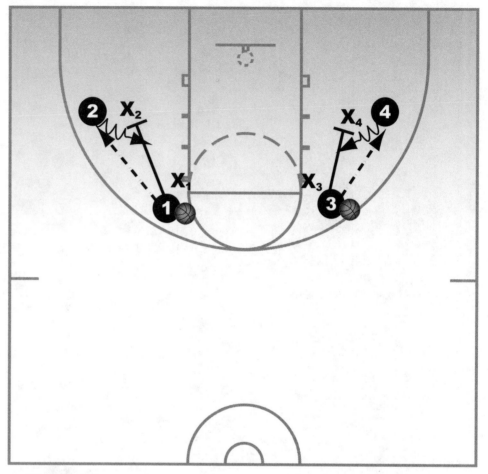

Diddle 1.3

SUMMARY

It is my opinion that no matter whether you are coaching a grade school team or a professional team, you must spend a great deal of time on the fundamentals if you desire to have a successful coaching career.

In addition to spending much time on the fundamentals, you must do two other things to become an outstanding coach. One is to be a keen student of the game; always strive to improve your coaching talents. Attend coaching clinics; talk basketball with other coaches; and read and study any written material on basketball that you can find. The other is to instill in your players that priceless attitude—desire. I don't think that an individual can be a great ball player unless he has desire.

SOURCE

Diddle, Ed. (1965). The Offensive Fundamentals in Basketball. In Hardin McLane (ed.), *Championship Basketball by 12 Great Coaches*. Englewood Cliffs, NJ: Prentice-Hall.

LEGACY OF
Bruce Drake

- Invented the shuffle offense, a five-player continuity offense.

- Led a national campaign in the 1940s to outlaw goaltending.

- Served as an assistant coach for the 1956 Gold Medal U.S. Olympic Team.

- Renowned for his sportsmanship and ethical conduct.

- Led the Wichita Vickers to the National Industrial League championship in 1957.

- Earned All-American honors as a basketball player at the University of Oklahoma.

Bruce Drake

*"Basketball needs to get rid of goaltending
—its leaping larceny at the lip of the goal"*
—Bruce Drake

BIOGRAPHY

Born: December 5, 1905 in Gentry, TX

Died: December 4, 1983

Inducted into the Naismith Basketball Hall of Fame in 1972

Bruce Drake was an outstanding athlete in basketball, track, and cross-country at Oklahoma City (OK) Central High School. He attended the University of Oklahoma and led the Sooners to an 18-0 season and the Big Six championship in 1928. In 1929, Drake was team captain and received All-American honors. Oklahoma went undefeated in the Big Six Conference and won the conference title. Drake was a champion pole-vaulter and won the Kansas Relays and Rice Relays. He also received two letters in football at Oklahoma, even though he never played football in high school. After graduation, Drake embarked on a coaching career, serving as freshman coach and assistant varsity coach at the University of Oklahoma. He was elevated to head coach in 1938 and stayed in that position for 17 years. Under Drake's direction, the Sooners won six conference championships and appeared in three NCAA tournaments. His teams competed in two Final Fours and were beaten by Holy Cross in the national championship game in 1947. Drake served as president of the NABC in 1951-52 and was chairman of the NCAA Rules Committee from 1951 to 1955. He led a national campaign to outlaw goaltending. Drake won a gold medal as an assistant coach for the U.S. Olympic Team in 1956. After retiring from Oklahoma, Drake coached the Wichita Vickers to the National Industrial League championship in 1957.

Bruce Drake...

Known for his aggressive and competitive spirit, Bruce Drake excelled in athletics before becoming one of America's most influential coaches. At Oklahoma City Central High School, Drake starred in basketball, track, and cross-country.

Drake then attended the University of Oklahoma and earned All-American honors in basketball in 1929. His four years at Oklahoma wasn't without its challenges. During Drake's first season on the varsity basketball team, coach Hugh McDermott started two lettermen ahead of Drake in an early-season game. Bruce walked to the locker room, took off his uniform, donned his street clothes and watched the game from the stands. After the game, "The Little Scotchman" McDermott met with Drake and informed the young player that he did not have the game experience needed to be a starter. Drake rejoined the team and worked hard every day in practice in preparation to be a starter. Later that season, Drake was elevated to a starter. It was a valuable lesson for the spirited young competitor.

In 1928, Oklahoma went 18-0 and won the Missouri Valley Conference championship. In 1929, Drake was selected team captain, and led the Sooners to a 10-0 record and the championship in the newly formed Big Six Conference. In the last game of the season, Oklahoma was trailing Missouri by three points late in the game. On two possessions, Drake dribbled the full length of the court through the entire Missouri team and scored the points necessary to lead Oklahoma to victory.

Drake also participated in football and track. He lettered two years as a quarterback, even though he never played high school football. In track, Drake was an outstanding pole-vaulter, winning both the Kansas Relays and the Rice Relays. As a senior, Drake earned the Letzeiser Medal for being the University's outstanding male in scholarship and non-academic activities.

After graduation, Drake went on to coach championship basketball on four different levels: college; AAU; Armed Forces, and the Olympics. He coached the freshman team and served as an assistant coach to McDermott at Oklahoma for ten years. In 1930, Drake married his high school sweetheart, Myrtle Tosho.

From 1938 until 1955, Drake held the head coaching reins at Oklahoma where he battled "Phog" Allen of Kansas and Henry Iba of Oklahoma A&M. They were brilliant years as Drake led Oklahoma to a spot in the upper echelon of basketball. During this perior, the Sooners won more than 200 games and had winning seasons in all but four years. This included six conference championships and a 6-3 record in NCAA tournament action. Drake's three loses in the NCAA tournament were all to the eventual national champion. In 1939, Oklahoma went to the initial Final Four and was beaten by Oregon, coached by future Hall of Famer Howard Hobson in the semi-finals. In 1943, his team lost to eventual champion Wyoming. In 1947, Drake led Oklahoma to the NCAA title game before losing to Holy Cross.

Bruce Drake was noted for his ingenious offenses that championed the case for the small player in basketball. His teams at Oklahoma were called the "Roundball Runts." He invented the five-player shuffle continuity offense called the Drake shuffle. It was designed to combat the advent of the big man in basketball and allowed smaller teams to be successful. The Drake Shuffle was the forerunner of the "flex motion offense" and many other continuity offenses. Joel Eaves at Auburn instituted Drake's offense in the SEC, where it became known as the "Auburn shuffle."

Drake was also the inventor of a novel way to attack a full-court press (Isaacs, 1975). It consisted of a pass from one player to another, while both players were standing out-of-bounds behind the baseline. The entry pass inbounds could then be made before the defenders had an opportunity to shift.

During the 1940s, Drake led a national campaign to outlaw goaltending at a time when tall players were changing the game. In the Big Seven Conference, seven-foot Bob Kurland from Oklahoma A&M was the best in the nation at goaltending. Legendary coach Henry Iba was never an advocate of a zone defense, but with Kurland's size, it made sense to design a defense to keep him near the basket. Iba installed a 1-1-3 zone with Kurland stationed under the basket. His job was quite simple. Every time a shot came near the goal, he was instructed to jump up and deflect it. Kurland forced Oklahoma's shooters to change the arc of their shots, and the Sooners were defeated 40-28. Drake was furious. He called the defensive umbrella formed by the tall players stationed near the goal and swatting away shots as "leaping larceny off the lip of the goal." Drake likened goaltending to a croquet player, thrusting his foot in front of the wicket after a perfect shot. He believed that once the ball left the shooter's hand, its course should not be violated or profaned. He called this period in basketball, "the rise of the goal robber."

Drake detested goaltending and decided to make a statement the next time Oklahoma and Oklahoma A&M played. He had one of his players take his pre-game warm-up shots on stilts in an attempt to distract Kurland. Drake also had a platform constructed behind the Sooner basket and had James St. Clair, the chairman of the NCAA Rules Committee, sit on the perch so he had a perfect vantage point of Kurland's thefts. Drake then proceeded to have his team hold the ball and shoot only when Kurland was screened away from the basket. Oklahoma A&M prevailed 14-11, and St. Clair watched Kurland use his goaltending technique only a total of three times (Bischoff, 1980). Nevertheless, the goaltending success of Kurland and his rival George Mikan caused a change in the rules at the end of the 1944 season. It was changed to the present rule—no defender can touch a shot on its downward path without a penalty of awarding the goal.

Drake also served as president of the National Association of Basketball Coaches (1951-52) and chairman of the Joint Basketball Rules Committee (1951-56).

In addition to coaching basketball, Drake started the University's golf and swimming programs. His golf teams won 33 consecutive dual matches and had one individual national champion. During the early years of the program, Drake personally transported his golfers to matches in the family car, a black Model "A" Ford sedan. The Oklahoma golf clubhouse is named after him. The swimming program set a couple of Big Six records and placed in the NCAA tournament twice, even though the Sooners didn't have a swimming pool. Drake was said to have trained his swimmers in a local pond until the University built a pool on campus.

After resigning in 1955, Drake had a successful year coaching the Air Force team to the Armed Forces championship and the Olympic Playoffs. In 1956, he was selected assistant coach for the U.S. Olympic basketball team. The head coach was Gerald Tucker, a former player of Drake's and All-American at Oklahoma. Together, they led the U.S to the Gold Medal. The U.S. Team averaged 99.5 points, while holding their opponents to only 44.9 points.

Drake's last coaching assignment was with the Wichita Vickers and he led them to the National Industrial League championship in 1957.

Drake was elected to the Helms Foundation Hall of Fame as both a player and a coach. His honors include induction into both the Naismith Memorial Basketball Hall of

Fame and the All-College Tournament Hall of Fame in Oklahoma City, and being the namesake of the Oklahoma basketball practice facility.

In 1958, Drake retired to life as an active community member and realtor in Norman. He continued to conduct coaching clinics around the world until his death at the age of 78.

Sources

Bischoff, John. (1980). *Mr Iba: Basketball's Aggie Iron Duke*. Oklahoma City: Western Heritage Books.

Isaacs, Neil. (1975). *All the Moves*. Philadelphia: J.P. Lippincott.

THE DRAKE
SHUFFLE OFFENSE

By Bruce Drake

Coaches hold divergent views on attacking patterns, but they all agree that the best offense is one that keeps all five players constantly occupied and one that works equally well against all defenses—man-to-man, zone, switching, or pressing.

After five years of experimentation, the coaching staff at Oklahoma has designed an offense that comes closer to meeting all the needs of the coach than any I've ever seen or personally tried. I call this offense the Drake Shuffle, because when my players start moving, it's impossible for anyone except myself to know where each player will be after several passes.

ADVANTAGES OF THE SHUFFLE OFFENSE

1. It will work against a switching defense just as well as against a straight man-to-man defense.
2. When operating from a single post (as we do), you don't have to get the ball into the post to make the offense successful.
3. It will work against a pressing defense, as well as a zone.
4. It allocates definite offensive rebounding assignments.
5. It enables us to freelance while still in our set pattern.
6. Its flexibility makes it tough to scout.
7. It affords a balanced attack with perimeter shooting, as well as driving opportunities.
8. All five players are moving all the time.
9. It is excellent for teams without a big player.
10. It prevents defenses from deploying its players where it wants them, unless it's playing a zone defense.
11. It reduces bad passing to a bare minimum.
12. It is very simple and easy to learn.

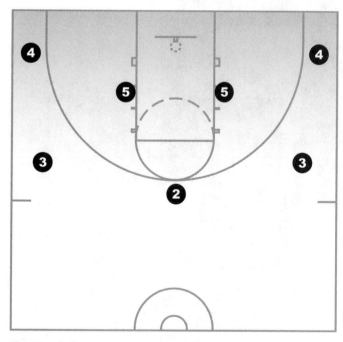

Drake 1.0

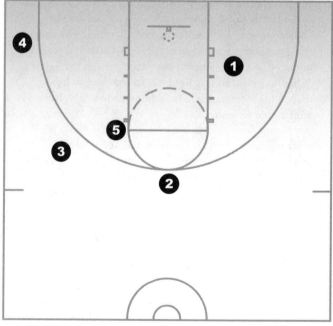

Drake 1.1

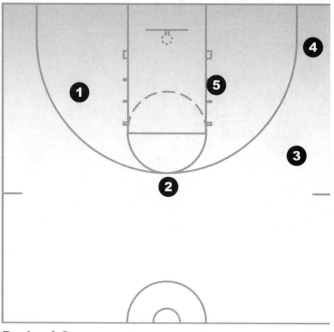

Drake 1.2

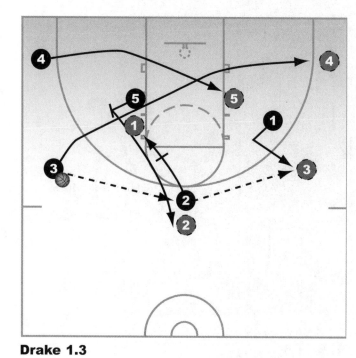

Drake 1.3

INITIAL ALIGNMENT AND DESIGNATED FLOOR SPOTS

In assimilating the shuffle offense, it is extremely important to proceed slowly so that everyone understands how we number our players. The number of the player corresponds with the spot on the floor that the player occupies. **Diagram 1.0** shows the designated floor positions regardless of whether we're lined up on the left or right side of the floor. As a player moves, his number changes to the floor spot that he is occupying.

Diagram 1.1 shows our numbering system when our initial alignment is on the left side. O1 is called the "weakside" player for the simple reason that he's the only player on that side of the court. O2 is always the player at the top of the circle. O5 is the post, whether he's lined up on the right or the left. The corners are always O4, and the wings are always O3. **Diagram 1.2** shows our numbering system when we align on the right side.

Memorize these spots, for reference to players later on will be by numbers, and these numbers will indicate the spots on the floor that they occupy.

CHANGE-OF-SIDES SERIES

In our change-of-sides play, we start overloaded on the left side and finish overloaded on the right, ready to continue with our pattern.

As shown in **Diagram 1.3**, O3 passes to O2 and receives a screen from O5, as O2 passes to O1. The first option is for O1 to pass to O3 for the open lay-up shot. If O3 isn't open, O1 dribbles out to the 3 spot, while O3 moves to the 4 spot.

O4 steps toward the baseline and then breaks to the 5 spot, after O3 clears through to the 4 spot. O2, after passing to O1, cuts down the lane and screens for O5. O5 comes to the top of the circle to the 2 spot. This completes the movements of all the players on the left side and puts them in position to continue the change-of-sides series on the right side.

This change-of-sides play must be mastered before anything else is added. The players must learn it from all positions, and to facilitate the learning process, I give the following guidelines to my players:

- O3 passes to O2, becomes the first cutter, and goes to the 4 spot.

- O4 is the second cutter and goes to the 5 spot.
- O1 receives the pass from O2 and goes to the 3 spot.
- O2 passes to O1, screens for O5, and is now in the 1 spot (weakside player).
- O5 uses the screen from O2 and goes to the 2 spot.

OTHER KEY TEACHING POINTS IN THE CHANGE-OF-SIDES SERIES

- Passes around the perimeter from O3 to O2 to O1 must be made rapidly.
- The position of O5 should be the free-throw line extended, approximately three to five feet from the lane.
- O3 must wait for O5's screen, run his defender into the screen, and then make the appropriate cut, depending on his defender's floor position.
- O1 must take the feed pass from O2 close to the lane—the farther out he receives the pass, the more difficult it is for him to make the pass to the cutter (O3).

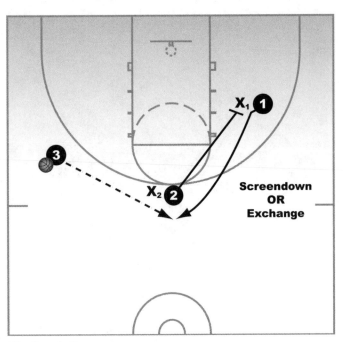

Drake 1.4

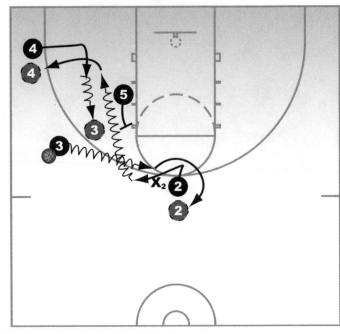

Drake 1.5

The nice thing about this simple movement is that we're really trapping the defensive player guarding O5. No matter what he does, it will be wrong. O5 will nearly always be open for a shot at the top of the circle when you run the change-of-sides. It doesn't make any difference whether the opponent is playing man-to-man straight or a switching defense. This is my starting point and a pretty fair offense in itself. If you get this simple pattern down, the rest of the offense will come easily.

OPTIONS AGAINST PRESSURE DEFENSE

There is no reason for a bad pass when running the Drake shuffle. I will explain four pressure release options that we utilize. First, let's take the situation where the defender covering O2 is playing him tight and denying the pass from O3. We do three things to eliminate a possible interception by X2.

1) SCREEN AWAY OR EXCHANGE POSITIONS

Anytime X2 is pressing O2 closely, O2 immediately exchanges positions or screens for O1. O1 comes to the 2 spot and

becomes O2. This will make an open passing lane from O3 to the top of the circle, as indicated in **Diagram 1.4.** We now have the ball in position.

2) DRIBBLE HAND-OFF

The second thing we do is have O3 dribble over to O2 and hand-off to him, setting a three-man roll, as shown in **Diagram 1.5**. When O2 sees O3 start dribbling toward him, he must not move toward him until O3 is about three feet away. At the same time O3 starts the dribble, O5 must take a position alongside the free-throw line.

When we run this roll, we are really freelancing, trying to score at any opportunity. For instance, O2 might dribble all the way in for a lay-up, or O4 might shoot over O2 on the roll. Even when this roll is in progress, the holes on the floor are always covered, and the change-of-sides may be run at any time.

In **Diagram 1.5**, O3 becomes O2. because he now occupies that spot. The original O2 becomes O3 until O4 takes the ball from him on the roll. Then, because he is occupying the 4 spot, he becomes O4. O4, who

took the ball from the original O2, becomes O3, since he's now occupying the 3 spot.

The three-man roll produces a lot of natural screens and floor balance. It is essential that O5 takes a position alongside the free-throw line and prepares to screen for O2 as soon as O3 dribbles toward the 2 spot.

As shown in **Diagram 1.5**, even though the players are moving rapidly, all the spots are filled. O4, who took the ball to the 3 spot, can pass immediately to the new player occupying the 2 spot, and everyone is in position to run the change-of-sides series.

3) "GO" CUT

The third thing we do to combat pressure is shown in **Diagram 1.6**. The play starts as before, with O3 dribbling over to O2. But instead of O3 giving the ball to O2, he tells O2 to "go." O3 fakes a pass to O2 as he goes by and passes to O1. Our change-of-sides series is now on, although it is set up in a different manner.

Frequently, after starting the change-of-sides, we won't be able to run it. For

LESSONS FROM THIS LEGEND...

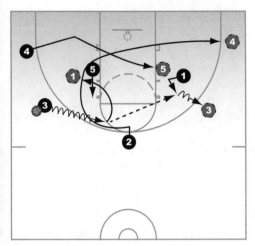

Drake 1.6

instance, suppose O3 passes to O2 and cuts for the basket, and O2 can't make the pass to O1. Now, the forcing play on the change-of-sides is on and must be executed. The type of pressure release we use in this situation is called the two-man roll.

4) DRIBBLE TO THE CORNER FOR THE TWO-MAN ROLL

If O2 can't make the pass to O1, he may elect to dribble to the corner to O4, thus starting our roll with only two players (see **Diagram 1.7**). When O1 sees that O2 can't pass to him, he immediately comes out to the 2 spot, thus balancing the court. The cutter, O3, stops at the 1 spot and becomes the weakside player.

The fact that we're always ready to go and always covering the spots makes this formation workable at all times. We know that we won't always be able to make the pass to O1 and also, from a timing standpoint, that O2 won't always be able to pass to O1 immediately.

Whenever O2 is delayed, he is not permitted to make the pass, for it will then be too late to feed O3. The success of the change-of-sides series depends greatly on a very rapid pass exchange from O3 to O2 to O1.

SOLO CUTS

Our solo cuts for the basket are part of our freelance. As shown in **Diagram 1.8**, O3

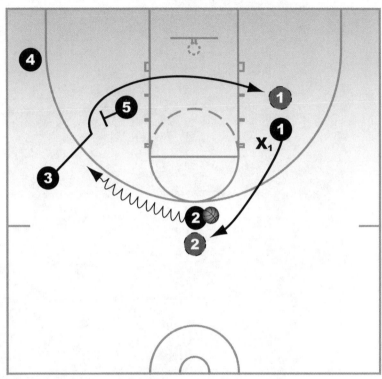

Drake 1.7

passes to O4, uses the screen of O5, and cuts to the basket. If O3 gets a step on his defender, O4 feeds him for the lay-up.

Anytime a solo cut is made for the basket, we fill in the holes left by the cutters. O2 moves over to fill the 3 spot, O1 comes to the 2 spot, O3 fills the 1 spot, and O5 holds his position. These solo cuts keep the defensive team constantly engaged.

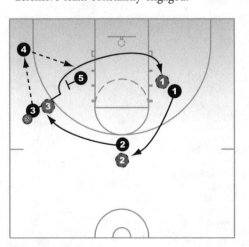

Drake 1.8

CLOSING

I believe the change-of-sides series, the rolling game, and the solo cuts for the basket will provide a very simple, but flexible, offense. Any number of plays may be run from this five-man moving offense. It's the most interesting offense I've ever coached, and one that comes closest to meeting all the needs of both high school and college coaches.

SOURCE

Drake, Bruce. (January 1966). The Original Shuffle. *Basketball Bulletin*.

95

LEGACY OF
Clarence "Big House" Gaines

- Mentored by John McLendon, the "Father of Black Coaches," and was one of the first coaches to break the color barrier in collegiate basketball.

- Spent 47 years at the same school and is the namesake of the C.E. Gaines Center at Winston-Salem University.

- Retired as the second winningest coach in college basketball history.

- Under Gaines' tutelage, his teams were nationally acclaimed for their up-tempo, fast-breaking style of play.

- Led Winston-Salem to the NCAA College Division national championship in 1967.

- Respected as an outstanding humanitarian who truly cared about his students and players.

- Enshrined in eight Halls of Fame.

CLARENCE "BIG HOUSE" GAINES

"Coaches come and go. Records come and go. But if you touch peoples' lives, they remember you."
—Clarence "Big House" Gaines

BIOGRAPHY

Born: May 21, 1923 in Paducah, KY

Inducted into the Naismith Basketball Hall of Fame in 1982

Clarence Edward Gaines was born just before the Great Depression of the 1930s. He attended Lincoln (Paducah, KY) H.S., where he was a star football and basketball player. Gaines then attended Morgan State (MD) College, where he played basketball for four years and excelled as a football tackle. After graduation in 1945, Gaines accepted a job at Winston-Salem College as an assistant coach in three sports: football, basketball, and track and field. In 1947, he was promoted to head coach in all three sports and eventually became athletic director, professor of physical education, and director of the physical education department. Gaines spent his entire career (47 years) at Winston-Salem, where his basketball teams were 828-447. By 1981, Gaines had become the nation's winningest active coach. His teams won 20 or more games 18 times and captured the Central Intercollegiate Athletic Association (CIAA) championship 12 times. In 1967, his team compiled a 31-1 record and became the first historically black school to win a NCAA national basketball championship (College Division). Gaines retired in 1993 with 828 wins, making him the second winningest coach in NCAA history at the time (behind legendary Adolph Rupp). He has been inducted into eight Halls of Fame, served as president of the NABC, and was selected National Coach of the Year in 1967.

Clarence "Big House" Gaines...

Clarence Gaines came from Kentucky Bluegrass Country with humble beginnings in Paducah. He played a lot of basketball as a youngster, even though he didn't have a real basket or even a ball. Gaines' father nailed a barrel hoop on a coal-house door, and they would shoot baskets with any kind of ball they could find.

Gaines starred in football and excelled in basketball at Lincoln (Paducah, KY) H.S. His inspiration was his mother, Olivia. She was an outstanding athlete and would play against Clarence in basketball, softball, and tennis. "I could never beat her," stated Gaines (2003). "Plus the most important thing was that she insisted that I practice and master the basic fundamentals of basketball."

As a young child, Gaines was taught to adhere to the Golden Rule. "My parents emphasized three key points," said Gaines. "Don't lie, don't cheat, don't steal. I've carried these values with me throughout my entire life."

After graduation from high school, Gaines enrolled at Morgan State (MD) College. He left home with 50 dollars in his pocket, driving an old Ford. Upon his arrival at the campus, Clarence stopped at the administration building to ask for directions from the school's business manager, Jimmy Carter. Upon seeing Gaines, he remarked, "I've never seen anything bigger than you but a house." Thus, the nickname "Big House" was originated, and it stuck. He left with a degree in chemistry and Little All-American status in football.

Following his graduation in 1946, "Big House" packed his bags for Winston-Salem State College in 1946, where he was to be assistant coach in football, basketball, and track and field. He planned to stay one year, just long enough to save money for dental school. Forty-seven years later, he was still at Winston-Salem (now a university). "I don't think I was meant to be a dentist," says Gaines, "Coaching is what the Lord called me to do."

What a fantastic forty-seven years it became. Gaines spent only two years as an assistant coach before being elevated to head coach of all three sports, common in those days. His stated goal became to "succeed not only as an athletic coach but also as a respected and significant asset to the university and community." He did that and more. At the time of his retirement, Gaines was the second winningest coach in college basketball history. He also held the positions of athletic director and chairperson of the physical education department and had attained the academic rank of professor of physical education.

In addition, he became a champion of youth sports, not only in the Winston-Salem area, but also in North Carolina. Clarence became a fixture in local youth sports programs and civic organizations. He was truly an educator who reached out to touch the lives and make a difference in the lives not only of his athletes and students, but also young people and others in his community.

"The greatest pleasure I got out of athletics was to see all the guys we work with, who weren't supposed to make it (by society's standards), grow into successful young men." said Gaines. "I've been around for a long enough time to have coached some of the guys who are now retired, and every time I see one of them, I just smile."

Coach Gaines developed an effective system of play, based on fast-breaking, up-tempo basketball. He emphasized ball movement and wanted his post players to flash toward the ball, rather than standing on the block. Gaines also used the "give-and-go play," one of the first plays ever used in basketball. Gaines said, "We did a lot of practicing with no dribbling allowed. The ball had to be passed, rather than dribbled. Players could not stand and wait for the pass. They had to move toward the ball to meet it."

Gaines also used the "four corners" offense popularized by Dean Smith at North Carolina. Hall of Fame coach John McLendon actually developed the concept and called the strategy "Jack in the Corner." Early in his career, Gaines was befriended and mentored by the legendary McLendon, who is called the "Father of Black Basketball Coaches."

Winston-Salem's star player on their 1967 national championship team was future Hall of Famer Earl "The Pearl" Monroe. Under Gaines' direction, Monroe was allowed to develop, perfect, and popularize the "spin dribble." Gaines said, "Earl was truly a 'pearl'—a coach's player. I never had a more conscientious player, a harder worker, or a player with a better personality."

Consistency and level-headedness were characteristics of "Big House" Gaines. He handled both victory and defeat with a level response. If the team won, he commended his players for good execution. If they lost, stress was placed on the part of their execution that could be improved. It was a very evenhanded approach that was one component that produced a local legend and a national treasure. Big House seemed always to praise his players and show appreciation for their efforts. Perseverance and humility were trademarks of his classy, professional approach. On the occasion of the New Year's Eve day before his team would achieve win number six hundred for him as a head coach, Clarence was asked how he nervously spent the day. He responded that he "scrubbed the kitchen floor," because his lovely wife, Clara, had asked him to do just that. Win number six hundred followed that night before a sparse crowd and honored only by a private party afterwards.

Clarence Gaines also was respected as a humanitarian. He regularly hosted the visiting coach after their game to get a barbecue sandwich or something to eat. Big House stated that he believed it was just the right thing to do. "We are both coaches of basketball, not going to war, but playing a game." He was so revered that he regularly was asked to speak at sports banquets, as are all coaches. But Clarence was asked to speak to rival schools (unheard of in coaching circles). As a humanitarian coach, he was most concerned about players' academic achievement, focusing on hard work. Gaines was especially honored with the prestigious Paul Robeson Award in this area of achievement.

His forty-seven year coaching career was also noteworthy because it occurred in the following challenging eras:

- **1947-57**, the "Dark Years," when the contributions of Black colleges in the United States were unknown and invisible. Black coaches had the added burden of travel, lodging, and board for movement between campuses and competitions in a very hostile social climate—"like a GI plotting a course through a minefield," avoiding and managing hostile racial confrontations and at the same time, maintaining a necessary role of respect, dignity, and leadership." (McLendon, 1982)

- **1960-70**, the period called the social revolution of protest or the "Turbulent Sixties." Victories were difficult in this time period, but a Gaines team reached the pinnacle of success by winning the 1967 College Division Championship.

- **1970-80**, the period of uncertainty and focus on "me" (the drug generation). Through this period of change (times/athletes/students/administrations/rules), the constant factor was Coach Gaines, a "Big House" on the scene—disciplined, adhering to moral coaching principles, unassailable integrity, and a style of gentle, yet firm, authority with class (McLendon, 1982). It was also said that his abilities as a coach were exceeded only by his integrity and his concern for the welfare and education of his athletes. "Gaines has done more to improve the quality of coaching and general conditions of play among predominantly black colleges than any other person" (Fritz, 1980). Big House, in his own way, was responsible for developing higher coaching standards, as well as higher academic and performance standards.

Throughout his career, Gaines was influenced by several future Hall of Fame coaches. The following examples illustrate his thoughts on some of the game's greatest coaches:

- "Coach John McLendon was a great innovator, mentor, and fundamentalist."
- "The most impressive clinician had to be Adolph Rupp. He could teach more basketball in 15 to 20 minutes than a lot of coaches could teach in two days. I learned all about the continuity offense from him."
- "Nobody ever wrote as many books and articles or ran more clinics both in the U.S. and abroad than Clair Bee. He also wrote the greatest series of juvenile sports novels ever published—the Chip Hilton series."
- "Everett Dean was another outstanding clinician. He wrote *Progressive Basketball*, which I consider the first 'scientific' textbook on basketball."
- "Another outstanding coach and person is Bob Knight. I believe he is the greatest humanitarian in basketball. He helps a lot of people and gets involved in a lot of good causes, without attracting attention to himself."

Gaines urges coaches today to teach fundamental skills and stress the importance of education. Gaines (2003) said, "The low graduation rates worry me. Education is the answer. Back in the old days, there was no professional basketball for black youngsters. We worked with everyone and stressed the importance of a college degree. We need to get back to emphasizing the importance of education."

Gaines would like to see two rule changes in the game of basketball. First, the distance of the three-point shot should be lengthened. Gaines would like to push the three-point arc back to the international distance. Second, the number of personal fouls allowed before disqualification should be increased, giving each player an extra foul—six instead of five.

Finally, notice should be made of the universal respect and recognition given to Clarence Gaines for his personal and professional accomplishments. He has been inducted into eight Halls of Fame, including CIAA, North Carolina Sports, Winston-Salem State University, National Association of Intercollegiate (NAIA), and the Naismith Basketball Hall of Fame. Uniquely, his nomination for the Naismith honor was sponsored by a rival institution in the CIAA conference, a real tribute to the respect earned by Clarence.

SOURCE

Fritz, Harry. (1980, May 29). Letter to Naismith Memorial Basketball Hall of Fame.

Gaines, Clarence. Vertical Files, Archives. Naismith Memorial Basketball Hall of Fame. Springfield, MA.

Gaines, Clarence. Interview with Ralph Pim. September 6, 2003.

Gaines, Clarence. (1994, April). Break Out at the Big House. *Scholastic Coach.*

McLendon. John. (1982, May 3). Presentation at the Naismith Hall of Fame.

LESSONS FROM THIS LEGEND...

FAST-BREAK BASKETBALL

By Clarence "Big House" Gaines

In basketball, the fast break is a widely known and used means of advancing the ball toward the offensive goal. The intent of the fast break is to outnumber the defensive players in the high-percentage scoring areas and score before the defenders are organized in their half-court defense.

FAST BREAK SITUATIONS

The fast break can be initiated from the following situations:

- Loose-ball situations
- Pass interceptions
- Stolen balls
- Jump ball situations
- Side-out-of-bounds in the back court
- After a missed free throw
- After a made free throw
- After a missed field goal
- After a made field goal

THE MAIN COMPONENTS OF THE FAST BREAK

DEFENSIVE REBOUND

The primary starting point of a fast break is the defensive rebound. From this point, regardless of any other opportunities, the fast break may be employed. The secondary starting point of a fast break is after a successful free throw or field goal by the opponents.

OUTLET PASS

The outlet pass after a rebound is the most crucial pass of the system. The best passers from the rebound position quickly determine the position of the outlet receivers and make the pass either right or left-handed. The two forwards and the center are the players who must be skilled in this technique. The outlet pass goes to a specified area where a receiver is waiting. Rebounds in the center and the right side of the rebound area are passed to the right (the passer's right when he faces down court); rebounds on the left are passed to the guard stationed on the left sideline.

OUTLET RECEIVER

The outlet receiver is either guard. His position varies from the corner baseline area to a position midway between the top of the key and the centerline (along the sideline), depending on the power, skill, and rebounding ability of the outlet passers, as well as the strength of the offensive rebounders. The more powerful the offensive rebounders, the closer to the baseline the outlet receiver positions himself. The optimum position to prevent defensive guard interference is at a point near the free-throw line extended .

GUARD OPPOSITE THE OUTLET-RECEIVING GUARD

The guard opposite the outlet receiver immediately breaks down court. He sprints down court to a position near the basket and stops there. His primary function is to make the defense drop back and thereby leave the center either open or defended by only one player. Getting the quick pass for a drive-in shot is of secondary importance. This player must be taught to appreciate this important function.

THIRD MAN IN THE FAST BREAK

The third man in the fast break is an extremely important part of the system. He is one of the rebounders, usually the one not engaged in the outlet pass phase. As the rebound is secured and before, or quickly after, the outlet pass, he sprints for the third or outside lane on the side of the outlet-pass receiver. He may cross in front of or behind the ball-handler as he dribbles to the middle and down the court. Very often, the outlet passer himself is in a position to follow his pass and becomes the first player in the third lane. On other occasions, the player whose opponent cannot or will not sprint back on defense may fill the third lane.

TRAILERS

The two remaining rebounders (trailers) may carry out any one of the following assignments: trail the break slowly and protect the back court; trail the break quickly and go to an intermediate shooting area for a field-goal attempt; drive into the scoring area for a pass from a four-on-three situation (the fourth lane is between the center lane and either outside lane); rush the offensive board after a field goal attempt; or move quickly to the regular set offensive position once the fast break has been stopped.

LESSONS FROM THIS LEGEND...

FAST BREAK FACTS

Guards do most of the ballhandling. The third man and the center-lane guard do most of the scoring. The center-lane guard is usually the leader in assists. The big rebounders do not handle the ball in the offense except for quick return passes, a drive-in shot, or an assist.

The driving lay-up is the key shot in the fast break. The driver must score or be fouled in the attempt. The second most important shot is the one from the foul circle by the center-lane guard.

The period of time directly after the fast break is stopped is an interim period during which the defense may be quite disorganized and opportunities for scoring are many. Good ball control during this period is essential.

The mechanics of the fast-break offense are as simple as any other offense; however, drills must be devised for each phase. The individual's ability to handle the ball under high-speed conditions requires thorough drilling in fundamental footwork and passing (especially avoiding traveling violations).

LITTLE MAN-BIG MAN DRILL

A single line is formed out-of-bounds along the sideline at the corner of the court. Each guard (little man) has a ball, and the center (big man) is positioned behind him. The guard dribbles the length of the court, shooting a right-hand lay-up shot or a short bank shot. The center runs downcourt immediately behind the guard. He rebounds the ball (if the shot is missed) and passes out to the guard, who has sprinted down the right sideline after his shot. If the shot is made, the guard will wait along the sideline, not farther than the mid-court line for the big man to take the ball out of bounds and throw a baseball pass to him. The guard then dribbles to the free-throw circle and passes off to the big man, who drives in from the outside lane for a lay-up shot (see **Diagram 1.0**).

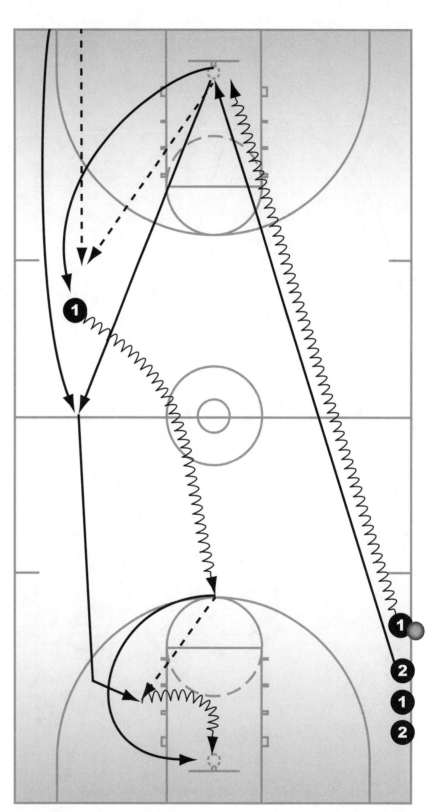

Gaines 1.0

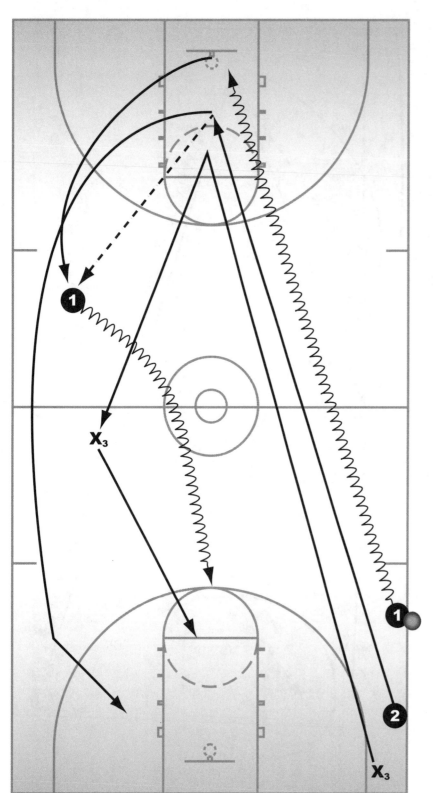

Gaines 1.1

LITTLE MAN-BIG MAN, PLUS ONE

A third player, usually a forward, is positioned behind the guard and the center. He is a defensive player who trails the two as they drive to the basket. He then attempts to: 1) rebound the ball if the shot is missed: 2) stop the outlet pass or the inbounds pass; and 3) stop the fast break back to the other end of the court (see **Diagram 1.1**).

SOURCE

Gaines, Clarence. (1980, Summer). Fast Break Basketball. *The Basketball Bulletin.*

LEGACY OF
James "Jack" Gardner

- Only coach in basketball history to direct two different schools to the Final Four at least twice.

- Built his teams on speed, quickness, and fast break basketball.

- Led Kansas State to the NCAA Finals in 1951.

- Nicknamed "The Fox" for his clever tactical abilities.

- Believed "details win games" and utilized statisticians to compile precise charts on every phase of the game.

- Known for his ritual of drinking milk during games to calm his ulcer.

- Revolutionized recruiting and was one of the first coaches to make home visits with recruits.

- Was the driving force behind the construction of new arenas at Kansas State and Utah.

JAMES "JACK" GARDNER

"Most players want to be winners, but it is the degree of commitment that determines the extent they will exceed."
—James "Jack" Gardner

BIOGRAPHY

Born: March 29, 1910 in Texico, NM

Died: April 10, 2000

Inducted into the Naismith Basketball Hall of Fame in 1984

Jack Gardner coached 36 years, and his teams registered an overall 649-278 record. He coached at Alhambra H.S. (CA), Modesto Junior College (CA), Kansas State University, and the University of Utah. Gardner spent twenty-eight years at the major college level, where his teams compiled a 486-235 record. He was the first coach to direct two different schools to the Final Four at least twice (Kansas State in 1948 and 1951 and Utah in 1961 and 1966). Gardner coached at Kansas State from 1939-1942 and 1946-1953, won three Big Seven titles, and led K-State to the 1951 NCAA championship game against Kentucky. During World War II, Gardner was a Lt. Commander in the Navy and coached some of the finest service teams in the country. During his 18-year tenure at Utah (1953-1971), Gardner's teams won seven conference titles and posted a record of 339-154. He coached ten teams to the NCAA or NIT tournaments. At the time of his retirement in 1971, Gardner ranked behind only Adolph Rupp and John Wooden as the winningest active coach in college basketball. During his retirement, Gardner served as a consultant for the Utah Jazz.

...SCOUTING REPORT.....SCOUTING REPORT.....

James "Jack" Gardner...

If you listened to pop music during the early 1960s, you will remember the lyrics of Barry Mann's hit song, *Who Put the Bomp*, asking the question,

"Who put the bop
In the bop shoo bop shoo bop?
Who put the ram
In the rama lama ding dong?
Who put the dip
In the dip da dip da dip?
Who was that man?"

For basketball fans during this period of time, there was no question who put the "run" in the "Running Utes." That man was James "Jack" Gardner.

Gardner's revolutionary fast-break style propelled Utah to two Final Four appearances and a record of 339-154 during his 18-year tenure (1953-71). From 1959 to 1962, Utah won 51 out of 56 games. His philosophy was built on speed, running, and hard-nosed basketball. In his words, he wanted to keep things "sound and simple," Gardner believed that the modern game demanded speed and quickness. He demanded that his players go up and down the court quickly.

"We plan on breaking every time we get the ball," said Gardner. "Keeping constant pressure on our opponents by fast breaking as soon as one of our players secures the ball is the rule. Psychologically, the threat of a fast break forces opponents to throttle their offense by constantly thinking of defensive balance and the necessity of speed in assembling their defensive formation."

Jack is the only coach to direct two different schools to the Final Four at least twice. Prior to his arrival at Utah, Gardner coached at Kansas State from 1939-42 and 1946-53 and led the Wildcats to the Final Four in 1948 and 1951. Kansas State was beaten in the 1951 NCAA championship game by Adolph Rupp's Kentucky Wildcats.

"I don't think there is any question that he was an outstanding coach," said Ernie Barrett, an All-American guard on the 1951 K-State team. "In those days, you had to fight for anything you could get, and he was pretty tenacious in that regard. One of the fun things with Coach Gardner was the rivalry that he had with the University of Kansas. He

and "Phog" Allen totally hated each other."

The intense rivalry between K-State and KU led Allen to mockingly call Gardner a "wonder boy." Undaunted by Allen's importance, the feisty Gardner won nine of 11 meetings from 1947 to 1951.

Gardner's engaging personality charmed prospects and parents, and he was nationally recognized as a great recruiter. He was one of the first coaches to make home visits with recruits. "His recruiting style was definitely years ahead of other coaches," said Barrett.

Gardner's recruiting success awakened Allen to the importance of hitting the recruiting trail. Phog hated the idea of recruiting. He normally sent a form letter back to prospects who contacted him, stating that he had never contacted a young man for his basketball playing ability. For years, Allen's philosophy was that young men in Kansas who wanted to play basketball should attend their state university and be pleased with their jobs working in the towel room for 35 cents an hour. Former Kansas assistant Dick Harp said, "Jack Gardner's teams ultimately changed Doc Allen's perspective. K-State had become more than a worthy competitor. Doc realized Jack Gardner was a real threat to the future, the first real threat he had ever faced. Before that, Doc had gotten most of the good players out of Kansas, and his coaching ability allowed him to dominate."

Gardner's players and peers affectionately knew the affable coach as "The Fox" because of his clever tactical abilities. *Sports Illustrated* claimed that Gardner was capable of winning with "an old maid in the post and four midgets."

An apostle of preparation, Gardner coached basketball as if it were a science. Jack believed that "details win games." His theory was "if it moves, chart it." During games and practices, he utilized statisticians to compile precise charts on every phase of the game. Gardner's office was referred to as a "Basketball Library of Congress," because there were neatly bound files containing game-by-game, minute-by-minute analysis of everything that had happened during Gardner's coaching career. He believed that keeping accurate records took a lot of the guesswork out of coaching.

Gardner considered rebounding as the most important single phase of the game. He told his players, "Your head height doesn't mean everything. Your reach, your arm spread, jumping ability (explosive power), and timing are more important. Timing can be developed through practice. Rope-jumping and weight lifting will improve your spring, as well as teach good footwork and coordination."

During games, Gardner called time-outs by waving a white handkerchief. Gardner remembered, "Over the years, this attracted some attention. Quite often, fans would wave back at me. But, the most comical experience I encountered with the hanky-waving took place when Dick Shores was playing for me. Dick stuffed a handkerchief in his basketball pants and when I waved for a time-out, he pulled it out, waved back, and continued on with the game."

Another memorable incident occurred when Gardner was coaching at Utah and his team was playing at the University of Wyoming. Jack always kept a bottle of milk under his seat and would frequently take swigs during the course of the game. On this night, some of the Utah players spiked his milk with a laxative, resulting in Gardner missing some of the second-half action.

Gardner was the driving force behind the construction of Ahearn Field House at Kansas State and the building of the Huntsman Center at the University of Utah. At K-State, Gardner invited members of the Legislature to attend a game at the tiny 2,800-seat Nichols Gym and then encouraged students to drop ketchup-soaked dummies from the rafters. His efforts, despite opposition from some university administrators and legislators, eventually led to the building of the 14,500-seat Ahearn Field House in 1950.

At Utah, the Huntsman Center was a "state-of-the-art" arena that included a spacious locker room for the home team. But for the visiting team, there was a room so small that the opposing players had to squeeze into the shower area or meet in the adjoining hallway for the pre-game talk. Rival coaches complained that it was just another way "The Fox" was trying to gain a home-court advantage.

Jack was a master at molding players into winning teams. "Most players want to be winners," said Gardner, "but it is the degree of commitment that determines the extent they will exceed. It is my job to enhance the qualities that will make athletes successful. Players must learn that only a maximum effort and positive attitude can bring winning results. But, they must also know that while winning is not everything, striving to is. And you cannot profit by losing unless you have extended yourself to the utmost to win. If you have done these things, you have won regardless of the score."

Gardner did not believe in many rules or regulations. "I never try to impose my will on a player," stated Gardner. "You can't get a player to play at the top of his natural abili-

ty if you try to rule him with an iron hand. I try to show the reason for doing certain things to the boy, and in that way, create the will to accomplish in him."

Gardner took great pride in preparing his players for life after basketball. "The mark of a coach is the men his players become," said Gardner.

Jack was born in New Mexico but spent much of his youth in southern California. Gardner credits Dick Lee, principal and basketball coach at Lincoln H.S. (CA), for fostering his love for the game of basketball. Lee opened the gym and provided Gardner with a ball so he could practice the sport whenever he desired. Gardner became an outstanding athlete and won 16 letters in four sports at Redlands H.S. (CA). He set the pole vault record that remained in place for 30 years.

Gardner attended USC and played for future Hall of Fame coach Sam Barry. At USC, he captained the 1932 basketball team and won the MVP award. Gardner began his coaching career as an assistant to Barry, while attending graduate school at USC. "Coach Barry," said Gardner (1961), "was one of the great minds of basketball and my inspiration and close friend."

Gardner then coached at Alhambra H.S. (CA) and Modesto Junior College. From 1935 to 1939, Gardner led his teams at Modesto to three state championships in basketball and three in baseball.

Gardner spent his entire life devoted to the game of basketball. He attended every Final Four for 58 years, starting with the first NCAA tournament in 1939. After his retirement from college coaching, Jack served as a consultant for the Utah Jazz.

At the time of Gardner's death in 2000, Kansas State president Jon Wefald said, "Coach Gardner will go down as one of the greatest coaches of all time. He's a legend, there's no question about it."

SOURCE

Gardner, Jack. (1961). *Championship Basketball with Jack Gardner.* Englewood Cliffs, NJ: Prentice-Hall, Inc.

Gardner, Jack. Vertical Files, Archives. Naismith Memorial Basketball Hall of Fame. Springfield, MA.

Kerkhoff, Blair (1996). *Phog Allen: The Father of Basketball Coaching.* Masters Press: Indianapolis, IN.

LESSONS FROM THIS LEGEND...

FAST-BREAK BASKETBALL

By Jack Gardner

The University of Utah Runnin' Redskins *(Authors' Note: The team is now called the Runnin' Utes)* really love to run. Our students and fans like to see us run, and the popularity of the run-and-shoot game in professional, college, independent, and high school basketball is further support for the fast break style of play. Although it requires a lot of hard work and that an athlete be in top condition to use the fast break, players like it because each one of them has a chance to get in on the play, to set up a teammate's scoring opportunity, or to make the basket himself.

We plan on breaking every time we get the ball. Keeping constant pressure on our opponents by fast breaking as soon as one of our players secures the ball is our rule. Psychologically, the threat of a fast break forces opponents to throttle their offense by constantly thinking of defensive balance and the necessity of speed in assembling their defensive formation.

The Go! Go! Go! Game means that a team takes off as soon as it gets possession of the ball and applies pressure all the way until the score is impossible. Only then does the fast break end and the set offense take over. Our specific approach to the fast break is covered in the following outline:

I. **Advantages:**
   a. Balanced attack demands it:
      i. Many teams can't stop it.
      ii. Failure to fast break would give opponents a rebounding advantage.
   b. The fast break is our KO punch:
      i. Close games can be broken open in a matter of seconds.
      ii. The fast break is demoralizing to opponents and is a tonic to the offensive players.
      iii. It is the best weapon against a press and/or a zone.
   c. Coming from behind to beat opponents:
      i. It is a means of catching up quickly when behind.
      ii. It is an excellent method by which to get the cheap basket.
   d. The fast break is a spectator's game:
      i. It provides thrills and daring plays.
      ii. It provides additional scoring opportunities and excitement.
   e. The fast break is a player's game:
      i. It gives the opportunist a chance to operate and score points quickly.
      ii. A fast-breaking and fast-moving offense permits more freedom, initiative, and the use of natural talents.
      iii. It is fun to play.

II. **The fast break is not a total or the only offense:**
   a. Twenty-three point five per cent of our scores have resulted from the fast break.

   b. The fast break keeps constant pressure on our opponents and has been the difference in many games.
   c. Good judgment is crucial, and players must know when the fast break advantage is lost.
   d. Good passing and shooting are musts. We do not want to be a "run-and-shoot-and-hope" team.

III. **Player requirements:**
   a. Quickness is more important than speed.
   b. Players must be alert and have excellent anticipation.
   c. Slow runners can excel in the fast break if they possess quickness and anticipation.
   d. Size and rebounding ability are essential. We must get the ball before we can start our break.
   e. Good ball-handling at top speed is necessary.

IV. **The fast break starts while on defense:**
   a. Players must be fast-break minded and look for opportunities to steal the ball.
   b. Play both the man and the ball. When defending a player without the ball, always maintain vision on the ball.
   c. Use pressure defense to create turnovers.

V. **Potential fast-break opportunities:**
   a. Following opponents' missed field goals
   b. Interceptions
   c. Held balls
   d. Following missed free throws
   e. After successful field goals
   f. After successful free throws

DEVELOPING FAST BREAK OPPORTUNITIES

Boxing-out and rebound positions are shown in **Diagram 1.0**. It is essential that all players box out. The first objective is the opponent—not the ball. Defensive players X1 and X2 are responsible for long rebounds in the free throw area. Defensive players X3, X4, and X5 block out and form a shell around the basket. As soon as we gain possession of the ball, our fast-break pattern begins to form. We want to initiate our fast break without delay, and that means all players hustle to fill the lanes.

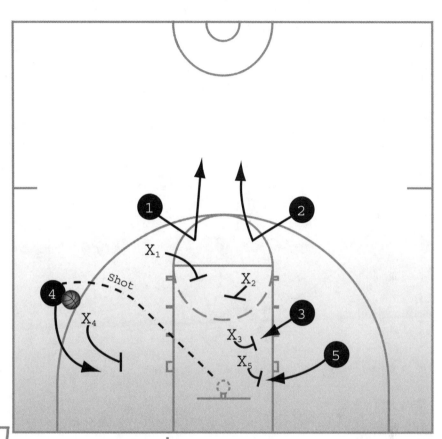

Gardner 1.0

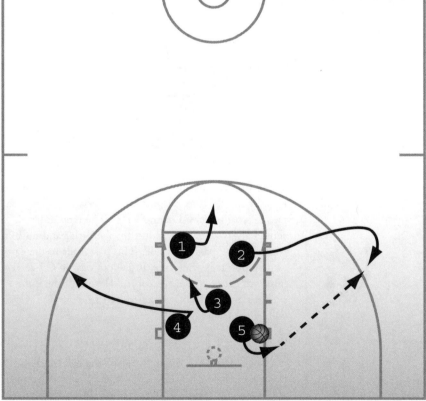

The most important pass in the fast break is the first pass. It must be fast and accurate. Baseball and hook passes are stressed. A good start leads to a good ending. In **Diagram 1.1**, O5 secures the rebound, turns away from the congestion under the basket, and looks to outlet the ball to O2. O2 breaks to the right sideline and anticipates the pass. O2 must meet the pass.

Gardner 1.1

LESSONS FROM THIS LEGEND...

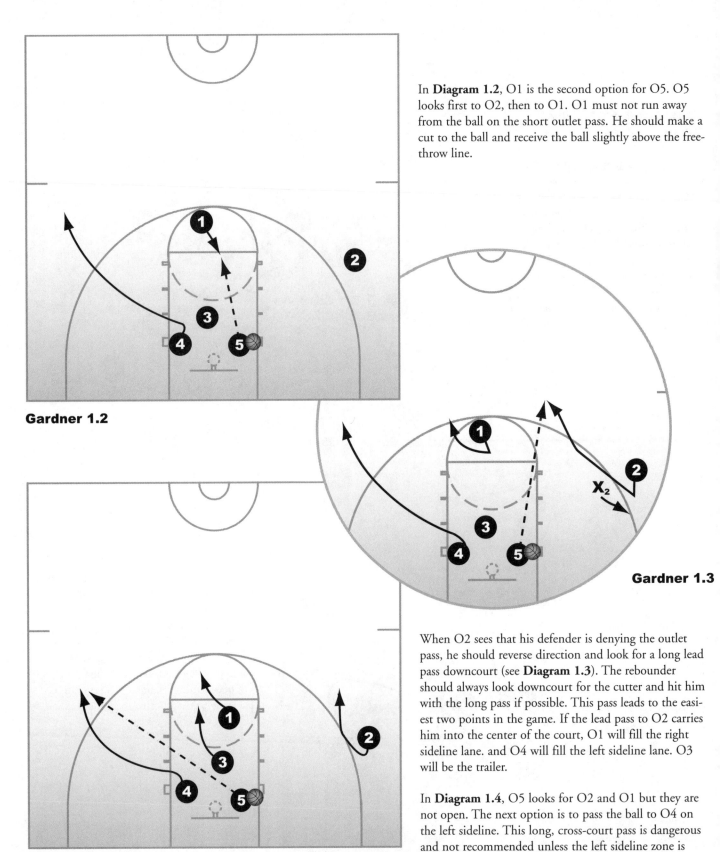

In **Diagram 1.2**, O1 is the second option for O5. O5 looks first to O2, then to O1. O1 must not run away from the ball on the short outlet pass. He should make a cut to the ball and receive the ball slightly above the free-throw line.

Gardner 1.2

Gardner 1.3

Gardner 1.4

When O2 sees that his defender is denying the outlet pass, he should reverse direction and look for a long lead pass downcourt (see **Diagram 1.3**). The rebounder should always look downcourt for the cutter and hit him with the long pass if possible. This pass leads to the easiest two points in the game. If the lead pass to O2 carries him into the center of the court, O1 will fill the right sideline lane. and O4 will fill the left sideline lane. O3 will be the trailer.

In **Diagram 1.4**, O5 looks for O2 and O1 but they are not open. The next option is to pass the ball to O4 on the left sideline. This long, cross-court pass is dangerous and not recommended unless the left sideline zone is wide open.

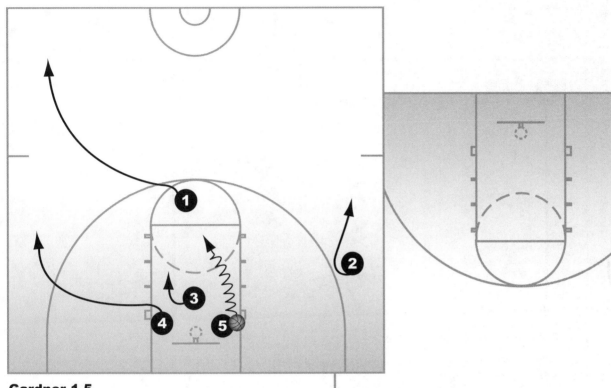

Gardner 1.5

Our first choice is always to pass the ball ahead to open teammates because it is faster and gets our fast break started quicker. However, when a pass is not possible, the next option is for the rebounder, O5, to start the fast break with a dribble. When O5's teammates see him dribble out from the basket and down the court, they fill the outside lanes (see **Diagram 1.5**). They must act quickly and adjust their cutting so the lanes are not clogged up with two or three players. If all the lanes are filled, the remaining players fill the trailer and the safety positions.

By the time the fast break reaches the midcourt line, we want to have the three lanes filled and the ball in the hands of the middle man. As shown in **Diagram 1.6**, when O2 receives the outlet pass, he looks for a chance to feed teammate O1. O1 may pass the ball to O4 or back to O2, but by the time we reach midcourt, we want the middle man to have the ball. This allows him to be in a position to pass off to either side at the end of the fast break. O1 must adjust his speed or the direction of his cut in order to get open for a pass back from the side lane. We believe in straight-lane fast breaks, and seldom have our players cross and exchange sides. Straight lines are quicker, and our objective is to get down to the other end of the court with an advantage—two-on-one, three-on-two, or four-on-three.

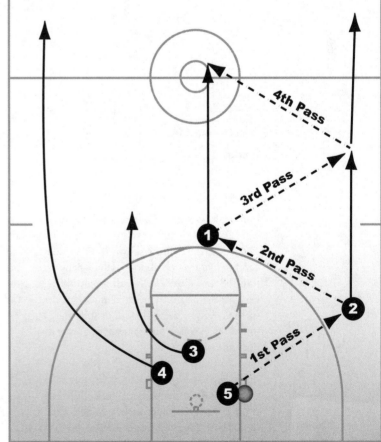

Gardner 1

LESSONS FROM THIS LEGEND...

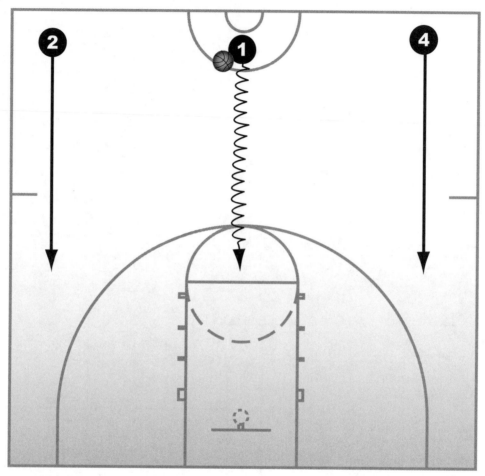

Gardner 1.7

Controlled speed is the key to a successful fast break. Without control, the fast break will become wild and result in erratic passing and loss of the ball. As shown in **Diagram 1.7**, we like for our middle man to penetrate into the top of the circle with the dribble, and prefer that our wing men are about two strides ahead of the ball. This enables the middle man to see his teammates, and it also puts more pressure on the defense. The wing men maintain a path along the sidelines until they reach the free-throw line extended and then cut to the basket. The middle man is the key player when the ball reaches the front court. He must approach the top of the circle with complete balance and under control. Then, he must quickly select the best option and execute it with confidence and control. The pass that leads to the shot is the second most important pass of the fast break. As in all offense, the defense determines the play. Their moves tell us what we can do.

Source

Gardner, Jack. (1961). *Championship Basketball with Jack Gardner*. Englewood Cliffs, NJ: Prentice-Hall.

LESSONS FROM THIS LEGEND...

TIPS FOR ATTACKING THE PRESS

By Jack Gardner

The lack of good passers and playmakers today has made pressing defenses more effective than ever before. You simply can't hide weak passers when playing against pressure defenses. So, unless a team works long and hard on good ballhandling, you might as well forfeit the game and go skiing, because the press will beat you.

The players must understand the objectives of the press, how it works, and what it is trying to accomplish in order to pick it apart. There are ways to beat any kind of defense if you understand it and are willing to spend time practicing sound habits. You must develop a positive attitude. If players fear a press, they are apt to panic, and that will be fatal.

UCLA coach John Wooden has been very successful using pressure defense. He told me that it has been the side effects of the press that have paid off so well for him. The constant pressure throughout the game makes most teams wear down or crack for short periods and then turn the ball over just enough to spell defeat. This has happened game after game for UCLA, with the turning point coming near the end of the first half or about the middle of the second half.

In preparation for pressure defenses, it is important to simplify your attack. For a few years at Utah, we had one pattern to attack man-to-man presses and another to attack zone presses. With the advent of so many variations and combination defenses used intermittently during a game or season, we have had to develop one attack and pattern that is simple and yet flexible enough to use against any type of pressure. We do favor a style that is most effective against the zone press, because it is more

frequently met and seems to be the most successful. There is simply not enough time, nor is it now practical, to teach a separate offense for each defense.

For two weeks in our pre-season drills, we spend a major portion of each session introducing our pressure attack. We continue working against various presses throughout the season. It has to be a top priority in your practice planning. Your players will develop confidence, and they will not panic when they encounter a press. The day of giving the ball to your best dribbler and letting him bring the ball up is gone forever. We also believe that we must practice our attack against pressure that begins anywhere from end line to mid-court. The front line of the defense may attack the ball at any place, and we must be prepared and practice accordingly.

A team must have a pattern and a plan of attack, but a coach must also provide a system flexible enough to allow players a certain amount of freedom. The presses are all different, each has strengths and weaknesses, and we want to take advantage of the opportunities that are presented. We want our players to use their own good talents and initiative. Poise and simplicity are two keys to success.

Here are my tips on attacking pressure defenses:

1. Get the ball in play quickly. Do not allow the defense time to set up.
2. Maintain proper floor spacing.
3. Avoid bringing your defender to the ball, because this creates trapping opportunities.
4. Be quick, but don't hurry.
5. Use fakes to create open passing lanes.
6. Move without the ball.
7. Meet all passes.
8. Always be balanced and move under control.
9. Pass to an open teammate before getting trapped.
10. Look for open teammates. Our primary objective is to safely advance the ball.
11. Pass and go away.
12. Look for the back-door cut. The back door is our counter move against an overplaying defender.
13. Use weakside action. The players positioned on the weakside can often get open by simply breaking for the basket.
14. Isolate a good dribbler, and let him bring the ball up against a man-to-man press.
15. Use passes to attack zone presses rather than dribbling. Zone presses eat dribblers for breakfast.
16. When you break the press, take the ball to the basket and look to score.
17. If you do not have an immediate scoring opportunity, move quickly into your half-court offense.
18. Never panic! It takes a cool head to play a hot game.

Source

Gardner, Jack. (1971). Presses: How to Beat Them. *NABC Coaches Clinic Program.*

LEGACY OF
Alexander "Alex" Hannum

- Excelled at blending the talents of his players and getting them to play together as a team.

- Had the uncanny ability to take floundering teams and turn them into champions.

- His moods on the bench—harshness, urgency, and concentration—reflected qualities that drove his teams to success.

- Became the first coach to win championships in both the NBA and the ABA.

- His 1967 Philadelphia 76ers set a record for regular season wins (68) and were selected the best team in the NBA's first 35 years.

- Voted NBA Coach of the Year in 1964 and ABA Coach of the Year in 1969.

- Coached 13 future Naismith Hall of Fame inductees.

ALEXANDER "ALEX" HANNUM

*"A player is supposed to perform
to the best of his ability.
It's the coach's job to see
that this gets done."*
—Alexander "Alex" Hannum

BIOGRAPHY

Born: July 19, 1923 in Los Angeles, CA

Died: January 18, 2002

Inducted into the Naismith Basketball Hall of Fame in 1998

Alex Hannum began his coaching career as a player-coach with the St. Louis Hawks during the 1956-57 season. He coached 16 years and compiled a 471-412 NBA record and a 178-152 ABA record. Hannum was the first coach in professional basketball history to win both an NBA and an ABA championship. He also coached the Wichita Vickers to the National Industrial League title in 1959. His 1967 Philadelphia 76ers set an NBA record for regular season wins (68) and were later voted the best team in the NBA's first 35 years. Hannum coached 13 Hall of Famers and was selected Coach of the Year in both the NBA (1964) and the ABA (1969). He played professional basketball for nine years. Hannum went to the University of Southern California to play for future Hall of Fame coach Sam Barry in 1941. He left school and served in the Army from 1943 to 1946. He returned to USC after World War II, received All-Conference honors in 1947 and 1948, and was the team's Most Valuable Player in 1948.

Alexander "Alex" Hannum...

Alex Hannum was an All-City performer at Hamilton High School (CA) and went to the University of Southern California on a basketball scholarship in 1941. After serving in the Army from 1943 to 1946, he returned to USC and graduated in 1948. Hannum played for Hall of Fame coach Sam Barry and was USC's MVP in 1948. He also earned All-Conference honors in 1947 and 1948. Other members of that USC team included Bill Sharman and Tex Winter.

Hannum played three seasons with the Los Angeles Shamrocks, an AAU team, and then joined the Oshkosh All-Stars in the NBL. During his NBA playing career, Hannum played for Syracuse, Baltimore, Milwaukee, Fort Wayne, and St. Louis. "I was a journeyman player in the truest sense of the word," said Hannum. "But I think it has made me a better coach, because I got to play with so many different players with different styles." (1969)

During his nine-year professional playing career, the 6-foot 7-inches, 220-pound forward was regarded as a hard-nosed defender and tenacious rebounder. "Alex was a tough, quality team player who gave his all," said Hall of Fame player Tom Gola. "Any team trying to overpower Alex was in for a tough night." (Gola, 2002)

Hannum began his professional coaching career with the St. Louis Hawks during the 1956-57 season. Coach Red Holzman was fired at mid-season, and star guard Slater Martin grudgingly accepted the coaching job. A week later Martin persuaded Hawks owner, Ben Kerner, to appoint Hannum as player-coach. The Hawks went on to win the Western Division title and were defeated by the Boston Celtics in the seventh game of the NBA Finals. The next year, Hannum began his first full season as head coach and guided St. Louis to the 1958 NBA championship. Hannum left St. Louis after the championship season because of Kerner's reputation as a compulsive trader and his impatience with his coaches. Kerner had released seven coaches during a seven-year period.

Hannum accepted a position at Wichita and coached the Vickers to the 1959 National Industrial League title. Hannum returned to the NBA in 1960 and directed the Syracuse Nationals to the play-offs three consecutive years.

Hannum possessed the ability to take floundering teams and turn them into champions. In 1963, Hannum

became head coach of the San Francisco Warriors, a team that had finished in fourth place the previous year, and led them to the Western Division championship. Under Hannum's guidance in San Francisco, Wilt Chamberlain altered his offensive-oriented game to one of defense, rebounding, and team play. Hannum convinced Wilt to concentrate less on shooting and look for open teammates when the defense converged on him.

Both Hannum and Chamberlain left San Francisco, but were reunited in Philadelphia in 1966. Soon, the Philadelphia attack became the most potent in the NBA. Although Chamberlain's scoring average dropped to only 24 points per game, the lowest of his career, he was credited with 630 assists, a career-high and the third-best in the NBA in 1967. Largely as a result of Chamberlain's unselfish play, Philadelphia won the 1967 NBA championship and compiled a 68-13 regular season record.

It has been said that one of Hannum's greatest coaching accomplishments was his "psychological conquest" of Chamberlain. Hannum disagreed (1968). "I do not subscribe to the theory that I was the only coach who could ever "handle" Wilt. Wilt will accept coaching, and he has tried, in his way, to cooperate with every coach he has ever had. Wilt has a fine mind and is quick to grasp ideas and offer his own suggestions."

The relationship between Hannum and Chamberlain was not without conflict and healthy debate, but since it was based on respect, mutual understanding, and common goals, it worked.Chamberlain called Hannum the best coach he had played for and presented Alex with a special trophy thanking him for his emphasis on team play.

Even though the 1967 Philadelphia 76ers were selected as the best team during the NBA's first 35 years, Hannum refused to take credit for the team's success. "I like to think I've added something," said Hannum, "but it hasn't been much. I keep the players hustling and enthusiastic about winning. That's the essence of a coach's job. The technical aspects of basketball can be gained from a textbook—it's the coach's job to make sure the players are always in the proper frame of mind."

In 1968, Hannum became the head coach of the Oakland Oaks in the upstart American Basketball Association. The year before Hannum's arrival, the Oaks finished in last place with a 22-56 record. With the addition of Rick Barry, Hannum led Oakland to a 60-18 mark and the ABA championship.

As a professional coach, Hannum (1969) believed that you "don't foul up the talent you've working with." He stated, "Over-coaching has ruined too many players. When we get a player in this league, he already is a polished performer. The only basic fundamental we have to deal with is defense. A coach is no more important than that of any player. I'm the 13th man on this team, and the only difference is that I have veto power over the other twelve."

Hannum earned the reputation as a tough-guy, but he also demonstrated qualities of softness and understanding. The keystone of Hannum's coaching success was his matter-of-fact- honesty. He was a take-charge type of coach who possessed excellent, up-front rapport with his players.

"You must be honest with your players in this league," said Hannum. "Let them be perfectly aware of your motives and then be dedicated and firm in accomplishing them. How else can you gain their respect?"Hannum blended the talents of his players into powerful teams. "He was a player's coach who, while making strong demands on each individual, got them to accept their roles and play together as a team," stated Hall of Fame coach Jack Ramsay (1996).

Hall of Fame player Nate Thurmond said, "I love Alex Hannum. He was so much a builder of men. I played with a lot of pain in my back. I did it for myself, for the Warriors, and for my teammates. Mostly, I did it for Alex.

With the pain, I'm not sure that I could have done it for anybody else."

John Kerr, former coach of the Chicago Bulls, described Hannum in these words, "He's a man's man. If you could pick a father, you'd pick Alex Hannum."

SOURCE

Hannum, Alex. Vertical Files, Archives. Naismith Memorial Basketball Hall of Fame. Springfield, MA.

Hannum, Alex and Frank Deford. (1968, November 25). Old Days and Changed Ways. *Sports Illustrated*.

Hannum, Alex. (1969). An Interview with Rockets' New Coach, Alex Hannum. *San Diego Rockets Game Program*.

Ramsay, Jack. (1996, May 15). Letter to Joseph O'Brien.

DOUBLE-SCREEN OFFENSE

By Alex Hannum

> I played for Hall of Fame coach Sam Barry at USC and incorporated many of his double-screen and triple-screen options in my offense. I call them the "roll-em" series and the "B" series. Both are very effective against a man-to-man defense and create high percentage shots for your shooters.

Hannum 1.0

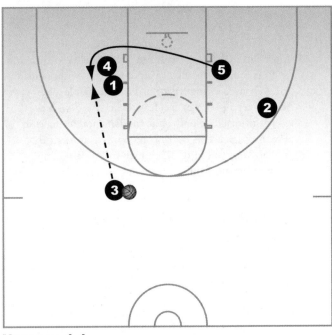

Hannum 1.1

"ROLL-EM" SERIES

1. DOUBLE SCREEN

As shown in **Diagram 1.0**, O1 dribbles to the left, hands off to O2, and continues on to the left side of the lane, where he joins O4 in setting a double screen on the left side of the lane. O2 dribbles right and hands off to O3, who dribbles to the left in the "dribble roll."

O5 has moved slowly down the right side of the lane. As soon as he sees the double screen set by O1 and O4, he cuts swiftly around the screen, where he receives the pass from O3. O5 can shoot over the screen, dribble over the top for a drive-and-shoot play, make a cross-court pass to O2 on the weakside, or pass back to O3 (see **Diagram 1.1**).

2. TRIPLE SCREEN

If O3 cannot pass to O5 coming off the double screen on the left side of the lane, he passes to O2 on the weakside and cuts around the triple screen to a post position on the right side of the lane (see **Diagram 1.2**).

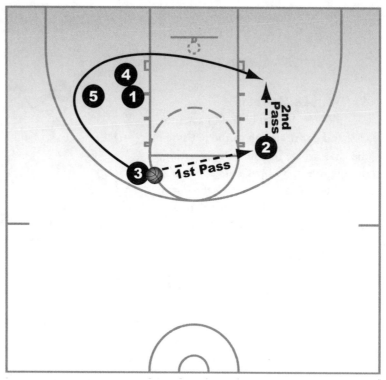

Hannum 1.2

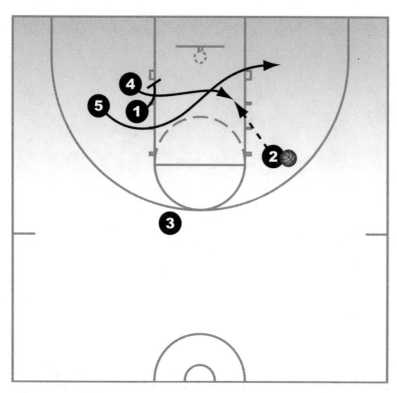

Another option for O3 is to pass to O2 and hold his position in the backcourt. O5 cuts in front of O1 and O4 and rolls across the lane. O4 breaks past a screen set by O1 and looks for the pass in the center of the lane (see **Diagram 1.3**).

Hannum 1.3

"B" SERIES

1. DOUBLE SCREEN

O1 initiates the dribble roll, passes to O2, and continues on to the left side of the lane, where he joins O5 in setting a double screen. O2 passes to O3 and continues to the corner. O4 cuts off the double screen and looks for the pass from O3 (See **Diagram 1.4**).

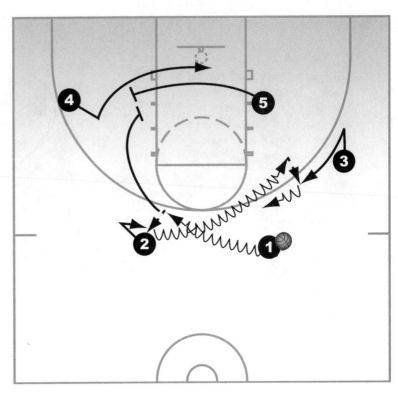

Hannum 1.4

2. REVERSE AROUND DOUBLE SCREEN

If O4 is not open coming off the double screen or if O3 is not able to get him the ball on the right side of the lane, O4 reverses his direction and uses the double screen again. O3 looks to pass to O4 coming off the screen (see **Diagram 1.5**).

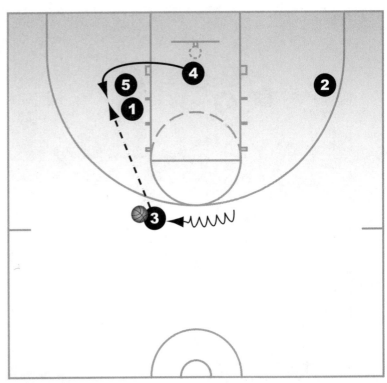

Hannum 1.5

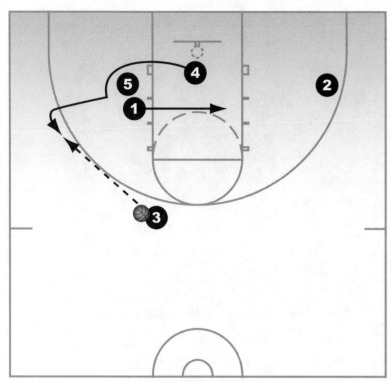

Hannum 1.6

3. FADE AND PASS TO PIVOT

If O4 does not receive the pass from O3 coming off the double screen, he should make a "fade" cut as shown in **Diagram 1.6**. The purpose of the "fade" cut is to get open on the wing. Immediately upon receiving the ball, O4 looks inside to O5. This pass is usually open because O5's defender usually tends to relax and is not in position to deny the pass.

Hannum 1.7

4. PIVOT PLAY

O1 has cut away from the double screen on the left side of the lane, leaving O5 alone and in good position for a pass from O4. In most cases, the defender guarding O5 is caught behind the pivot man and has no opportunity to advance to the side or in front of O5 to contest the pass (see **Diagram 1.7**).

SOURCE

Bee, Clair (ed.). (1963). *Winning Basketball Plays*. New York: Ronald Press.

121

LEGACY OF
Marv Harshman

- Compiled 642 wins at Pacific Lutheran, Washington State, and Washington.

- Selected NCAA Division I Coach of the Year in 1984.

- Respected as a teacher, philosopher, and strategist.

- Directed basketball programs that reflected dignity, honesty, and class.

- Originated the match-up zone defense in the Northwest.

- Considered an offensive genius for his high-low system of play.

- Led Pacific Lutheran to NAIA Finals in 1959.

- Served on the U.S. Olympic Committee from 1975 to 1981.

MARV HARSHMAN

*"Players know how to dribble, shoot and pass.
The challenge is to teach them why they should do it
a certain way, and when they should do it."*
—Marv Harshman

BIOGRAPHY

Born: October 4, 1917 in Eau Claire, WI

Inducted into the Naismith Basketball Hall of Fame in 1985

Marv Harshman lived in Wisconsin, Montana, and Minnesota before his parents, Claude and Florence, set-

tled in Lake Stevens, Washington. Harshman attended Lake Stevens (WA) High School from 1931 to 1935,

where he was a four-year starter in football and a three-year all-conference performer in basketball. He briefly

attended the University of Washington in 1935-36 before dropping out to work and help at home. Marv

went back to college and graduated from Pacific Lutheran in 1942. He was a star performer in football and

received Little All-American honors in basketball. Harshman was in the Navy during World War II and then

returned to Pacific Lutheran to begin his coaching career. In a distinguished 40-year career, Harshman won

642 games at Pacific Lutheran (241-121), Washington State (155-181), and Washington (246-146). At

Pacific Lutheran, Harshman's 1957 team finished 28-1, and his 1959 squad finished runner-up for the NAIA

national championship. At the University of Washington, four of his teams won 20 or more games, and he

was selected PAC 10 Coach of the Year in 1982 and 1984. Harshman is a member of the NAIA National

Hall of Fame.

Marv Harshman...

Claude and Florence Harshman were hardy and hard-working German-Dutch folks who had four children; one of which was born October 4, 1917 in Eau Claire, WI. They named this boy Marvel Keith, who later become known as Marv for obvious reasons. Father Claude moved throughout the upper Midwest, until finally bringing his family west and settling in Lake Stevens, Washington, on a small farm of eight acres, just as the Great Depression began. Marvel and older bother Sterling dominated the sports scene at Lake Stevens High School and excelled in football, track, and basketball. Marv stated, that his Lake Stevens years were in a "do-it society that gave you the appreciation of things you were able to do, but also what your neighbors and others had done. It was a genuine appreciation, because you recognized how much they had put into it" (Mosher, 1994).

Harshman was a marvelous athlete who was 6 foot 1 inch and 210 lbs. and could run a 100-yard dash near 10 seconds flat. His hard-working heritage and athletic prowess made him an all-sport performer in football, baseball, and track—one of the best in the history of Lake Stevens, from where he graduated in 1935.

Marv or Harsh, as he was called, entered the University of Washington to play basketball and football in 1935-36, but dropped out mid-year due to academic struggles and financial pressures at home. He worked for the Civilian Conservation Corps (CCC) and lumber mills before returning to college, this time at Pacific Lutheran College, where he excelled in football and track for four years and baseball (one year). He was All-League for three years and Little All-American in 1941, his senior year. Harsh was especially noted for football, where his 1940 PLC team went undefeated, defeating powerful Gonzaga University (16-13), who were led by All-American Tony Canadeo, in a special postseason game played in Tacoma, Washington before 15,000 fans. In three seasons, PLC football teams lost only one game.

But, he was also an excellent basketball player. "He reminded me of Elgin Baylor, Seattle University All-American. He was long and slender and could jump like a deer. He was just fabulous—behind-the back passes and one-hand shots," said one observer. Still, he was drafted by the old Chicago Cardinals in football.

WWII interrupted those plans, so he spent the next three years in the Navy. He returned to Pacific Lutheran College, where he became a head coach in three sports, the athletic director, and an instructor in physical education. He remained at PLC for thirteen years.

His PLC teams were 242-121 and won four district championships, taking them to the NAIA National Tourney in Kansas City four times. His 1957 team came within a whisper of winning it all, losing by one point in the semifinals to eventual champion, Tennessee State, who won three consecutive championships under future Hall of Fame coach John McLendon. PLC led all the way until All-American Dick Barnett hit a shot in the final seconds to win 71-70. Tennessee State easily won in the finals the next night.

Harshman was selected as NAIA District I Coach of the Year seven times, even though his teams won only four championships. It was a sign of the respect he was earning. His NAIA tourney team in 1948 was the first to use his unique contribution to the game—the high-low post offense. It captured the fancy of fans in the 32-team tournament. Harshman exploited defenses by placing two offensive players in a high-low formation. Then, he taught players how to play, why they are doing things and when to do them. He said, "My golden rule of offense is that a defense tells you what to do." The formation dictates where the defense has to be and then you make the right move at the right time.

From 1958 until 1971, he coached at Washington State University, where he produced three second-place finishes during the Wooden era at UCLA, when only the champion could go to postseason play. It was a challenging place to recruit players, located in a remote spot in Eastern Washington, at the very edge of the state line in the rolling hills of wheat country. In his second year, after getting drubbed by eventual NCAA Champion

California, 37-61, at home, Harshman was humiliated and disconsolate. Future Hall of Fame Coach Pete Newell came by and sat down with him. "Coach, there is nothing wrong with what you are doing. You just don't have any players. It doesn't matter how much you know about the game—what you are doing is very good." In 1965, Jud Heathcote arrived from West Valley High School in Spokane, and the recruiting level went up. Marv's teams were always competitive after that, and WSU became well known for "getting the most" out of their talent. His WSU teams were the first to beat Wooden at UCLA (Wooden's first year) and the last to beat him in 1975. John Wooden and Harshman became respected friends, with Wooden one of his biggest boosters. Wooden said, "Marv Harshman qualifies for what our favorite American, Abraham Lincoln, once said, "There's nothing stronger than gentleness. In his quiet way, that was Marv, and will always be Marv."
Heathcote gave him the highest compliment, "He's the best friend a guy could ever have, and he's the best guy a friend could ever have."

Marv Harshman made a difficult departure from his beloved Cougarville to become coach at archrival University of Washington. It was caused by changes in the WSU administration, both athletic and presidency. His Washington teams were 246-146 in his 13 years there; four of his Husky teamswon 20 games, and UW claimed two PAC 10 titles during Harshman's tenure at Washington. He was selected conference coach of the year three times and NABC National Coach of the Year in 1984. Harsh coached the USA team to the Pan-American Games gold medal in 1975 and was NABC President in 1981. Marv Harshman was a player's coach who earned player respect. He said, "the basis of respect is honesty. Players make their own decisions, based on our actions and how you treat them and how you conduct yourself in the whole situation." He did earn that respect with dead honesty, warmth, high moral convictions, and the straightforward philosophy developed from his humble beginnings. (Mosher, 1994).

He was quoted in 1994 as saying, "If anybody remembers me at all, I think it'll be as good teacher. I think the thing I've done is teach some people to be better than they might have been in basketball, and, hopefully, as people." He also stated that he felt sports is only important if and how they help people. His career has validated this value of sport.

SOURCE

Harshman, Marv. Vertical Files, Archives. Naismith Memorial Basketball Hall of Fame. Springfield, MA.

Harshman, Marv. Personal Interview.

Heathcote, Jud. Personal Interview.

Mosher, Terry. (1994) *Harsh: The Life, Times, and Philosophy of Hall of Fame Coach Marv Harshman.* Mo Books.

HIGH-LOW POST OFFENSE

By Marv Harshman

INTRODUCTION

This offense was developed at PLC where we had few athletic players and needed an offense which was simple, utilized role players, and was built on the concept of counter options. I set up the spacing and positions to take advantage of the potential for creating two-on-one opportunities.

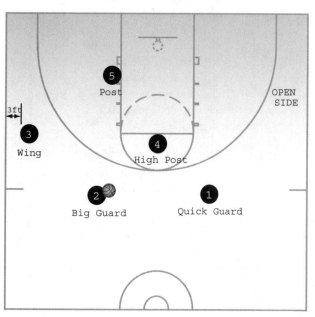

Harshman 1.0

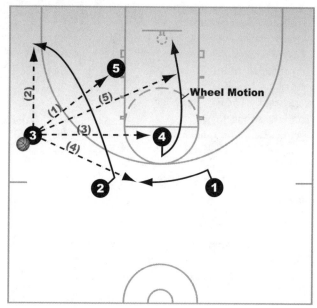

Harshman 1.1

BASIC SET

Diagram 1.0 shows the original set. The basic options from this set were:

1. O2 to O3 entry—pass to the wing.
2. O2 to O4 entry—pass to the high post.
3. O2 to O3 entry—pass to the post, O5.
4. O3 to O1 swing—pass to the quick guard for a baseline drive.

WING ENTRY

After receiving the pass from O2, O3 has the following options (see **Diagram 1.1**):

1. Pass inside to O5
2. Pass to O2 after he has made a cut to the corner.
3. Pass to O4 at the high post.
4. Pass to O1 at the point.
5. Pass to O4 on the "wheel move" (the "wheel move" is used when O4 is overplayed).

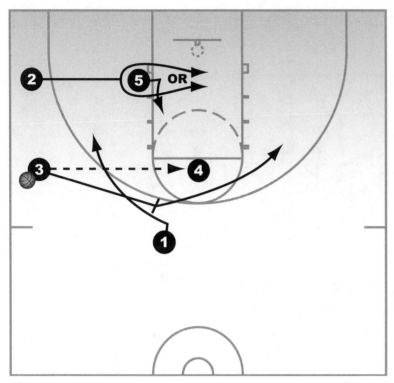

Harshman 1.2

WING TO HIGH POST OPTION

After receiving the pass from O3, O4 faces the basket and looks for the following scoring options (See **Diagram 1.2**):

1. O2 runs a baseline shuffle cut, using O5 as a screener, followed by a "duck-in," post-up move by O5.
2. O1 breaks off the screen set by O3.
3. After setting the screen for O1, O3 slips to the open side for a possible shot.

COUNTERS

Players begin to realize that when the defense takes something away, they give you something else. Role players then learn to read defenders and make corresponding counter moves. An example would be for O2 to use the "second-side" cut on the high post option, when the defenders switch on the "split-the-post" move.

This keys the "second guard around" counter to the switching defense (see **Diagram 1.3**).

Another key, as with any offense, are the following nuances: spacing, timing, rebounding, and floor balance. These critical components must be worked out, depending on the talent available. An important adage that must be taught is "the defense tells you what to do."

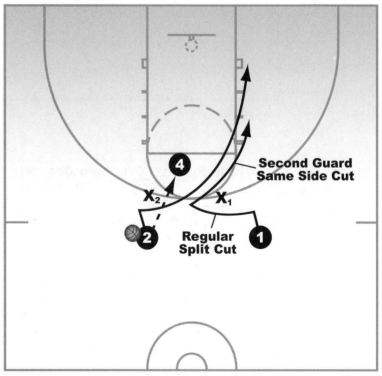

Harshman 1.3

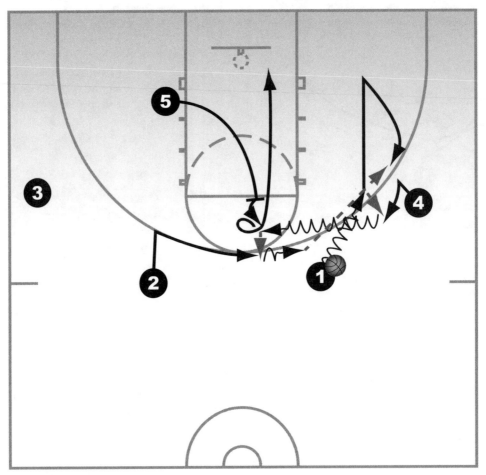

Harshman 1.4

HIGH POST TO OFF WING OPTION

The sequence of events in the high post to the off-wing option is as follows
(see **Diagram 1.4**):

1. O1 dribble penetrates, hands-off to O4, and continues toward the
   baseline.
2. O4 dribbles toward the middle of the floor for a hand-off with O2.
3. O5 breaks up from the low post and prepares to set a back screen on
   O4's defender.
4. O1 breaks out to the wing and receives the pass from O2.
5. O4 uses a reverse pivot and drives his defender into O5's screen.
6. O4 cuts to the basket, looking for the pass from O1.

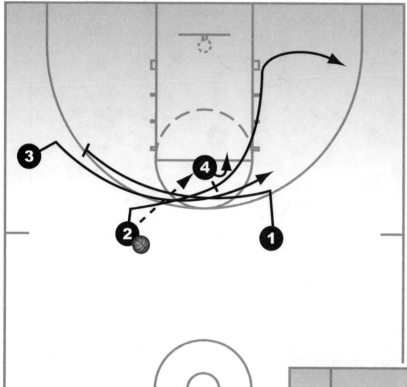

Harshman 1.5

HIGH POST SPLIT

The following sequence of events occurs in the high post split is as follows (see **Diagram 1.5**):

1. O2 passes to the high post, O4.
2. O4, after receiving the pass, pivots to the open side and faces the basket.
3. O2 becomes the first cutter and attempts to cut past the outside foot of O4.
4. O1 fakes a backdoor cut to the open side and then split-cuts over the high post (O4).
5. If O1 does not receive the ball from O4, he will screen for O3, who cuts over the high post for a possible shot.
6. After passing to O3 on the open side, O4 screens down for O5 and then looks to roll/slip to the basket (see **Diagram 1.6**).

Harshman 1.6

LESSONS FROM THIS LEGEND...

WEAKSIDE ENTRY TO HIGH POST

Diagram 1.7 shows the following sequence of events when the ball is passed into O4 from the weakside guard O1:

1. O1 makes a backdoor cut to the basket, looking for a return pass.
2. If O1 does not receive the return pass, he sets a cross-screen for O5.
3. O5 breaks across the lane, looking for the pass from O4.
4. O3 sets a down-screen for O1.
5. O1 breaks out to the wing, looking for the pass from O4.
6. After setting the down-screen, O3 "ducks-in" and looks for the pass from O4.

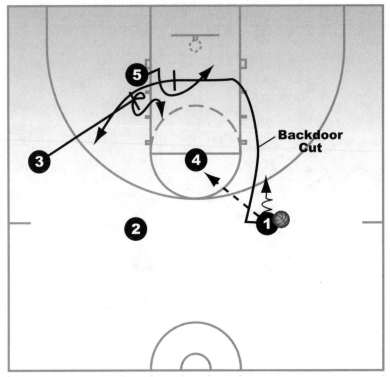

Harshman 1.7

OVER PLAY

When O3 is denied the pass at the wing, the following options are available (see **Diagram 1.8**):

1. O5 breaks to the high-post elbow.
2. O2 passes to O5 and screens away for O1.
3. O3 makes a backdoor cut to the basket, looking for the pass from O5.
4. O1 comes off a staggered double screen set by O2 and O4.
5. O3 comes off a double screen set by O4 and O2.

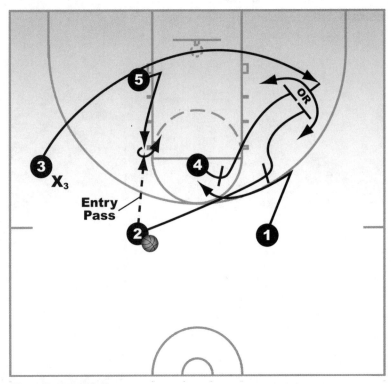

Harshman 1.8

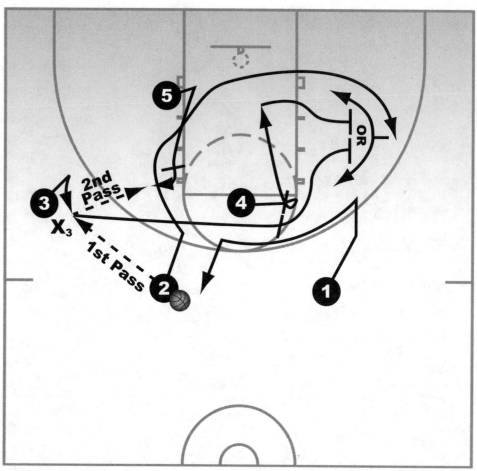

Harshman 1.9

GO-BALLSIDE SHUFFLE CUT

If O2 passes to the wing and his defender is playing tight defense, the following options are available (see **Diagram 1.9**):

1. O2 runs a shuffle cut off the screen set by O5 and looks for the pass from O3.
2. O2 has the options of stopping at the block and posting up or breaking to the open side of the floor.
3. When O3 passes to O5 at the high-post elbow, this keys the double screen option for O2 on the open side of the floor.
4. O3 breaks across the floor and sets a double screen with O4 for O2.
5. O2 can either break high or low off the screen.
6. Variation: O4 must learn to "read" his defender. When his defender helps too early on the double screen, O4 should "slip" to the basket for the easy basket.

SOURCE

Harshman, Marv. Interview by Jerry Krause, June 2003.

LEGACY OF
Edgar "Eddie" Hickey

- Built his patented three-lane fast break on excellent passing and precision ballhandling.

- Led St. Louis to the NIT championship in 1948.

- Called "The Little General" because of his small stature and demanding personality.

- Became the first coach in basketball history to lead three different teams to the NCAA tournament.

- One of the early originators of the match-up zone defense.

- Selected National Coach of the Year in 1959.

- Known for his organization and attention to detail.

EDGAR "EDDIE" HICKEY

*"The key to the fast break is simple -
Get there firstest with the mostest."
—Edgar "Eddie" Hickey*

BIOGRAPHY

Born: December 20, 1902 in Reynolds, NE

Died: December 5, 1980

Inducted into the Naismith Basketball Hall of Fame in 1979

During his prolific 35-year coaching career at Creighton, St. Louis, and Marquette, Edgar "Eddie" Hickey compiled an overall record of 436-231. He was the first coach to lead three different universities into the NCAA tournament. At Creighton, Hickey's team won four Missouri Valley Conference titles and appeared in two NITs and one NCAA tournament. During Hickey's 11-year tenure at St. Louis, the Billikens never had a losing season, won three Missouri Valley Conference championships, and appeared in six NITs and two NCAA tournaments. In 1948, St. Louis won the NIT championship and recorded a 24-3 record. At Marquette, Hickey led his team to two NCAA tournaments and one NIT appearance. He was named National Coach of the Year in 1959 by the USBWA and the NABC. Hickey was president of the NABC in 1953-54, served on the NABC Rules Recommendation committees, and was a member of the NABC Ethics committee. He was the chairman of the All-American Selection committee from 1955 to 1964.

Edgar "Eddie" Hickey...

Edgar "Eddie" Hickey spent the first 14 years of his life in Reynolds, Nebraska and then moved to Iowa, where he was a three-sport standout at Trinity College Prep in Sioux City. During his senior year, Hickey was the team captain in football, basketball, and baseball.

Hickey played basketball at Creighton for two years, but his best sport was football. He was the North Central (now the Missouri Valley) All-Conference quarterback for three straight years. During his senior year in college, Hickey launched his coaching career at Creighton Prep, where he was the head basketball coach.

Hickey graduated cum laude from the Creighton Law School in 1927 and planned to join a law firm. The sudden death of his father several weeks before graduation changed his plans, and he decided to continue in the coaching position that he held during his senior year. Hickey compiled a 115-26 record at Creighton Prep from 1926-1934, and his teams won the Omaha City League championship in 1929, 1932, and 1934.

In 1934, Hickey returned to Creighton as their head football coach. Hickey's association with football had an ironic twist later in his career. A year after he joined the staff at St. Louis and Marquette, the schools dropped their football programs. "I was renowned during my career," Hickey said with a laugh. "I got the reputation that wherever Eddie Hickey went, football would soon be eliminated. Of course, I never had anything to do with that—it was just a coincidence."

Hickey became the head basketball coach at Creighton in 1935, and it marked the beginning of his highly successful 35-year collegiate basketball career. Known as a disciplinarian and perfectionist, Hickey was called "The Little General." During games, Hickey used chalk to draw plays on the court. His teams were well prepared, and Hickey's brief-case was always filled with scouting reports and diagrams.

Hickey changed the complexion of the game by designing the three-lane fast break. "Everything was controlled,"

said Hickey. "One man brought the ball up in the middle of the floor, and there was a player on each side in the wings. The man in the middle could either stop and pass off or go all the way himself." (Sholtys, 1979)

All-American and Hall of Famer "Easy" Ed Macauley who played for Hickey at St. Louis remembered Hickey as being a very dominating and demanding coach; he insisted that everything be done just right. Regarding the fast break, Macauley (2003) said, "We had the best fast break in the country. Every player understood his responsibilities. I usually got the rebound and quickly passed

to the player at the wing. There would be a player breaking into the middle for the next pass and another player filling the other outside lane. As soon as I rebounded the ball, my teammates took off. That was the key to our fast break. We got down the floor so quickly that we often outnumbered our opponent. Hickey's fast break was built on speed. We had to be fast and pass the ball ahead to open teammates. We knew what we were going to do and simply outran our opponents."

"Probably of all the fast-break coaches of his era, Coach Hickey's team more clearly showed the stamp of their coach in their precision and ballhandling in their fast break," said Hall of Fame coach Pete Newell. "He certainly was a leading exponent of the passing fast break and his principles are widely accepted today, as the proper way to run the fast break. (Newell, 1973)

Hank Raymonds, who won over 71 percent of his games while coaching at Marquette from 1977-83, played for and coached with Eddie Hickey. "If I could select a coach to prepare a team for one game, I would most definitely pick Coach Hickey," said Raymonds. "He was thorough and so precise. He was years ahead of coaches with his organization and attention to detail. We would watch game films every day. In fact, I remember spending Christmas Day at his house watching films. Eddie Hickey was all business." (Raymonds, 2003)

"Eddie Hickey was a great, great basketball coach," said Macauley (2003). "He had a meticulous mind and taught us how to play together. We bought into his philosophy, and we had the perfect personnel to run Hickey's style of play. We won the NIT in 1948 and beat NYU, the sentimental favorite of the fans at Madison Square Garden. We played one of our best games and won going away. It was the greatest thing that ever happened to St. Louis. Over 15,000 fans were waiting for us when we returned from New York. We had a parade through the city. It was probably one of the best basketball experiences that Eddie ever had."

During the early years of Hickey's tenure at St. Louis, he accepted an invitation to be an instructor at Springfield College during summer school. It provided an opportunity for Hickey to work with Edward Hickox, former NABC president and basketball coach at Springfield. For many years, Hickox also served as the NABC historian. During the time that Hickey taught at Springfield College, Hickox was involved with an alleged claim that the game of basketball originated in Herkimer, New York and was not the invention of Dr. James Naismith. Hickey worked diligently with Hickox and eventually substantiated the inaccuracy of the Herkimer claim.

During his coaching career, Hickey saw the game of basketball evolve through various rule changes. Jump balls were eliminated after every basket, the free-throw lanes were enlarged to 12 feet, and the three-second violation was instituted. "The rule changes have been to motivate the big players, to challenge their playing skills," stated Hickey. "The changes kept them from having an advantage just because of their size. There is no question basketball is a better game because of the changes." Hickey believed there was still a place for the "little man." Hickey spoke fondly of the little man in basketball because at the height of 5 foot-5 inches, it was the role that he played.

"When I played, I was usually the high scorer in the game," Hickey said. "But when I played, one player shot all the free throws, and I usually did that because I was a pretty good shooter."

While coaching at Creighton, Hickey developed a 3-2 match-up zone that stifled opposing teams. Hank Raymonds (2003) stated that many opposing teams refused to schedule Creighton because of the effectiveness of their match-up defense.

Eddie Hickey left his mark as an educator, mentor, and leader just as much as he left his mark as a coach. He was as fanatical about his players receiving their degrees as he was about them scoring baskets. In his 11 years at St. Louis, where six of his teams qualified for the NIT and two of his squads for the NCAA tournament, every player that lettered for the Billikens received a degree. "The only reason you can justify athletics in school is because it is a portion of an education, and it is helping develop students in every respect. I wanted my players to be good students first."

In 1979, Hickey offered a word of caution to college basketball administrators. "I don't think they should ever overlook the fact that the only real purpose of basketball is to fatten and develop the overall education for the boy who is using athletics as a part of his over-all education."

Concerning the role of a coach, Hickey said, "I always felt that part of the duty of a coach is to develop a Christian man." You should look at life from all sides and all angles." (York, 1979)

SOURCE

Hickey, Eddie. Vertical Files, Archives. Naismith Memorial Basketball Hall of Fame. Springfield, MA.

Macauley, Ed. Interview by Ralph Pim, September 5, 2003.

Newell, Pete. (1973, August 6). Letter to the Naismith Memorial Basketball Hall of Fame.

Raymonds, Hank. Interview with Ralph Pim, July 17, 2003.

Sholtys, Gordie. (1979, April). Time Won't Forget Mesa Man Who Saw Basketball Grow Up Fast. *East Valley Tribune*.

York, Randy. (1979, February 4). *Lincoln Sunday Journal and Star*.

THE THREE-LANE FAST BREAK

By Eddie Hickey

The St. Louis fast break may be broken down into two phases—the initial stage (backcourt) and the scoring area (front-court).

KEY POINTS IN THE INITIAL STAGE

1. The fast break may start from any of the following: defensive rebound, interception, loose ball recovery, out-of-bounds play, jump ball, or after a score by the opponents.
2. The best opportunity for initiating the fast break comes from the defensive rebound. The principles covering this situation will also apply to the other possibilities. The fast-break offense will generally follow a free-lance pattern but should observe the practice patterns that will be explained later.
3. Remember, the fast break cannot be initiated without first obtaining possession of the ball. (Hence the best defense against the fast break is a possession game.) Any player may initiate the fast break with the outlet pass. The patterns of these outlet passes will be thoroughly described later.
4. The backcourt has been divided into the following specific outlet areas (see **Diagram 1.0**):
   a. Right side, short and long (best)
   b. Inside, short and long
   c. Left side, short and long
   d. Baseline, right and left
5. The outlet pass must be quick and sharp, but not too long. Use of

the long area comes only after full development. A "relay" outlet (extra pass) will be effective at times in the baseline area.
6. A player without the ball must quickly react toward the outlet area as his teammates move to fill unoccupied lanes.

7. A prospective receiver must not run downcourt away from the ball. In other words, he shouldn't anticipate the outlet pass and "release" downcourt. Remember, the potential receiver must get to the outside of the court using the correct footwork.

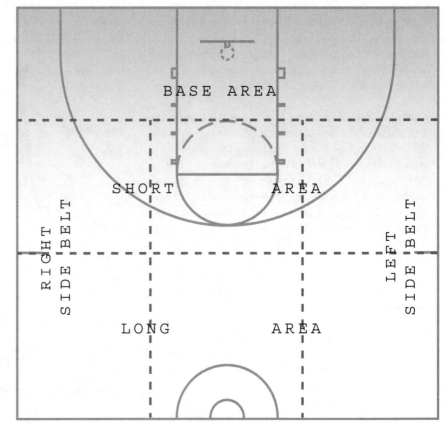

Hickey 1.0

LESSONS FROM THIS LEGEND...

PLAY PATTERNS FROM A 2-3 DEFENSE

The following various play patterns can be utilized from a 2-3 (single pivot) defense:

1. "A" PATTERN

As shown in **Diagram 1.1**, the defensive center is the rebounder, and the outlet pass is made to 02 in the side belt.

2. "B" PATTERN

As shown in **Diagram 1.2**, the defensive center is the rebounder, and the outlet pass is made to 01 in the inside area.

3. "C" PATTERN

As shown in **Diagram 1.3**, O1 secures the rebound and initiates the outlet pass into the opposite side belt.

4. "D" PATTERN

As shown in **Diagram 1.4**, O4 secures the rebound and makes the outlet pass to O2 in the side belt. O2 then passes to O1 in the middle.

PLAY PATTERNS FROM A 3-2 DEFENSE

The fast break works even better from the 3-2 defense because the three lanes for the first wave down court are already established (see **Diagram 1.5**). The fast break from this type of defense possesses fewer variations with regard to filling the lanes. Depending on the location of the rebound, the players will use either the "A", "B", "C", or "D" pattern.

KEY POINTS IN THE SCORING AREA (FRONTCOURT)

1. Stay wide when advancing down the court.
2. Don't run downcourt even with an opponent. Sprint and get ahead of him. If this is impossible, you may use a change-of-pace tactic to create an open passing lane.
3. If you can't get a three-on-one or three-on-two situation, give up on the break. Remember, this is a controlled fast break.

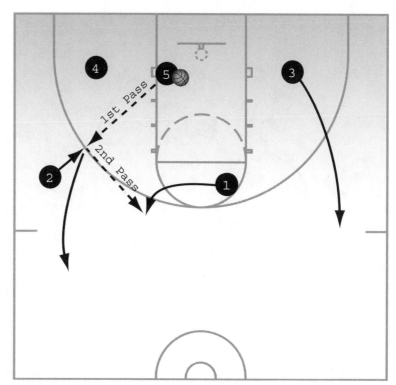

Hickey 1.1

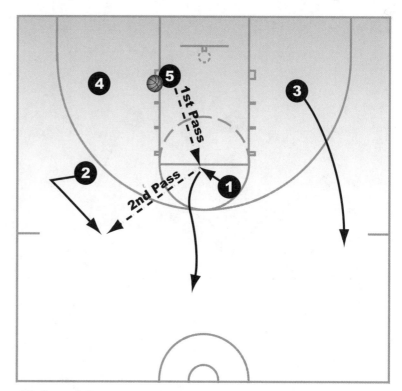

Hickey 1.2

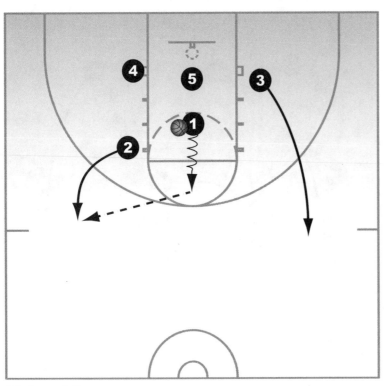

Hickey 1.3

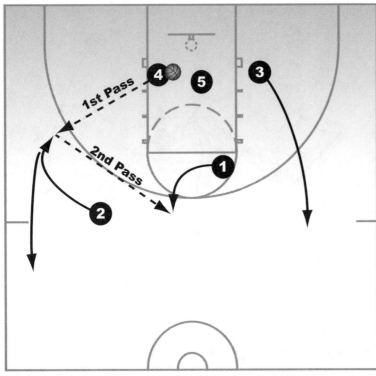

Hickey 1.4

4. It is preferable for the players in the outside lanes to be slightly ahead of the player in the middle lane.

5. The middle lane player should hold up at the top of the circle, with or without the ball. He should go to the basket only under the following conditions:

   a. With possession of the ball to score

   b. To rebound after a shot, regardless of who shoots
   If the middle lane player finds himself too tight to the basket, he should retreat quickly.

6. Don't pass from one outside lane to the other (cross-court pass) until you're close to the basket.

7. If you find yourself ahead of the pack (the ball is being handled by players in the three lanes behind you), run straight ahead and off the court, then swing around and back out to the trailer position. Don't stop short, lest you obstruct the breaking of the players behind you.

8. When filling the "blind" side late (either wing), communicate out so that the middle lane man will be able to anticipate a pass to you. Often the blind side will never handle the ball in the fast-break attack until he takes the pass to score.

9. Dribble as little as possible. Use the dribble in the following situations:

   a. To secure safe possession

   b. To assist timing or spacing

   c. To make the defensive man commit himself to cover you and thus open the breaking lanes for your teammates

   d. When challenged by a defensive player (one who tries to jam your possession)

   e. When a teammate to whom you would like to pass is challenged by his defender

LESSONS FROM THIS LEGEND...

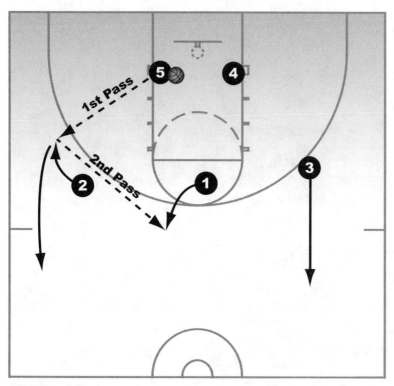

Hickey 1.5

and you need to create an open passing lane

f. When an opening for a drive to the basket presents itself

10. Don't let the fast break become helter-skelter. Remember, it's a controlled break working for an early-scoring opportunity. The ball must be slowed down, and possession retained whenever a good scoring opportunity isn't completely certain.

11. The best place for the ball when approaching the scoring territory is in the middle lane.

12. Every scoring opportunity does not have to be a lay-up shot. Open, high-percentage shots are encouraged, especially when we have a rebounding advantage.

13. Players should talk to each other on the break and call out the type of defense, such as: "three-on-one," "three-on-two," or "three-on-three."

14. Don't force the fast break. Slow it down rather than force a bad shot or pass.

15. When the break is underway, the ball must always be advanced toward the scoring end of the court.

16. Free-lance opportunities will often be possible. Look to capitalize on scoring opportunities. Be willing to take a chance occasionally.

17. Always have two trailers and do not allow them to follow the front line too closely. Trailers are responsible for good defensive balance on the end of the break and should always be ready for the development of various options.

18. The trailers should keep an equal spread across the court, about 17 feet in from the sideline (one-third of the width of the court).

SOURCE

Hickey, Eddie. (1955, December). St. Louis' Controlled Three-Lane Fast Break. *Scholastic Coach.*

LEGACY OF
Paul "Tony" Hinkle

- Garnered more than 1,000 victories coaching football, basketball, and baseball at Butler University.

- Developed the Hinkle System, a style of offensive play based on constant ball movement, screening, and accurate shooting.

- Respected by his peers for his ability to get the maximum from his players.

- Led Butler to the national basketball championship in 1929.

- Developed the concept of using an orange-colored ball.

- Retired as the "Dean of Indiana College Coaches."

- Namesake of the Tony Hinkle Memorial Fieldhouse at Butler University, longtime site of Indiana's State High School championships.

PAUL "TONY" HINKLE

*"It makes no difference how many baskets you make
...only what you make of yourself.*
—Paul "Tony" Hinkle*

BIOGRAPHY

Born: December 19, 1898 in Logansport, IN

Died: September 22, 1992

Inducted into the Naismith Basketball Hall of Fame in 1965

Paul "Tony" Hinkle was an institution at Butler University. He arrived in 1921 and never left, except for duty in World War II from 1942 to 1945. Hinkle was forced into mandatory retirement from coaching in 1970, but became a special assistant to the president, a position he held until his death in 1992. Hinkle coached three sports, served as the athletic director, and taught physical education classes during his Butler tenure. His teams won more than 1,000 games. In basketball, Hinkle compiled a record of 560-392. The Veterans Athletic Association of Philadelphia declared his 1929-team national champions. He developed the Hinkle System of offensive play that greatly impacts how basketball was played in the State of Indiana. More than 200 of his former players and students became teachers and coaches. Hinkle was called the "Dean of Indiana College Coaches." He served as president of the NABC in 1954-55 and was chairman of Rules Committee from to 1948 to 1950. In 1952, Hinkle received the NABC Metropolitan Award for his contributions to basketball. He was an outstanding athlete at the University of Chicago where he earned nine letters (football, basketball, and baseball). Hinkle was named Helms Foundation All-American in basketball in 1920.

Paul "Tony" Hinkle...

The game of basketball was only seven years old when Paul "Tony" Hinkle was born in Logansport, Indiana. Tony's first introduction to the game came as a youngster growing up on the south side of Chicago. He would go to a park where an instructor allowed boys to play basketball after a session of calisthenics. Tony fell in love with the game, but his father, who was a teacher, did not highly encourage his participation in athletics. Tony spent most of his time during the summer doing chores on the farm in north central Indiana where he was born.

Hinkle attended Calumet (IL) High School and participated in basketball, baseball, golf, and soccer (football had been dropped before Hinkle's arrival at the school because team members were caught cheating on an exam). He led his soccer team to the city high school championship and his basketball team to the final game of the city championship.

Tony's father encouraged him to attend the University of Chicago because it was an outstanding institution academically, plus the campus was only four miles from the Hinkle house, and money could be saved if Tony lived at home. It was at the University of Chicago that Hinkle met and played for the legendary football coach Amos Alonzo Stagg. Stagg had been a professor at Springfield College and even played in the very first basketball game in 1891. Stagg was later elected into the Naismith Memorial Basketball Hall of Fame. John Wooden said, "Tony Hinkle is a true disciple of Amos Alonzo Stagg, both as a coach and as a man, and I feel that is about as high a compliment that one can give."

Tony earned nine letters at Chicago, three each in football, basketball, and baseball. The only other University of Chicago athlete that earned that distinction was Fritz Crisler, a teammate of Hinkle's who later became a highly successful football coach and athletic director at the University of Michigan. In basketball, Hinkle was twice selected All-Big Ten and was a member of the Big Ten

championship team in 1920. The Helms Foundation named Hinkle a basketball All-American in 1920.

It was during Hinkle's second year at the University of Chicago that he was given the nickname "Tony." Basketball coach Harlan "Pat" Page started calling him "Tony" when he saw Hinkle come out of a restaurant carrying an extra serving of spaghetti and meatballs. The nickname became a permanent part of Hinkle's life, although his parents and sisters never really accepted it.

In baseball, Hinkle's specialty was the spitball pitch. The spitball was perfectly legal until 1921, when it was outlawed for anyone going into professional baseball. Hinkle learned how to throw it during his teenage playing days. He chewed slippery elm, and then would moisten the ball with its juice. Major league baseball manager John McGraw was so impressed with Tony's spitball that he wanted Hinkle to report to the New York Giants. When the spitball was banned, the Giants withdrew their offer.

Hinkle majored in oil geology at the University of Chicago but decided to accept a coaching job with his college coach, Pat Page, who was hired at Butler University. Tony served as assistant athletic director and assistant coach under Page's supervision. Page's basketball teams produced the best records that the school had even seen. In 1924, with Hinkle as his assistant, Butler won the AAU national championship.

Hinkle's starting salary was only fifty dollars a week, so he looked for ways to supplement his income as long as it did not interfere with his work at Butler. He played professional basketball with several midwestern teams and officiated high school games. Tony also spent one summer playing minor league baseball.

Page resigned just before the last basketball game in 1926, and Tony was named acting athletic director and head football and basketball coach. In 1928, Butler University introduced one of the premier basketball facilities in the nation. Twelve thousand fans watched Butler defeat Notre Dame, 21-13, in the opening game. Butler Fieldhouse was the site for the Indiana High School Athletic Association's annual basketball championships from 1928 to 1994. To show their appreciation for Hinkle's loyalty and hard work, Butler renamed the facility the Hinkle Fieldhouse in 1965.

During Hinkle's first three years as basketball coach, Butler won 52 out of 61 games. Hinkle enjoyed one of his greatest moments in 1929, when the Veterans Athletic Association of Philadelphia named Butler national champions. During that memorable season, Butler defeated defending national champion Pittsburgh and their future Hall of Fame coach, "Doc" Carlson.

Tony's basketball offensive system, called the Hinkle System, blossomed in the 1930s. Hinkle's players consisted mostly of Indiana players, and he very rarely had tall men. He developed versatile players who were well schooled in the fundamentals. Hinkle designed a five-player continuity offense that had constant movement of the ball between pairs of players. Tony developed 14 two-man plays that were designed to screen defensive players. The system, called the Fifth Way, concentrated on getting high-percentage shots for all players, some more than others. It was described as "everybody moved, everybody handled the ball, and everybody got to shoot." There was constant ball movement, and all positions on the floor were interchangeable.

The Hinkle System was a perfect fit for the players who attended Butler. It was not dependent upon size and speed, like Ward "Piggy" Lambert's fast break at Purdue. As John Wooden put it, "Coach Hinkle's teams were always looking for the shot. Players knew where to go and how to get there with the purpose to score."

Hinkle gave many coaching clinics and kept no secrets about the Hinkle System. Herb Schwomeyer, a former assistant coach and legendary historian of basketball in Indiana, believed the key was Tony's ability to teach his system. He focused on perfect execution, and through daily repetition, his players learned how to move and recognize shooting opportunities. The Hinkle System enabled Butler to compete against larger universities and defeat squads with better talented athletes. Butler earned a reputation as "Big Ten Giant Killers" during Hickey's tenure.

Hinkle was very influential in the development of the game. He served as chairman of the Rules Committee and was the president of the NABC in 1954-55. Tony also campaigned to standardize the color of the ball. He wanted to brighten the ball so the spectators could see it better. The Spaulding Company worked on perfecting a ball that met the requirements that Hinkle wanted. It was tested at

the 1958 NCAA Finals in Louisville in 1958. Members of the NCAA were impressed, and the color orange was adopted. Hinkle also persuaded the NCAA to standardize the color of the rim. The NCAA mandated that all rims must be painted orange.

It seemed like Hinkle wore a permanent scowl, but his mind was full of fun. He could needle, be blunt and firm, or be a practical joker. He once had someone plant a pair of women's panties in the luggage of one of the shyest members of the team. Checking out of the hotel, Hinkle declared a luggage check to ensure nothing was taken from the hotel. Much to the embarrassment of the young man, the panties were discovered, and everyone had a big laugh.

Rather than use a player's first name, Hinkle normally called everyone, "Kid." He did this to emphasize their team role, instead of their individual name. Hinkle also liked to use expressions, such as "you couldn't guard a lamppost because even the light would fake you out," to make his points.

One of Hinkle's greatest legacies was the large number (over 200) of former players and students who went on to become coaches. One of his former players, Marvin Wood, went on to coach at Milan High School, when the tiny school captured the state title in 1954, and became the real-life inspiration for the 1980s movie, Hoosiers.

Hall of Fame coach Bob Knight said, "Tony Hinkle may well be the most remarkable coach in American collegiate athletic history. Certainly no man has been involved with more athletes in more sports over a longer period of time than he. Because of all the championships his teams won, and all the players whose lives he affected in all the sports that he coached, Tony Hinkle stands alone as The Coach." (Caldwell, 1991. p. ix)

Source

Caldwell, Howard. (1991). *Tony Hinkle: Coach for All Seasons.* Bloomington, IN: Indiana University Press.

Hinkle, Tony. Vertical Files, Archives. Naismith Memorial Basketball Hall of Fame. Springfield, MA.

THE HINKLE SYSTEM

By Leroy Compton

Author's Note: This 1971 version of the Hinkle System was refined by Leroy Compton of Proviso West, H.S. (IL).

The Hinkle System was Tony Hinkle's offensive strategy. Herb Schwomeyer, who played for Hinkle and served as his assistant for six years, explained it as constant movement of the ball between pairs of players. Essentially, the man with the ball dictated the two-man plays by the pass made and the cut taken. These two-man plays produced picks and screens on defenders.

The system focused on getting high-percentage shots and scoring opportunities. It was based on the following concepts: all five players were interchangeable; everybody moved; everybody handled the ball; everybody got to shoot; everybody had a place to go; and the ball kept moving.

The two-player drills to teach the system were used every practice for the whole season. This produced players who could react automatically to the correct option according to how the defense played. It was ideal for the all-around players from Indiana who really knew how to play the game and could play inside or outside.

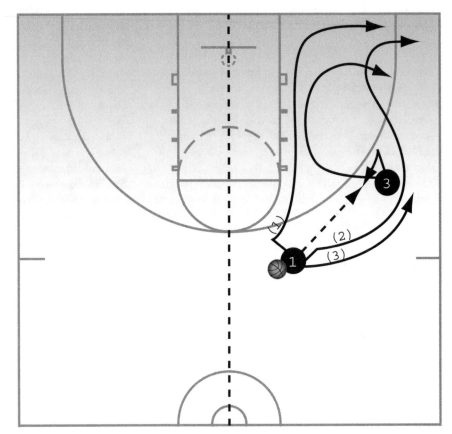

Hinkle 1.0

The advantages of the Hinkle offensive basketball system were:

1. Opportunities for all players
2. Incorporates all basic offensive phases
3. Takes advantage of individual strengths
4. Allows offensive players to exploit defensive weaknesses
5. Provides effective offensive rebounding
6. Allows for good defensive transition
7. Adaptable against all defenses
8. Each player learns to play every position
9. Gives players and the coach a feeling of offensive confidence and security
10. Provides inside scoring opportunities
11. Provides outside scoring opportunities
12. Provides driving opportunities
13. Takes advantage of defensive mismatches
14. Uses strongside and weakside options
15. Can be used as a delay game

In coaching the system, Hinkle recommended daily drills; first against man-to-man defense (all variations), then combination, pressing, and zone defenses. The defense will create scoring opportunities; the offensive players must learn to read the defenders and react accordingly.

LESSONS FROM THIS LEGEND...

There are three rules of movement for the two-man plays:

1. When making a "same-side" cut, use only one-half of the court. If you don't receive the ball, go to the same side (see **Diagram 1.0**).

2. When making a "through" cut, move from one-half of the floor to the other half. Cut to the opposite side of the floor from where you started your cut (**Diagram 1.1**).

3. When you pass the ball out (see **Diagram 1.2**), move away from the basket and the player who caught the pass.

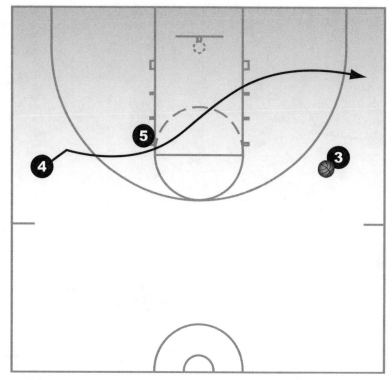

Hinkle 1.1

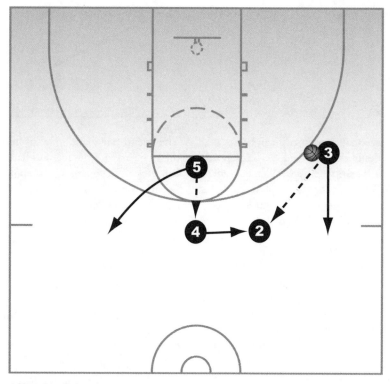

Hinkle 1.2

LESSONS FROM THIS LEGEND...

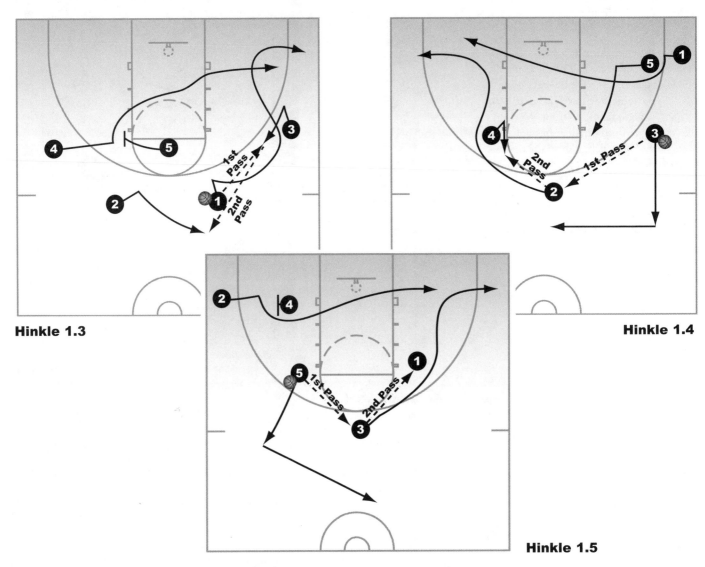

Hinkle 1.3

Hinkle 1.4

Hinkle 1.5

The player-pair movements can be run on both sides of the floor and can be grouped in series. The first series is called the "guard around" and occurs when a player in a guard position passes to a player in a forward position (see **Diagram 1.3**). All series occur from a 2-3 set, including the "guard-around" series. When the passer initiates this pass-and-cut series, 03 can return the ball to 01 who is "turning the corner," pass to 01 in the corner, or pass the ball back out to 02 after 04 makes an opposite-side cut. The "pass-ball-out" option is triggered by the 03-to-02 pass which initiates another "guard-around" series and "opposite-side" cut as seen in **Diagram 1.4**. This motion can continue with all five players moving and ball reversal again, as shown in **Diagram 1.5.**

The "guard-handback" series is initiated by the G-F pass and the forward handing the ball back to the guard at that spot on the "guard-around" cut. This keys the forward cutting options shown in **Diagram 1.6**, with the "opposite-side" cut and "pass-out" option remaining the same.

On the G-F entry, the guard can use a variety of options to counter defensive play, including:

1. G-F entry pass or G-F backdoor pass
2. G dribble entry pushes F into the "handback" series
3. Dribble weave toward other guard
4. Dribble penetrate to middle of lane for "dribble and dump" pass

5. G-G entry pass at high post

The receiving forward on the G-F entry also has a number of options to counter defensive play, including:

1. Regular G-F entry catching a pass from G at free throw line extended
2. F backdoor pass from G on defense overplay
3. Catch, face basket and shoot or drive (middle or baseline)
4. Interchange with the high post/center on extreme overplay
5. Return pass to the cutting guard:
   - Guard hand-back series
   - Give-and-go/pass and cut-on-guard overplay (**Diagram 1.7**)

LESSONS FROM THIS LEGEND...

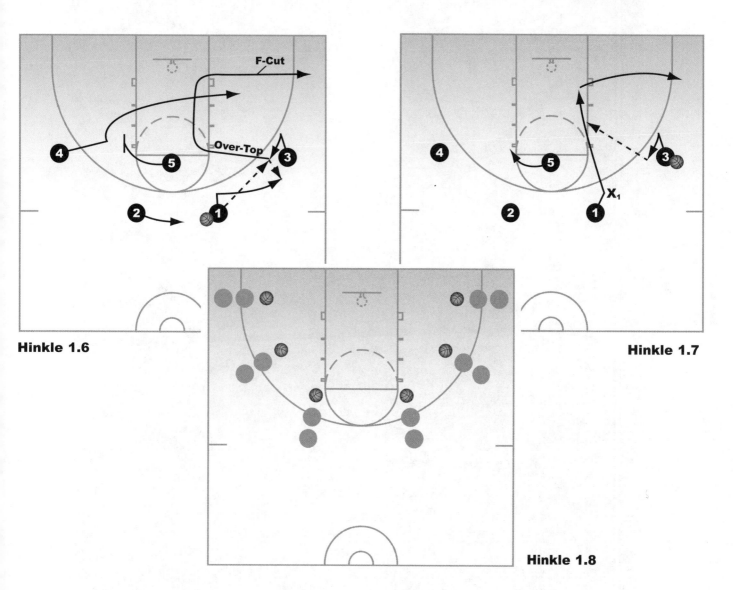

Hinkle 1.6

Hinkle 1.7

Hinkle 1.8

The guard and forward also have a number of options on the "guard handback" series, including:

1. G hits F on a return pass-over-the-top move to basket (see **Diagram 1.6**) or passes to F on a post up move or hits F who has moved out to corner
2. Guard shoot or drive
3. Weakside F on "opposite cut"
4. Pass-out option on ball reversal

In all options, the player filling the center position has a number of options:

1. G-C entry pass near high post:
   • Face basket and score
   • Pass to F on backdoor move
   • Guards split-post moves

2. Screen away for weakside F and slip the screen or backdoor to basket
3. Rebound on the weakside

It can be seen that the Hinkle System has 14 basic player-pair movements, with the system keyed and controlled by the man with the ball and the choices that player made in response to the defense.

Herb Schwomeyer also provided a shooting drill used by Hinkle before each practice (**Diagram 1.8**). In this drill, six groups of three players each shot/drove from all offensive positions so they would be able to handle the ball and shoot from all angles/spots in the Hinkle offensive system.

SOURCE

Schwomeyer, Herb. (2003, July). Personal Notes.

LEGACY OF
Nat Holman

- Became national hero during the 1920s and was nicknamed "Mr. Basketball."

- Played with the Original Celtics, the most celebrated barnstorming team of their day.

- Considered the finest passer and playmaker in basketball and was the game's first superstar.

- Led a double life of professional basketball player and college basketball coach.

- Coached 37 years at CCNY and compiled a 421-190 record.

- Only coach in basketball history to lead his team to both the NIT and NCAA championship in the same year (CCNY in 1950).

- At CCNY, developed a street-smart style of play known as "The City Game."

NAT HOLMAN

"To be a coach is to be a teacher. You have to teach people from different backgrounds to work together for the common good."
— Nat Holman

BIOGRAPHY

Born: October 19, 1896 in New York, NY

Died: February 12, 1995

Inducted into the Naismith Basketball Hall of Fame in 1964

Nat Holman was a national hero during the 1920s and earned the title "Mr. Basketball" for his playing excellence. He was one of the game's most accurate shooters and dazzled fans with his wizardry ballhandling and passing. Holman played the majority of his career with the world-famous Original Celtics, and made the team virtually unbeatable. He was one of the great pioneers of professional basketball, and his creativity on the court helped developed the pivot play in basketball. From 1919 to 1933, Homan lived the double life of professional basketball player and college coach. At the age of 32, Holman ended his professional playing career to concentrate on his coaching job at CCNY. During his 37-year coaching career at CCNY, Holman compiled a 423-190 record. Without question, the greatest thrill in Nat Holman's life happened in 1950. His CCNY team won, what has been called the "Grand Slam in College Basketball," the NIT and the NCAA tournaments. Holman is the only coach to ever win both titles in the same season. It will never happen again, since a team can no longer participate in both tournaments during the same year. Holman was an international ambassador for basketball and held coaching clinics in Israel, Japan, Turkey, Korea, Taiwan, Mexico, and Canada. He wrote four basketball books, served as president of the NABC in 1941, and was presented with the Helms Foundation Award in recognition of his contributions to basketball. In 1951, Holman was selected National Coach of the Year.

Nat Holman...

Nat Holman grew up on New York's Lower East Side with his parents, six brothers and three sisters. By the time Holman was twelve years old, he had earned the reputation as an excellent basketball player. He obtained that reputation the hard way—playing in the rough neighborhood games against men much older and bigger than him.

Even though the game of basketball was in its infancy, "It was not a new game on the Lower East Side," Holman said. "It was very popular. We played basketball all year around, indoors, and outdoors. It was at the Settlement Houses that I really got my start. Saturday night was a big night out. We would schedule a game, and there would be a dance before the game, between halves, and after the game. Thanks to the Settlement Houses, we always had a place to play basketball." (Healy, 1988)

Holman recalled how difficult it was playing on a court with dance wax. "I cut two holes in the sole of each basketball shoe and filled them with petroleum jelly," Holman said. "This allowed me to have better traction."

A key person in Holman's life was his playground instructor, Jim Gennitty. "I really must tip my hat to him. I can honestly say he inspired me so much that I patterned my lifestyle after him," said Holman. (Healy, 1988)

While in the High School of Commerce, he earned the nickname "Kid" Holman for his athletic exploits. In football, he was the All-Star halfback; in soccer, he was the all-scholastic goalie; in baseball, he starred as a pitcher and his team came within one game of winning the city championship; and in basketball, he received his first taste of what might be considered professional basketball by playing on a touring team called the Busy Izzies that featured future Hall of Fame players Barney Sedran and Marty Friedman.

After Holman graduated from high school, the Cincinnati Reds offered him a baseball contract, but instead, he enrolled in the Savage School of Physical Education. While an undergraduate, Holman played basketball for Savage, and one of his teammates was future Hall of Fame referee, Dave Tobey. Holman financed his education by barnstorming with several professional basketball teams.

While in graduate school at New York University in 1919, Holman assumed the basketball coaching duties at the City College of New York (CCNY). From 1919 through 1933, Holman led a double life of professional basketball player and college coach. "Those were busy days," explained Holman. "There were times when I'd rush to

New Jersey after a game at the college and get into my pro basketball suit in an automobile, while crossing the 125th Street Ferry." (Strauss, 1959)

Holman was one of basketball's most accurate shooters and the finest passer and playmaker of his era. Holman reached the top as a player with the Original Celtics, a team that won 720 games out of the 795 played between 1921 and 1928. The Original Celtics never lost a series and frequently played up to 150 games a year, averaging five or six games a week, including two on Sunday. "You had to be in good condition," Holman stated. "Your body would adjust. Saturday, we learned to hit the sack early to prepare for Sunday's two games. We'd play one at 2 p.m. and then rest before the next game at 8 p.m."

Holman was a national hero in the 1920's and was called "Mr. Basketball." Wherever the Original Celtics played, their clean-cut hero was the main drawing attraction.

The Original Celtics, as well as other teams in that era, wore heavy, woolen uniforms. They had padded pants, kneepads, and some players even wore elbow guards. "We had to wear heavy, woolen uniforms," Holman recalled. "We played in armories, dance halls, and even on theater stages. The temperature would vary from one place to the next. In fact, in many of the armories, the fans would wear overcoats, and we'd be playing in shorts and a sleeveless top." (Healy, 1988)

.....SCOUTING REPORT.....SCOUTING REPORT...

The highlight in Holman's coaching career occurred in 1950, when his CCNY team won both the NIT and the NCAA championship for the first and only time in basketball history. "What a great thrill it was that night," remembered Holman. When we left Madison Square Garden, the students and fans were on Seventh Avenue waiting for us. Flags were being waved, and the students were singing our Alma Mater. I will never forget it."

Holman was an outstanding teacher whose devotion to detail was overwhelming. CCNY was different from most schools. There was no tuition, so only the top academic students could gain admission. Holman did not have the best talent, but he masterfully developed his players into beautifully drilled teams that won far more games than they were entitled to win. His teams always portrayed his poise, confidence, and toughness. Even at the age of 60, Holman would often get on the floor during practice and show his players what he wanted and how to do it.

Early in his coaching career, Holman believed in the patient, deliberate Eastern style of play, but later installed the Western style that featured the fast break and the one-hand shot. To Holman, the five most important ingredients in the game were ballhandling, shiftiness, endurance, shooting ability, and poise.

Holman's teams operated with very few set plays. "I want resourceful, flexible thinking teams that are never stuck for an idea on what to do next." Said Holman. "I teach my players to recognize situations and know what will develop from a particular floor pattern. All basketball is a pattern. Get in that pattern, and then you're going." (Padwe, 1970)

Holman retired from coaching in 1960 with an overall record of 421-190.

Holman believed there were many contributors to the game of basketball during his lifetime, but Hank Luissetti and Ned Irish were at the top of his list.

"Hank Luissetti of Stanford will be remembered for his famous one-hand shot," said Holman. "In my time, this was the first man who brought something new to the game. I tip my hat to him for all the thrills he gave me."

"Ned Irish made basketball a big-time sport," stated Holman. He organized the first college doubleheader in Madison Square Garden in 1934, and in the 1940s, he introduced college basketball to television."

In 1949, one year after the birth of the State of Israel, Holman launched the nation's first basketball program. He has been recognized as the Father of Israeli Basketball. Holman served as president of the United States Committee Sports for Israel (USCSFI), an organization established to promote athletics and physical education both in the United States and Israel. In 1972, on only four hours notice, Holman flew to Israel to attend the memorial service for the Israel athletes slain during the Olympics in Munich. He was the only non-member of the Israel Olympic Committee who was invited to address the body during its days of grief.

Holman's contributions go far beyond his accomplishments on the basketball court. He worked more than half a century as director of Camp Scatico, a private summer children's camp in Elizaville, New York. His interaction with campers, counselors, and parents brought him great joy.

Holman said, "I loved every minute of it. You talk about recruiting basketball players. I recruited counselors! I spent a great deal of time looking for the right person to work with the campers. I wanted a person the campers could look up to and would be proud to introduce to their parents."

Nat Holman was a special human being. He was a gifted leader who touched every person he met. To each, he imparted that special "Holman magic," the power to believe, and the urge to excel and exceed self-imposed limits.

SOURCE

Healy, Jerry. (1988, September 12). *Nat Holman...Player and Coach*. Naismith Memorial Basketball Hall of Fame News Release.

Holman, Nat. Vertical Files, Archives. Naismith Memorial Basketball Hall of Fame. Springfield, MA.

Padwe, Sandy. (1970). *Basketball's Hall of Fame*. Englewood Cliffs, NJ: Prentice-Hall.

Strauss, Michael. (1959, February 8). Holman Figures His Age by Games. *New York Times*.

THE PIVOT PLAY

By Nat Holman

A revolutionary change in any sport requires a long period of adaptation, in which time the entire game frequently undergoes a revision of style. Such an innovation was that of the forward pass in football. It opened up new fields of offensive strategy and created innumerable difficulties for settled systems. But these difficulties have been overcome, and the forward pass is now an indispensable part of the gridiron game. So too, when the pivot play was introduced into basketball seven years ago, it necessitated a drastic rearrangement of offensive play. It has made a noteworthy and probably lasting imprint on the game.

The Original Celtics, who for many years were the professional basketball champions of the world, introduced the pivot play in 1925. The play was not an amazing overnight discovery, but came about through a slow process of evolutionary change, though the final result was of itself both startling and original. The Celtics made constant and important use of the play in which one man moved slowly across the foul-line territory near his own basket, received a pass, and made a quick return play. This might be termed a moving pivot play. However, the player moving across the court, either by accident or through an economy of unnecessary movement, finally came to stop at the foul line, where he stationed himself firmly, received passes from his teammates, and made himself the central point in the offensive orbit. Thus was introduced the pivot play. The Original Celtics, with "Dutch" Dehnert in the pivot position, developed this into the most damaging scoring play ever devised and did much to bring the play to its present state of comparative success.

Simple as does the play appears, its effects have been of signal significance and have made marked impressions on the progress of basketball. Fundamentally, it has altered the old five-man style of offense, since it has taken one player completely out of the cutting end of the offensive play. But, it has had the all-important effect of encouraging cutting on the part of the moving players, since it has provided them with a definite target for passes made preparatory to breaks for the basket. It has placed an important premium on speed and deception. It has also made a potentially dangerous scoring man out of the pivot player, who is in a position to use his size and strength for quick pivots and shots at the goal, though it should be kept in mind, that the pivot play is essentially a team offensive strategy, rather than a medium for individual scoring efforts.

REQUIREMENTS FOR THE PIVOT POSITION

- The pivot player must be able to catch and hold a ball expertly.
- The pivot player needs to be able to pass sharply, adeptly, and accurately. He must be cool and a good ballhandler, but paramount to all other attributes, he must have a keen passing sense.

HOW TO GET INTO PROPER POSITION IN THE PIVOT

- The pivot player does not go directly to his station, which is ordinarily on or about the foul line.
- To be most effective, he should first run down the side of the court, and then reverse and break for the foul line.

PASSES TO THE PIVOT PLAYER

- The most effective pass is a bounce pass because it is less liable to interception.
- The passer must make sure the path to the pivot man is open.
- The pass should be sharp and clean, and aimed in accordance with the pivot's expressed wishes.
- As soon as the pass is made, the pivot man should take two quick steps forward to receive the ball.

THE PIVOT PLAYER'S PASS TO CUTTERS

- Once the pivot man has the ball in his possession, his ability to see the floor comes into play. It must be remembered from the outset that he need not feed a cutting man on each and every play; he must use his judgment and pass the ball out to a teammate in the backcourt if all the cutters are covered.
- The pivot player's most important assignment comes after he has made his pass. If he has thrown the ball to a cutting teammate on his left, he reverses immediately to the right, and cuts in towards the basket, where he is in position either for a return pass or to rebound a missed shot.

LESSONS FROM THIS LEGEND...

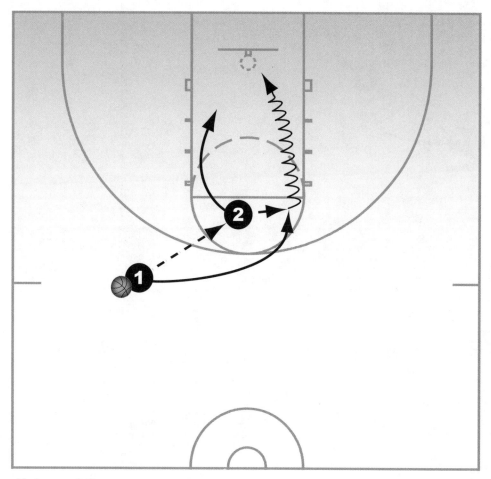

Holman 1.0

PIVOT PLAY OPTIONS

In **Diagram 1.0**, O1 makes his bounce pass from the side and cuts directly around the pivot man, O2, for a return pass. The cutter should keep close to the pivot man so that his defender's path is blocked. On this play, as in every other, the pivot reverses in the direction opposite to the cutter, and cuts under the basket to recover the ball if the shot is unsuccessful.

LESSONS FROM THIS LEGEND...

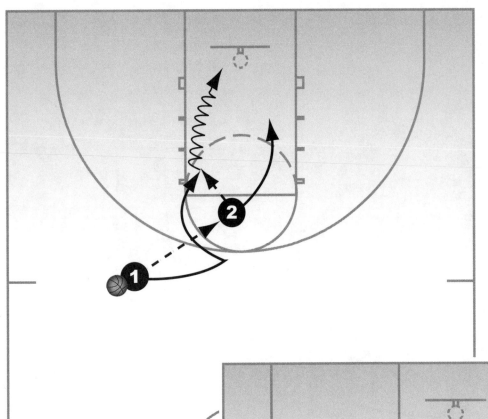

In **Diagram 1.1**, O1 passes to the pivot, O2, cuts directly towards him, and then reverses on the same side. It is advisable in this situation for the pivot player to use the back-bounce pass to the cutter.

Holman 1.1

In **Diagram 1.2**, O1 passes to the pivot, O2, from the left side, and cuts across the pivot on the right side. He then makes an abrupt stop, feints in the direction of his cut, changes direction, and swings over to the left side.

Holman 1.2

LESSONS FROM THIS LEGEND...

In **Diagram 1.3**, O1 passes to the pivot, O2. As soon as the pass is completed, both O1 and O3 cut simultaneously and cross each other in front of the pivot player. The pivot player uses his judgment as to which one is free for a pass.

In **Diagram 1.4**, if the pivot man O2 is being crowded by his defensive man who is attempting to intercept a pass on the left side, the pivot man should turn right and go in towards the goal, ready to receive a loop pass from O1.

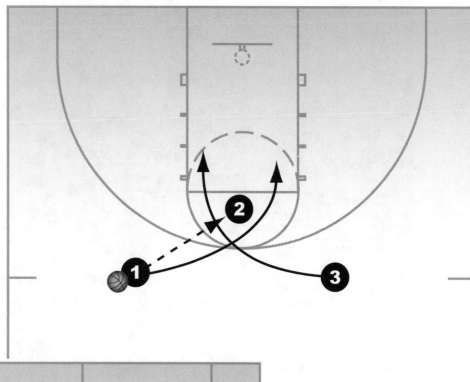

Holman 1.3

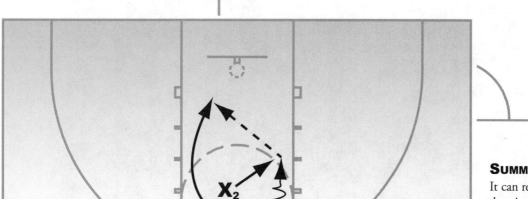

Holman 1.4

SUMMARY

It can readily be seen from the foregoing description that the pivot play has infinite possibilities. The pivot man can be used as the starter for many variations of plays. It lends itself easily to deceptive plays and the faster the attack, the more confused will it leave the defense. For greater effectiveness, however, the play should be alternated with the normal five-man style of attack and should not be used when the defensive team is successful in intercepting passes to the pivot man.

SOURCE

Holman, Nat. (1932). *Winning Basketball*. New York: Charles Scribner's Sons.

155

LEGACY OF
Frank Keaney

- Called the "Father of the Fast Break."

- Changed basketball from a slow, deliberate game to one of full-court defensive pressure, fast breaks, and high scoring.

- Known for his eccentricity, creativity, and showmanship.

- Inspired his players by reading poetry during his pregame talks.

- Invented the "Keaney Rim," an attachment that fit inside the rim and made the diameter of the goal two inches smaller.

- His 1939 Rhode Island squad was the first team in history to average more than 50 points per game, and his 1943 squad averaged almost 81 points per game.

- Led Rhode Island to the 1946 NIT finals.

FRANK KEANEY

*"The more you shoot,
the more points you make."*
— *Frank Keaney*

BIOGRAPHY

Born: June 5, 1886 in Boston, MA

Died: October 10, 1967

Inducted into the Naismith Basketball Hall of Fame in 1960

Frank Keaney was the head basketball coach at the University of Rhode Island from 1920 to 1948 and never had a losing season. He is credited with changing the game of basketball from a slow, deliberate-type to a fast-paced, full-court, high-scoring game. Keaney's fast break was triggered by quick, long passes to open receivers streaking down the floor. Keaney's racehorse basketball earned him the title, "Father of the Fast Break." His 1939 squad, called the "point-a-minute" team, was the first to average more than 50 points per game. By the time opponents started to catch on to his "run-and-shoot" offense, Keaney had his team scoring two points per minute. In 1943, Rhode Island averaged almost 81 points per game and earned the nickame, "The Firehouse Gang." Keaney compiled an overall coaching record of 401-124 and led Rhode Island to four NIT tournaments. In 1946, Rhode Island lost in the NIT Finals to Kentucky, 46-45. When Keaney arrived at Rhode Island in 1920, he was the head coach of all sports, athletic director, and teacher of chemistry. In 1953, Rhode Island dedicated their new gymnasium in Keaney's honor. It marked the first time that a campus building was named for a living faculty member. Keaney was the first coach ever signed by the Boston Celtics, but was unable to take the position due to medical reasons. Frank was enshrined in both the Helms Foundation Basketball Hall of Fame and the Naismith Memorial Basketball Hall of Fame.

Frank Keaney...

Frank Keaney was a Phi Betta Kappa graduate of Bates College, where he starred in football, basketball, baseball, and track. During the 1910 baseball season, Keaney's batting average was .480, and he set a school record with 38 stolen bases. After college, he directed high school athletic programs in Putnam, Connecticut; Woonsocket, Rhode Island; and Everett, Massachusetts, all in the northeast.

Keaney began his collegiate coaching career at Rhode Island in 1920 and was commonly referred to as the "nation's greatest one-man coaching staff." He served as track and cross country coach for five years, football coach for 19 years, baseball coach for 26 years, and basketball coach for 28 years. Keaney's cross country teams were never defeated. His football teams were known for their fast, tricky plays, and some people claim that he was using the triple-wing formation before others took credit for it. In baseball, Keaney used hit-and-run plays, delayed steals, and squeeze plays and compiled an overall record of 197-97. In basketball, Keaney pioneered the fast break and emphasized the concepts of conditioning, speed, quickness, full-court defense, and sharp passing 25 years before they became the norm.

When Keaney arrived at Rhode Island and looked over his squad of athletes, he said, "I can't make them any taller, but I can have them better conditioned than our opponents." Working on this premise, Keaney or "Menty" as he was affectionately called, produced superbly conditioned teams. Prior to the season, Keaney ran his players up and down the football stands until they were in shape. During the season, his players scrimmaged for two and a half hours every day.

Keaney conceived the idea of the fast break in basketball as he watched a Boston Bruins' ice hockey game in 1928. He watched quick skaters poke at the puck and make steals before any offense could be mounted. Keaney envisioned a similar strategy in basketball and immediately went to work designing a system that utilized full-court defensive pressure and quick scoring opportunities.

Keaney wrote the following in his personal journal regarding his creation of the fast break (Woodward, 1991):

"My wife just said, 'You are a dreamer. What are you dreaming now?' She had been reading a book with a glance now and then at me. Sure, I had been daydream-ing. I was thinking of my team and how I could improve the skill of the players. My mind was wondering; I thought various thoughts; I thought up all kinds of ideas. I was confused. My mind seemed amusing to me. I thought of all kinds of plays. Some seemed good; some seemed terrible. My wife was right—I was dreaming. I asked her what she meant. 'Your mind is all action,' she said. 'You seem to have many thoughts. Why don't you wake up and concentrate on one idea.' I replied, 'My thoughts are amusing to me. I am seeing all kinds of ways to help my boys win basketball games.' And while I was talking, I did get a stimulus—I said, 'I have it.' I rushed to my desk; out came the checkers that I used as players, and after an hour, I had planned the "quick break" in basketball. It was only the start, and in my first practice on the "fast break," I knew it would revolutionize the game. I sure am a dreamer."

The baseball pass was the primary weapon in Keaney's fast break. He believed that you must have at least three players who could throw an overhand catcher's throw with speed and accuracy the full length of the court. Receivers had to be able to catch the ball on the run and shoot while moving at full speed. Keaney's (1956) fast break system required: 1) speed of thought; 2) speed of foot; 3) long passes; 4) little dribbling; and 5) accurate shooting on the run. Keaney's theory was to get the ball into the offensive end of the floor as quickly as possible and then attack the basket. The faster the ball reached the front-court, the more likely the offensive players would outnumber the defensive players. He insisted that his team attempt more shots than the opponent, because he believed that was the key to victory.

Skeptics and traditionalists scorned and doubted Keaney's innovative methods. Many coaches and writers called it "crazy basketball." Traditional physical educators predicted that his players would die of weak hearts due to the fast pace of the game, but the high-scoring Rams soon caught the attention of basketball fans. Keaney's 1921 squad stunned the basketball world by scoring 87 points in a single game. By the mid 1930's, Rhode Island was known as the "Point-A-Minute" Rams. With the elimination of the center jump, some teams managed to catch on to his "point-a-minute" ways, but by that time, Keaney's club averaged "two points-a-minute." A team high was reached in 1947 when Rhode Island averaged over 82 points per game.

Keaney's system called for full-court defensive pressure the entire game. The objective was to try to force opponents into turnovers, which would provide additional scoring opportunities for Keaney's team. Another objective was the try to accelerate the tempo of the game and make the opponents play a run-and-shoot game.

Even though Keaney's players lacked height, he always had one player who not only secured the defensive rebound, but also was able to throw a basketball almost the length of the court. Perhaps the best at this was Keaney's son Warner, an exceptional athlete at 300 pounds, who could also drop kick a football from midfield. Young Keaney would snatch the rebound and quickly pass it to a teammate streaking down the court. This long pass was the trigger for the fast break that the Rams could run the entire game.

It was a "Keaney Rule" that every player was expected to play the entire game unless sidelined by fouls. His squads were never larger than seven or eight players, which sometimes caused anxious moments when players fouled out. Against Northeastern, Keaney found himself with only four players left on the floor. The officials demanded that he send in a substitute. Keaney placed a chair on the floor and told the officials that was his fifth player and to carry on with the game. The officials were so startled that they resumed play with the chair becoming an active player for the first time in history.

Keaney was an unforgettable personality. His eccentricity, creativity, and zest for life endeared him to his students, players, and the entire sports world. Sportswriters referred to his original expressions and never-ending slogans as Keaney-ana. Keaney called a player that liked to show-off "Fancy Willie." A foolish player was "Fried Banana." The team manager was "MG apostrophe R." Cigarettes were "Coffin Nails."

A fiery leader, Keaney's pre-game and halftime talks to his teams were masterful. He was such an excitable showman on the bench that many fans attended the games largely to enjoy his gestures and outbursts. On game nights, Keaney often pinch hit as an usher so he could squeeze as many fans into Rodman Hall as possible. He also was known to take over the ticket seller's job if he thought that individual was too slow in making change.

Keaney often strayed from tradition and built his own. He disliked the school colors and changed them to turquoise blue—which now bear the name of "Keaney-Blue." In 1928, Keaney learned that the election of captains sometimes created strife so he junked the system and personally made his own selections. Some years, he selected a half-dozen team captains. When faced against DePaul's All-American George Mikan, Keaney had a 5-foot 4-inch

player jump center against the 6 foot 11 inch Mikan. To help his players become better shooters, he designed an attachment called the "Keaney-rim," a device that fits inside the rim and made the diameter of the goal two inches smaller.

Besides his coaching responsibilities, Keaney was a chemistry instructor for 14 years. He invented various liniments that he used to treat his players. In 1931, he developed one of the first cures known for "athlete's foot," and he often received requests from people throughout the country who learned of his formula. Keaney suspected that some people might attempt to analyze the ingredients and market the cure for personal profit, so he always added certain elements to make it difficult for someone to discover the secret of his formula.

Keaney was the first coach ever signed by the Boston Celtics. Walter Brown was impressed with Keaney's Rhode Island teams and signed Keaney to coach his Boston club. Unfortunately for the Celtics, Keaney's doctor refused to let him take the job.

Keaney and his wife, Winnie, were married over 50 years; Winnie was the director of the women's athletic department at Rhode Island and coached every sport for 13 years.

Keaney was an inspirational mentor and advised his students that their goal in life should be to reach home plate and never become satisfied by only reaching third base.

SOURCE

Keaney, Frank. (1956, September). Frank Keaney Outlines His Fast Break. *Basketball Bulletin.*

Keaney, Frank. Vertical Files, Archives. Naismith Memorial Basketball Hall of Fame. Springfield, MA.

Woodward, William. (1991). Keaney. Wickford, RI: *The Dutch Island Press.*

LESSONS FROM THIS LEGEND...

FIRE-HORSE BASKETBALL

By Frank Keaney

To win basketball games, players must throw that ball through the hoop. Therefore, as coaches, we point to the basket and then to the floor and explain to our players the methods necessary for advancing the ball up the floor and toward the basket. In other words, we think it is good teaching to show our players the final result, and then break our teaching down into smaller essentials.

BASKETBALL ESSENTIALS

The essentials for the game of basketball are passing, cutting, dribbling, and shooting. These fundamentals should be practiced and practiced until every player can execute them skillfully. My philosophy is simple. Get your players in shape, run your opponents into exhaustion, and shoot the ball whenever possible.

GETTING THE BALL UP THE FLOOR USING THE "FIRE-HORSE" METHOD

The "Fire-Horse" way of getting the ball up the floor is one of the many ways of approaching the basket. It is called "fire-horse," because it looks like a

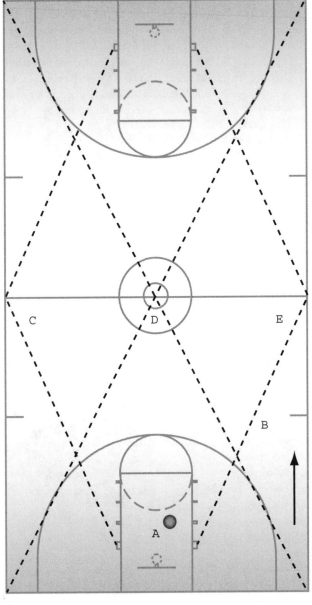

Keaney 1.0

wild and haphazard method of speeding up the floor, with all five players running here and there without any fixed methods of approaching the final goal. If this so-called

method is tried, it will be found that it will take long hours of practice to bring a team up to a fair degree of perfection. It looks easy from the bleachers, but coaches find there is a great amount of teaching to be done, and many mistakes to be rectified.

Diagram 1.0 gives the approximate positions in which we expect our players to be immediately after the opponents have scored or missed a basket.

KEY POINTS IN FIRE-HORSE BASKETBALL

1. Get the ball up the floor in as few passes as possible.
2. Throw passes straight down the court—do not make crosscourt passes.
3. Use the overhead catcher's pass.
4. Make it a bullet pass—snap your wrist the moment the ball leaves your hand.
5. Throw the ball head-high to the receiver.
6. Whenever possible, throw passes that cover one-half the length of the court.
7. Receivers should catch the ball with their fingers spread and their feet apart.
8. After catching the ball, immediately pivot, with your toes on the floor and your heels raised high and look for another open teammate.
9. See the entire floor—always look toward your basket and use split vision to locate open teammates.
10. Rebound if the basket is missed—always be in strategic positions to secure the ball after a basket is missed.

LESSONS FROM THIS LEGEND...

FIRE-HORSE OPTIONS

Look at **Diagram 1.0** again. If player A recovers the ball after a basket by an opponent or by a missed basket, he does not dribble to the corner, but looks toward his basket and by split vision, looks up the whole floor at his basket. Player A has the following options:

1. Throwing the length-court pass to C, D, or E:
   - This pass should be used when C, D, or E can jump his guard.
   - This pass takes practice, but is worth practicing, as it pays dividends.
2. Throwing an overhand bullet pass to B:
   - After making the pass, A cuts behind B.
   - After receiving the pass, B immediately pivots and looks to throw a long overhand pass to C, D, or E.
   - If the players down the floor are not open, B push-passes back to A and then cuts behind A, as A looks to throw a long pass.

Authors' Note: The phrase "jump his guard" refers to the ability of an offensive player to get open and secure the pass.

TEACH THE PROPER FUNDAMENTALS

Coaches should be certain to teach their players to throw the ball correctly, using the one-handed catcher's pass. For the inexperienced coach may I say that the pass is hard to master, but any player who likes the game, and is willing to practice, can conquer it. There are several key points to emphasize with the catcher's pass:

- Hold the ball correctly using both hands, one is the guide hand and the other is the throwing hand.
- Throw it overhand and not sidearm, as a sidearm pass will curve.
- Take just one step as a baseball catcher does.

- Follow through as a catcher does.
- Throw the ball hard and fast.
- Throw it head high.
- Catch the ball with the fingers spread.

ALL PLAYERS MOVE WITH SPEED

I hope the readers can see why it is called "fire-horse" or "race-horse" basketball. We get the ball, pass it a couple of times, and shoot it up at the basket. All players move and move with speed. They are positioned so they are ready for a rebound if the basket is missed. At times, the players will make many mistakes, but I wish a few of the readers would try it out.

ADVICE TO YOUNG COACHES

If you think the fast break is just "helter-skelter, razzle-dazzle, shoot-at-will" basketball, then forget it. I worked on this many years. It took many trials and errors before I discovered the right method. It is essential that you teach your principles to your players. The following are the five essential keys in fast break basketball:

1. You must have at least three guards who can throw an overhand catcher's pass with great speed and accuracy. I want my players to be able to throw this pass the length of the court.

2. You must develop an outstanding playmaker. He is the key to success with the long passes. He must be a team player and have the ability to throw the ball one-handed at least 50 feet. He should also be able to dribble and advance the ball quickly when necessary. This player must be able to see the entire court. A great playmaker will create many outnumbering situations for your offense.

3. You need forwards who can sprint down the floor, cut to the basket, catch the ball, and score. They must have great timing and be able to lay the ball up on the board with a "gentle touch."

4. Your players must know how and when to fast break. They must be able to recognize 5-on-4, 4-on-3, 3-on-2, or 2-on-1 situations.

5. Always remember the fast break requires speed of thought and speed of foot. It may be one long pass to a cutting forward, or a pass to the playmaker. The quicker you can get to your basket, the better. Too many passes or too many dribbles take time. Always remember that you can throw it faster than you can dribble it.

LAST BUT NOT LEAST

They call me the "rugged individualist," the "old philosopher," or the "old psychologist." My wife calls me "the dreamer," or the "lover of life." So to the young coaches, I will say:

1. Inject the "will to win" in all your players.

2. There are no short cuts to success.

3. Games are lost, because we think they are lost.

4. Without superb conditioning, you will fail. Not just good conditioning, but superb conditioning. It is every coach's duty.

5. Don't lose the game before it is played.

6. Love luck, because it is careful hard work.

7. Be full of intuition, illumination, inspiration, and initiative.

SOURCE

Keaney, Frank. (1944, December). Fire-Horse Basketball. *Athletic Journal.*

Keaney, Frank. (1956, September). Frank Keaney Outlines His Fast Break. *Basketball Bulletin.*

LEGACY OF
John Kundla

- Created the NBA's first dynasty by leading the Minneapolis Lakers to four league championships in a five-year span.

- Designed the power forward position in basketball.

- Guided the Lakers to six league championships (NBL-1948, BAA-1949, NBA-1950, 1952, 1953, 1954).

- Coached the U.S. to the gold medal in the 1965 World University Games.

- Respected by his peers for his ability to blend athletes with diverse personalities into a championship team.

- Selected as one of the top ten coaches in NBA history.

- Was a humble, quiet coach who always kept an even demeanor on the court.

JOHN KUNDLA

"Blending the talents of your team members is crucial to basketball success."
— *John Kundla*

BIOGRAPHY

Born: July 3, 1916 in Star Junction, PA

Inducted into the Naismith Basketball Hall of Fame in 1955

John Kundla's playing and coaching career spanned five decades and included a Big Ten title, four NBA championships, one NBL championship, and one BAA crown. Kundla was named head coach of the Minneapolis Lakers at the relatively young age of 31. He went on to one of the greatest head coaching careers in professional basketball and was the architect of the NBA's first dynasty. Kundla compiled a 466-319 record, including a 70-38 playoff record. He led the Lakers to six league championships and coached six future Hall of Famers. Kundla coached in four NBA All-Star Games. Following his NBA career, Kundla coached nine years at his alma mater, the University of Minnesota. As a collegiate player, Kundla led the Gophers to a share of the Big Ten title in 1937. An all-conference performer in 1938 and team captain in 1939, Kundla led the team in scoring all three years. After his playing days were over, he took his passion for the game to the sidelines and was an assistant coach at Minnesota from 1939 to 1942 and again in 1945-46. From 1942-45, Kundla coached De La Salle High School, and led the school to two state championships in three year. Kundla coached the Moroccan National Team in 1983-84. In 1999, he was named by *Sports Illustrated* as one of the top 50 greatest 20th-century athletes in the State of Minnesota. He was selected as one of the top ten coaches in NBA history as part of the "NBA at 50" celebration in 1996. Kundla is enshrined in the University of Minnesota Hall of Fame, the Minnesota Hall of Fame, and the Naismith Memorial Basketball Hall of Fame.

John Kundla...

John Kundla starred in basketball and baseball at Central High School in Minneapolis. He continued his athletic career at the University of Minnesota, where he was a standout in both sports. In basketball, Kundla helped Minnesota win a share of the Big Ten Conference in 1937. He was named All-Confernce in 1938, and led the Gophers in scoring all three years. Kundla received the Big Ten Conference medal for scholastic and athletic proficiency in 1939.

After graduating from Minnesota in 1939, Kundla coached at Ascension Grade School and was also on the staff at the University of Minnesota. In 1942, John became head basketball coach at De La Salle High School in Minneapolis and led his team to two state championships in three years. He served in the Navy and then returned to Minnesota for the 1945-46 season.

Kundla accepted the head coaching position at St. Thomas College (MN) in 1946 and compiled an 11-11 record during his first year. It was at this time that professional basketball first came to Minnesota. Ben Berger and Morris Chalfen purchased and relocated a near-extinct National Basketball League franchise, the Detroit Gems, to Minneapolis. They talked with Kundla several times about becoming head coach, but he was not eager to take the job. Finally, he agreed, and the first NBA dynasty was in the making.

What caused this dynasty that some said blazed the trail for the acceptance of professional basketball as a major sport? One reason was the outstanding play of future Hall of Famers George Mikan, Vern Mikkelsen, Jim Pollard, Elgin Baylor, Clyde Lovellette, and Slater Martin. Another reason was the leadership and coaching of John Kundla. He blended great players with strong personalities into a unified team.

George Mikan, who was selected as the greatest player in the first 50 years of the NBA, said, "John's a great person and a smarter basketball man than you'll ever know."

Ray Meyer, the legendary coach from DePaul, said, "He took All-American superstars and merged them into a unit that played well together."

Arnie Ferrin, who played on the Lakers under Kundla from 1948-51, stated, "To blend the idiosyncrasies and strong personalities of the players he coached into a winning team was remarkable."

Kundla was well respected by his coaching peers. He emphasized defense and held his players accountable. On the floor, Kundla wasn't boisterous and coached in a rather low-key manner. He was the quiet force behind the Laker's success.

Unfortunately, Kundla never received the credit he deserved for leading Minneapolis to five NBA titles in six years. Many individuals erroneously thought that any coach with George Mikan, Jim Pollard, and Vern Mikkelsen would win titles without much work.

Boston Celtic's icon "Red" Auerbach didn't buy that type of thinking. "I've seen a lot of great teams, at least on paper, that won nothing," Auerbach said. "Sure, Kundla had a great team, but he did great things with them."

Two college coaches played a part in the success of the Lakers. One was Ray Meyer, who coached Mikan at DePaul, and the other was former Kentucky coach Adolph Rupp. Meyer coached George Mikan at DePaul and was instrumental in his development as a player. Kundla occasionally called on Meyer to help coach Mikan, either during practice sessions or games. During the playoffs, Meyer would often join the team and sit on the bench. His role was to make sure that Mikan played up to his ability.

Adolph Rupp played a big role in helping the Lakers get prepared for the season. Kundla arranged to have the Lakers conduct preseason workouts at the University of Kentucky. At that time, the NBA did not have any rules against professional players working out with college teams. Rupp was nationally recognized for his dictatorial style of coaching, and he assisted Kundla in getting the Lakers in prime physical condition for the season.

Kundla was the architect of the prototypical modern team. He was the first to include the distinct positions of power and quick forwards. In the 1940s, any player, 6'6" or taller, was a candidate to play center. Kundla had the NBA's best center in George Mikan, but he also had a tall, talented player named Vern Mikkelsen. Kundla moved Mikkelsen to a position that hadn't been invented yet—

the power forward position. Instead of having Mikkelsen inside with his back to the basket, Kundla placed him away from the lane, facing the basket. Although he was not the focus of the offense, Mikkelson became one of the key components in making Kundla's offense successful.

Mikkelsen (Kirscht,1998) stated, "One day, John gets up and says, 'We've got to have a play for Mikkelsen,' and I got all excited. So, he went on and told me to set a pick here, and then go set a pick over there. I finally asked, 'Yeah, coach, then what?' John looked at me and said, 'Then, go get the rebound.' But you know what? It worked."

The play was nicknamed "Askov," after Mikkelsen's northern Minnesota hometown, and it did work. Mikkelsen was among the NBA's top 10 rebounders four times in his career.

"John didn't really know what he was putting together back then," said Mikkelsen. "But, this is the model for basketball today."

Kundla was among the first NBA coaches to design plays, a strategy that earned the Lakers' coach some criticism around the league. He kept the offense simple, choosing to depend on a pick-and-roll play down low with Mikan and Jim Pollard. If the defenders switched, leaving Mikan against a smaller forward, Pollard would pass the ball to his center and watch him score.

"If the defense didn't switch, it meant an easy drive to the basket for the quick forward. "It was a simple little play," Kundla said. "But, it was very successful."

Kundla also substituted frequently, a strategy that later coaches would attempt to duplicate. He was a master at getting players to accept roles within the framework of the team.

As he approaches his 88th birthday, Kundla's passion for the Gophers, Lakers, and Timberwolves remains strong. He attends as many collegiate and professional games as he can.

When asked about the good and bad changes that he has seen in the game of basketball, Kundla (2004) stated, "Wow, over the years the game has changed so much. I think more than anything on the court, the biggest change is the lost art of passing. No one passes like they used to any more. The bounce pass has gone by the wayside, and I cringe when I see how guards are giving entry passes nowadays. The other big change from when I was

around is the three-point shot. I would love to see what a guy like Trent Tucker would have done with a three-point line in college. Off the court, the biggest change is the way players are recruited. These AAU tournaments are great experiences for everyone, but it puts a lot of pressure on guys knowing that coaches are watching them. I am shocked that my grandson, who is a sophomore, already has scholarship offers. I guess though if one coach does it, it forces every coach to do it."

Kundla said, "On the professional level, the two recent players that I could watch every night are Kevin Garnett and Tim Duncan. Both players are outstanding role models. Every time I talk with Garnett, he always refers to me as "Sir" or "Coach." Most guys at his level wouldn't even know who I am, but he has a sense of basketball history. I admire that."

John Kundla, the quiet and humble architect of the NBA's first dynasty, never stops coaching.

Source

Kirscht, Aaron. (1998, May 14). "Hall of Famers Reflect on Bygone Era." *The Minnesota Daily Online.* Web site: <http://www.mndaily.com/daily/1998/05/14/sports/laker/>

Kundla, John. Vertical Files, Archives. Naismith Memorial Basketball Hall of Fame. Springfield, MA.

Kundla, John. (2004, May 3). *Where Are They Now?* Web site: <http://www.GopherHole.com.>

LESSONS FROM THIS LEGEND...

MY FAVORITE PLAYS

By John Kundla

In these offensive sets, John Kundla featured post man George Mikan, who was selected "The Greatest Player of the First 50 Years in the NBA. Mikan was an exceptional scorer and passer.

In **Diagram 1.0,** O1 passes to teammate O3 and cuts to the outside. O3 fakes a return pass to O1 and passes back to teammate O2. O2 passess to teammate O4 who is breaking out to the ball. O4 passes to teammate O3, who is cutting into the lane around the screen set by the post man, O5.

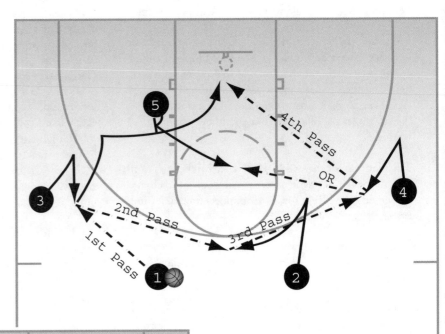

Kundla 1.0

In **Diagram 1.1**, O1 passes to teammate O3 and cuts to either side of the post player, O5. O3 passes to teammate O5, who breaks out and then faces the basket with the ball. Player O3 sets a screen on the left side of the lane and teammate O1 breaks around the screen and toward the ball. O5 passes the ball to teammate O1 if he is free for a shot.

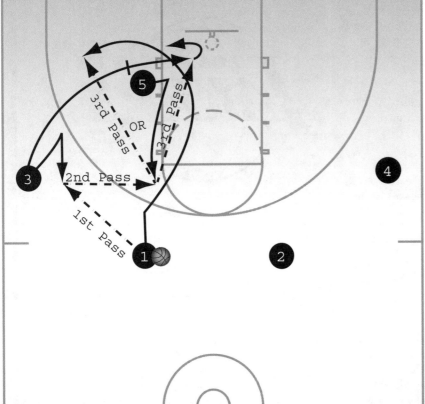

Kundla 1.1

LESSONS FROM THIS LEGEND...

In **Diagram 1.2.** O1 passes the ball to teammate O3 and cuts to the outside. O3 then passes to teammate O2, who is moving toward the ball and then sets a pick against teammate O1's guard. Post man, O5, now breaks out and receives the ball from guard O2. O1 reverses and breaks around the screen set by O3 and receives the ball from the post man, O5, for a shot.

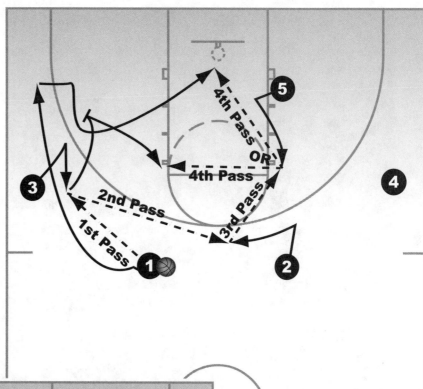

Kundla 1.2

In **Diagram 1.3,** backcourt players O1 and O2 exchange positions by means of a dribble. When O1 receives the ball, he dribbles toward teammate O4 on the right sideline. O4 starts out, reverses, and sets a double screen on the right side of the lane with the post man, O5. O3 breaks around the double screen for a pass from O1.

SOURCE:

Bee, Clair, ed. (1963). Winning Basketball Plays. New York: Ronald Press.

Kundla 1.3

LEGACY OF
Ward "Piggy" Lambert

- Pioneered the fast break in the Midwest and his system became known as "racehorse-style" basketball.

- Built his teams on size (for controlling the defensive boards) and speed (for quickly advancing the ball).

- Coached 29 years at Purdue and led the Boilermakers to 11 conference championships.

- Directed Purdue to the Helms Foundation national championship in 1932.

- Was an energetic, animated bench coach, who demanded precision and execution from his teams.

- Authored *Practical Basketball,* a legendary basketball textbook. (His All-American player, John Wooden, later wrote a classic basketball textbook entitled, *Practical Modern Basketball.*)

WARD "PIGGY" LAMBERT

"Basketball is a mental game."
— Ward "Piggy" Lambert

BIOGRAPHY

Born May 28, 1888, in Deadwood, S.D.

Died: January 20, 1958

Inducted into the Naismith Basketball Hall of Fame in 1960

Ward "Piggy" Lambert grew up in Indiana during the formative years of basketball. He was introduced to the game at the local YMCA and Crawfordsville High School. Lambert played basketball at Wabash (IN) College. He went on to receive his master's degree in chemistry from the University of Minnesota in 1912. His first coaching position was at Lebanon (IN) High School. In 1916, Lambert accepted the position as head basketball coach at Purdue University. With the exception of three years spent in World War I and three years in professional basketball, Lambert spent the rest of his career at Purdue. He helped put the Big Ten Conference on the basketball map with his powerful Purdue teams. In 29 years as coach, the Boilermakers won or shared 11 Big Ten titles and posted 371 victories with only 152 losses. Lambert led Purdue to the national championship in 1932. He pioneered the fast-break style of play, and his teams were noted for their great speed. In 1946, Lambert left Purdue to become the commissioner of the National Professional Basketball League. He returned to Purdue in 1949 as head freshman basketball and baseball coach. He gave up his basketball responsibilities in 1955, but continued coaching baseball until his death in 1958. Lambert authored *Practical Basketball,* one of the early "Bibles" of the game. He served as chairman of the Rules Committee for the National Association of Basketball Coaches. Lambert is enshrined in the Helms Foundation Hall of Fame, the Indiana Hall of Fame, and the Naismith Memorial Basketball Hall of Fame.

...SCOUTING REPORT.....SCOUTING REPORT.....

Ward "Piggy" Lambert

Ward "Piggy" Lambert was born in Deadwood, South Dakota, but in his youth, his family moved to Crawfordsville, Indiana. Lambert was three years old when James Naismith invented the game of basketball at Springfield College. The Crawfordsville YMCA was said to be the first YMCA in Indiana to adopt the new game. Lambert played the game in a city basketball league that began in 1898. He watched basketball start as a gym group game and later develop into seven-man teams. During his lifetime, he had seen, played, or coached through all the major rule changes in the game.

Lambert went to Wabash College as a short, but determined, 114-pound youth. He led the Little Giants in scoring as a basketball forward and also played football and baseball. During his senior year in 1911, Lambert even coached the basketball team as a player-coach.

Following graduation from Wabash, Lambert was awarded a scholarship to the University of Minnesota, where he took post-graduate work in chemistry, which he intended to follow as a life profession.

In 1912, Lambert accepted a position as teacher of chemistry and physics, and coach of the athletic teams at Lebanon (IN) High School. Lambert's basketball teams compiled outstanding records and attracted the attention of administrators at Purdue University. In the fall of 1916, Lambert began his career at Purdue as head basketball and baseball coach.

Even though Lambert was nicknamed "Piggy" because of his small size and round stature, his coaching accomplishments were huge. In 29 seasons, Lambert compiled a record of 371-152 and led the Boilermakers to the Helms Foundation national championship in 1932. Lambert bucked the prevailing style of ball control and continuity offenses. He introduced the fast break to the Big Ten Conference, and his system became known as "race-horse-style" basketball. Lambert recruited players that fit into his coaching philosophy. He wanted big players who could control the defensive boards and quick, aggressive perimeter players who could run his fast break.

Two of Lambert's star players were Charles "Stretch" Murphy and John Wooden. Murphy was 6'6"—the perfect player to rebound and quickly initiate the fast break. "Stretch" was a Helms Foundation All-American in 1929 and 1930 and led Purdue to three Big Ten championships. In 1929, Murphy set the Big Ten record for points scored in one season.

John Wooden came to Purdue as a legendary high school player from Martinsville (IN) High School. Wooden brought speed and quickness, both offensively and defensively to the Boilermakers. Lambert claimed that Wooden ran "like he had an outboard motor attached to him."

Wooden was a three-time Helms Foundation All-American, the National Player of the Year in 1932, and led the Boilermakers to the national championship in 1932. Wooden, who went on to become one of the all-time greatest coaches in the history of the game, won 10 national championships at UCLA. He cites "Piggy" Lambert as being his "greatest influence, both from the standpoint of playing and coaching." Wooden also said, "Coach Lambert had higher principles than anyone I knew."

Purdue's success during the late 1920s and early1930s captured the attention of coaches, and Lambert's style of play soon replaced the "Doc" Meanwell era of ball control.

Lambert was an energetic coach who nervously paced the sidelines during games. He demanded precision and execution from his teams. Wooden said, "Coach Lambert had a fetish for details."

Lambert believed that "half-hearted players were a detriment to the squad." He demanded that his players had the proper mental attitude, worked hard, and were enthusiastic.

"The best player who lacks enthusiasm cannot do his best," stated Lambert (1932). "The coach must be aggressive in practice and stimulate enthusiasm by encouragement. There is no human who does not like credit for good work, and the coach who continually tells his players that they are 'rotten' is sure to make them so. A coach has to develop pride in cooperation and team play, and create the desire to win. A player must understand that all that can be expected of him is to perform up to his capability, regardless of the success of the other team. When the mental courage of a player is destroyed, he is indecisive. If the mind is not aggressive, the drive in the legs is gone."

Lambert also cautioned coaches about overcoaching. "Overcoaching may be more injurious than undercoaching," Lambert stated. "Players may easily be overburdened with too much knowledge, which will cause them to lose the spirit of play and competition."

.....SCOUTING REPORT.....SCOUTING REPORT...

There have been many "Piggy" Lambert stories passed down through the years, but one of the best describes the time when Lambert gave his pre-game talk from a bathtub. "Piggy" was watching a preliminary game but was standing too close to the timer. At the final gun, signaling the end of the game, Lambert was sprayed with gunpowder resulting in hives and an eye infection. "Piggy" got into a bathtub to ease his discomfort and decided to give his players their final instructions from that location.

Lambert was not a supporter of postseason competition. He did not think college games should be played off campus because he felt intercollegiate athletics was for the students and the alumni. Even thought Purdue won the Big Ten in 1940, Lambert did not take the team to the NCAA tournament. Indiana went on to win the national championship even though it had finished second in the conference.

Lambert's book, *Practical Basketball*, became one of the great basketball textbooks. His star pupil, John Wooden, later wrote a classic basketball book, entitled *Practical Modern Basketball*, in honor of his former coach.

At the first meeting of the National Association of Basketball Coaches, Lambert was elected chairman of the Rules Committee. He also served on the Board of Directors of that organization.

In 1945, Lambert was named the nation's outstanding basketball coach in a poll conducted by *Esquire*.

Lambert will also be remembered as the pioneer of the fast break in the Midwest. His Purdue teams changed the style of play in the Big Ten Conference. But just as importantly, Ward "Piggy" Lambert will be remembered as a man of the highest principles.

Source

Lambert, Ward L. (1932). *Practical Basketball*. Chicago: Athletic Journal Publishing.

Luisetti, Hank. (1946). *Famous Play Patterns by America's Most Famous Coaches*. San Francisco: Mercury Press.

TEAM OFFENSE

by Ward Lambert

Authors' Note: This lesson selection focuses on the Lambert legacy—the aggressive, fast-breaking offense, with emphasis on the offensive fundamental skills he favored. Team Offense, in the preface of his book, Practical Basketball, details his approach to offense and the fast break. As he stated in the preface, "the fast break, with dependence upon initiative of players rather than set formations, is, in my opinion, the ideal system if the coach has the necessary material." This article is a classic on the origins of the fast break.

TEAM OFFENSE AND FAST BREAK

HISTORICAL DEVELOPMENT

In the early years of the game of basketball, the organization of team offense was not well developed. Rather, it consisted of rapid passing of the ball from one offensive man to another. The defense was a man-to-man assignment, that is, the guards guarded the forwards, the forwards guarded the guards, and the center guarded the center. When a team lost control of the ball, each player picked up his man at once, on any part of the floor, and stayed with him.

As the game progressed, we had various systems of team offense, which were developed to overcome the defense. In turn, various systems of defense were developed to stop the new systems of offense. We saw various blocking systems of offense arise because the team defensive idea was man-to-man; these were aimed at the chief weakness of the man-to-man system. We saw zone defensive systems arise, first, to protect against the short shot, and second, as a defense against blocking and crossing systems of offense. Special offensive arrange-

ments were developed to combat certain defensive strengths, and vice versa. Some offensive systems were found to be most effective only when the offensive team was ahead in the score. Some defensive systems likewise were discovered to be usable only when the defensive team was ahead.

This continual combat between the offensive and defensive ideas not only caused many changes in the rules of the game so that the offensive and defensive balance might be maintained, but it was responsible for rapid development of the game in a scientific manner.

By close observation of the game and its development, we are sable to arrive at certain conclusions regarding the essentials that should be contained in an offensive system.

GENERAL ESSENTIALS

There are certain essentials that are included in practically all systems of team offense. In the discussions of team offense that follow, the use of these essentials are reviewed.

BREAKING

When a defensive team secures the ball through fumbles, by intercepted passes, or from the bank on rebounds, it becomes then an offensive team in possession of the ball. Whether the reaction to break for the offensive basket is fast or slow depends upon the habit the coach decides to develop in the players. In order to develop fast-break habits, the coach should use such expressions as "look first; dribble last," and "pass through rapidly and run."

Have your team break fast on intercepted passes! There is always a fast-break situation presented to your team because the opponent for whom the pass was intended is off balance for defense. There will be a chance for 2-and-1, 3-and-2 or 4-and-3 situations on offense. In my opinion, looking for fast-break opportunities first should be a part of any offensive system. The habits developed by the fast break are valuable, both offensively and defensively for the reactions established.

CONTROL OF THE BALL

Having possession of the ball, the players should be impressed by the coach with the importance of retaining it. The importance of passing and its relation to offense have already been stressed. In starting an offense, the first pass must be accurate.

Otherwise, there can be no offense. There must be no short passes underneath the opponents' basket. Interception here is most dangerous. To prevent a dangerous interception, the players must throw the first pass a distance of twenty to twenty-five feet toward the sidelines or middle of the floor, or long into offensive territory.

In order to insure that the first pass will be accurate, players require practice in putting themselves in position to meet a pass from their teammate who has gained control. If the first pass is to be met on the side of the floor, the player receiving the ball breaks to the sideline, and then from the sideline to receive it. Sideline huggers receiving passes allow for a better chance of interception and are jammed against the sideline and slowed in their attempts to start the offensive. When breaking from the sideline and

LESSONS FROM THIS LEGEND...

meeting the ball, players put their bodies between the ball and prospective interceptors of passes. In starting the offense, the first one or two passes should carry the ball from dangerous territory into offensive territory. If the training on the first one or two passes is fast, a fast break can be developed; if players dribble to the corners from the break to insure possession, then the break is slow. The manner in which players break first to and then from the sidelines in the fast break is illustrated in diagrams shown later.

Players who continually play together establish their own habits of breaking and receiving passes, and, by long association, develop a system of offensive team play. This may consist only of an understanding of the individual characteristics of the team members.

If the players who are to make-up a team have already established habits, and if these players do not understand the characteristics of one another, then there must be some unified system of habits furnished these various individuals. This is the job for the coach. The habits to be established by the coach should be good habits; it is just as easy to teach bad habits. Basketball is surely a game of habits, and whether the habits performed are good or bad depends upon the systematized teaching that is used to develop them.

FOUNDATION OF FUNDAMENTALS

The offensive team which is successful in scoring a great many points in any one contest generally accomplishes this by the execution of fundamentals alone. That is, it does not need the so-called strategy, center-tip plays, and out-of-bounds plays to win the easy game. From observation, I believe that close contests also are won on the proper execution of fundamental habits during the game, and not because of strategy, or tip-off or out-of-bounds plays, or out-guessing the opponent. Under the discussion of fundamental habits of passing (meeting the ball and looking before the pass), basket shooting, dribbling and offen-

sive footwork, the point was emphasized that the establishment of correct habits is an offensive system in itself, if the players have the opportunity of understanding each other by playing together.

COORDINATION OF OFFENSE AND DEFENSE

The system of offense supplied by the coach must call for such an arrangement of players that they may be in position to break into offense from defense, or vice versa, in reverse order; that is, if an offensive man is expected to be first into the offensive territory, he is logically expected to be the fifth man back on defense. A balance of position between offense and defense should be maintained at all times so that neither will suffer by change from one to the other.

Authors' Note: This is what modern coaches would call "transition."

DEVELOPING PSYCHOLOGICAL REACTIONS

Most offensive systems of basketball contain principles of passing and meeting the ball in such a manner that the pass is forward and the man meeting the ball angles toward the pass and the basket at the same time. Such principles create an aggressive, forward, mental drive for the basket, when drilling establishes the habit and insistent driving expressions are used by the coach. If a system is used which allows for and even calls for a predominance of passes back, then the psychological reaction is to destroy the aggressive, forward, mental drive.

Since the short shots have a greater percentage of success than the long shots, most set offensive systems have, as an essential, such an arrangement and movement of players as to create openings under the basket for short shots. A player may be started from beneath the basket toward a pass to draw a defensive player away, and thereby, clear floor space underneath the basket, so that a teammate may have that space in which to

receive a pass for a short shot. If the defensive player is not drawn, then the successful long pass received by the player moving from the basket will have the proper psychological reaction upon the defensive man to draw him out.

A close study of the following discussion and explanation of various types of offense will disclose the fact that the aforementioned essentials are included. Fast breaks and slow-break set formations are shown in which all of these essentials are used to advantage.

COACHING ADVICE

With experience in developing basketball teams, we realize that the position of the coach first of all is that of a teacher. He must realize at the start that basketball is a habit game, and that it is just as easy to teach bad habits as good ones. Bad habits surely result if the players are allowed to execute fundamentals incorrectly.

The basketball game is a mental contest, and proper mental training must be given by the teacher or coach. My experience has been that the process of teaching and developing players is a gradual one, and requires much patience by the coach. In other words, players should not be driven in the execution of fundamental plays until the lessons have been well learned. If we hear the expression, "They went up in the air," used in referring to a team, we know that team had not learned its lesson in fundamental execution and mental control. One of the dangers in teaching is overloading players with knowledge. Some inexperienced coaches try to teach young players everything they know about the game. Most young players cannot absorb all of this knowledge, and there is more danger in over-coaching than in under-coaching.

MOLDING INDIVIDUALS INTO A TEAM

Having drilled properly in individual techniques and fundamentals of passing, foot-

LESSONS FROM THIS LEGEND...

work, and basket shooting, a coach must then take advantage of the strength of the various individuals to mold them into a unified system of play, which we call the team offense. He must give to the players a picture of this offensive system by explanation, diagram, and demonstration on the floor. He must be sure that all of the individuals thoroughly understand the working principle of this system of play. After that, much practice on the various play possibilities of the system is required for proper execution and timing.

The selection and placing of the various individuals on the squad in certain positions is a subject for which there is no definite recipe. This is a problem more for every individual coach to decide, but the following suggestions may be helpful.

One of the first requirements of a basketball player (the same is true of athletes in other types of sport) is courage, which is mental, not physical. The coach should teach players that courage is mental stability, and make them realize that they are able to play up to their maximum capability, regardless of the success of the opponents. The fight is mental and not physical, if we take for granted, of course, that the individuals are in top condition. Brains and character are the most valuable assets. Players having these qualifications will perform up to their expected capabilities in close contests, and even rise to higher planes in cases of extreme stress.

Natural physical abilities, or cleverness, is an asset, but the player of ability without courage and brains is not apt to perform well under trying conditions. Although size is important, the coach should have an open mind as to size of players and not exclude small, fast men because of this factor alone. Many small players are valuable, even though they have a disadvantage of size in guarding around the basket. It is true, nevertheless, that the good big man is better than the good little man, other qualifications being equal.

THE PLACING OF PLAYERS

CENTER. The selection of a center is an important factor, and, in this selection, we must not be deceived by height alone. A tall man playing center has a considerable bearing on the control of the ball at the center tip, but the fact that he can control the ball is not sufficient reason that he is the man for the position. Many tall men lack aggressiveness in offense around the basket, particularly in following shots, and in the defensive duties they must perform. They may also lack accuracy in passing and basket shooting. Jumping on center plays is also needed.

FORWARDS. First of all, forwards should be good shots; tall men are more valuable than short men on following shots, if they are equal in speed, offensive footwork and ability to guard.

GUARDS. In practically all defensive systems, at least one tall, rugged, hard-fighting guard is required. Because of his height, a great deal of responsibility is put upon a back guard of this type to protect against short shots around the basket and to secure rebound shots which will assure a starting of the offense. If two guards of this sort are obtainable, the greater becomes the defensive strength around the basket, and the greater is the assurance of possession of the ball on rebounds. Size in guards, while most valuable, should not be attained entirely at the sacrifice of speed and footwork. Many systems of play use a guard known as the "floor guard," or "running guard," who not only has ability in defensive work, but who is qualified as well to be used extensively in the offense. A floor guard of this type should be fast. He should also be a good, aggressive ballhandler and a good shot when used in the offense, as well as an excellent passer, who is able to use sound judgment in his play.

It has already been said that over-coaching is one of the dangers in basketball. It is best to use a few strong plays that are well learn-

ed, rather than a large number in which there is not perfect execution. Strong plays will have balance of offense and defense at all times.

In order that the individuals of a team may use an offense to best advantage, the coach must prepare the minds of the players for the various styles of defense they may meet. This should be done in early season practice to avoid, if possible, any surprise defense that may be thrown against them. Having been pre-warned and taught the offensive tactics to be used against any defense, the players should be able to react properly to any situation. Under the discussion of types of offense, special offensive methods are shown for use against zone defense. Likewise, special defenses for the various offenses are shown. The counter attack for each of these special defenses should be taught.

After the individuals have been drilled and molded into a team, practice should first be carried on without resistance of the defense to develop accuracy and speed, and then it should be followed with a dummy scrimmage. After this, scrimmages should be held to attain proper execution under practice that approaches game conditions as nearly as possible.

While scrimmages are being carried on, the coach should insist upon the rudiments of offense by giving such reminders as these:

1. Stay six feet from the sidelines on dribbles.
2. Make no short passes under the opponents' basket. Follow your shots.
3. No offense without accurate passes, Look first, dribble last.
4. Don't take wild shots.
5. Don't pass to sideline huggers.
6. Meet the ball.
7. Break from the sidelines to take passes.
8. Break fast and pass fast on intercepted passes.

LESSONS FROM THIS LEGEND...

SELECTING A STYLE OF TEAM OFFENSE

With the foregoing discussion of essentials of team offensive and advice in its development, we are ready to present an analysis and discussion of the various offenses, which include both fast-break and slow-break types and also formations which may spread mass defense when the offense is ahead in the score.

In going into the explanation of these offensive systems, it is to be understood that in the systems other than that used by the Purdue team only a general conception of the fundamental working principles is given. There is no intention to criticize any system destructively, but each is presented with the idea of giving the reader a broad insight into various offensive systems and, if possible, of pointing out the particular offensive strength or weakness with respect to the defense that may be most effective.

You should select a type of offense which will conform to the ability of your material and have an effective operating plan against specific and collective styles of team defense you may meet. No one experienced teacher of basketball may say, "This is the only system." We are compelled to have an open mind and sometimes adapt our convictions to material and competition.

FAST-BREAK

In the discussion of essentials of offense, it is pointed out that a fast break should be a part of the offensive system. In the development of a fast break, it is quite necessary to have the players distinguish between a fast-break opportunity and the lack of this opportunity. In the latter case, they should bring the ball up slowly. In order to have a fast-break opportunity, the players must realize quickly the advantages of a fast break; that is, when they may be able to get two offensive players against one defensive player, or three against two, or four against three. In trying for such situations, players are apt to make mistakes, and the coach may

defeat his own purpose by "second guessing" on players who make mistakes. In any fast break, these mistakes are apt to happen, and it is a question of percentage of opportunities during the progress of the game.

Some coaches believe that in order to eliminate these possible mistakes, the ball should be brought up slowly, and set formations of various types be used entirely. This is a matter of opinion. From my experience, I have learned that opportunities for 2-and-1, 3-and-2 and 4-and-3 situations are overlooked. If players try for these opportunities, they will find them. If the ball is brought up slowly and a definite plan of attack used, a number of shots may be obtained outside of the foul circle, but many similar shots may be obtained by use of the fast break.

Whether a fast break is successful depends entirely upon the habits developed by the offensive team using it, and upon those members of the defensive team that may or may not be trained in fast-break habits. The players of the opposition may fully realize that a fast break is to be used against them, but it is a question of whether their daily practice has prepared them for a real fast break. No fast break is efficient unless the players are well drilled in the habit of looking for a fast-break opportunity when they first secure possession of the ball off the defensive basket; that is, guards and forwards as well must be trained, when they get a rebound from the defensive basket, to look first for this opportunity and cock the arm for a pass.

A fast break starts with possession of the ball at the defensive basket. Many opportunities are lost because players, after recovering the ball, bounce it once or twice toward the side of the court. Accordingly, it is necessary to drill players to be able to pivot quickly and make a hook pass to start the fast break.

Aside from possession of the ball off the bank, fast-break opportunities are presented on fumbled balls and intercepted passes. It should be drilled into players, when these

situations arise, to pass ahead rapidly, or drive fast into offensive territory with a dribble. The fast break offense requires a great deal of drilling. In the drills discussed in the following paragraphs, defensive men are not started underneath the basket with the offensive players shown in the diagrams until after the essential habits have been developed in the offensive players.

LONG PASS FAST-BREAK

The following discussion shows the development of the long-pass and short-pass cross combination of the fast break. In using a long pass as an offensive weapon in the fast break, we must take into consideration our competition, remembering that it is of college and high school type and not of the expert, professional type with a high degree of accuracy.

In your competition and mine, the passing is not always accurate, nor the basket shooting perfect. Our competition is such that the average basket shooting is between twenty and forty percent; that is, the opposing players make approximately one basket in four trials (1920's & 1930's). So if they miss, and we receive the ball off the backboard, providing we are well drilled in a fast-break and long pass, we may succeed with one long pass in making the short set-up shot. With this realization, we lay our center back in offensive territory, expecting him to receive a long pass from one of his teammates. Success in this strategy will force one of the opponents to stay with the center; as a result, the opposition's offense will contain only four with whom our four defensive men have to contend.

The long pass is very similar to the punt in football. One long pass from the defensive basket into scoring territory and possession by our center takes the ball from the dangerous territory of the opponents into our scoring territory immediately. Theoretically, if five men of the offense take the ball up the floor on a fast break against our four men, they should retain possession until they have scored; but, in actual practice,

LESSONS FROM THIS LEGEND...

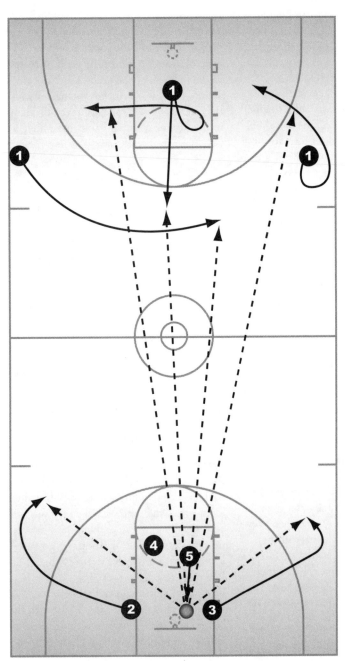

Lambert 1.0

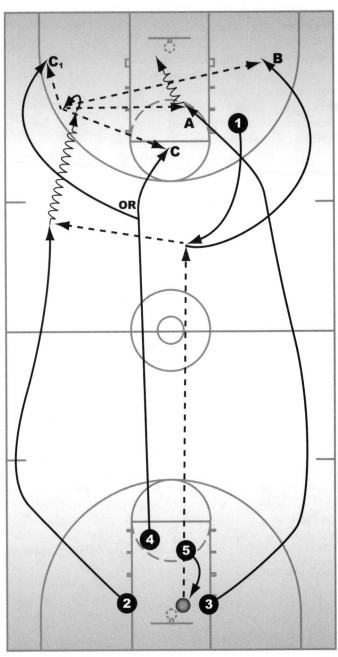

Lambert 1.1

when they do not score, and we obtain possession and make one long pass to our center under the basket, they are forced to drop a fifth man back with the center.

In **Diagram 1.0,** we have a simple illustration of a play in which, after a shot is taken by the opponents, No. 5, presumably a big guard and trained in rebound shots and the hook pass, passes down the floor to No. 1,

the center, in one of the possible positions shown; that is, No. 1 may be any position indicated. With practice, No. 1 learns to fake and cross-over and break from the endline or sideline, timing himself with the back guard to receive the pass. This requires much practice, and it is essential that the center time himself with the man taking the ball from the bank. The diagram also

shows, aside from the long pass to the center in offensive territory, the possible passes to forward No. 3, forward No. 2, and floor guard No.4, who in turn upon receiving the ball should look through and pass through to No. 1 and run. It is to be understood from this diagram that 3, 4, or 2 may take the ball off the bank and react to the situation the same as 5.

LESSONS FROM THIS LEGEND...

Authors' Note: In this early version of the fast break, it relied completely on the long pass to the center, eventually evolving into the more common short pass outlets to 2 or 3.

In **Diagram1.1** we have an illustration of a play in which No. 1 has broken out to a position outside of the foul circle to receive a pass from No. 5. No. 3 and No. 2, also expecting a pass from 5, have broken to the sidelines. From the sidelines, when they see that 5 has control of the ball, they run straight down the floor, because traveling the straight line is the quickest way in which to get into offensive territory. With No. 1 having control of the ball, they may have a possible 2-on-1 or 3-on-2 situation.

The illustration shows that the center, No. 1, is successful in meeting the pass from 5. He passes to 2, running rapidly into offensive territory. No. 2, in turn, dribbles for the basket, but is shut off by X1, who originally was guarding 1, and is forced to stop and turn. 3, seeing the pass from 1 to 2, watches for the stop, and turns and crosses to receive a pass from 2 at A. 1, after the pass to 2, breaks to the outside of the court opposite the pass, ready to feed in to receive a pass from 2 at B. No.4, the floor guard, feeds in as the fourth man on offense, ready to take a pass from 2 at position C or C1.

Diagram 1.2 shows a long pass play from No. 5 to No.1, in which X1 has followed 1 out, thinking to intercept the pass. 1, having received the pass, is forced to land and pivot. 3 and 2, seeing this slight delay, cross in front of 1, so that 1 may pass to either 2 or 3. The diagram shows a pass from 1 to 2, who dribbles. If 2 is forced to stop, 3 is in position to cross to meet a pass; also 1, having taken the opposite side from 2, who received the pass from him, is in position to feed in and around the basket and receive a pass from 2. 4, the floor guard, breaking down the middle of the floor behind the ball, is in position to receive passes from 2 at either position A or A₁.

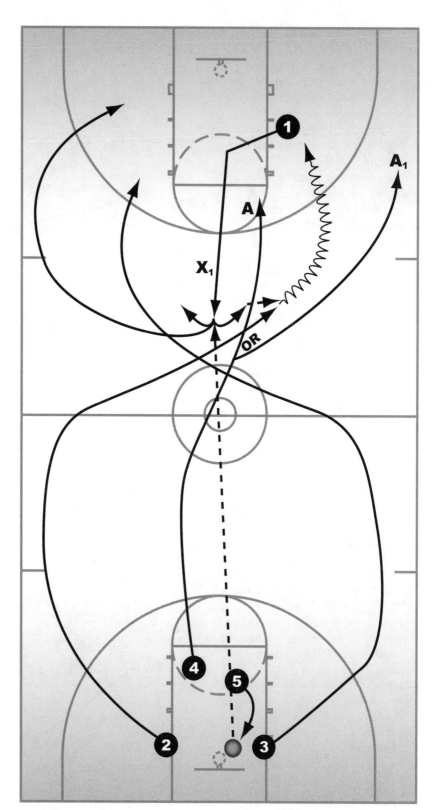

Lambert 1.2

LESSONS FROM THIS LEGEND...

SHORT PASS CROSSING

In the drill on the fast break shown in **Diagram 1.3**, a simple illustration is given of a pass from the back guard to the forward to the other forward to the center. In the drill, forwards 2 and 3 are placed under the basket, with floor guard 4 on the foul circle and back guard 5 on the foul line. 4 takes a shot at the basket, and, when he misses, 5 follows the shot and hook passes out to 3, who breaks first to the sideline and then from the sideline to take the pass. Forward 2, also expecting a pass, does as 3 does.

The reason for breaking first to the sideline and then away from the sideline is that breaking from the sideline to receive a pass is a principle of offense which gives a player the possibility of putting his body between any defensive man who may be ready to intercept the pass.

When 3 receives a pass in a fast break, his first reaction should be to look through and pass to 1 if possible. The fast break is better if 3 throws the ball to 1 at once and runs to get a possible 2-on-1 situation with him, than if he dribbles or passes to 2. Passing to 2, then, is merely optional. In this drill, having looked through to see if he can pass to 1, 3 passes to 2. 2 should, in turn, see if he can pass rapidly on through to 1 and then run. The diagram assumes that 2 dribbles toward the basket and is forced to stop and turn or hook pass to 1, who is breaking from the position he took on the sideline when the first pass went to 3. 1, it is understood, went to the side of the floor opposite that from which the first pass was thrown.

In **Diagram 1.4,** we have the pass going from forward to forward to floor guard to center. 4 takes a shot at the basket; 5 follows for the rebound and hook passes to 3, who, in turn, passes to 2. 2 dribbles and is forced to stop and turn. Now, the floor guard, 4, comes through as a trailer and receives a pass from 2 on the outside at position A, or through the middle at position B. 4 dribbles for the basket and is forced to make a pass to 1, using a stop jump or a hook pass.

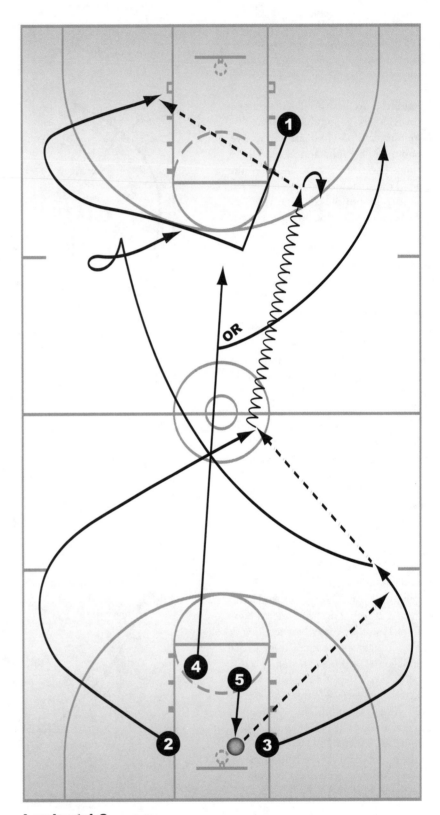

Lambert 1.3

LESSONS FROM THIS LEGEND...

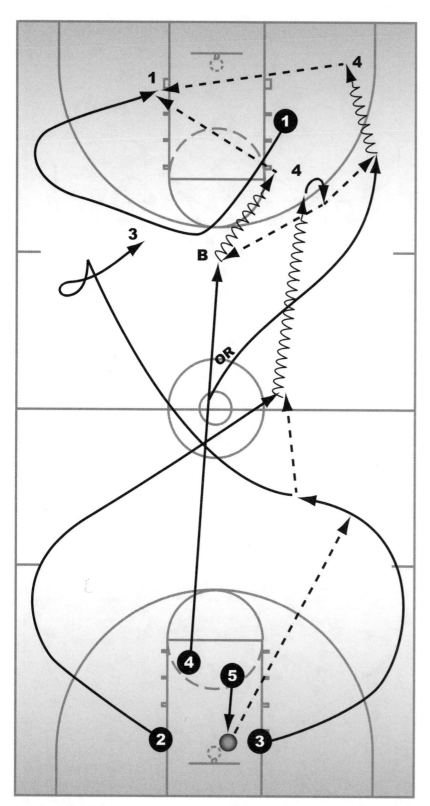

Lambert 1.4

Authors' Note: During this early era of basket-ball, the "jump/quick stop" and pivot was commonly used in the fast break and regular offense by ballhandlers.

PRINCIPLE OF CROSSING

We see in **Diagram 1.4** that 3 crosses the floor following his pass. The assumption here is that 3 passes to 2 because he is stopped by a defensive player and cannot pass on through to 1. If 3, while in the act of crossing the floor, is stopped by a guard on the inside of him (that is, between him and the basket), he puts the guard on the outside of him by pivoting so that he is between the guard and the basket. This action of 3 illustrates the principles of crossing.

Keep in mind that the action is rapid. The guard must drop in behind 3 in order to get between 3 and the basket again. With the same relative speeds of 3 and the guard who picks him up, 3 may gain the advantage at any point in the crossing to drive straight ahead.

In **Diagram 1.5**, we assume that as 3 crosses the court, he watched 2, who has the ball for a time but who may be forced to stop. We also assume that the defensive man taking 3 has been able to get between him and the basket; so we see in the diagram that 3 uses a pivot with the inside foot, or a change of direction turn, in order to get between the guard and the ball. He crosses again and may receive a pass from 2. This change of direction or pivot footwork may allow the guard to break so that 3 may be able to receive a pass from 2. Running in a semi-circle will never get such a break for 3. If 3 is successful in losing his guard, whether he receives a pass from 2 or not, he will carry the defense in the direction of 2 so that the floor guard, 4, may be able to receive a pass at B.

In the drill shown in **Diagram 1.5** we have a pass from back guard 5 to forward 3 to forward 2 to forward 3 to floor guard 4 to center 1. It is assumed that forward 2 has been forced to stop and turn and pass back to 3, who has crossed and executed the footwork

179

LESSONS FROM THIS LEGEND...

described in the preceding drill, and who, in turn, is forced to stop and turn and pass back to 4 at B with a hook pass. 4, driving in with a dribble toward the basket and faking a shot, passes to 1, who is breaking from the sideline. As an alternative, 4 may take the outside of the floor to receive a pass from 3 at A.

In **Diagrams 1.3, 1.4 and 1.5**, both forwards, the floor guard and the center are drilled so that they respond to a pass from the bank by 5 to forward 3.

In developing the execution of the floorwork and passing necessary for this fast break, the coach may call out "forward to forward to center"; "forward to forward to floor guard to center"; "forward to forward to forward to floor guard to center." By the combination of these drills, habit is so developed in players that they respond rapidly to the passes, or the positions from which their teammates are coming to meet passes, or are breaking in to the basket to receive them.

This short-pass crossing offense, combined with the long pass, gives a fast-break system of offense, which, of necessity, is based entirely upon habit. No fast break is efficient unless the players respond rapidly to the habits formed. The diagrams presented here show the first pass going to forward 3. Similar diagrams apply when the first pass goes to forward 2.

The drill shown in **Diagram 1.6** sums up the possibilities of passes when the ball is first received by 3. 3 may pass directly through to 1 at A. He may pass to 2, who dribbles until he is forced to stop, and who, in turn, may pass to 1 at B, to 3 at C, or to 4 at D or E. 3, having received the ball from 2 at C, may pass to 4 at F, or 1 at G. 4, having received a pass from 3 at F, may pass to 1, who is cutting in under the basket.

In all of these drills, 1 has been shown breaking out from underneath the basket to receive passes; this has been for convenience in the diagram. As shown in the diagram for the long pass, 1 may be in any position

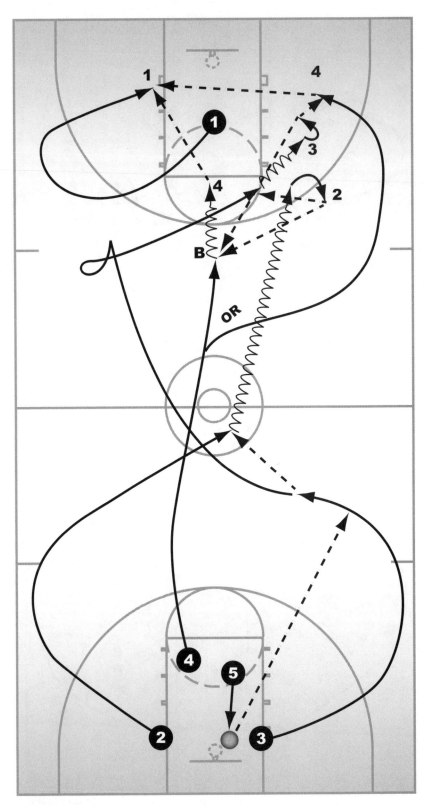

Lambert 1.5

LESSONS FROM THIS LEGEND...

at that end of the floor, breaking from the sidelines or endline to a point around the foul circle. 1, when he takes the side of the court opposite that to which the first pass goes, is careful not to wander in underneath the basket. He sticks to the sideline and then breaks fast from the sideline to receive a pass when the opportunity arises.

Having practiced the drills for a long-pass and short-pass cross with their various possibilities, the coach will find that the next step in the development of the fast break is to combine them. Now, the back guard, floor guard or forwards, in taking the ball on rebound from the bank, are given the option of passing to any teammate. The center is laid back in offensive territory. A guard is put with him to give him practice in faking and timing himself to break and expect a pass when his team comes into possession of the ball.

Upon possession of the ball by any man on the team, all of the other offensive men are expecting the pass and likewise are getting into position to receive the ball. If the back guard should take the ball off the bank, he may then pass long to the center, to either forward breaking from the sideline, or to the floor guard. The fast-break habits developed by the foregoing drills should then be carried out at the discretion of the players.

The assumption is now that the players have formed habits of getting the ball into scoring territory rapidly, and the drilling they have had has taught them to know where teammates are coming from to receive passes. Suppose two forwards are caught on defense on the same side of the floor, and the pass goes to one if them. The floor guard, in this case, should cross and meet a pass and follow the same habits of crossing that the forwards have acquired. The other forward would then become the floor guard and act as he does in the fast break.

As soon as the players have acquired proper execution in passing and have learned to react properly to the situation, defensive

men are placed at the basket where the fast break is to start. A shot is taken by one of the players, and all try for possession of the ball on the rebound. If the team working on the offense gets possession, the men at once start their fast break and carry through until either a basket has been made, or they have lost control of the ball.

In trying for these fast breaks and knowing the value of possession of the ball, the players soon learn to distinguish between an actual fast-break opportunity and a situation in which they should keep possession of the ball and go into a set formation. The coach emphasizes speed, accuracy, and footwork. After a fumble occurs, the play stops and begins over. This impresses the players with the sin of fumbling.

Source

Lambert, Ward L. (1932). *Practical Basketball*. Chicago: Athletic Journal Publishing.

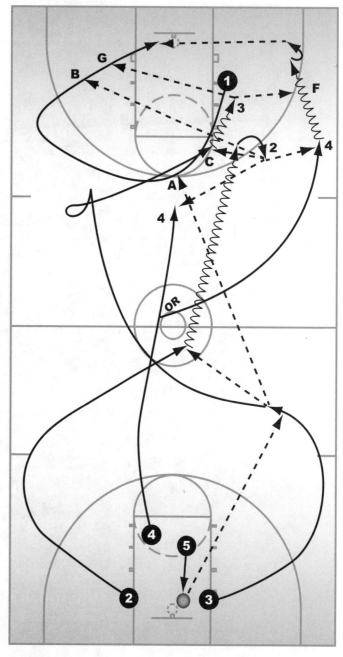

Lambert 1.6

LEGACY OF
Kenneth "Ken" Loeffler

- Developed an offensive system called "incentive basketball," which featured a continuity offense based on team play.

- Believed every player must be versatile and able to execute all the skills of the game.

- Directed LaSalle to the NIT championship in 1952 and the NCAA championship in 1954.

- Considered himself a basketball visionary and preached that the ball should be in the center of the court when initiating a play pattern.

- Believed the future of basketball was dictated on speed and quickness.

- Known for his outspokenness, flamboyance, and many talents (basketball coach, law professor, poet, musician, writer, baseball scout, telecaster, and dude ranch operator).

KENNETH "KEN" LOEFFLER

*"Balance is the most important requisite
in any offensive attack."*
— *Kenneth "Ken" Loeffler*

BIOGRAPHY

Born: April 14, 1902 in Beaver Falls, PA

Died: January 1, 1975

Inducted into the Naismith Hall of Fame in 1964

Kenneth "Ken" Loeffler was a flamboyant coach who had an affinity for bow ties and poetry. The scholarly Loeffler received a law degree from the University of Pittsburgh at the same time that he was coaching basketball at Geneva College. He led Geneva to two conference championships and seven consecutive winning seasons. Loeffler then went to Yale University, where he was the head basketball and baseball coach and assistant football coach. At Yale, Loeffler roomed with future President of the United States, Gerald R. Ford. After serving in the Army Air Corps during World War II, Loeffler coached professional basketball with the St. Louis Bombers and the Providence Steamrollers. He returned to the college-coaching ranks in 1949 at La Salle University and led the Explorers to six straight 20-win seasons. From 1952 to 1955, La Salle was a national power. The Explorers won the NIT title in 1952, and the NCAA championship in 1954, and finished second in the NCAA in 1955. Loeffler completed his 22-year coaching career by spending two years at Texas A&M, from which he retired in 1957. He authored a comprehensive coaching book entitled, *Ken Loeffler on Basketball*. Loeffler is enshrined into the Helms Foundation Hall and Fame and the Naismith Memorial Basketball Hall of Fame.

Kenneth "Ken" Loeffler...

Loeffler was one of the most colorful figures in basketball and a man of many talents. Besides being a masterful basketball coach, Loeffler was a law professor, poet, musician, writer, professional basketball player, dude ranch operator, baseball scout, and telecaster.

As a youth, Loeffler's ambition was to become a lawyer, so he attended Pittsburgh Law School at the same time he coached basketball at Geneva College. Upon graduation from law school in 1934, Loeffler was offered a position with the Federal Bureau of Investigation, but opted to coach the basketball team at Yale University.

Loeffler joined the Army Air Corps during World War II and was discharged in 1945 as a major. In 1946, a new professional basketball league was formed, and Loeffler was hired to coach the St. Louis Bombers. During the summer months, Loeffler operated a dude ranch in Wyoming and also worked for the New York Yankees in their try-out camps.

Loeffler coached at La Salle from 1949 to 1955 and led the Explorers to six-straight 20-plus win seasons. He spent two seasons at Texas A&M, before retiring from coaching in 1957.

Outspoken and opinionated, Loeffler always stated what he believed was the truth. When his statements created controversy, Loeffler responded "if speaking the truth makes me controversial, then I am that, because truth is so rarely heard in this world of mice. I've been criticized for sounding off, but I've never said anything I didn't believe." (Loeffler, 1955, pp. 2-4)

Regarding the coaching profession, Loeffler had these words, ""What should be a noble profession, the genuine influencing of young men toward the goal of living a life of sportsmanship in a needy world, has become a rat race to oblivion—a vicious cycle of wins and, if you fail to win enough, the sack. To me, there can be only one sensible goal for competitive sports: a fair field, no favorite, and may the best team win after it has been trained and schooled in the best techniques possible by the teacher-coach." (Loeffler, 1955, pp. 187-188)

Loeffler always possessed a sharp tongue and a quick wit. In 1951, Loeffler took La Salle University to Raleigh, North Carolina and lost a close contest to North Carolina State 76-74. Loeffler was in an uproar over what he considered was terrible officiating. He was convinced the officials had taken the game from his team and complained, "This is the biggest steal since the Louisiana Purchase." (Loeffler, 1955, p.2)

The flamboyant Loeffler loved the glory that surrounded his success. His detractors described him as arrogant and egotistical, but Loeffler said his attitude was one of supreme confidence and assurance.

Loeffler's tactical legacy was an offensive system that he called "incentive basketball," which featured a continuity offense based on team play. "Incentive basketball" required each player to execute every skill: screening, shooting, flash-pivot play, and rebounding. Loeffler described his system in the following words, "Each man is a balanced performer and equipped to execute all the skills of the game. This creates a greater incentive to master them. Every player is a king. He is no longer a supporting actor. He is just as important as the set pivot man" (Loeffler, 1955, p. 19). Loeffler's system helped La Salle win 145 out of 175 games during a six-year period. This included the NIT championship in 1952 and the NCAA championship in 1954.

All-American Tom Gola credited Loeffler and his offensive system for helping him become a complete player. "At La Salle, we played a five-man weave," Gola said. "Anybody could bring the ball up, and we all had places to go on the court. We had nobody sitting in the pivot, and the middle was always open to drives if you got by your man. So, that's how I learned how to handle the basketball, how to shoot from the outside and eventually how to play guard for ten years in the NBA." (Gutman, 1989, p. 94)

Loeffler's system was in direct contrast to the offenses that became popular due to the influence of tall players, such as George Mikan and Bob Kurland. He vehemently opposed an offense that was designed for a tall player to do the majority of the scoring, while the other players served only in support roles.

The cerebral Loeffler considered himself a basketball visionary. He believed the future of basketball was dictated on speed and quickness. Loeffler also predicted that he was "fifteen years ahead of the game," with his theory that the ball should be in the center of the court when initiating a play pattern. In such a position, a point guard was able to pass to either forward in order to start his continuity offense.

Loeffler, a man who loved bow ties and poetry, struggled throughout his career with physical ailments. He suffered from bleeding ulcers, pneumonia, phlebitis, and a permanently numb leg that occurred when trying to break a horse on his dude ranch. In the 1954 NCAA title game, Loeffler kept a bottle of milk and blue ulcer pills alongside the bench. Loeffler always claimed that he'd rather die on the bench than in a hospital bed. (Loeffler, 1955, p. 10)

SOURCE

Gutman, Bill. (1989). *The Pictorial History of College Basketball.* New York: Gallery Books.

Loeffler, Ken. (1955). *Ken Loeffler on Basketball.* Englewood Cliffs, NJ: Prentice-Hall.

LESSONS FROM THIS LEGEND...

THE SCREEN-WEAVE OFFENSE

By Ken Loeffler

I am not a proponent of the set-play style of offense. A set-play offense alone is easily defended. In addition, the set-play offense leads you to the use of specialists, like the pivot. It takes away, at least from my point of view, the genuine balanced team play. I believe set plays revolving around any one or two men tend to take the interest of the game away from the other men on the team. Of course, this hits on the very theme of this advanced discussion of basketball techniques that I call "incentive basketball." Every player becomes a threat to score in the "incentive-basketball" style of play.

A CONTINUITY OFFENSE NEVER ALLOWS THE DEFENSE TO REST

Any type of basketball pattern that involves the use of set plays only and is dependent entirely on the resetting of these plays is lacking in offensive balance. When the set plays fail and have to be re-executed, the defense has the opportunity to recover and reset to defend. The goal is to keep the defense confused and unsettled. You can accomplish this only by using a continuity offense, one that never allows the defense to think, let alone rest.

A set-play pattern defeats the very idea of the offense, which is to catch the defense out of position and off balance. You lose this opportunity with a set-pattern system. On the other hand, if you use a continuity series like the screen-weave, the defense has no chance to stop and regroup. Before they recover from the first maneuver, a second one is in process. The continuity offense keeps both the offense and the defense alive. It makes for a much more interesting game for the spectators and develops the thought processes of the players.

SET PATTERNS AS A SUPPLEMENT TO YOUR CONTINUITY OFFENSE

Lest I mislead you, let me say that set patterns are a necessary part of basketball, as is the fast break. But, they should be used as a supplement to continuity offensive patterns. Set patterns are better for young, inexperienced players who are just mastering the fundamentals of passing, dribbling, shooting, cutting, reversing, and screening. Set plays are often introduced to make them team conscious as an initial step toward a continuity offense. Set plays are used to defeat defensive blocks that have been thrown up to defeat the continuity offense. Remember that set patterns supplement the moving pattern offense in order to keep the defense in a constant state of flux. They help to confuse the defense, which is the primary object of any offensive pattern.

SCREEN-WEAVE PATTERN

The screen-weave flash-pivot pattern is a compromise between the set play and random patterns. Remember that your set-play pattern is weak because it allows the defense to readjust and recover after one play has been operated. The random offense fails to coordinate the thinking and maneuvering of the five men on the court. I believe the screen-weave pattern is a compromise between the latter two methods of offense.

Balance is the most important requisite in any attack. A team must have its players situated on the court so as to spread the defense and must allow itself ample space to maneuver the offense. An offense that positions four men on the same side of the court is unbalanced. It defeats itself by con-

gesting the area in which it wants to operate. In effect, by jamming one section of the court, the offense limits its own ability to move in several directions.

Whether you use a five-man, four-man, or three-man weave pattern, the ball must be localized as close to the center of the court as possible. It is logical to assume that a greater defensive burden is placed on your opponent if you force him to defend from both sides of the court, rather than from only one. My teams start the weave from a semi-circle, with two men spread almost to the corners on each side of the center man, who has the ball. From this pattern, we have our choice of a number of screens, give-and-go plays, set shots, pivot plays, etc.

The type of screen-weave pattern to be employed depends on four factors: 1) the material available; 2) defensive strength and personnel of the opponent; 3) the amount of time to play, which brings into consideration the physical condition of your players and the opponent; and 4) the personal foul count on your opponents and the score of the game (if you have several opponents with four fouls, it might be well to use a pattern that could force these players to foul out).

If all five players are able to execute the fundamentals of the screen-weave pattern, use the five-man pattern. On the other hand, if one of your players is unable to work the weave to shoot from the outside, or to screen, but is adept at rebounding and corner shooting, the weave should be limited to four players. If you have two players unsuited to the weave pattern, they should be used inside to flash pivot, corner shoot, and rebound. No matter if you use the five-man, four-man, or three-man pattern, the

LESSONS FROM THIS LEGEND...

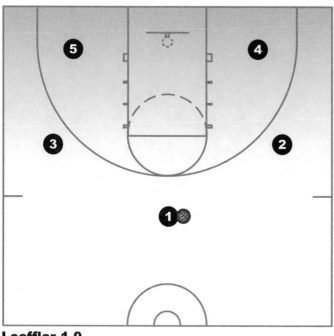

Loeffler 1.0

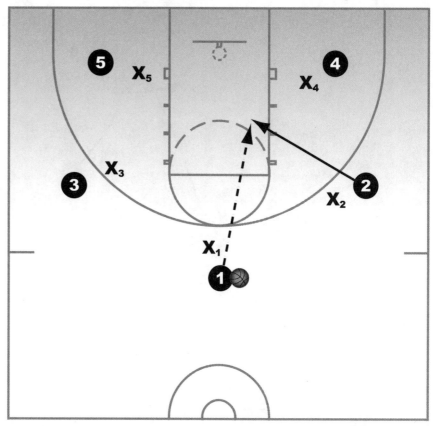

Loeffler 1.1

middle of the floor must be kept open, because it creates driving opportunities. This is the basis of all incentive basketball.

OPTIONS IN THE SCREEN-WEAVE PATTERN

1. Initial Alignment

The screen-weave offense has five perimeter players (see **Diagram 1.0**).

2. Pass and Screen on the Ball

O1 passes to O2 and sets a screen on X2. O1 then moves and screens for O4. O4 uses a head fake and sets up his defender prior to O1's screen (see **Diagram 1.1**).

3. Back Door Cut by O2

When X2 is denying the pass from O1 to O2, O2 should break toward the basket, looking for a pass (see **Diagram 1.2**).

4. Back Door Cut by O1

O1 passes to O2. X1 anticipates the screen on X2 and overplays. O1 reads his defender and breaks to the basket (see **Diagram 1.4**).

Loeffler 1.2

LESSONS FROM THIS LEGEND...

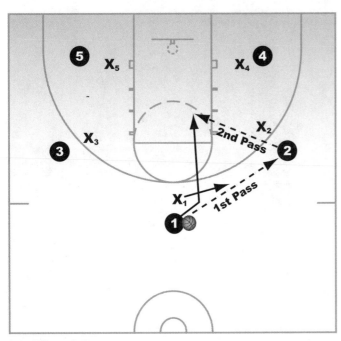

Loeffler 1.3

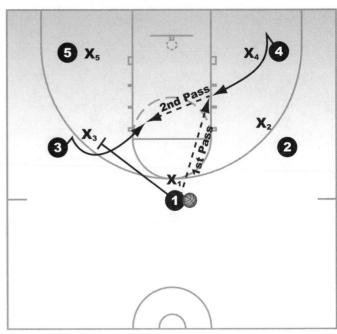

Loeffler 1.4

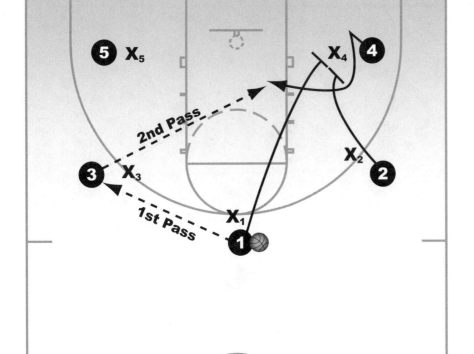

Loeffler 1.5

5. Flash Pivot by O4

O1 passes to O4 in the post and screens for O3. O3 comes off the screen and looks for a pass from O4 (see **Diagram 1.4**).

6. Pass to the Weakside and Double Screen

O1 passes to O3. O1 and O2 set a double screen for O4 (see **Diagram 1.5**).

KEY TEACHING POINTS IN THE SCREEN-WEAVE PATTERN

In our screen-weave pattern, the ball is passed, half-passed, or handed off to a teammate just before the passer moves toward his teammate's opponent to set a screen. The player who receives the ball thus is able to go in two directions. This pass is very important in the screen attack. In making the pass, the passer should never look at his teammate, but rather at his teammate's defensive opponent, whom the passer will attempt to screen after passing the ball.

LESSONS FROM THIS LEGEND...

The ballhandler must be able to change his mind at the last moment. Besides passing to a forward, the point guard has the option of throwing a bounce pass to the corner pivot player, or driving to the basket if the opening presents itself. When driving to the basket, most young high school prospects are unbelievably surprised to learn that, with the proper shooting fake prior to their drive, they can go to the basket from a distance of twenty feet in one dribble. In our screen-weave pattern, most of the maneuvering is done with either one or two dribbles. If the dribble is employed, it should be started from the triple-threat position.

The ability of the player to maneuver without the ball is the mark of a great basketball player. Jim Pollard, George Mikan, Bob Cousy, and Tom Gola owe much of their greatness to this ability.

However, teaching the skill of "moving without the ball" is a real problem for the college coach. The reason is that most high school stars become stars with the ball. They achieve publicity through their shooting, passing, dribbling, or rebounding. But in college they are told there is another road to greatness, and it's hard for them to believe it. They must now, at the college level, relate their movements to those of their teammates, whether they have the ball or not.

The man without the ball should be head faking his opponent to: 1) set him up for screening situations; 2) acquire a backboard rebounding advantage; 3) acquire a temporary pivot position; and 4) acquire cutting and reversing positions.

Dribbling, although it appears sensational and serves a purpose when used properly and not to excess, is not so dominant a part of basketball as most fans think it is. The reason for this is that too much dribbling promotes individualism. And individualism has a bad psychological effect on the rest of a team. Most players resent a dribbler who shows off. They feel he is hogging the ball. So, they don't bother to try to maneuver without the ball. They feel the dribbler is so occupied with his dribbling that they will not be seen anyway if they free themselves to receive a pass. A dribble, therefore, should be used only in cases of emergency such as: 1) to prevent traveling with the ball; 2) to aid in taking a better screening or passing position; 3) and to drive to the basket for a lay-up shot. In our screen-weave offensive pattern, particularly in the frontcourt, most of the maneuvering is done with the aid and use of a single dribble or, at the most, two dribbles.

SUMMARY

We normally start the game with the five-man screen-weave pattern and then adjust into either the four-man, or three-man pattern. The middle is always kept open to provide driving opportunities. Should you find a weak defender, the weave would have to be adjusted to take advantage of that weakness. An important theory in basketball is that a superior offensive player will continually beat a weaker defender. Many games are won with just this theory.

When using the screen-weave offense, all players, except the flash pivot, must completely face the basket. They do this in order to be a constant offensive threat. This is probably the most difficult thing to teach in the screen-weave pattern of play. But once taught, each player remains a constant threat and an ever-ready help to your key player, who cannot be double-teamed. If one of your players allows his defensive opponent to double-team, he defeats the system. Part of Tom Gola's greatness was enhanced by the fact that his teammates, Charley Singley, Charley Greenberg, Alonzo Lewis, Fran O'Malley, Frank Blatcher, and Bob Maples, were all constant threats.

SOURCE

Loeffler, Ken. (1955). *Ken Loeffler on Basketball*. Prentice-Hall, Inc.: Englewood Cliffs, New Jersey.

LEGACY OF
Frank McGuire

- First coach in basketball history to lead two different universities to the NCAA Finals.

- Compiled an overall 550-235 record and led his teams to 15 postseason appearances (8 NCAA tournaments and 7 NITs).

- Led North Carolina past Wilt Chamberlain and the University of Kansas in triple overtime to win the 1957 National Championship.

- Believed the best basketball players in the nation came from New York City and established a recruiting pipeline known as "The Underground Railroad."

- Charismatic, confidant coach who appeared to have stepped out of the pages of *Esquire*.

- Known as a master psychologist and motivator.

- Believed a good team could only become a great team by playing top-ranked opponents under adverse conditions on the road.

FRANK McGUIRE

"The reason I recruit New York players is because they have to be quick in order to dodge the eighteen thousand cabs that run around New York."
— *Frank McGuire*

BIOGRAPHY

Born: November 8, 1916 in New York, NY

Died: November 11, 1994

Inducted into the Naismith Basketball Hall of Fame in 1977

Frank McGuire was the first basketball coach in history to win 100 games at three different universities, and also was the first coach to lead two different universities to the Final Four. During his 31-year coaching career, McGuire coached at St. John's (1948-1952), North Carolina (1953-1961), and South Carolina (1964-1980). In the 1952 NCAA Tournament, McGuire led St. John's to an upset win over top-ranked Kentucky and advanced to the NCAA Finals before being stopped by Kansas. In 1957, McGuire led North Carolina to the NCAA title and one of the greatest upsets in college basketball, when the Tar Heels beat the Wilt Chamberlain-led Kansas Jayhawks, in triple overtime. McGuire compiled a 550-235 career record and guided his teams to 15 postseason tournament appearances (8 NCAA tournaments and 7 NIT tournaments). McGuire was named National Coach of the Year in 1952 (St. John's), 1957 (North Carolina), and 1970 (South Carolina). South Carolina honored McGuire by renaming their coliseum the Frank McGuire Arena in 1977. Frank started his coaching career at St. Xavier (NY) High School, where he compiled an eleven-year record of 126-39. McGuire also coached Philadelphia in the NBA in 1962 and led the Warriors to the Eastern Conference Finals. McGuire is enshrined into the St. John's, North Carolina, South Carolina, and the Naismith Memorial Basketball Halls of Fame.

Frank McGuire...

Frank McGuire grew up in Manhattan's Greenwich Village, the 13th child of a New York City policeman. As a youngster, McGuire played basketball morning, noon, and night in New York's Lower West Side. He attended St. Xavier Prep in New York, a Jesuit military school, where he captained the football, basketball, and baseball teams.

McGuire attended St. John's University and received a Bachelor of Science degree in 1936. At St. John's, he was a four-year letterman in basketball and baseball, serving as captain of both sports his senior year. After graduation, McGuire coached eleven seasons at St. Xavier Prep and compiled a 126-39 record. In a game against St. Cecilia in Englewood, NJ, he made the reporter from the St. Xavier student newspaper sit at the scorer's table and watch the clock. McGuire was cautious of any home team's timekeeper, even when the St. Cecilia basketball coach that night was also its football coach, the legendary Vince Lombardi.

McGuire played professional basketball from 1936-1938 in the American Basketball League and was selected as the League's best defensive player.

From 1948 to 1952, McGuire was the head coach at St. John's University and led his teams to an impressive 103-35 record. At St. John's, he coached the brother combination and future Hall of Famers Dick McGuire and Al McGuire. *(Authors' Note: Dick and Al were no relation to Frank).* In 1952, St. John's upset defending national champion and number-one ranked Kentucky in the NCAA East Regional. Earlier that season, Kentucky had humiliated St. John's 81-40. St. John's beat number two-ranked Illinois 61-59 in the semi-finals, and then lost to Kansas in the NCAA title game. McGuire's teams played a rugged, physical style of play, and Kansas's legendary coach "Phog" Allen compared McGuire's players to "vicious alley-cats" (Mayer, 1952). At St. John's, McGuire also coached the baseball team, and his teams won more than 77 percent of their games. Hall of Fame coach Lou Carnesecca was a second baseman on McGuire's baseball team that played in the 1949 College World Series.

In 1953, McGuire accepted the challenge of building the basketball program at the University of North Carolina. He was attracted to Chapel Hill because he was stationed there during World War II and believed it would be a great location to raise his family. McGuire immediately changed the fortunes of Tar Heel basketball. He insisted on doing things the right way and refused to accept second-class citizenship for his basketball program. His teams had the sharpest uniforms, the best equipment, and ate at the finest restaurants. McGuire dressed exquisitely for games and insisted that his staff always came to work in coats and ties. His charisma and winning ways made basketball the top sport at UNC.

His first basketball challenge was to beat the powerful teams at North Carolina State coached by Everett Case. In McGuire's initial game against their archrival, the Tar Heels ended a 14-game losing streak with a 70-69 victory over the Wolfpack. McGuire's philosophy was simple: "Recruit the best players." And that he did. McGuire went back to his hometown contacts and developed what was referred to as "The Underground Railroad," a recruiting pipeline from the playgrounds of New York City to Chapel Hill. McGuire emphatically announced to his rivals, "New York is my personal territory. Duke can scout in Philadelphia, and North Carolina State can have the whole country. But if anybody wants to move into New York, they need a passport from me."

McGuire believed the best basketball players in the nation came from New York City. He felt that he had better rapport with players from New York and also thought they were quicker and tougher than players from other places. McGuire would comically say, "The reason I recruit New York players is because they have to be quick in order to dodge the eighteen thousand cabs that run around New York." (Smith, 2002)

McGuire loved New York so much that he had a provision in his contract that allowed him to spend every summer at his beautiful home on Greenwood Lake, located on the border of New York and New Jersey.

McGuire helped popularize the game of basketball in the South by bringing in his "New York" style of play. "To play our kind of basketball," said McGuire, "you've got to have discipline above everything else. Basically, we play the same kind of game that I was born to, that I learned from Buck Freeman at St. John's. It's the New York, the metropolitan kind of game that concentrates on controlling the ball above everything else. One way of explaining it is to say that on offense, we've got five forwards, and on defense, we have five guards. We cherish the ball. We treat it like a gold piece. We take only the good shots and try to teach every boy to know his good shot." (Morris, 1988)

The 1957 North Carolina team, led by five starters from New York, won 32 straight games, including the triple-overtime victory over Wilt Chamberlain's University of Kansas team for the national championship. Chamberlain scored a game-high 23 points and accounted for half of his team's rebounds, but North Carolina had four players in double figures and won the rebounding war 42-28 in the 54-53 victory.

Before the championship game, McGuire talked only about Chamberlain. He said North Carolina didn't have a chance unless his entire team defended Wilt at all times. McGuire put three men around Chamberlain everywhere he went. When a shot went up, there would be one man in front and one on either side of him.

The championship game started with one of the most unforgettable sights in Final Four history. McGuire decided to challenge Wilt Chamberlain's pride instead of his muscle and sent his smallest starter, 5-foot 10-inches guard Tommy Kearns, to jump against the 7-foot center. "I told him if he jumped high enough," said McGuire, "he might reach Wilt's stomach" (Gergen, 1987). The move, designed to distract the Kansas star, brought smiles to the faces of the North Carolina players. The Tar Heels went on to shoot 65 percent from the field during the first half, while Kansas made only 27 percent of its attempts.

The night before the championship game, North Carolina beat Michigan State in triple overtime. Michigan State led the Tar Heels by two points with eight seconds remaining in the second overtime. Johnny Green of Michigan State was at the free-throw line shooting one-and-one. His shot bounced off the rim into the hands of North Carolina's Pete Brennan, who dribbled the length of the court and made the lay-up to send the game into the third overtime. The Tar Heels outlasted Michigan State by the score of 74-70.

For nine seasons, McGuire's North Carolina squads compiled a record of 164-58. From 1956 to 1961, McGuire's teams won 85 percent of their Atlantic Coast Conference games and captured four regular season ACC championships.

In 1962, McGuire coached the Philadelphia Warriors in the NBA, led by future Hall of Famers Wilt Chamberlain, Tom Gola, and Paul Arizin. McGuire's only season in the NBA was Wilt Chamberlain's best statistically. Wilt averaged 50.4 points and 25.7 rebounds per game, including his record setting 100-point game against the New York Knicks.

Chamberlain said, "Mr. McGuire told us he'd never coach anything but a happy team and that a happy team sticks together. He talked pretty blunt. He has a code of ethics and you know he's going to stand by those ethics, win or lose. You have to respect this man." (Anderson, 1994)

McGuire returned to the college coaching ranks in 1964 at the University of South Carolina and compiled a 283-142 record. He became the first coach in ACC history to win conference championships at two different schools.

McGuire was a master psychologist and motivator. He delegated responsibility to his assistants and sometimes would stand up in the bleachers during practice with a megaphone in his hand and supervise. It was McGuire's belief that all of basketball starts and ends with the players. It is the player who plays the game, not the coach. He wanted his players to play freely, without fear of making a mistake.

McGuire's basketball philosophy was reflected in his words: "I believe that it is my job to instill spirit and enthusiasm in my players, inspire them with the intense desire to be the best players in the world, and imbue them with a winning spirit. I believe that it is important to pour it on my players and make them work hard. I also believe that it is my job to so convince them that hard work pays great individual and team dividends that they will want to work hard. Along this line, I believe that a player remembers and respects most the coach who drills him hard and, through repetition, makes him do it right. Happy players are good players. Practices and games should be fun. Too much work and too little fun result in boredom and staleness. I like to plan my practices so they will not become monotonous. I keep the workouts hopping, shifting rapidly from one drill to another, accompanied by a lot of good-natured yelling and player enthusiasm." (McGuire, 1966)

A dapper dresser in his blue double-breasted suits and black alligator shoes, McGuire was just slightly larger than life. Dean Smith (2002) said, "Picture a guy with an easy charm and utter confidence who appeared to have stepped out of the pages of *Esquire* magazine, and that was Frank. His clothes hung on him just the way they did on the store mannequins, and his rich reddish-brown hair seemed to naturally fall into a swirl. He could have done anything he wanted, in any field. He looked like success."

SOURCE

Anderson, Dave. (1994, November 12). Missionary of New York Basketball. *New York Times.*

Gergen, Joe. (1987). *The Final Four.* St. Louis: The Sporting News

Mayer, Bill. (1952, March 27). Matchless Jawhawkers Subdue Powerful St. John's of Brooklyn. *Lawrence Journal-World.*

McGuire, Frank. (1966). *Team Basketball: Offense and Defense.* Englewood Cliffs, NJ: Prentice-Hall.

Morris, Ron. (1988). *ACC Basketball: An Illustrated History.* Chapel Hill, NC: Four Corners Press.

Smith, Dean. (2002). *A Coach's Life.* New York: Random House.

LESSONS FROM THIS LEGEND...

WEAVE, POST, AND PIVOT OFFENSE

By Frank McGuire

Our offense at North Carolina is a free-lance affair commonly identified as "Eastern Style" basketball. Developed by the old-time professional teams in the East and Midwest, it exploits all of the players' individual brilliance—enabling them to make maximum use of their clever ball-handling, dribbling, faking, feinting, and footwork.

By free-lance, we do not mean an offense that lets the players play "by ear." We provide them with a flexible pattern that permits them to exercise their individual initiative. In this basic pattern, our players set up in a loose 3-2 spread. As shown in **Diagram 1.0**, we place three players out near the center of the court and one man in each corner.

O1, our best passer, is the quarterback and playmaker; O2 and O3 are the perimeter shooters and drivers; and O4 and O5 are the corner men. The latter two must be able to set up pivot plays, as well as rebound strongly.

From this basic formation, we go into our weave. Developed at St. John's years ago by coach Buck Freeman, who is now my assistant at North Carolina, it is called "weave circulation" by some coaches and the "Figure 8" by others. The latter is a misnomer. It is not the Figure 8 invented by the great Dr. H.C. Carlson at Pittsburgh. After listening to Dr. Carlson at the All-American Basketball School conducted by Clair Bee the past summer, I can safely say there's little connection between our weave and the Figure 8.

As shown in **Diagram 1.1**, the playmaker, O1, starts the weave either to the left or

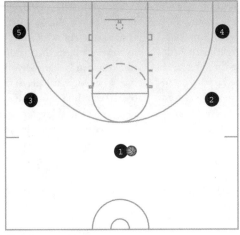

McGuire 1.0

right, and then continues on through with an inside moving screen. In the old days, the inside screen was called "picking off without contact."

Next, O2 who has received the ball from O1, passes to O3 and continues on to set an inside screen in that direction. O4 comes up from the corner and gets into the circulation by receiving the pass from O3. O4 then passes to O5, who has moved up from the opposite corner.

This is the basic weave from our "horseshoe" formation. Note that the order of the

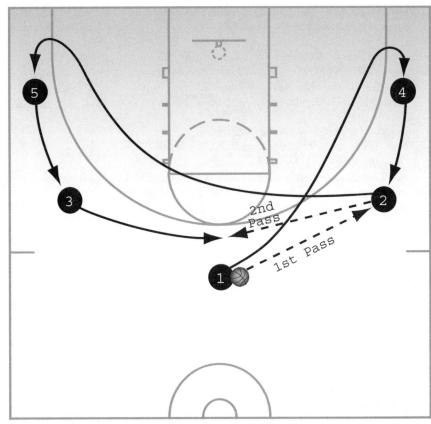

McGuire 1.1

LESSONS FROM THIS LEGEND...

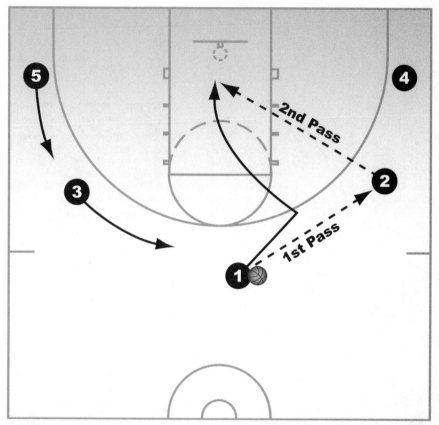

McGuire 1.2

ers know when to change from a full weave to a screening, perimeter-shooting game.

We have found that the weave offense is most effective against man-to-man defenses that do not properly slide and switch. These teams are constantly picking each other and running into one another. There's nothing more demoralizing than discovering they can't get out of each other's way.

Another outstanding advantage of this formation is that the center—the area immediately under the basket—is always open. This is very important for the cutters and drivers, as they can really move under when the center is open.

This isn't the case when you have a pivot player in the area. The defensive player guarding him can now switch to any free player driving to the basket. With the middle open, a good driver has only his defender to beat.

passes corresponds to the numbering of the players. In short, O1 passes to O2; O2 passes to O3; O3 passes to O4; and O4 passes to O5.

The ball is worked into the basket for the ultimate objective–a lay-up shot. If we do not get the ball into the basket, we start our weave over again, using the same principles.

Sometimes, a good change of direction will catch a defensive opponent flat-footed and enable our player to get inside for an easy lay-up. As shown in **Diagram 1.2,** it is a simple stunt—one of the outside players stopping quickly and cutting in the opposite direction.

From this weave, we can screen for our perimeter shooters. We find shooting over set screens very effective from this position (see **Diagram 1.3).** On long shots, the other players in the weave change positions in order to form a triangle for rebounding purposes. From constant practice, our play-

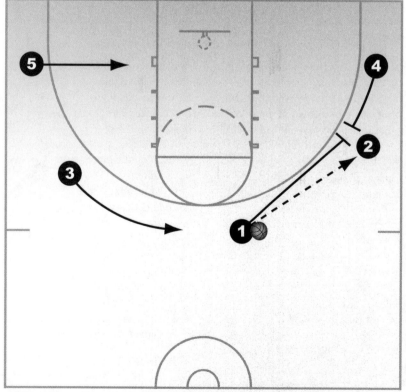

McGuire 1.3

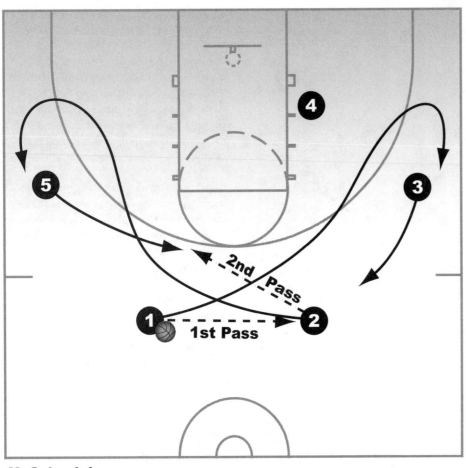

McGuire 1.4

the pivot man, who buttonhooks as the driver passes him. The pivot must always face the ball when the dribbler drives by him. This puts him in position for a return pass.

We also want our pivot man to feed or pass back to the player who originally gave him the ball, setting the outside man up for a perimeter shot.

Our pivot player is taught to keep moving in figure-8 fashion under the basket, going over to the weakside and then coming back to the strongside. With all the strong defenses being utilized against pivot players today, it's almost impossible to feed a stationary pivot. That's why we want our pivot player moving and getting into good position. **Diagram 1.5** shows a single-pivot triangle offense against a zone defense.

Our next variation in our attack is a post offense. A post player, according to our way of thinking, is a player away from the board or to the side or rear of the front court, with his back to the basket. This player may also be permanently stationed on the foul line.

After the weave has been going for a while, you can start springing a lot of good give-and-go plays. In fact, they work best from this 3-out and 2-in formation. Some of the teams that make effective use of give-and-go plays are: Duquesne under Dudey Moore, Dartmouth under Doggie Julian, City College of New York under Nat Holman, and Navy under Ben Carnevale.

To summarize what I have described so far, our weave offense starts from the center-open formation. This is considered part of our inside attack. It may then change to produce perimeter shooting opportunities over screens, plus give-and-go tactics with its hard cutting and driving.

The next phase of our attack is the single-pivot roll offense shown in **Diagram 1.4**. Whenever we throw our big man into a pivot on either side of the basket outside the

lane, it becomes his divine right to shoot. His teammates know this and feed him from the sides of the court.

We employ the pivot in various ways: (1) we can feed him for direct scoring; (2) cross-cut or scissors off him, feeding the first or second cutter whoever breaks loose; or (3) have our cutters or drivers break by him and note whether the pivot's guard switches.

If the defensive pivot does switch, the driver hooks a pass back to

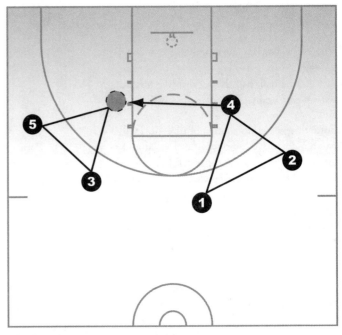

McGuire 1.5

We employ these post players in many ways, for example, (1) cross-cutting plays, (2) double-cross cutting plays, (3) single cuts in which the defensive players are run into the post, and (4) a great deal of optional plays that are developed by the players themselves in pre-season practice.

We alternate the single-pivot offense with the post offense to give versatility to our attack. Sometimes a good pivot player can add to his effectiveness by improving his post play on the foul line. This intensifies the defensive problem, since the man facing him will find it extremely hard to manipulate around a player who is good at both spots. The post player can also get off a variety of jump shots from the lane or foul line.

Nearly every college team uses some form of the fast break, and we're no exception. We try to organize our fast break from the well-known defensive triangle, as we feel this is the best way to control the boards. You must control the defensive board to have a good fast break.

Assuming that we get the rebound, we use a baseball pass out to the wing man on whatever side the ball comes off, and then immediately pass back to the middle man, who's the key player in our fast break.

Though we teach everyone to play the middle, we prefer to have our best dribbler or quarterback in that spot. This middle man has two options. One of these is the dribbling fast break, which means he dribbles as fast as he can to the foul line. If he's unopposed, he continues to the basket for a layup or jump shot. If he's picked up, he stops at the foul line and passes to either wing player. The latter runs in a straight line to the corner and then comes in to the basket at a right angle (see **Diagram 1.6**).

The other option on a fast break is the swift passing exchange, popularized by Ed Hickey at St. Louis University when he had Ed Macauley. The middle man in this fast-break pattern passes back and forth to the wing men until he reaches the foul line, where once more, he stops and either

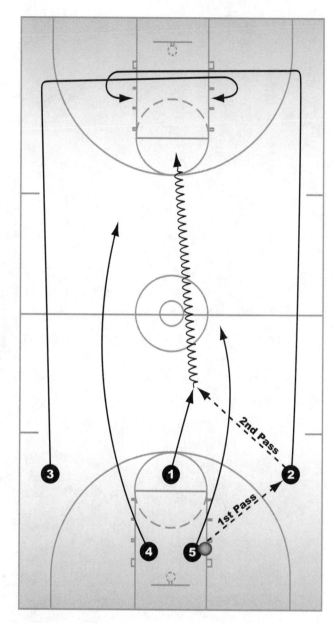

McGuire 1.6

shoots or passes to an open wing man. These wing men sometimes cross under the boards and buttonhook.

I have tried to give you a picture of our offensive strategies—the weave, single pivot, alternating pivot and post offense, and fast break. If you'll concentrate on these basic patterns within the framework of free-lance offense, you'll develop a sufficiently varied attack that will work well against any man-to-man defense.

SOURCE

McGuire, Frank. (1954). North Carolina's Weave, Post and Pivot. *1954-1955 Seal-O-San Basketball Coaches Digest*. Huntington, IN: Huntington Laboratories.

LEGACY OF
John "Johnny Mac" McLendon

- Pioneered integrated basketball and heightened awareness of basketball at predominately black institutions.

- Led Tennessee A&I (now Tennessee State) to three consecutive NAIA national championships (1957,58,59).

- Compiled a college-coaching record of 523-165 during his 25-year career.

- Studied under Dr. James Naismith at the University of Kansas.

- Became the first black head coach in the ABL with the Cleveland Pipers in 1961.

- Advocated a fast-break offense, and coached teams that always featured superior conditioning and pressure defense.

- Possessed exceptional knowledge of the game, and had an engaging personality that made him one of basketball's leading ambassadors.

- Namesake of the basketball arena at Cleveland State University.

JOHN "JOHNNY MAC" McLENDON

"Nils Desparandum, words I always heed;
My inspiration, prayer and creed;
Life's storms cannot my aspirations dim
For these are words I hear from him"
— John McClendon, Jr

BIOGRAPHY

Born: April 5, 1915 in Hiawatha, KS

Died: October 8, 1999

Inducted into Naismith Basketball Hall of Fame in 1979

John McLendon grew up in racially segregated Kansas in the early 1900s. McLendon began his coaching career as an undergraduate student and directed Lawrence Memorial High School to the Kansas-Missouri Athletic Conference championship in 1936. His first head-college coaching job was at North Carolina College, where he compiled a record of 264-60 in 12 years. From 1952 to 1954, McLendon coached at Hampton Institute and led his teams to a 32-14 record. He achieved national prominence at Tennessee A&I from 1954-59 (now Tennessee State University), when he became the first college coach to lead teams to three consecutive NAIA National Championships (1957-59). McLendon pioneered integrated basketball and heightened awareness of basketball at all-black colleges. John was selected National NAIA Coach of the Year in 1958. He compiled a lifetime college coaching record of 523-165. McLendon coached professional basketball with the Cleveland Pipers and the Denver Rockets. Cleveland won the NIBL and AAU championships in 1961. McLendon wrote *Fast Break Basketball,* which is still a primary text for any coach wanting to develop the fast-break attack. He was elected to the Helms Foundation Hall of Fame and the Black Sports Foundation Hall of Fame.

John "Johnny Mac" McLendon....

Born in Hiawatha (KS), John McLendon was raised in Kansas City, when Kansas was still racially segregated, and blacks were not allowed sport opportunities, especially in basketball. Who would have thought that diminutive "Johnny Mac" would become the black pioneer who broke the barriers for persons of color to help make basketball truly "a game for everyone."

"Johnny Mac" graduated from Sumner High School in Kansas City in 1932 and enrolled in Kansas University (KU) as a physical education student. At the time, blacks weren't allowed to play basketball (intramural or intercollegiate) at KU. In fact, he became the first black person in the physical education program. However, good fortune came his way, when his college advisor was none other than the inventor of basketball, Dr. James Naismith. He became a direct link to the legendary Naismith, learning all he could about the game directly from him, even mowing his lawn. McLendon also became a close observer of future Hall of Fame coach Phog Allen, then coaching basketball at Kansas. John had two excellent basketball mentors, but times were still not easy. In a required physical education swimming class, other P.E. majors refused to enter the pool when McLendon swam. Even though humiliated and scorned, Johnny Mac completed all swim-test requirements with special provisions with the instructor and him using the pool (hardly a crucible of fair play to foster optimism against bias). Yet somehow, McLendon thrived and developed. The determination was strong to become the person who other black coaches affectionately called "Coach Mac."

In fact, he eventually became the beacon of hope for black coaches everywhere. It all started at Kansas, when he began his eminent career coaching the Lawrence Memorial High School team his junior and senior years in college. They were 13-3 in 1936 and won the Missouri-Kansas Conference title. John went to the acclaimed physical education master's degree program at the University of Iowa and obtained his degree in 1936-37. He coached from 1937-52 at North Carolina College, becoming head coach in 1940. This is where he began to break down barriers for blacks—originating and organizing the National Basketball Committee in 1949. This group of black coaches and administrators became the change agent for addressing inequities imposed on predominately black colleges, one of which was access to national tournament play. This allowed Tennessee A&I to play in the national NAIA tourney for the first time in 1952-53. He also coached at Hampton Institute from 1952-54. In 1954, Coach Mac moved to Tennessee A&I, and A&I became the first black team to receive an invite to the NAIA Invitational tip-off in Kansas City—he accepted on the condition that his team would be housed in downtown K.C. with seven other teams. A&I won the tournament, and another hotel-restaurant barrier was broken. From 1957-59, Coach Mac's Tennessee A&I team won three straight NAIA National Championships; he became the first coach in history to accomplish that feat and the first coach to win a national-integrated tourney in basketball.

The barriers to blacks continued to come down with coach John McLendon, Jr. playing the key role:

- First black to coach and win an integrated national tournament
- Coach of the first black college team to attain a #1 UPI ranking (Tennessee A&I, 1959)
- First black coach to become head coach of a post-college team (Cleveland-NIBL)
- First black pro-coach—Cleveland Pipers title team (1962) and Denver Rockets of ABA (1968-69)
- First black coach to serve on U.S. Olympic Basketball Staff (1968)
- First black coach to write a basketball coaching book (1965)
- First black head coach at a predominately white university (Cleveland State, 1966-69)

Is there any doubt that "Coach Mac" earned the title as "Father of Black Basketball (and Coaches)" in the United States? He indeed paved the way for all.

Mac went on to complete an illustrious 34-year coaching career with the Cleveland Pipers of NIBL (1959-61), the Cleveland Pipers of NBL (1961-62), Kentucky State College (1963-66), Cleveland State University (1966-69), and the Denver Rockets of the ABA in 1969. His cumulative career record was 729-240 (.752), which he garnered while also teaching physical education and administering programs in a variety of positions. During his career, his teams won 22 of 29 tournaments they qualified for or entered. Clair Bee, in the twilight of his years in 1972 said, "I have known John for over 35 years. His contributions and accomplishments have been beyond comparison. He is a fine gentleman and an honor to basketball in every respect."

What did "Coach Mac" bring to the game. Neil Isaacs (1975) summed it up best, "to talk about basketball without John McLendon is like talking about the interpretation of dreams without Freud." Mac attributes his legacy to Naismith and Kansas basketball (one-hand shooting, rugged rebounding, and great tradition). His teams always ran and pushed the ball up the floor—one of his North Carolina College teams won the 1947 CIAA tourney, with four players 5 feet 7 inches or under. They were called the "Mighty Mites" and were so balanced none made the all-conference team. Mac pioneered the full-court game— fast breaking, full-court pressure defense (including the early zone press), the revolving pivot/post, multiple offenses, and superb conditioning.

The little known trademark of McLendon teams was exemplary team sportsmanship and bench decorum. He was often characterized as a gentleman and fine sportsman. This almost seems incongruous with the many barriers he must have faced and disadvantages he overcame. But a reality it was; "Coach Mac" became a mentor and model for all. As a symbol of the respect he had earned, his Hall of Fame nomination had the unanimous endorsement of every active black basketball coach and all black institutions in the United States. In the vast network of basketball played in inner cities, most leagues have adopted what is called the"McLendon Rule," which holds

that if a coach draws a technical foul, every player on that team roster is accessed a foul. What a tribute to "Coach Mac's" mentorship!!! Leroy Walker, President of North Carolina Central College and former U.S. Olympic Track and Field Coach said of him, "McLendon's impeccable character and great personal traits have permitted his basketball genius to shine through at all levels and among all people."

SOURCE

Isaacs, Neil. (1975). *All the Moves - A History of Basketball.* Philadelphia: J.B. Lippincott.

McLendon, John. Vertical Files, Archives. Naismith Memorial Basketball Hall of Fame. Springfield, MA.

LESSONS FROM THIS LEGEND...

FAST BREAK CHAMPIONSHIP STYLE

By John McLendon

There are almost as many ways to play basketball as there are coaches to coach the game. However, various systems of offense and defense have been devised by individuals in the profession who have attempted to express, through team action, some game philosophy, some set of principles, or some group of objectives. The fast-break offense is an example of one of these systems. In each instance, the performances by individuals who adhere to these objectives and by coaches who direct them serve to emphasize the strength and weaknesses of the system employed. The fast break has been tried, tested, and found true. Many coaches and players have made their contribution to this type of game by developing the tremendous number of skills and techniques that are necessary for this system of play. My version of the fast break is simply the result of trying to keep the good, eliminating the ineffective, and staying with those practices that make the system most likely to succeed regardless of the defenses applied against it.

Coaches and players alike are marked by the type of play that brings them attention and success. Opponents devise many tests for a coach's system; some are orthodox, some unorthodox, some sound, and some outright gambles. Each attack brings an answering adjustment, which

solidifies the system, strengthens it, makes it adjustable, and flexible to the degree that it can remain a known weapon in the coach's arsenal. This is what has happened in my own experience. I am sure it has happened to many others in theirs.

Basketball is ever changing. No one offense is versatile enough to withstand, without adjustment, the onslaught of the multiple defenses and defensive variations employed by teams today. Yet, no offense should be so fundamentally weak that it must be completely abandoned or made unrecognizable at the first sign of a change in defensive tactics. The principles of offensive play should maintain their identity regardless of the situations met. The fast-break system used by my teams over the years has the same objective it has always had. The mechanics change to meet various defenses, and some ways of executing a particular skill have been adjusted to keep the fast break moving; certain techniques have a flexibility about them which allows game-by-game changes and within-the-game variations, but the original intent of the fast-break offense still requires more men on offense in the close-to-the-goal, high-percentage, scoring area than there are defensive men in the same area.

LESSONS FROM THIS LEGEND...

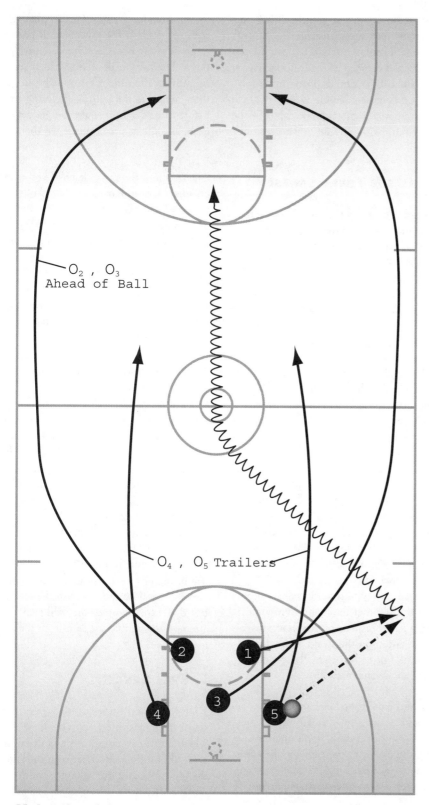

O₂ , O₃
Ahead of Ball

O₄ , O₅ Trailers

McLendon 1.0

In looking at the entire idea of the fast-break offense, I am positive that part of its soundness as a game stems from the loyalty one has to the principles underlying it. No matter what the opponents do to force a change in techniques used, the basic objectives must remain constant. To accomplish this, the following ideas are to be continuously activated:

1. GO OUT AND GET THAT BALL!

We will begin with a full-court defense, the kind best adapted to our personnel, and one with which all the players have been familiarized and trained to execute. We will try for the ball in the deep backcourt, the three-quarter court or half-court. We plan to continue in the frontcourt to attack aggressively the offense, making an effort to force a drastic change in their game and to drive them will yield the ball to us. When we get it, we will quickly and aggressively attack the optimum scoring area. We want that ball, and we want to get it into that basket!

2. GET THE BALL OFF THE BOARD!

If it takes three rebounders, four rebounders, or five, you must get the ball if you plan to use the fast break from the defensive board. Failure here cuts down over half of your fast-break possibilities.

Against larger teams, we will use a rebound plan where the entire team positions itself inside the three-second lane while the ball is in flight after a field-goal attempt. In other words, we zone the rebound, regardless of the defense we are otherwise using. Both guards are in the circle, one at the bottom of the free-throw circle, the other just below the foul line. The "inside" guard (the best rebounder) makes a try for all rebounds which rebound over the heads of the three players in the rebound triangle. The "outside" guard goes for the long rebound and also takes the outlet pass to either side of the court (see **Diagram 1.0**).

LESSONS FROM THIS LEGEND...

Against teams that do not have the height-size advantage, (i.e., those which are more our size), we use the regular rebound triangle by our forwards and center. The guards follow up any offensive field-goal attempt to the top of the foul circle and then immediately go to their next assignment (which is either receiving the outlet pass or taking an outside lane downcourt fast).

We want the ball more than the defensive rebound and the made field-goal afford. We must employ harassing defenses to multiply our own offensive opportunities. Part of the fast-break offense is an aggressive defense. We must have that ball!

3. GET IT OUT!

The position of the ball as it rebounds determines the side to which the outlet pass will be released. If it rebounds to the left or center (as you face the goal), the outlet pass receiver will take his receiving position along the left sideline. If it rebounds to the right, the outlet pass goes to the right sideline. The actual position of the receiver from corner baseline to midcourt is determined by the ability of the defensive rebounder, by the type of defense employed against the receiver, and by the size, strength, and aggressiveness of the offensive rebounders. There is an outlet-pass receiving position for every situation. The receiving guard hustles every time to receive this all-important pass. We use the station on the sideline opposite the top of the circle most frequently. It seems to be the best position, all factors considered. (Our team considers a rebound as valid only when it is secured and immediately released to a receiver.) When a field goal or free throw is made, we use an offensive, right sideline station for the quick endline throw-in by a designated rebounder.

4. GET DOWN COURT!

Whenever interceptions, loose balls, recoveries, or steals are involved, we quickly fill the three fast-break lanes. Our dribbler

takes the center lane or ends up in the center lane by the time he reaches the pass-off area, which begins a few feet above the top of circle and extends to the foul line (see **Diagram 1.0**). A similar procedure is followed on defensive rebounds after the field-goal attempt, and after the field-goal made and free-throw made. Get down, in front of the ball!

5. FILL THE THREE LANES!

The center lane and the outside (sideline) lanes must contain three players, two of whom are ahead of the ball or who are sprinting for such a position (see **Diagram 1.0**).

The guard, other than the one who stations himself on the sideline for the outlet pass, is the "guard going" each time he anticipates possession or each time possession of the ball is actually obtained. He speeds quickly downcourt, his primary function being to depress the defense (at least one defender usually goes with him). His secondary function is to receive the long pass, which is unlikely and seldom accomplished, but possible on occasions.

Only one of the guards may be particularly adapted to the outlet-pass receiving responsibilities. That is, only one may be able to handle the center lane. In that case, each guard will be assigned to do one thing— one will break each time, and one will take the outlet pass each time. Needless to point out is the fact that the inability to interchange guard responsibilities places a serious limitation on the speed with which the fast break can be launched. Two good guards are invaluable.

The third lane is the key lane. It is this lane which gives the 3-on-2 situation. Of course, if the 2-on-1 or 3-on-1 situation arises, so much the better, but a team should strive for the 3-on-2 fast break since it gives an advantage over the defensive alignment of "2 back," which all teams strive for as a normal, defensive beginning against the fast-break attack.

To put it another way, all teams plan to have two men in the backcourt or prepared to get into the backcourt for defensive purposes. The fast-break offense that is successful most of the time is one which can get three men into the optimum scoring area before three defensive men can get between them and the goal and organized themselves.

The fastest of the three defensive rebounders fills the third lane (or whoever of the three can fill this lane earliest after the rebounder chore has been taken care of). Under certain conditions, the third man may be a specifically assigned player, for example, when his opponent is physically lacking in stamina and fails to run consistently to a defensive position, or when the offensive player is more skilled in the scoring department than his teammates.

6. TRAILERS, FOLLOW UP!

In all of the fast-break plans (with one exception), our rebounders go to the lane to which the outlet pass is thrown. In fact, they are to compete against each other in the first half of the full court to see which can be the third man on the fast break. The two rebounders who fail to become a part of the first three men down then move out of the third lane to fill lanes four and five. From lanes four and five, they will remain in the backcourt to protect against a return fast break, or follow through to the scoring area for the close shot, or rush the offensive board as a follow-up to the field goal attempt, or shoot as a trailer from the intermediate area.

7. FREE LANCE!

Look for opportunities to follow the initial stages of the fast break with free-lane moves which result in a continued assault on the goal. Utilize the period between the end of the fast break and the beginning of the secondary offense by taking advantage of defensive errors and misplacements which may occur as the defense reorganizes itself.

LESSONS FROM THIS LEGEND...

(The defense is often busy trying to match up or re-form itself.) Keep the pressure on! Move from the fast break, to free-lance, to set offense, with continuous, threatening maneuvers.

8. FATIGUE IS A PSYCHOLOGICAL PHENOMENON!

Superior conditioning, achieved through cross-country running which precedes the season's opening by three to four weeks, is a must. Some games, we plan to beat teams with better players by running them into errors and misjudgments, solely as a by-product of fast-break-induced fatigue. Our team, however, cannot admit fatigue as a factor in their own performance. It is non-existent as long as the desire to excel is uppermost in the player's mind. A player does not tire if he wants to win badly enough. Our conditioning objective is to have each player on the squad in such a state of physical readiness that he can play 40 minutes of full-court offense, combined with full-court defense. When the player can manage this performance, he is ready for any game, since all other games are less demanding.

SOURCE:

McLendon, John B. Jr. (1965). *Fast Break Basketball*. West Nyack, NY: Parker Publishing.

LEGACY OF
Walter "Doc" Meanwell

- Directed Wisconsin to three Helms Foundation national championships (1912, 1914, and 1916).

- Radically changed the game of basketball with his disciplined offensive patterns which were predicated and short, crisp passes.

- Became one of the most influential coaches in the country during the 1910s and 1920s.

- Developed a valve-free, hidden-lace ball that replaced the old-style rawhide laces and ensured a true bounce every time.

- Led an unsuccessful campaign in 1929 to eliminate dribbling from the game.

- Regarded as a strong disciplinarian and perfectionist.

- Earned five nicknames during his career (Napoleon of Basketball, Doc, Little Doctor, Little Giant, and The Wizard).

WALTER "DOC" MEANWELL

"A team well versed in fundamentals, especially in passing and shooting, is difficult to beat, regardless of the style of offense or defense it employs."
— Walter "Doc" Meanwell

BIOGRAPHY

Born: January 26,1884 in Leeds, England

Died: December 2, 1953

Inducted into the Naismith Basketball Hall of Fame in 1959

Although he never played the game, Walter "Doc" Meanwell coached at the Baltimore Settlement House while in medical school, and directed his teams to a record of 61-1. In 1912, Meanwell became the first basketball coach at the University of Wisconsin and quickly captured the attention of basketball fans nationwide, as his teams compiled a 44-1 record during his first three years. He led the Badgers to the Helms Foundation national championship in 1912, 1914, and 1916. Meanwell was one of the game's most innovative first-generation coaches. He designed a disciplined, ball-control offensive system called "scientific basketball." Meanwell disliked dribbling and built his offense on criss-cross patterns and short passes. During the 1920s, Meanwell lobbied the Rules Committee to limit players to a single bounce. So heated was the debate that the National Association of Basketball Coaches was formed to protect the sport against the anti-dribbling forces. Meanwell guided Wisconsin to eight Big Ten championships. He also coached at the University of Missouri for two years (1918-1920) and led the Tigers to a 34-2 record. During his 20-year coaching career, Meanwell's teams won 70 percent of their games. He served on the National Rules Committee for both basketball and wrestling. Meanwell wrote a popular basketball book in 1924 entitled, *The Science of Basketball.* Meanwell was enshrined into the Helms Foundation, Wisconsin, and the Naismith Memorial Basketball Halls of Fame.

...SCOUTING REPORT.....SCOUTING REPORT.....

Walter "Doc" Meanwell...

Walter Meanwell was born in Leeds, England, and was three years old when his family arrived in America. He was raised in Rochester, NY and became involved in athletics as a young boy. Meanwell won boxing and wrestling championships for the Rochester (NY) Athletic Club and also participated in baseball, basketball, and gymnastics.

Meanwell graduated from Deichmann College Preparatory School in 1905 and received his medical degree from the University of Maryland Medical School at Baltimore in 1909.

Although he never played the game in college, Meanwell coached basketball at the Baltimore Settlement House while attending medical school. His teams won sixty-one out of sixty-two games using a system new to the game of basketball. Meanwell instituted an offense based on short, accurate passes and unmolested lay-up shots. He trained his players to move in precise patterns and utilized screens to create scoring opportunities. Basketball historian Peter C. Bjarkman said, "It was Meanwell in Wisconsin, more than any other figure, who entrenched the earliest notions of the basketball coach as an artistic choreographer. (Bjarkman, 2000, p. 254)

The elements of the Meanwell system—the short pass, the pivot, the criss-cross pass, dribble, and short shot, radically changed the game of basketball. It was a far contrast to Dr. Naismith's original offense that specified players as "backs, centers, or forwards." When Naismith's "backs" recovered the ball under their opponent's basket, they passed to a teammate positioned in the middle of the court called a "center." The "center" would then throw a long pass downcourt to a "forward," who attempted to score.

Meanwell taught basketball according to the book—his own book. He was regarded as a perfectionist and demanded that his players play according to his ideas. A player shooting a one-hand shot rather than the two-handed set shot, or making a long pass instead of a shorter one, received the wrath of Meanwell. He strongly believed that any player who was going to play basketball for him, would either play it his way, or not at all. The 5-foot 6-inch demanding coach didn't have just one nickname, but five: "Doc," "Napoleon of Basketball," "Little Doctor," "Little Giant," and "The Wizard."

"Doc" became head coach at the University of Wisconsin in 1912 and led the Badgers to the Helms Foundation mythical national championship in his rookie campaign. In Meanwell's first three years at Wisconsin, the Badgers won 44 games and lost only one. An upset loss at the University of Chicago in 1913 was the only blemish on an otherwise perfect three-year record. No coach in the history of the game reached the top of the coaching profession faster than Meanwell. During his first six years, Meanwell led Wisconsin to a record of 63-9 and won four conference titles.

Meanwell left Wisconsin to enter the Army as a captain in the Medical Corps. While on leave from Wisconsin, Meanwell coached the University of Missouri to two conference championships and a 32-2 record. In 1920, Meanwell returned to Wisconsin as basketball coach and medical supervisor of athletics.

Meanwell established himself as the most influential coach in the country. Head coaches from the East Coast to the West Coast copied his methods, and during the 1920's, all of the nation's basketball roads seemed to lead out of Madison, Wisconsin. Universities and colleges throughout the country began hiring Meanwell's former players in order to emulate his winning style of play. Bud Foster and Harold Olson played for Meanwell at Wisconsin and were later enshrined in the Naismith Basketball Hall of Fame for their outstanding contributions to the game, coming out of the Meanwell basketball coaching family tree.

Meanwell set his mark in basketball history with his offensive system, but he was also a masterful teacher of defensive tactics. His defensive system was called the "five-man, two-line" defense. Three players spread across the court formed the first line of defense, while two players formed a second line of defense, about twelve feet back of the front line. Wisconsin led the nation in defense in 1923 by allowing only 14 points per game.

In 1929, Meanwell led a nearly successful campaign to eliminate dribbling from the game of basketball. He strongly believed that dribbling took away from the aesthetic beauty of the sport and wanted to limit players to a single bounce. Meanwell convinced the Collegiate Joint Rules Committee to vote by a slim 9-8 margin in favor of eliminating the dribble as a legal offensive maneuver. Nat Holman, a star player for the Celtics and coach at City College of New York (CCNY), made a powerful speech stating that college players were not prepared for success on the professional level and needed the dribble as a strategy. The vote was retaken and the dribble supporters prevailed, thus ending what was called "the last great dribble debate." (Bjarkman, 2000, p. 10)

Dr. Meanwell was one of the first coaches to conduct coaching schools in the summer and traveled nationwide, teaching his basketball system. Knute Rockne, the legendary football coach from Notre Dame, joined him at many of the schools.

Meanwell retired from coaching at the end of the 1934 season, concluding 20 years as Wisconsin's basketball coach. He was athletic director until 1936 and then resigned to practice medicine in Madison, Wisconsin.

SOURCE

Bjarkman, Peter K. (2000). *The Biographical History of Basketball.* Chicago: Master's Press.

Meanwell, Walter. Vertical Files, Archives. Naismith Memorial Basketball Hall of Fame. Springfield, MA.

LESSONS FROM THIS LEGEND...

PASSING AND CATCHING

By Dr. Walter E. Meanwell

Skill in catching and passing the ball is more necessary to success than almost any other element in basketball. Ability with the ball breeds confidence and morale. Fast, accurate passing will bring the ball frequently to within such close distances that even an ordinary shooter can score. Therefore, the poorer a team is at shooting, the more time and attention should be devoted to improving the handling of the ball and speeding up the pass. Usually however, low-scoring teams devote most of their practice to basket shooting. The latter takes a long time to develop, while passing and team play improve immediately under intensive training and are more certain to produce increased scores. A good passing team is usually a steady, closely cooperating, five-man affair, while the good shooting team is more individualistic, more inclined to unexpected off nights, and less reliable. Accordingly, teams should spend considerable time on passing practice.

CATCHING

Learn to catch and pass from any position and with either or both hands. In catching the ball, the fingers and thumbs should be well spread and the palms well cupped. In catching, the hands are usually parallel and the palms turned in towards each other. To correct fumbling, drill each player to keep his eye on the ball. Most fumbling results from the player failing to watch the ball until it strikes his hands.

On receiving the ball, the player's arms should give slightly at the elbow to lessen the shock, but always in a direction and in such a manner as to make this receiving movement the initial part of the passing or shooting action that should immediately follow.

PASSING

There are a variety of ways to pass the ball, of which all but the overhand hook pass come quite naturally to most players. The shove, underhand, overhand, bounce, and hook passes are all used quite commonly.

The shove pass is merely a rapid deflection of the course of the ball made by the receiving player shoving or "stiff-arming" the ball for a pass without first catching it. The shove is usually made by using both hands and is particularly useful in close-in, fast passing near the basket. It is also commonly used when players are dashing up the floor in straight lines and abreast.

The underhand pass is generally the best for the pivot and short-pass game, when rapid-fire passing is employed. It is made underhand with either one or both hands, preferably both. The ball should travel moderately fast, on a line, and from waist to shoulder height.

The bounce pass is particularly efficient in out-of-bounds work, in offensive play near the goal, and when the attack is passing through the first line of a five-man defense. The bounce pass should frequently be preceded by a feint with the eyes or hands. The bounce pass must be used as a variant to the underhand and shove passes and not as the predominant type of pass. The ball should strike the floor four or five feet from the receiver. If the bounce pass is to be a long one, it should be made with a downward motion of the fingers, rotating the ball away from the passer. This gives a "hop" to the ball and adds speed and accuracy to the pass. If the pass is to be a short one, reverse the spin by pulling the thumbs

down and in towards the body. This "kills" the ball and causes it to bounce high and slowly. The receiver may handle it more surely.

The overhand shoulder pass can be made with either one or two hands. It is the most natural method of passing and the one most commonly used. However, I believe that it is best restricted to use in the backcourt and from out-of-bounds. The underhand, the shove, and the bounce passes can all be made more quickly and accurately.

The one-hand shoulder pass is valuable in both long and short passing. Its good points are its naturalness and power. Quite often, the long overhand pass is made much as one would throw a baseball. Objections to this pass are its comparative inaccuracy and the length of time required for its execution.

The two-hand shoulder pass is a short or moderate distance pass. It is very useful because of its accuracy, ease, and speed of execution, and for fast passing near the goal. The ball is held in both hands, with the fingers pointing upward. The thumbs are behind and below the ball and are pointing inward. The elbows are almost fully flexed and are held down toward the waist and below the ball. The shoulders and upper arms participate but little in the pass, which is executed primarily by a short, quick extension of the elbows and by a wrist snap. The ball is held quite close to the body, about shoulder height, until thrown. The pass is very accurate, is readily learned, and can be made with nice adjustments of speed.

The overhand hook pass is perhaps the fastest and most accurate one for long dis-

LESSONS FROM THIS LEGEND...

tances and, when skillfully made, is almost impossible to block or guard successfully. It is especially useful in getting the ball out of the backcourt after a recovery of a missed shot. The hook pass is made by holding the ball in the throwing hand, waist high, with the fingers spread, and the ball held against the wrist. If the right hand is used, turn the left side to the opponent and take one step away from him with the right foot. Jump high in the air and execute the pass by swinging the fully extended arm from the waist upward and overhead. Do not bend the elbow. The fingers are brought downward and under the ball as it leaves the hand. A major point is the snap of the fin-

gers down and underneath the ball as it is thrown. This pass is fast, accurate and exceedingly difficult to guard.

HINTS ABOUT PASSING

Improvement in passing is to be gained chiefly by eliminating the stop that so often occurs between the receipt of the ball and its subsequent delivery to a teammate. Receive the ball and pass it with one motion and from the position in which it is received.

The basis for a successful offense is skill with the pass. The players must be able to

pass quickly and accurately and to that end, sufficient practice must be directed. Next in importance come the stops and turns, and finally, shooting. It has been my principle that almost anyone can make a basket if the ball is brought close to the goal. Therefore, I spend most of my time on the other fundamentals and on floor work, and much less time on shooting practice.

SOURCE

Meanwell, Walter E. (1924). *The Science of Basketball*. Madison, WI: Democrat Publishing.

LEGACY OF
Billie Moore

- Succeeded in bringing women's basketball into the modern era.

- Led the first U.S. Olympic women's basketball team to a silver medal in 1976.

- Became the first coach to lead two universities to national women's basketball championships (Cal State-Fullerton in 1970 and UCLA in 1978).

- Compiled a 436-196 record during her 24-year career and guided her teams to postseason play 16 times.

- Enshrined into the Women's Basketball Hall of Fame with the inaugural class.

- Recognized as an outstanding teacher and clinician.

- Believed the keys to success were commitment to excellence, attention to detail, and discipline.

BILLIE MOORE

*"It is important to find what you love and
then love doing it."*
— *Billie Jean Moore*

BIOGRAPHY

Born: May 5, 1943 in Westmoreland, KS

Inducted into the Naismith Basketball Hall of Fame in 1999

Billie Jean Moore began her 24-year basketball-coaching career at Cal State-Fullerton. In her first season, she guided her team to a 17-1 record and the 1970 AIAW National Championship. Moore led Cal State-Fullerton to eight consecutive conference championships and an amazing 140-15 (.903) record. Billie accepted the UCLA job in 1977 and in her inaugural season, led the Bruins to the 1978 AIAW National Championship. Moore's postseason coaching record was 59-18, including two national championships (1969, 1978), two third-place finishes (1972, 1975), one fourth-place finish (1979), and one fifth-place finish (1971). At a time when women's basketball was searching for an identity and credibility, Billie Moore provided both. She was a coaching pioneer whose tireless efforts succeeded in bringing the women's collegiate game into the modern era. She served as head coach of the U.S. World University Team in 1973 and 1975 and was an assistant coach for the U.S. Pan-Am team in 1975. Moore was named head coach of the first U.S Olympic women's basketball team in 1976 and directed the team to a silver medal. She was selected 1978 National Coach of the Year in women's basketball. Moore was the first woman inducted into the Washburn University Athletic Hall of Fame. In 1999, Moore was part of the inaugural class of inductees into the Women's Basketball Hall of Fame in Knoxville, Tennessee.

Billie Jean Moore...

Billie Jean Moore grew up in the small town of Westmoreland, KS. Her father, a high school principal who coached basketball on the side, sparked Billie's initial interest in basketball. When her family moved to Topeka, Billie faced the challenge of playing basketball in a city with no competitive school teams for women's basketball. She played AAU basketball, at a time when girls played the old half-court game. Moore was also an outstanding third baseman on a nationally known women's fast-pitch softball team in Topeka called Ohse Meats.

After graduating from Highland Park High School in 1962, Moore attended Washburn University and majored in physical education. "It never occurred to me during those times, even as an undergrad at Washburn, that coaching was even an avenue I could follow," said Moore. "I finished college in 1965, and my first job was teaching in a junior high." (Norwood, 1999).

Billie went on to receive a master's degree in physical education from Southern Illinois University in 1968. Her first collegiate position was at Cal State-Fullerton, as head basketball coach and assistant athletic director. In 1970, at only 25 years of age, Moore won a national championship in her first year as a college coach. That paved the way for more success, as Moore led Cal-State Fullerton to eight consecutive conference championships and compiled a phenomenal 140-15 (.903) record.

Moore traces the evolution of women's college basketball back to small schools that had strong physical education departments. "At schools like Long Beach, Fullerton, and Immaculata, the basketball program just became an extension of the physical education department," Moore said.

Title IX changed the future of women's sports in 1972. "Title IX brought awareness," stated Moore. "You weren't going to see dramatic changes unless the universities wanted to see them, and once they were aware of the major inequity, a lot of schools acted quickly. It took time to filter down, but it did."

In 1976, Moore served as the head coach for the first-ever United States Olympic women's basketball team. Billie captured the attention of basketball fans internationally, as she led the Americans to a silver medal. The team members were living out a dream of their own; however, it was not a life of luxury during the six-week training period. The players endured grueling practices and were funded with only $500 in cash and the personal American Express card of Bill Wall, then the head of USA Basketball.

Moore's professionalism and drive made an impression on Pat Summitt, whose teammates on the Olympic team included Hall of Fame members Nancy Lieberman and Ann Meyers. "I never played for a coach who could get more out of me, said Summitt. "I'd never conditioned or trained or worked as hard as I did as an Olympic athlete. I think she believed we would have to overachieve to get a medal. That's what we did. We came together as a result of all the tough practices—and there were days when we had to give each other pep talks to get through those tough workouts."

Moore's next coaching position was at UCLA. In her first season, she led the Bruins to the 1978 AIAW National Championship, and the following year, she guided UCLA to a fourth-place finish. Overall, Moore's 16-year coaching record at UCLA was 296-181.

Many of Moore's former players (Ann Meyers, Denise Curry, Anita Ortega) have gone on to excel in athletic endeavors including college coaching, professional basketball, radio/television broadcasting, and community service.

Ann Meyers-Drysdale remembers Moore's toughness and her will to succeed. "She was always tough," stated Meyers-Drysdale, "and she knew the game. She was the kind of coach who was a teacher. That was what always set her apart. I don't know if people teach as much now. There was a purpose to her toughness, and that was to succeed."

Denise Curry, currently an assistant at Long Beach State, praises Moore's technical abilities - particularly when it comes to analyzing videos. "She can watch 20 seconds of videotape and dissect 50 things when I am lucky to catch two or three." Curry said.

In 1993, emotionally worn by the death of her father and her mother's cancer diagnosis, Moore opted for early retirement. She has remained close to the game that she loves. Billie has directed camps and clinics for the Women's Basketball Coaches Association, and does consulting work for college and professional teams. She has had numerous opportunities to return to coaching, but she is happy and content with her life. Moore enjoys passing on her knowledge of the game.

"People took a chance on me," said Moore. "What I've tried to do is give someone an opportunity the same way it was given to me." (Norwood, 1999)

Pat Summitt said, "Billie Moore has had more influence on my coaching career than anyone. She was my mentor and has had a huge impact on my coaching style. She may be retired, but I keep her busy, asking her questions and getting her opinions. Billie's ability to challenge and bring out the best in players was second to none."

Moore said, "If there's anything I miss about coaching, it's the teaching and the opportunity to deal with young people. When you finish coaching, and if all you have is your championships and victories, then you've ignored a lot about coaching. Coaching is about the fellowships and friendships you gain. And that's what I really miss." (Tran, 2002)

In 2002, Billie was the recipient of the Atlanta Tipoff Club's Naismith Outstanding Contribution to Basketball

Award. "She is one of the sport's pioneers," said Jackie Bradford, president of the Atlanta Tipoff Club. "She had achievement in the early days of women's basketball, and she was a powerful figure in the development of sports in general. Her accomplishments speak for themselves. She has set a standard of excellence for years to come." (Tran, 2002)

A plaque, that used to hang on the wall in Moore's UCLA office, probably described her best: "I have the simplest of tastes—I only want the best."

Source

Moore, Billie. Vertical Files, Archives. Naismith Memorial Basketball Hall of Fame. Springfield, MA.

Norwood, Robyn. (1999). Winning Time. Naismith Memorial Basketball Hall of Fame Enshrinement Program.

Tran, Bruce. April 4, 2002. UCLA coach given national honor. *Daily Bruin Online*. Web address: http://www.dailybruin.ucla.edu/news/articles.asp?id=19052

1-4 ZONE OFFENSE

By Billie Moore

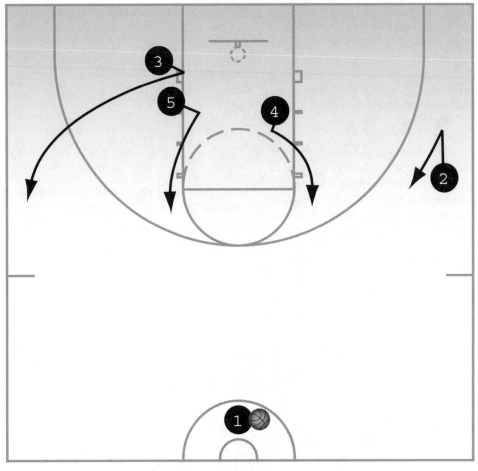

Moore 1.0

One of the major considerations facing a coach is that of selecting which offense her team will employ. This selection process usually involves a careful evaluation of the personnel so as to utilize each individual to her maximum. It is usually necessary to employ an offense which will be equally effective against both zone defenses and player-to-player defenses. Since the basic premise in attacking a zone defense is to align the offense into a mismatch or over-load situation, the best approach is to utilize one zone offense that will be successful against all types of zone defenses. It is not advisable to attempt multiple offensive sets to use against each type of zone, but rather to select one that can be universally effective with only minor adjustments.

At UCLA, consequently, we employ a 1-4 zone offense as our primary offense and find it very effective against all types of zone defenses. It thus saves us from having to refine and develop the necessary timing for several offensive patterns.

The concept of our 1-4 zone offense is to utilize player movement, ball movement, and overload principles. The pattern is very basic, with several options off each pass. As it is a continuity offense, we are able to reset and begin with little adjustment in the placement of the players.

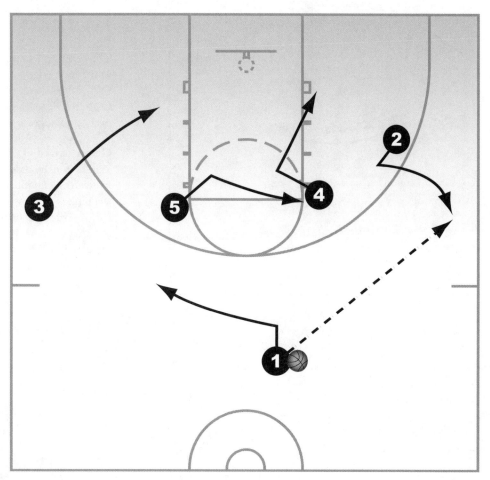

Moore 1.1

The basic set is shown in **Diagram 1.0,** with the first option being the pass to position 2 (see **Diagram 1.1**). In **Diagram 1.0,** the players in positions 3, 5, 4, and 2 may be initially set from any position. We utilize the free-throw line as the reference line, because it allows us room to execute the backdoor series, as well as keeping the players within excellent shooting range of the basket. The position of the players in the initial set can easily be adjusted to match the specific skills of your personnel.

In **Diagram 1.1**, the first pass is made from O1 to O2. On the pass, O4 and O5 cut simultaneously to their respective areas. On the cuts of O4 and O5, O3 steps down into the passing lane from O2 (with the ball). O2 now has the option of passing to 4, 5, or 3. If none is open, 2 return-passes to 1 (see **Diagram 1.2**).

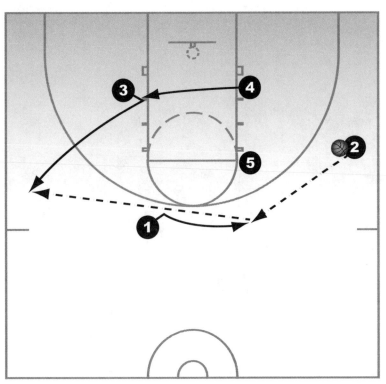

Moore 1.2

This basic movement concept is the foundation for the offense. The timing and execution of the various cuts, in relationship to each pass, dictate the success the offense will enjoy. The pass from position 1 to position 2 or 3 is the primary option in our 1-4 zone offense.

The other option is for the pass to be made to the high-post position (either O4 or O5). When the defenders deny the pass to O2 and O3, O1 looks to pass to the high post (see **Diagram 1.4**).

On the pass to O4, O2 cuts backdoor, looking for the pass, and O5 cuts diagonally down the middle of the lane, with O3 stepping into the vacuum created by O5's cut. If nothing is open, O4 returns the pass to either O2, O1, or O3. If the pass is made to O3, we are right back in our offense as shown in **Diagram 1.4**. The

As soon as the pass is returned to O1, she immediately swings the ball to O3. If O3 does not have the shot, she looks for O4, who is cutting across the lane in the low-post position (see **Diagram 1.3**). In case O4 is not open, the pass is returned to O1, with O4 cutting to the high-post position, and we are ready to reset to continue the offense as shown in **Diagram 1.3**.

The offense may continue with a pass either to position 2 or 3, using the same movement pattern as shown in **Diagrams 1.0 - 1.3.** If the pass is made to O3, the offensive pattern is that of **Diagram 1.1.** The key for the cuts inside by O4 and O5 is that they move simultaneously on the pass. The player on the side opposite the ball always has the responsibility of stepping down toward the basket into the open passing lane, and then stepping out wide enough to be open for the return pass.

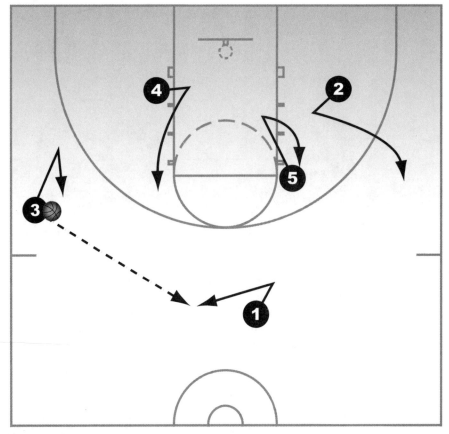

Moore 1.3

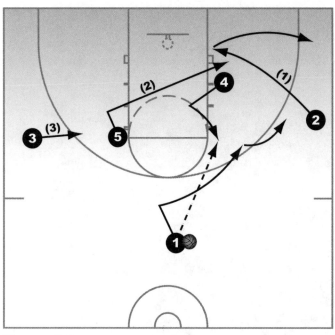

Moore 1.4

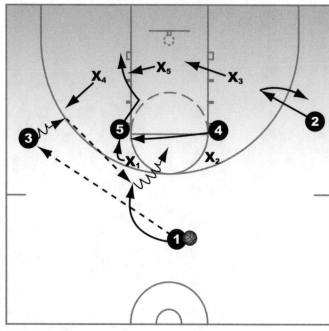

Moore 1.5

players must react accordingly. If the pass is returned to O3, it is merely a matter of O4 sliding across the key and O5 cutting high for us to reset.

These two options are what we utilize in our 1-4 zone offense. As I indicated in the beginning, this offense is very basic and simple. Success is dependent upon the timing and execution of our players in relationship to the defense being employed against them. It is important that this offense utilize a good balance of options one and two, so as to take advantage of defensive weaknesses.

There are minor adjustments you can make in the offensive pattern that will make your offense more successful against whichever zone defense you encounter. One adjustment is the angle of the cuts by the two inside players (O4 and O5), especially in the backdoor series (option two). The angle of these cuts will be dictated by how each opponent employs its 2-3, 1-3, 2-1-2, or 1-2-2 zone. Your wing players (O2 and O3)

also will need to adjust their movements; the open area each moves into on each pass will be different for each zone, so it is imperative that your wing players be able to recognize, and move to, the open area in each zone.

As your players become familiar with the basic movement pattern and learn to recognize the open areas of each zone defense, you will find more and more options available off each pass and off each situation. Again, the key here is for your players to learn to react correctly to the defensive situation which faces them.

It is important that each aspect or option of the offense be executed properly. To insure this, it is essential that you take each pass individually and set up appropriate drills. For example, with the first pass to the wing (see **Diagrams 1.1 and 1.2**), it is important that O4 and O5 learn how to get open, as well as how to position themselves for the pass and their subsequent shot attempt. **Diagram 1.4** shows an appropriate drill for

this pattern. The players should then exchange positions and sides of the floor and practice this option.

The same type of drill can be set up for the second option in the offense by utilizing the movement patterns shown in **Diagram 1.5.**

To repeat, it is important that your players exchange positions and sides of the floor in each of these drills. By drilling, each individual player learns to perfect the timing necessary for each aspect of the offense. Using the isolated drills will help your players develop the overall timing essential for the total offense to be successful.

SOURCE

Moore, Billie. (1982). 1-4 Zone Offense. *Medalist Flashback Notebook.*

LEGACY OF
Pete Newell

- First coach in basketball history to win the "Triple Crown" of coaching - NIT championship in 1949, NCAA championship in 1959, and the Olympic gold medal in 1960.

- Recognized as one of the all-time greatest teachers in the game of basketball.

- Directed the University of California to four consecutive Pacific-8 championships and back-to-back appearances in the NCAA Finals in 1959 and 1960.

- Led San Francisco to the NIT championship in 1949.

- Considered America's "Basketball Guru" and "Coach of Coaches."

- Selected National Coach of the Year in 1960.

- University of California's basketball court was renamed Newell Court in 1987.

PETE NEWELL

"I believe there is less individual teaching of footwork than ever before. The skills of clever movement and good balance have been sacrificed in many coaches' minds for high jumping and physically overpowering skills."
— Pete Newell

BIOGRAPHY

Born: August 31, 1915 in Vancouver, BC, Canada

Inducted into the Naismith Memorial Basketball Hall of Fame in 1979

Pete Newell was the first coach in basketball history to win the "Triple Crown" of coaching: NIT championship (1949); NCAA championship (1959); and the Olympic Gold Medal (1960). In the basketball world, Newell is considered America's "Basketball Guru" for his teaching ability, innovative coaching techniques, and his aptitude in evaluating talent. He coached at San Francisco, Michigan State, and California at Berkeley and was chosen National Coach of the Year in 1960. At California, Newell compiled a 119-44 record and directed the Golden Bears to four consecutive Pac-8 titles and back-to-back appearances in the NCAA championship game. He has worked in the NBA as a scout, general manager, and director of player development. In 2003, Newell and his late wife, Florence, were honored with the Nell and John Wooden Humanitarian Award for Lifetime Coaching Achievement.

Peter "Pete" Newell.

Pete Newell was born in Vancouver, B.C. in 1915 and was the youngest of eight children. A year later, his family moved to Los Angeles. Pete's mother was very determined to get her children into show business and would often take them for tryouts. Pete captured the attention of Hollywood directors and became a child actor during the silent-film era. He had parts in around a dozen feature films and nearly stole the starring role in "The Kid" from Jackie Coogan.

For Newell, it wasn't a part of his life that he looked back upon fondly. "I felt like a freak," said Pete. "I didn't want to see myself on the screen. All I wanted to do was go out and play baseball with the other kids. Instead, I had to get up at 4:00 in the morning and have my mother put on all the makeup. And the worst thing was, you had to have a Buster Brown haircut. I started acting when I was about three years old, and I guess I was seven or eight before I was able to get out of the damn thing." (Jenkins, 1999)

Former *San Francisco Chronicle* sports editor Art Rosenbaum said, "I think that experience (as a childhood actor) shaped his relationship with the public. He became an actor for life, I think. He always had such great presence. And even today, the way he carries himself, people say he reminds them of an actor. He's an equal in any company." (Jenkins, 1999)

Pete attended St. Agnes High School and excelled in football, baseball, and basketball. After graduation, Newell accepted a job as a deck cadet on one of the biggest trans-Pacific steamship carriers. "I graduated from high school right after the Depression, jobs were tough to come by, and my family didn't have the money," remembered Newell. "Back then, college wasn't a right. It was a privilege."

After two years of seeing places like Shanghai, Hong Kong, and Honolulu, Newell decided it was time to attend college. Pete selected Loyola of Los Angeles and played basketball for legendary coach Jimmy Needles. Needles had earned the reputation as one of the finest basketball minds on the West Coast and was selected to coach the first U.S. Olympic basketball team in 1936. "Jimmy and I used to sit down and talk basketball, or just life, for four or five hours at a time," said Newell. So many of the things I utilized as a coach later in my career—the reverse-action offense, weakside help on

defense, the stall, positioning for the transition game, getting players to think for themselves instead of relying on timeouts—they all came from Jimmy."

One of Newell's teammates at Loyola was Phil Woolpert. Woolpert later led San Francisco to back-to-back national championships and was also inducted into the Naismith Basketball Hall of Fame.

Newell was a switch-hitting center fielder on Loyola's baseball team and played one season of minor league baseball in the Dodgers' organization. "My season with the Dodgers' club I was so beat up that I could hardly even run or catch the ball. It was about that time that I decided that I'd like to be a coach someday."

Newell's first coaching job was at St. John's Military Academy in Los Angeles. He coached four sports—football, basketball, track, and softball—and in Newell's two years there (1940 and 1941), the school went undefeated in all four.

In 1942, Newell enlisted in the Navy and with the help of USC coach Sam Barry, he was assigned to Great Lakes, Illinois. "I played on the basketball team under Tony Hinkle, who became a great coach at Butler," remembered Newell. "It was the biggest Naval base in the country, and there were college all-stars all over the place. I met people like Johnny Mize, Bob Feller, Joe Kuharich, and Red Auerbach."

At the completion of his training, Newell joined the amphibious operation out of Coronado, California. "I was on ship for about a year and a half," said Newell. "It seemed like ten years. We went straight to the Philippines, and got involved in the second Manila operation and the

landing at Okinawa when the battle was still going on. I was a different man when I got back to the Bay Area. I swear, that experience aged me at least ten years."

Newell accepted a job at the University of San Francisco in 1946 as the head coach of basketball, baseball, and golf. During Newell's fours years at San Francisco, his bas-

ketball record was 70-37, and his 1949 team won the NIT championship.

His basketball team was subjected to Newell's intense conditioning program. The cornerstone of Newell's conditioning was a drill known as "Hands Up." Players were required to stay in the defensive stance with their hands held high for long periods of time. "I'd start the "Hands Up" drill on the first day of practice for about three minutes," stated Newell. "We eventually worked up to 20 minutes at a time."

From 1950 to 1954, Newell coached at Michigan State University. He compiled a highly respectable record of 45-42, considering the school's poor reputation in the sport. In 1951, the Spartans finished second in the nation in overall defense. In 1953, Michigan State scored a shocking victory over Kansas State, which was ranked number one in the country at the time.

Gus Ganakas, who coached the Spartans from 1969 to 1976, said, "Pete was way ahead of his time. He introduced reverse-action offense and pattern basketball at Michigan State, when everybody was fast-breaking and freelancing. It was like going to a basketball clinic, and there were so few people at games, you could sit just about anywhere. Even after what he'd done at USF, Pete wasn't any kind of name. He was unappreciated in our state. People still don't realize that he coached here." (Jenkins, 1999)

Newell's players at Michigan State have never forgotten the impact Coach Newell made on their lives. For 50 years, this group of athletes have gathered together annually to relive the past and give thanks to their coach. Ricky Ayala, the first African American to play basketball at Michigan State, said, "If you ask me the most significant thing about Pete at Michigan State, I'd say there wasn't one man who got a varsity letter during that period who did not graduate. You were a student. You had to be. Every year after summer vacation, there'd be a note in your box. You had an appointment with Pete, and if you were smart, you'd get there 10 minutes early. He'd spend 45 minutes talking about life, where you stood in the world. Then much later: 'Now, let's talk a little basketball.' Coach Newell always stayed in your mind." (Jenkins, 1999)

Pete could not tolerate complainers or negative thinkers. He demonstrated this prior to a game at the University of Wisconsin. One of his starters returned to the bench during warm-ups complaining about the rims. Newell immediately went to the scorer's table and announced a change in his starting line-up. "I don't want people having emotional problems when they go on the court." Newell told him. "You seem to have one with the backboards and rims here, so I'm going to take that problem away from you. You'll watch the game with me tonight."

Newell never did play that player that night. "I was trying to teach him—and all my players—that you can't have everything you want in life. If the rims aren't right, so be it. If it means a longer rebound, you make that adjustment."

Newell, the master teacher, used what is called today the part-whole teaching method. Newell said, "Part-method teaching tells a kid why he's doing something. In five-on-five drills, you're not teaching, you're coaching. Break it down to one-on-one, two-on-two, three-on-three, go through every option of the offense and defense, and the players will understand why you're doing it. And if they make mistakes, you can point it out. The parts make the whole. It's like your car engine; you work on the spark-plugs or the carburetor or whatever's causing the problem. You don't have to get rid of the whole motor."

"I got a taste of part-method teaching from Jimmy Needles, but I really learned it from Tony Hinkle when I played on his Navy team at Great Lakes, and to this day, it's the whole basis of my coaching."

Newell coached at the University of California at Berkeley from 1954 to 1960 and directed the Golden Bears to back-to-back appearances in the NCAA championship game in 1959 and 1960. His record at California was 119-44. Newell's 1959 team won the national champi-onship with no All-Americans or even any first-team All-Pac-8 Conference players.

During games Newell nervously chewed towels. "When I first started coaching, my palms would get sweaty, my mouth would get dry and I'd drink some water and have a towel to wipe my hands," said Newell. "Finally, I got a towel that was wet at one end and dry at the other. I'd suck on one end and dry my hands on the other, and it became a crutch."

Newell retired from active coaching after just 14 seasons on the collegiate level. The stress of coaching took its toll. Newell's coffee-and-cigarettes diet was well documented: During a two-day period he would consume 40 cups of coffee and six packs of cigarettes. *(Authors' Note: Newell quit smoking for good in 1974).* He'd eat his last meal on

Thursday night, and then suffer through the game days of Friday and Saturday without food. I wanted to be able to eat, but I could never keep anything down," stated Newell. "I was an emotional wreck."

Newell's wife, Florence, revealed some of the family frus-tration only weeks before he retired in a 1960 *Sports Illustrated* article entitled, "My Husband is a Nervous Wreck." Florence described Pete's game-day behavior as a "totally preoccupied trance." She went on to say, "Ordinarily, Pete is a gregarious, likeable guy, eager to play practical jokes and enjoy life. As I watch the fun fade from his eyes during the basketball weekends, I wonder, is this a way of life? How often does a man have to kill him-self for a paycheck?" (Jenkins, 1999)

Today, Newell is considered the sport's foremost expert on post play and has worked with hundreds of NBA players. It began as a private workout for Kermit Washington who needed help in making the transition from college center to NBA power forward and grew into a Big Man Camp for college and NBA players. "The chance to spend a week with Pete Newell is like a student of literature get-ting to spend a week with Hemingway or Frost," said NBA coach Rick Carlisle. "The man is the greatest treas-ure we have in our sport. He is the godfather of modern basketball." (Bucher, 2002.)

Newell constantly emphasizes the importance of proper footwork in his Big Man Camp. "I want players to under-stand they play 100 percent of the time with their feet, and 10 percent of the time with the ball," said Newell. (DeCourcy, 1997)

"I believe there is less individual teaching of footwork than ever before," added Newell. "The skills of clever movement and good balance have been sacrificed in many coaches' minds for high jumping and physically overpow-ering skills. There is a tendency to emphasize the height of a player's leap to the detriment of his balance and movement."

When asked what advice he would give young coaches today, Newell (2003) responded. "First and foremost," said Newell, "Be a teacher. Today, there are so many time demands on coaches that they don't make the time to teach. It's too bad because the rewards that you get are the friendships you have with players that played for you 20 or 30 years ago. You get a different relationship with play-ers when you teach, rather than just coach them. That definitely is the most important. Be a teacher. I always felt I was a teacher more than a coach."

.....SCOUTING REPORT.....SCOUTING REPORT...

No report on Pete Newell could be complete without mentioning the beautiful relationship he had with his wife Florence. Pete said, "I was so lucky to have a wonderful woman like Florence." They were a perfect compliment to each other, and Pete was at a loss when she died in 1984. "I was shattered," said Newell. "I cannot explain the emptiness."

Florence's best friend, Barbara Benington, said, "You know what I'll always remember about those two? How they never lost sight of their love affair. As preoccupied as Pete could get, Florence would not allow them to lose one bit of the way they felt back then. She looked at Pete, 40 years later, the same way she looked at him when they fell in love."

"Florence may be the most impressive woman I ever met," said Bob Knight. "She was brilliant, extremely well-read, and knew sports inside and out. She raised all of Pete's kids, and she was sort of a second mother to anyone who ever came in contact with the family. In fact, I think Florence thought I was one of her kids." (Jenkins, 1999)

SOURCE

Bucher, Ric. (2002, September 17). The Godfather. *ESPN The Magazine.*

Jenkins, Bruce. (1999). *A Good Man: The Pete Newell Story.* Berkeley, CA: Frog, Ltd.

Newell, Pete. Interview with Ralph Pim. September 28, 2002.

Newell, Pete. Iterview with Ralph Pim, September 5, 2003.

Newell, Pete. Vertical Files, Archives. Naismith Memorial Basketball Hall of Fame. Springfield, MA.

REVERSE-ACTION CONTINUITY PATTERN

By Pete Newell

Basketball is essentially a game of percentage based on sound habits of play—a thorough working knowledge of the fundamentals and the proper reactions to game situations. There is just one way to develop these habits—through rigorous, repetitive work in daily practice sessions.

At San Francisco, this training is accomplished through a series of practice drills, predicated closely upon our offensive pattern. To approximate game conditions still further, we always have our offensive players working against defensive resistance.

Since our drills furnish the keystone to our system, I will describe each drill and show how it fits into our team play. Later on in the article, I will paint in the broader aspects of the system.

ONE-AND-ONE DRILL

The one-and-one drill, embracing an offensive forward, a defender, and a feeder, comes first. All action is confined to the forward's normal operating area, which we term the forward's quarter of the offensive court (see **Diagram 1.0**).

To create the proper lead, the forward finesses the defender in the area of the baseline and breaks to receive the ball. Upon reception, the forward attempts to create a good shot through individual skill. The defensive player contests the lead pass from the feeder and then tries to defend against a good-percentage shot.

This drill enables us to improve the following offensive skills:
- Proper footwork. When receiving the ball, the forward comes to a jump stop, assuming a flexed knee

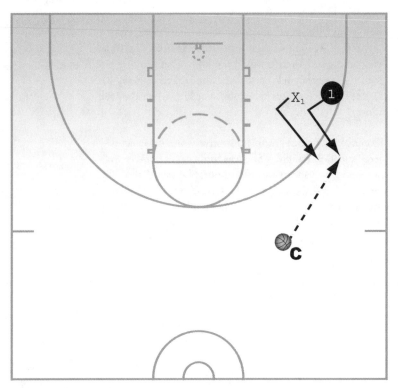

NEWELL 1.0

position, with the inside foot advanced as the pivot foot. This position enables the forward to protect the ball from the defender and establishes the proper base for a reverse turn or a drive across the defender, should the latter fail to adopt a balanced defensive stance.
- Proper body position in the reception of the ball.
- The variable use of individual skills in finessing the defender.
- Percentage shooting from a normal operational zone.

When receiving the ball from the feeder, the forward is held responsible for the creation of a good passing lane. To accomplish this, the forward must fake the direction of

movement. While this seems comparatively simple, the habit can be developed only through constant practice. Many close games are lost through failure in adhering to this elementary fundamental of "meeting" the ball.

Defensively, much can be accomplished in the correction of poor defensive habits, such as:
- Over-commitment on fakes
- Unbalanced position of feet in contesting the lead pass or shots at the basket
- Improper body balance and court position in covering the offensive player, with or without the ball
- Laxity in maintenance of mental and physical poise

LESSONS FROM THIS LEGEND...

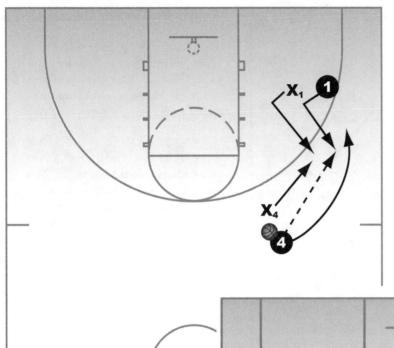

Diagram 1.2 outlines the ensuing play. O1 hands off to O4, who proceeds to dribble as far as possible. O1 breaks to the foul line and attempts to create a passing lane for the dribbler. If O4 is tied up with the ball, a two-man action between O4 and O1 develops.

The objectives are to perfect timing in handoffs between the guard and forward and to create good shooting opportunities by clever two-man action. Particular emphasis is given to proper steps and reverse turns by the dribbler and good faking and change of direction in the cut of the breaker. The offensive movements must, of necessity, adjust to the type of defense encountered.

NEWELL 1.1

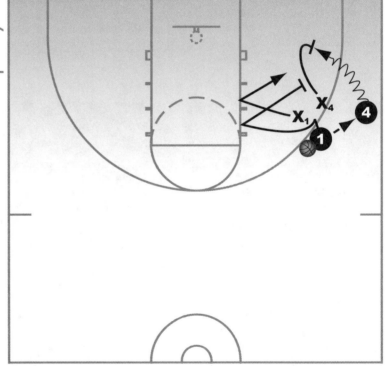

NEWELL 1.2

The importance of good individual play magnifies upon reflection of the great advancement in scouting. Competent scouts don't restrict themselves to an analysis of only the offensive and defensive patterns, but carefully note the weaknesses and strengths of each player.

TWO-AND-TWO DRILL

The two-and-two drill, in which a forward and a guard on offense work against a forward and a guard on defense, comes next (see **Diagrams 1.1 and 1.2**).

Again, the action is confined to a forward quarter of the offensive court and a shifting or a straight man-to-man defense may be employed.

In **Diagram 1.1**, O4 (guard) passes to O1 and rolls to the outside. The path of the cut (toward the basket) is important, as the player should be heading in that direction in the event of a hand-off. O1 makes a fake toward the center and advances to meet the ball.

Defensively, team play is stressed. Coordination of movement between frontline and backline defenders is developed. The defender on the ball must adjust position to allow the defender on the cutter to slide through. The backline defender calls all shifts on defense by these two players.

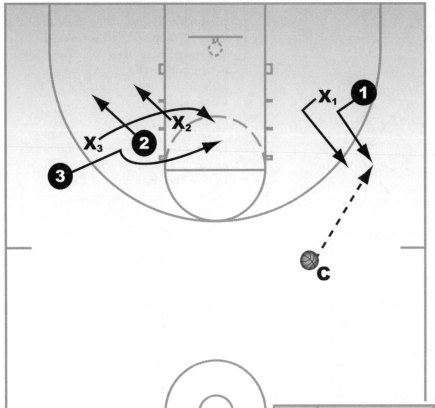

NEWELL 1.3

THREE-AND-THREE DRILL

Two forwards and a center now work against three defenders. A feeder is used to pass the ball to the offensive players, and inside offense is accentuated with emphasis on timing between the passer and cutter.

A passing lane must be opened as the cutter advances to the basket area. This requires split-second timing and coordination, which can be acquired only through practice under the variable situations of defensive play.

In **Diagram 1.3**, the feeder passes to O1, who advances to meet the pass. The receiver now has three options: 1) to create a shot through individual action; 2) to pass to O3 breaking across O2's screen into the basket area; or 3) to return pass to the feeder. O2 slides to the weakside after setting the screen and looks for a pass from the feeder.

In **Diagram 1.4,** the ball is reversed from O1 to the feeder, and then to O2. O2 now has the same options as O1 in **Diagram 1.3.**

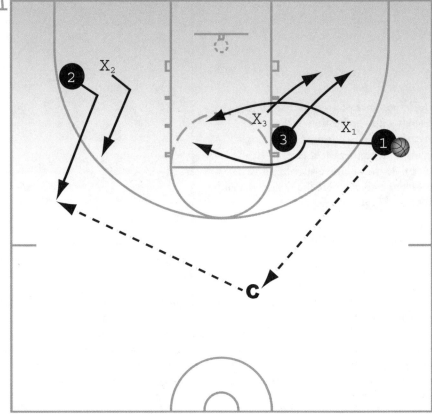

NEWELL 1.4

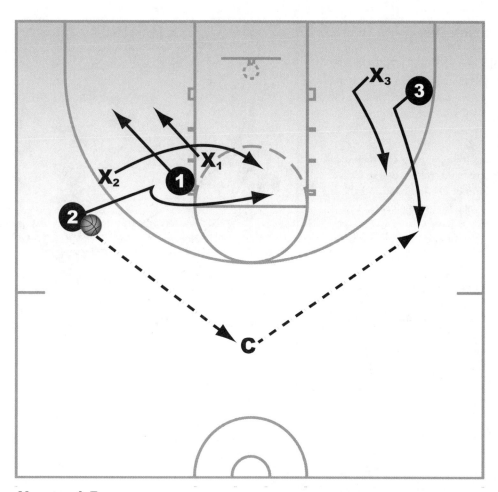

NEWELL 1.5

In **Diagram 1.5**, O3 now has the same options that O1 and O2 had in the preceding diagrams.

As the diagrams indicate, three inside players can sustain the continuity through a constant interchange of positions. A good court balance is maintained, which insures correct rebounding balance.

Forced passing is strictly taboo, because an optional lead (to the feeder) always exists. The inside screener does not pick, but establishes a screen as a result of the movement of the cutter. Here again, the feint in direction of movement before the cutter's break is very important.

This drill affords the opportunity to stress rebounding, coverage of the rebound area after a shot, and defense. One of the primary fundamentals of sound defense, peripheral vision, is strongly emphasized, as well as team deployment in relation to the position of the ball, individual tactics in covering the cutter, sliding through screens, and rebounding position.

When a shifting of defensive responsibilities is called for, we stress alertness in calling the switch and quick adjustment.

LESSONS FROM THIS LEGEND...

THE DRIBBLE ROTATION DRILL

This drill, shown in **Diagrams 1.6 and 1.7**, is accorded a great deal of time. In this maneuver, two forwards and two guards operate offensively against two defensive forwards and guards. The guard with the ball initiates the action.

In **Diagram 1.6**, O4 fakes to the outside and then dribbles toward the middle and hands off the ball to O5. O5 dribbles in the direction of O1 and hands off the ball to O1. O1 must first fake toward the center and then come back to receive the hand off from O5. Upon receiving the ball, O1 dribbles toward O3, who is coming to meet the ball.

In **Diagram 1.7**, O1 hands off to O3 and assumes the same path as O4 did in **Diagram 1.6.** O3 dribbles in the direction of O5 for a hand off. Again, we have a continuity of pattern, with attention given to good faking and timing in the handoffs. The proper movement of the personnel, rather than pickoffs, creates the defensive mistakes that open the alley for a drive to the basket or a close-in shot.

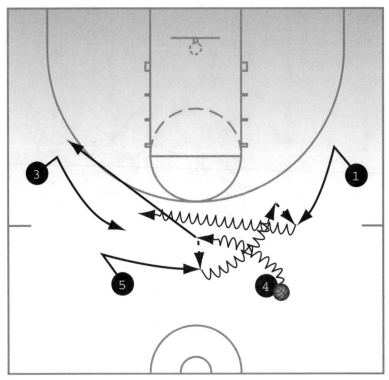

NEWELL 1.6

NEWELL 1.7

The fake before the break is again demanded here, and the correct protection of the ball by the dribbler and the use of the outside hand (the hand away from the defender) are emphasized. Fingertip control of the ball in the handoff insures a light ball easily handled by the receiver.

Dribble rotation is adaptable to action off the post player or center. Upon cessation of the movement, the post adjusts his position in order to receive the ball. A pass to this post player can initiate an action that will force the defense into quick adjustments, thus producing errors in position and creating openings for scoring thrusts.

Slow reactions on defense can be corrected during this drill. When sliding through screens, stress should be placed on snapping at the ball. There must be a coordinated movement between defensive players that will permit the player off the ball to slide past the defender on the ball, without causing congestion or a collision between the two.

LESSONS FROM THIS LEGEND...

ESTABLISHING SOUND HABITS

A system of play patterns will not by itself assure victory; neither will outstanding personnel. These are important to a successful style of play, but equally important is the individual's habit of play. This must be developed into skills that are usable regardless of the defensive pressure. Furthermore, your style of play must be flexible enough to both minimize the strength of your opponent and to play to his predetermined weaknesses.

OUR BASIC SET PATTERN

Our basic set pattern is referred to as "reverse action." In this pattern, we attempt to keep the ball in motion in order to keep the defense in motion. If you allow the defense to set up on you, your problem of opening passing lanes becomes much greater. But, if you can force all five defensive players to move, your chances of penetration will naturally increase.

In our reverse action, we operate both single and double screens. All screens are stationary and, as previously explained, we try to congest the defense rather than "block" them. Relatively few screening fouls are called against us.

Our inside players employ a constant "Figure 8," with our guards rolling to the outside. This gives us good rebound position and court balance, which allows a balanced retreat in the event the opponents recover the ball.

KEY TO THE KINGDOM

The key to our offense is essentially proper timing between passer and cutter. Although all offenses are based on this principle, we attempt to cultivate it through constantly doing it in our daily drills. Very little time is spent diagramming responsibilities. You can't make a player meet the pass through the medium of chalk, but it can be accomplished through repetitive drill work.

Along with our reverse action, we employ a dribble rotation, as was shown in **Diagrams 1.7 and 1.8**, with a moving post. Against certain types of defenses, this pattern creates many fine shooting opportunities. The success of this movement is predicated on the individual ballhandling and dribbling of the four outside players.

Our system is based upon the following principles:
- High-percentage shots
- Offensive rebounding
- Flexibility

We attempt to get the good shot, with a reasonable chance at the rebound or tap in. We also have the flexibility to operate against radical defensive measures. Without such flexibility, a team will encounter serious trouble against smart opponents.

SOURCE

Newell, Pete. (December 1949). San Francisco Continuity Pattern. *Scholastic Coach.*Vol. 19, (4)

LEGACY OF
Adolph Rupp

- Nicknamed the "Baron of the Bluegrass."

- Retired as the all-time winningest coach in college basketball history.

- Feisty, controversial coach whose basic tenet was "Play to Win."

- Produced fundamentally sound, fast-breaking teams.

- Namesake of Rupp Arena on the University of Kentucky campus.

- Led Kentucky to four NCAA championships (1948, 1949, 1951, 1958).

- Compiled a record of 876-190 (.822) at Kentucky.

- Was a master at developing local talent. He took more than 80 percent of his players from the hills of Kentucky and turned them into champions.

ADOLPH RUPP

*"I know I have plenty of enemies,
but I'd rather be most hated coach in
the country than the most popular one.
Show me a popular coach and
I'll show you a loser."*
— Adolph Rupp

BIOGRAPHY

Born: September 2, 1901 in Halstead, KS

Died: December 10, 1977

Inducted into the Naismith Memorial Basketball Hall of Fame in 1969

Adolph Rupp coached 42 years at the University of Kentucky and made Kentucky basketball synonymous with greatness. His teams won 876 games, including NCAA championships in 1948, 1949, 1951, and 1958. Rupp also led Kentucky to the NIT title in 1946. Nicknamed the "Baron of the Bluegrass," Rupp was a master of developing homegrown talent. Over 80 percent of his players came from the state of Kentucky. Rupp's teams appeared in 20 NCAA tournaments and won 27 SEC titles. Rupp retired as the all-time winningest coach in college basketball. He was regarded as one of the fiercest competitors in the game of basketball. As a college player, Rupp played for future Hall of Fame coach "Phog" Allen on the 1922 and 1923 Kansas teams that were named national champions. Rupp co-coached the 1948 Olympic team to a gold medal.

Adolph Rupp...

Adolph Rupp was raised on a farm in Halstead, KS and, at a young age, began playing basketball, using a homemade ball and a barrel nailed to a barn door. He attended the University of Kansas and formulated much of his basketball philosophy from future Hall of Fame coach "Phog" Allen and the game's inventor, Dr. James Naismith.

Rupp received his degree in business from the University of Kansas and had no intention of entering the coaching profession. He discovered quickly, during this period before our country's depression, that jobs were scarce in the banking business. Rupp returned to the University of Kansas as an assistant instructor. He then accepted a position at Burr Oak, KS, teaching history and coaching all sports. Rupp soon discovered that there was no place to play basketball. The only facility was a renovated barn that had been converted into a skating rink. Basketball was only played when no skating was scheduled. Rupp knew that this was not the place for him and eagerly accepted a position at Marshalltown High School in Iowa. He was disappointed again when he arrived, only to find out that he was to coach wrestling, not basketball, as he had anticipated. Totally unfamiliar with the sport of wrestling, Rupp purchased a wrestling book and then coached his team to the state championship.

Rupp moved the following year to Freeport High School in Illinois and led his basketball teams to a 67-16 record. While coaching at Freeport, Rupp attended summer school at Columbia University and received his master of arts degree. Rupp learned that John Mauer was leaving the University of Kentucky for the head-coaching position at Miami of Ohio. He applied for the job at Kentucky and was named head coach in May of 1930. He was given a two-year contract for $2,800 a year. Rupp was 28-years old and had no college coaching experience. When asked why he should get the Kentucky job, Rupp responded, "Because, I'm the best damned basketball coach in the nation."

One of Rupp's first moves after arriving on campus was to call Carey Spicer, the team's captain, and tell him of the fast break and man-to-man defense that the Wildcats would use. Rupp made an instant impact in the South, when his Kentucky team won their first ten games and advanced to the finals of the Southeastern Conference, before losing to Maryland on a last-second shot.

At Kentucky, Adolph Rupp became one of the all-time most powerful men in sports. Rupp ruled with an iron fist and was basketball's version of General MacArthur and General Patton rolled into one. When he issued a compliment, it was worth something. When he talked, people listened, for he was a man of authoritative expression. Critics accused Rupp of taking the fun out of the game, but he countered by saying that "his boys" get their fun by playing for national championships. "We do not wish merely to participate in sports," stated Rupp. "We wish to be successful in sports. In order to be successful, we must create within these boys the competitive spirit that will bring success. Defeat and failure to me are enemies. Without victory, basketball has little meaning." (Padwe, 1970)

In opponents' gymnasiums, Rupp was the hated enemy. Auburn fans threw tomatoes at him. During World War II, Tennessee fans gave him the ultimate insult by linking his name with Adolph Hitler. Rupp's strength, dedication, and confidence prevailed against all those who attacked him. "To sit by and worry about criticism, which too often comes from the misinformed or from those incapable of passing judgment on an individual or a problem, is a waste of time," Rupp said. "I've gotten a lot of publicity for being a mean man. But, it's not true."

"I have always thought that an excerpt from Parkenham Beatty's *Self Reliance* contained a good philosophy for every coach," said Rupp:

> By your own soul learn to live,
> And if men thwart you, take no heed,
> If men hate you, have no care,
> Sing your song and dream your dream,
> Hope your hope and pray your prayer.

"I am sure if a coach will follow this philosophy of life, he will be successful," stated Rupp. (Rupp, 1958)

Rupp was rough on his players, and they often didn't understand their coach until after their playing days were over. "He wanted everybody to hate him—and he succeeded," said former Wildcat star Bill Spivey. "He called us names some of us had never heard before."

All-American guard Louie Dampier said, "Coach Rupp was a very strict disciplinarian. He was tough to play for, and a lot of guys left because they didn't like it. I never crossed paths with him when I was playing, but I never developed much of a relationship with him then either. It wasn't until after I graduated that I got to meet him on different grounds, as a man, and I grew to love him then."

Practices under Rupp were long and hard, and, above all, they were silent. "It is generally understood out there," Rupp explained, "that no one is to speak unless he can improve on the silence...Why should boys constantly chatter in a class in basketball any more than they do in a class in English?"

Hall of Fame player Cliff Hagan (2003) described practices as extremely demanding. "It wasn't a whole lot of fun," Hagan said. "It was work, work, work, and more work. Scrimmaging and playing the games were about the only thing that were fun when playing for Coach Rupp. But, it was worth it, because Coach Rupp was something special."

When asked what were Rupp's greatest qualities, Hagan quickly listed six that stood out above the others:
1. "He was a perfectionist and never settled for anything less.
2. He was exceedingly demanding of his players and himself.
3. He was exacting in the drills. Our plays were part of our practice drills. It became second nature to go right from the drills into our plays.
4. Conditioning. We believed that we were in better condition than any team we played against.
5. He was very bright. He was probably brighter than most people he was coaching against.
6. He was a good recruiter. He could recognize talent."

Rupp pushed his players to great levels of success. Twenty-four players earned All-American honors, seven captured Olympic gold medals, and 28 played professional basketball. Legendary coach "Red" Auerbach said, "Rupp-trained players are better grounded in the fundamentals than any others."

Rupp stated, "It's the work we give them in the fundamentals, there's no other way. The first thing you have to do is curtail the individual desire of the boy in the interest of team play. Then, you have to correct two deficiencies every boy has—in playing defense and in recognizing the value of ball possession."

Rupp was a colorful collection of rituals and superstitions. He always wore a brown suit to games and attended every practice dressed in khaki pants. On game days, Rupp would not step on the court without a buckeye, a rabbit's foot, and a four-leaf clover in his pocket.

Rupp declared his biggest thrills in basketball came when he and his five Kentucky players won Olympic gold medals and when he occupied a front row seat at a U.S. Armed Forces track meet in Frankfort, Germany in 1945, along with George S. Patton and 20 other World War II generals.

Rupp was a strong advocate of the fast break and a tough man-to-man defense. From an offensive standpoint, Rupp believed the greatest offense was the pivot-post offense. Rupp said, "We employed the pivot-post at Kentucky the entire time I coached there. The Original Celtics made the offense perfect. I studied that play with them many nights, talking and talking into the wee hours. I discovered that if you don't have a good pivot man, you're not going to get anywhere with it. We had ten basic plays with the pivot-post offense that we worked on and worked on....not only hours, but hundreds of thousands of hours in order to perfect them." (Rupp, 1976)

Hall of Fame coach Ray Meyer (2003) said, "I played and coached against Mr. Rupp, and I consider him one of the fiercest competitors in the game of basketball. I always liked to play his team early in the season, because he would always tell me what was wrong with my team."

The "Baron of the Bluegrass" established a legacy that few can match. His teams won 876 games, while losing only 190 for a winning percentage of .822. He retired as the winningest coach in college basketball. Adolph Rupp made Kentucky Basketball synonymous with winning.

SOURCE

Hagan, Cliff. Interview with Ralph Pim. September 5, 2003.

Meyer, Ray. Interview with Ralph Pim. September 5, 2003.

Padwe, Sandy. (1970). *Basketball's Hall of Fame.* Englewood Cliffs, NJ: Prentice-Hall.

Rupp, Adolph. Vertical Files, Archives. Naismith Memorial Basketball Hall of Fame. Springfield, MA.

Rupp, Adolph. (1958, December 8). Defeat and Failure To Me Are Enemies. *Sports Illustrated.*

Rupp, Adolph. (1976). Reflections. *The Basketball Bulletin (Winter Edition).*

LESSONS FROM THIS LEGEND...

KENTUCKY'S FAST BREAK

By Adolph Rupp

During the past five years, the fast break has provoked a lot of controversy among the coaching fraternity. At one time, it represented the chief scoring threat and practically the only offensive maneuver that most teams had. Then, came the era of the slower, or deliberate, type of offense. At times, this game became so mechanical that the opportunity to fast break was never exploited. As a result, the fast break became practically an obsolete weapon.

But, today the fast break has arisen from the dead. It has become the most popular attacking pattern in the game. Thanks to the enormously accelerated tempo of play, scoring has increased tremendously.

THREE SCHOOLS OF THOUGHT ON THE FAST BREAK

The advocates of the fast break claim that it is a desirable weapon because basketball is essentially a game of action and people like that type of play. There are three schools of thought on this.

First, there are those who contend that the more deliberate the offense, the sounder it is. Their reasoning is simple. They point out that the fast break tends to promote ballhandling errors and militates against careful planning of the attack.

Another school of thought maintains that the fast break is the easiest way to score and should be employed whenever the opportunity presents itself. Some teams, of course, depend entirely upon the fast break; and when it fails, they mill around until a shot can be obtained.

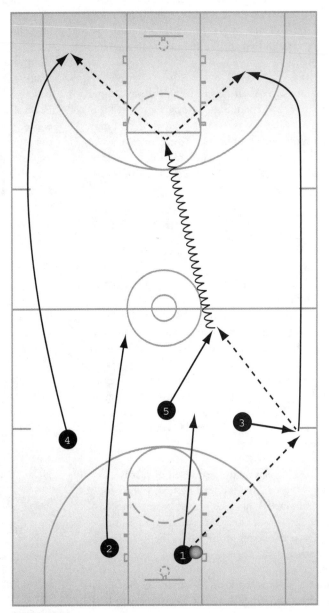

Rupp 1.0

The third school believes that an ideal mixture of the fast break and the set offense produces the best results. In other words, if you have a good fast-break opportunity, use it. But, if a good scoring chance doesn't present itself, don't throw the ball away carelessly; bring it back out again and go into a deliberate pattern of play.

KENTUCKY'S FAST BREAK

We believe in the third school of thought. If a scoring opportunity doesn't present itself from the fast break, we bring it out and go into our set patterns. That's the way we operate at Kentucky.

In teaching the fast break, don't become discouraged if at first it looks ragged and disorganized. Once the players learn exactly what's expected of them, the break will take definite shape. It will develop into a potent, beautiful-to-watch attack.

Diagram 1.0 shows how the fast break may be worked off a zone defense. Let's assume in this case that it's a 3-2 zone. Suppose our opponents have taken the shot and player 01 has taken the ball off the board.

It is now up to the three players in the frontline to carefully check to see where the outlet pass will go. If possible, we want to get the pass to the player in the center and let that individual advance the ball from there by means of a dribble.

However, if we cannot get the ball to the player in the center of the court, we like to have the players go to the sidelines, receive the pass, and work it to the center player as fast as possible. In **Diagram 1.0**, the ball is thrown from 01 to 03, who turns and passes to the center player, 05, for the break.

Diagram 1.1 outlines the fast break from a defensive setup for a free throw. The same pattern prevails whether the toss is made or missed. Again, we try to get the ball out to the side and then bring it to the center.

Should the fast break prove fruitless, we

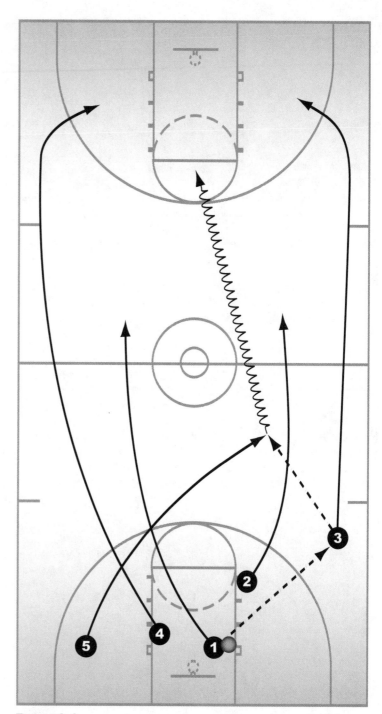

Rupp 1.1

bring the ball out and set up in the pattern we use for all our set plays, with the two guards out and the big center near the pivot line in our single-post offense.

In our basic setup for a free throw, we keep all five players fairly close to the basket area.

Some coaches prefer to keep at least one player farther up court to offer a greater scoring threat once possession is obtained. We like to line up as shown, because we believe it better enables our out-men to pick up loose balls for positive ball-control.

LESSONS FROM THIS LEGEND...

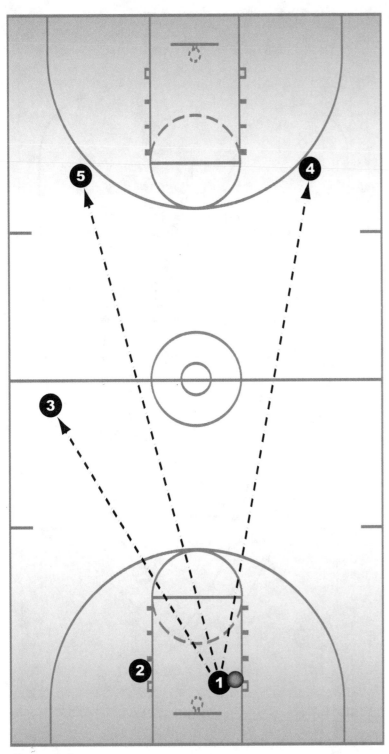

Rupp 1.2

A radical, offensive-minded free throw setup is illustrated in **Diagram 1.2.** This spread formation permits a team to get off a long outlet pass that will by-pass the greater portion of the defensive strength. Some high school teams with good ball-handers use this pattern in the hope of demoralizing the defense and at the same time harass the free-throw shooter.

By dropping player 03 almost as far out as the center line, you'll tend to worry the free thrower, inasmuch as he'll be forced to get back to cover this player. Once the pass is received, 03 will be in an excellent position to dribble toward the basket and force a three-on-two situation. However, many teams prefer to throw the length of the floor to one of the two downcourt players.

As you can see, it's necessary to keep two defensive men back in this situation. Should the opponents try to defend by putting one player on 03 and the other between the two downcourt players, you can use one of the latter as the outlet player; this will immediately give you a two-on-one situation.

SOURCE

Rupp, Adolph. (1951, December). Kentucky's Fast Break. *Scholastic Coach*.

LEGACY OF
William "Bill" Sharman

- Became only the third person in basketball history to be elected to the Naismith Basketball Hall of Fame, as both a player (1976) and a coach (2004).

- Only coach to win championships in three professional leagues (ABL in 1962; ABA in 1971; and NBA in 1972).

- Introduced an innovative training session on game days called the "shoot-around."

- Played in eight NBA All-Star Games during his 11-year NBA career.

- Ranked among the top NBA free-throw shooters of all time with a spectacular .883 percentage.

- Selected in 1996 as one of the 50 Greatest Players in NBA History.

- Helped lead the Boston Celtics to four NBA championships (1957, 1959, 1960, 1961).

WILLIAM "BILL" SHARMAN

"Being a winner in basketball comes down to three things: conditioning, fundamentals, and teamwork."
— *Willian "Bill" Sharman*

BIOGRAPHY

Born: May 25, 1926 in Abilene, TX

Inducted into the Naismith Basketball Hall of Fame as a player in 1976

and as a coach in 2004

In 2004, Bill Sharman joined John Wooden and Lenny Wilkens in the Naismith Basketball Hall of Famer as both a player and a coach. Sharman is the only coach to win championships in three professional leagues (American Basketball League in 1962; American Basketball Association in 1971; and the National Basketball Association in 1972). In 11 seasons coaching in the ABL, ABA, and NBA, Sharman compiled a regular-season record of 509-379 and a post-season record of 62-42. During the 1972 season, he led the Los Angeles Lakers to a 69-13 record, including an NBA record 33-game winning streak. Sharman was a four-year letter-winner at the University of Southern California under future Hall of Fame coach Sam Barry. He was a basketball All-American and the Pacific Coast Conference Most Valuable Player in both 1949 and 1950. Sharman was also an outstanding baseball player and played both sports professionally for five years. In 1955, Sharman abandoned his baseball career to concentrate on basketball. In an 11-year NBA career played mostly with the Boston Celtics, Sharman was voted to the All-NBA first or second team seven times, and he played in eight All-Star Games. He led the NBA in free-throw shooting percentage a record seven seasons and shot .883 (3,143 of 3,559) from the line during his career. Sharman teamed up with Bob Cousy to form one of the most formidable backcourts in NBA history, helping the Celtics win four NBA championships during his tenure. Sharman was named one of the 50 Greatest Players in NBA History, and the Celtics retired his jersey number.

William "Bill" Sharman...

William "Bill" Sharman started playing basketball on a playground near his home in Lomita, California when he was about ten years old. He enjoyed all sports, but basketball caught his attention because it was a sport that he could practice by himself. "In those years, I was somewhat on the bashful side," said Sharman (1975). "My father helped me build a backboard and hoop in my backyard, and I was out there practicing in the mornings and the evenings. Anytime I could get a spare minute, I'd be out there shooting the ball. If there were five minutes before dinner was ready, I'd be out there. It was a perfect opportunity for me to progress and develop my own skills without the help of others."

The first organized basketball games for Bill occurred in junior high school when several teachers organized a basketball league during lunch hour. This became one of his favorite activities, and he played with tremendous intensity and enthusiasm. "Even today, I remember my junior high experience very strongly," said Sharman. "I believe this lunchtime league probably sparked the fires of competitive basketball in me."

At Porterville (CA) High School, Sharman won 15 varsity letters. In basketball, Sharman was his team's leading scorer and captain for three consecutive years and was also selected All-Conference each year. Sharman graduated from Porterville in 1944 and served in the Armed Forces for the next two years.

Sharman attended the University of Southern California where he was a standout athlete in both basketball and baseball. He was unsure which sport to pursue after graduation and signed a minor league baseball contract with the Brooklyn Dodgers in 1950. Later that year, the Washington Capitals drafted Sharman in the second round of the NBA Draft. For the next five years, Sharman played both professional baseball and basketball.

Sharman was a promising outfielder in the Dodgers organization. In September 1955, Brooklyn called up Sharman to the Major Leagues for the final month of the season. During one game, the umpire became so upset with the players on the Brooklyn bench, that he ejected every one, including Sharman. Because of his expulsion, Sharman's name became the answer to the following baseball trivia question: "Who was the only player to be thrown out of a Major League game without ever playing in one?"

In the NBA, things were different for Sharman. He joined the Boston Celtics in 1951 and teamed up with Bob Cousy to produce one of the NBA's greatest backcourt combos. Sharman's deadly jump shot blended perfectly with Cousy's ballhandling wizardry in Red Auerbach's vaunted fast-break offense. Future Hall of Famer Bill Russsell would control the boards and quickly outlet the ball to Cousy, who would speed dribble downcourt, with Sharman trailing. Then, Cousy would either drive for the basket, or flip the ball back to Sharman for his patented jump shot.

Sharman was unquestionable one of basketball's greatest pure shooters of all time. He led the NBA in free-throw shooting percentage seven times, including a stretch of five years in a row. During his 11-year NBA career, Sharman shot a spectacular .883 percentage from the charity stripe.

He was also respected for his fierce, aggressive defensive style. "Bill was tough," said Hall of Fame player Jerry West. "You did not drive by him. He got into more fights than Mike Tyson. You respected him as a player."

Sharman was a fitness zealot and maintained a physical conditioning regime that bordered on being obsessive. He believed that conditioning was something that had to be worked on every day. "A coach can offer advice," said Sharman (1975), "but individuals must motivate themselves. You have to do certain things in order to keep in condition."

"First, you have to learn to take care of your body," said Sharman. "That means good eating habits. You should know the basics of nutrition and vitamins, as well as the value of good food, so you can perform better at each game and in each practice session.

"Second," continued Sharman, "you should acquire good sleeping habits. You should know how much sleep you need the night before a game, how much of a nap or rest you need the afternoon of a game. You should know how to control your social activities so they don't interfere with your playing during the season."

"And third, a player should know the value of self-pride," said Sharman. "I feel this is a big factor. It means getting ready mentally and emotionally for the game so you can do the very best you can in every aspect of the contest."

Sharman retired from the NBA in 1961. During his 11-year career, he played in eight All-Star Games and helped Boston win four NBA championships.

Sharman's professional playing career didn't end when he left Boston. He was hired by the Los Angeles Jets of the American Basketball League (ABL) to be a player-coach for the 1961-62 season. Sharman appeared in 19 games for the Jets, but when the franchise folded midway during the season, his playing days officially ended. He remained in the ABL that year, however, moving over to coach the Cleveland Pipers. Under Sharman's leadership, the Pipers won the ABL Championship.

After the ABL folded, Sharman became a head coach on the collegiate level at Cal State-Los Angeles and compiled a two-year record of 27-20. Sharman's next head coaching position was with the San Francisco Warriors, where he guided the team to an 87-76 record. Sharman left the Warriors to take control of the Los Angeles Stars of the American Basketball Association (ABA). The franchise moved to Utah, and Sharman directed the Stars to the 1971 ABA Championship over the heavily favored Kentucky Colonels.

The following year, Sharman became head coach of the Los Angeles Lakers in the NBA. The team went two months without losing a game, and set an NBA record of 33 victories in a row. Led by Wilt Chamberlain, Jerry West, and Gail Goodrich, the Lakers went on to win the 1972 NBA Championship, and Sharman was selected NBA Coach of the Year.

Chamberlain described Sharman as an "astute basketball man." Wilt also said, "Sharman knows personnel and how to deal with the individual. He gets players to do what he thinks is best for the team. He also listens to what players have to say to make it a better unit."

Sharman gave up his coaching duties after the 1976 season and became the Lakers' general manager. During that span, Los Angeles drafted Magic Johnson and won the NBA championship in 1980 and 1982. Sharman then became club president and helped the Lakers capture three more championships in 1985, 1987, and 1988. Sharman retired in 1988 but has remained with the Lakers as a special consultant.

Jerry West probably described Bill Sharman best when he said, "I have been around a lot of coaches but none like him. He's a remarkable guy. He doesn't miss a thing. He has the ability to get the most out of people. Bill always sees a bright spot, even when things are darkest."

Bill Sharman will go down in history as a player and coach who brought an untiring quest for perfection and a winning attitude to basketball.

Source

Sharman, Bill. (1965). *Sharman on Basketball Shooting.* Englewood Cliffs, NJ: Prentice-Hall.

http://www.baseballlibrary.com/baseballlibrary/ballplayers/s/sharman_bill.stm

http://www.nba.com/history/players/sharman_bio.html

LESSONS FROM THIS LEGEND...

FREE-THROW SHOOTING TECHNIQUES

By Bill Sharman

I am sure every basketball player, coach, and fan has had nightmares about the missed free throw that cost his team a valuable victory. Free-throw shooting is directly responsible, as well, for many victories during the season, and many coaches feel that it is the most important factor in winning any close game.

All coaches should emphasize that free-throw shooting can be improved more than any other phase of shooting. It is the only shot that remains the same on every attempt. Ten seconds are allowed to prepare and execute the shot; no defenders are allowed to hinder the shot; and the distance and position on the court are always the same.

I urge that every player be coached on the fundamentals of the free-throw technique. The shot is truly a feat of muscle memory and repetition. I like to compare it to a person giving a speech: the more he practices, the better his delivery will be. The same applies to shooting free throws. The more it is practiced, the better it becomes. There is no substitute for hard work and desire in any sport.

While every player has his own style for shooting free throws, there are certain basic principles that can be applied to all styles. This article will deal with the psychological and technical aspects of shooting free throws.

GENERAL FREE THROW HINTS

1. SHOOT WITH RHYTHM AND SMOOTHNESS

I firmly believe that rhythm and smoothness are the keys to successful free-throw shooting, assuming of course, that the shooter is using proper fundamentals. Golf instructors always stress that the swing should be very smooth and executed with a definite rhythm. This also applies when shooting a basketball, especially on the free-throw line. Any movement that is hurried or jerky will definitely handicap accuracy and control.

2. TRAIN YOURSELF TO CONCENTRATE

As in all sports and activities, a successful basketball player must learn how to think, as well as how to go through the motions. He must learn to concentrate in order to reach his highest potential. When a player is fouled, and is awarded a free throw, he must immediately start concentrating on the execution of the shot. If he just walks up to the line and thinks, "I hope it goes in," he will undoubtedly be shooting far below his maximum ability, and he will probably have a tendency to tie himself up psychologically.

3. LEARN TO RELAX AND BE COMFORTABLE

Any player who does not feel relaxed and comfortable will not reach his highest degree of efficiency. This is a very common observation that applies to free-throw shooting. If the player feels cramped or tied up, his confidence and control will suffer, and many unnecessary misses will result.

Correct practice methods and mastery of the fundamentals are the answer to this problem. Each player should pretend he is shooting the crucial or winning free throw every time he shoots a practice throw. He should experiment with different techniques and methods in order to discover his most relaxed and comfortable position at the free-throw line.

4. ESTABLISH A DEFINITE ROUTINE

The necessity for each player to develop a good sound routine is one of the most abused phases of shooting free throws. Too often, I have observed potentially good free-throw shooters merely go through the motions, without establishing a good pattern that would regulate their thoughts and actions before shooting. It is important for each player to realize that he will be shooting free throws under different conditions

LESSONS FROM THIS LEGEND...

each time. One time he might get fouled near the end of the game, when he is very tired. Therefore, he should work on a routine that will help him feel the same way each time he steps up to the free-throw line, regardless of the circumstances. There are numerous methods for doing this:

- Take a few deep breaths.
- Bounce the ball a few times.
- Waggle the ball before shooting.
- Take a comfortable stance before receiving the ball from the official.

The main point here is that the player must use the same routine in practice, as well as in the game, so that he gets the same feeling every time he shoots.

5. TAKE ADVANTAGE OF THE 10-SECOND TIME LIMIT

The main thing a player should learn about the 10-second rule when shooting free throws is neither to shoot too quickly nor to wait too long. A player can sometimes become too deliberate and lower his accuracy by "posing" in one position longer than he should. This usually results in his shooting short of the basket.

Of course, a rushed shot—where the player doesn't take enough time—will also hamper accuracy. A player should learn to use the amount of time that best suits his style and form when shooting free throws.

6. DON'T HAVE TOO MANY THOUGHTS BEFORE SHOOTING

A player can lower his proficiency simply by trying to cover too many things at once just prior to shooting. The time to think and work on weaknesses or checkpoints is during daily practice sessions. Probably not more than one or two fundamentals should be in the players' mind just before the free throw. This does not contradict the idea that a basic routine must be established.

This rule compares favorably with correct golfing methods. Most golf instructors and

pros advocate that the player have a single thought when he actually starts his swing; usually this thought involves the determination to keep every motion as smooth as possible. The thought is applicable to shooting free throws as well.

7. LEARN HOW TO KEEP YOUR HEAD AS STILL AS POSSIBLE

Another golf fundamental that certainly applies to shooting a basketball is the necessity for the shooter to keep his head still. Arnold Palmer has written that keeping the head still while putting is probably the most important factor in that phase of the game. Obviously, shooting a basketball requires more body action than putting a golf ball; however, the principle of holding the head as still as possible is equally applicable and will help to improve accuracy at the free-throw line.

8. KEEP BALL AIMED STRAIGHT FOR THE MIDDLE OF THE BASKET

The technique that has helped me the most while shooting a free throw is that of keeping the ball aimed straight for the middle section of the rim. If the ball strays to one side or the other, the chances of its going through are tremendously reduced.

9. LINE UP BALL PROPERLY

There is a distinct advantage in lining up the ball in a similar position for each free-throw shot. Extra confidence can be gained by placing the fingers either across the seams or parallel with them each time a shot is attempted.

The player should also make sure his hands and the ball are as dry as possible each time he shoots. This can become a problem with those players who perspire a lot in an over-heated gymnasium. The player can wipe his hands on his shirt, pants, or socks before shooting, or he might ask the official to wipe off the ball first or ask him for permission to use a towel.

10. WALK SLOWLY TO THE FREE-THROW LINE

Often a player will miss a free throw just by not being ready to shoot when he receives the ball from the official. Therefore, he should walk slowly to the free-throw line in order to prepare himself mentally and physically. If he rushes to the line and does not prepare himself thoroughly, he will surely perform far below his peak potential.

FREE THROW COACHING METHODS

If a player has already achieved an accurate free-throw style, the coach shouldn't try to change it. There are many successful unorthodox performers in all sports, and basketball is no exception.

If a player has developed a fairly successful technique but is using some improper fundamentals, the coach should make an adjustment in his form, rather than completely changing his style. If a coach tries to completely change a player's style, it may destroy the player's self-confidence and sense of timing. A slow, gradual adjustment gives the player a feeling of comfort and also bolsters his morale. The coach should always explain the reasons for any change he advises, so that the boy will understand why such a change will help his shot.

The coach should set definite free-throw percentage goals for each player. Conscientious players who often practice by themselves do not always have the advantage of competing against teammates. Setting individual goals during practice sessions can compensate for this. If a player is working on free throws, he should have a definite goal in mind. This helps to maintain his concentration during shooting practice.

SHARMAN FREE-THROW TECHNIQUE

My free-throw method is an accumulation of the fundamentals that I found to work best for me. I will go over my method step-by-step.

LESSONS FROM THIS LEGEND...

1. When I am fouled after running real hard, I always take a little more time to walk to the free-throw line. This extra time gives me a chance to catch my breath and to collect my thought before attempting the free throw.

2. I then take the stance I find comfortable and suitable to me, and line up in the same position each time.

3. I always bounce the ball a few times to get the feel of it, and also to loosen up my wrist.

4. I then assume the starting position, with my body and the ball held correctly.

5. I take one or two deep breaths. This helps to calm my body and respiration.

6. I always strive to achieve the same feeling each time I shoot a free throw.

7. I then waggle the ball a few times. Because the ball sometimes feels different—slippery or slick with perspiration. This gives me a better feel of the ball just before shooting. Like the waggle in golf just before the start of the swing, it also tends to loosen up the player and offers a smoother shot.

8. I then sight the basket and concentrate on pinpointing my target.

9. I always think about keeping the ball straight when aiming.

10. Next, I make sure my elbow moves under the ball, instead of staying behind it. This corrects the wrist cock for a successful release.

11. I always try to exaggerate the backspin on the ball (for a smoother, more accurate shot) by letting the ball roll off my fingertips and giving a good strong wrist snap.

12. I build up my concentration to a peak, just at the instant the ball actually leaves my fingers.

13. I always make a complete follow-through, which is necessary for maximum control and accuracy.

14. I always notice exactly where the ball lands. If I miss the basket or target, I am then prepared to make the necessary adjustments before taking my next shot. That way I do not lose confidence in my shooting—as I might if I wasn't aware of my error or didn't know how to correct it.

FREE THROW SHOOTING DRILLS

The key words in successful free-throw shooting are competition, relaxation, fundamentals, pressure, and simulation of game conditions. These are some of the elements that should be considered and used in free-throw shooting drills.

1. PARTNER SHOOTING

One of the best methods for getting players interested and concentrating on each shot is to divide the squad into teams of two, matching strong and weak shooters in each pair. Then, one team challenges another after the regular practice session is over. The winning group gets to go shower, but the losing group has to stay and challenge another losing group until it finally wins. I usually set the first game at 30, which means each player has to shoot 30 free throws, two at a time. After shooting two, he then rotates with his opponents and his partner, so he is shooting two out of every eight shots taken. I usually drop the second round to 20 shots each. Then, the third-round losers shoot 10 free throws each, until finally the last two players on the same team will have to compete against each other, with the loser shooting an extra 10 by himself.

2. ELIMINATION CONTEST DRILL

This drill is similar to the partner shooting drill, except each player competes against another player. Each player shoots 30 free throws, two at a time. The winner can go shower or have free time to practice some other phase of the game. The losers must challenge another loser for a second round. This continues until every player on the team has won a match (some other penalty can be used for the losing man in the last pair).

3. DAILY CHARTS

Daily charts of each player's free-throw shooting can be very useful and beneficial. They let the players and the coach know who the best free-throw shooters are and also identifies which players need special work and instruction. Approximately 50 shots each day is a good number to start preseason training. The charts should be posted in the locker room, so each player can check his daily and weekly progress.

4. SHOOT UNTIL MISS

Having players divide up and shoot free throws at separate baskets right after a hard practice can simulate game conditions. One method of improving their concentration is to have them continue to shoot as long as they make the basket. If they miss, they have to give up the ball.

LESSONS FROM THIS LEGEND...

5. FREE-THROW LADDER

A free-throw ladder can be fun and very useful to the players, the coach, and the team. Naturally, certain players will dominate the top spots, but letting the other players challenge for higher positions can serve to motivate them. Penalties and rewards can also be used very effectively in this method of shooting free throws.

6. INDIVIDUAL FREE THROWS

Complete concentration is always the best method of making any shot, especially free throws. If a player is practicing by himself, he should set a definite goal before he begins, and make it a habit not to quit until he reaches this predetermined number. The player should always strive to increase his regular-shooting percentage by setting goals a little higher than his average.

Source

Sharman, Bill. (1965). *Sharman on Basketball Shooting*. Englewood Cliffs, NJ: Prentice-Hall.

LEGACY OF
Everett "Ev" Shelton

- Directed the University of Wyoming to the NCAA championship in 1943.

- Innovative coach who developed a five-man weave called the "Box Weave."

- Served as president of the NABC (1959-60) and created the position of National Rules Interpreter (today called the Rules Secretary/Editor).

- Compiled an 845-492 record in 46 years of coaching at the high school, college, and AAU levels.

- Led the Denver Safeways to the 1937 National AAU Championship.

- Coached Kenny Sailors, the player most credited with developing the first jump shot in basketball.

EVERETT "EV" SHELTON

"I believe in a ball-control, patterned offense, but our offense is not so strict that it takes away the individual ability and freedom of a player."
— *Everett "Ev" Shelton*

BIOGRAPHY

Born: May 12, 1898 in Cunningham, KS

Died: April 16, 1974

Inducted into the Naismith Basketball Hall of Fame in 1980

Everett "Ev" Shelton began his coaching career at Claremore (OK) High School in 1923. The following year, Shelton returned to his alma mater, Phillips University, where he served as the head coach for all sports for three years. From 1927-29, he coached AAU basketball, where one of his players for Sterling Milk was future Hall of Famer, Henry Iba. Shelton returned to the high-school coaching ranks from 1929 to 1936. During this stint, he led Christian Brothers (MO) High School to three city titles and a second-place finish in the state tournament. Shelton developed the five-man weave offense in 1932, which he later used to direct the Denver Safeway Stores to the 1937 AAU National Championship. In 1939, Shelton began the first of 19 seasons at the University of Wyoming. He led the Cowboys to 328 victories, eight Skyline Conference championships, eight NCAA tournament appearances, and the 1943 NCAA title. Shelton completed his coaching career at Sacramento State College from 1959 to 1969. He led Sacramento State to the Small-College NCAA Finals in 1962. Shelton compiled an 845-492 record in 46 years of coaching at the high school, college, and AAU levels. He served as president of the NABC in 1959-60 and was a member of the NCAA Tournament Committee from 1954 to 1959. In 1969, Shelton was selected the first commissioner of the Far Western Conference. He is enshrined into the Helms Foundation and Naismith Memorial Basketball Halls of Fame.

Everett "Ev" Shelton...

Everett "Ev" Shelton was born and raised, immersed in the rich heritage of basketball, in the Great Plains of Kansas. He attended Cunningham (KS) High School from 1912 to 1916, and garnered four letters each in football, basketball, and baseball. Shelton served in the U.S. Marine Corps and then entered Phillips University in Enid, Oklahoma. He graduated in 1923, with a degree in chemistry, and he also earned four letters each in football, basketball, and baseball. This formed the basis of an illustrious 46-year coaching career in high school, college, and AAU basketball.

Shelton was an innovative coach and was always looking for new strategies and techniques. In 1932, he developed a five-man weave offense, which he later used with the Denver Safeway Stores to win the AAU national championship in 1937. Shelton believed in a patterned, ball-control offense, but most importantly, he wanted to provide individual freedom for a player to utilize his strengths and exploit defensive mistakes.

Shelton was also a big believer in scouting reports, and he used that information to formulate game planes based on the strengths and weaknesses of his opponents. He wanted to know the type of defense employed by his opponent, as well as the weakest defenders on the team.

Shelton instructed his players on the correct techniques for shooting because he preached that shooting accuracy was the most important part of the game. Shelton stated, "We have a theory that all shots should be from the finger tips, rather than from the palm of the hand." Shelton wanted his players to catch the ball on their fingertips and be ready to initiate the shot from that position.

The 1943 season was, perhaps, Shelton's most successful year as a coach. He led the University of Wyoming to the Skyline Conference championship, won the NCAA

Western playoffs, and then defeated Georgetown for the NCAA national title. The following week, Wyoming was pitted against St. John's, the winner of the NIT tournament, in the first Red Cross Benefit game. The Cowboys prevailed over St. John's in a classic match-up of champions, and Wyoming earned the title of "World Champions." During the 1943 season, Wyoming also swept two games from the AAU champions, Phillips 66ers.

Diminutive Kenny Sailors, the Most Valuable Player of the NCAA tournament and College Player of the Year, led the 1943 team. Sailors also took his place in basketball history. When he was 13 years old, his older, taller brother, Bud, often dominated Kenny. When they played on their farm in tiny Hillsdale, Wyoming, Bud would block one shot after another. Kenny decided if he could jump high enough, he might be able to get the shot off. Kenny's theory worked, much to the surprise of his brother. He went on to develop the jump shot and later became the star of the Wyoming Cowboy's national championship team. In that era, leaving the ground to shoot was unthinkable; two-handed set shots and a few hook shots were the norm. Sailors, under the tutelage of Everett Shelton, changed all of that. Basketball would never be the same with the advent of the mid-range jump shot. Other key developers of the shot were Hank Luissetti of Stanford, who first popularized the standing one-hand set shot, and Joe Fulks from Murray State University.

Following Wyoming's national championship, Sailors, along with most team members, enlisted in World War II, and the 1943-44 season was suspended. Shelton spent the year coaching the Dow Chemical AAU team and guided his squad to the AAU national finals.

Shelton left Wyoming in 1959 and coached at Sacramento State until 1969. He led Sacramento to the small-college NCAA National Finals, where Mount St. Mary's defeated them by one point in overtime.

When Shelton served as president of the NABC (1959-60), he convinced the NCAA to create a permanent position called the National Interpreter of Basketball Rules. John Bunn first filled the position, followed by Ed Steitz.

Together, they had a combined tenure of over 50 years in this position and were later inducted into the Naismith Basketball Hall of Fame.

After retiring from coaching with an overall record of 845-492, Shelton became the first commissioner of the Far Western Conference. He stayed close to the game he loved by giving coaching clinics and writing technical articles.

Source

Shelton, Everett. Vertical Files, Archives. Naismith Memorial Basketball Hall of Fame. Springfield, MA.

Shelton, Everett F. (1946). Five-Man Weave Pattern. In Hank Luissetti (ed), *Famous Play Patterns by America's Most Famous Coaches*. San Francisco: Mercury Press.

LESSONS FROM THIS LEGEND...

WYOMING'S BOX WEAVE

By Everett F. Shelton

Authors' Note: Coach Everett Shelton developed his form of the five-man weave offense called the box weave. He described it as an offense, that had twenty different options depending on what the defense did. These options, generally broke down into five basic two-man plays, a dribble penetration to the middle or outside from the guard position, and an option chosen according to how the defense reacted to the box weave. All five players were interchangeable. This article was written at the conclusion of Shelton's 1943 NCAA Championship season.

In this article, I will discuss how we play basketball at the University of Wyoming Ever since Dr. Naismith put a peach basket at each end of the gymnasium at Springfield College, offense has been playing against defense. We arranged our offense in reference to the team defense of our opponents, and also, in reference to the individual defense of our opponents.

First, we will consider the individual defense. From our scouting reports, we will identify the slow defensive man. This is the man who is slow to take a defensive position, the careless defensive man, the man who is careless about staying in position, and what we call the "lazy defensive" man. He is the one who will cover very closely for three or four times and then for a couple of times is lazy about covering. We also evaluate the defensive forward and want to know how fast he reacts to the side on which his foot is back. Then, we will form our offense in reference to these particular traits of defense individually.

The most important part of our basketball game is the ability to shoot accurately. We have a theory that all shots should be from the fingertips, rather than from the palm of the hand. Most young players, when they come to you, because of their lack of ability to shoot long, will pull the ball down in their lap, so to speak, to start their shot. We don't believe this helps the shot in any way, and it takes much longer to get the shot away. We teach our boys to catch the ball on the fingertips, and if the ball is caught below the shoulders, start the ball up and release it with the fingers and wrist snap. If you change a boy's shooting and start him with short shots, you'll be surprised how quickly he will develop into a long shooter. There is no preliminary movement, therefore, your guard cannot know when the ball is going to be released toward the basket.

We do a lot of one-handed shooting because of our style of offense. This shot is quicker and softer than the two-handed shot. When we teach a player how to shoot, we have him catch the ball on the axis in his fingers. As the ball goes up, the ball is rotated. If the boy is right-handed, he is taught to get his right hand behind the ball. As the ball rolls off of his fingers, the player finishes with a snap of the wrist. He guides the ball up in both hands until the left hand is about face high, and then the right hand follows the ball through. As a player develops, if he is right-handed, he will catch the ball with his right hand back of the ball and his left hand on the side. Then, he will shoot the ball the same as described, although there is no rotating to get the hand behind the ball. This year, our squad members all shot one-handed and had the highest percentage of accuracy of any squad I have coached in twenty years.

As for team defense, we like to be able to tell by our scouting reports if defensive men are assigned to our offensive players before the game starts—if they try to cover straight through the whole game by assignment, or if they will pick up the offensive man as he goes into the offensive territory; if the opponent's defense will change men as we run a screen, or if they will try to give-and-take and cover the same man.

As for arranging the offense in reference to the defense we have scouted, if our opponents have a defensive man who is slow, we will arrange our offense so he will have to cover our fastest offensive man. Against the defensive man who is careless about position, we arrange our offense to have our quickest shooter play against him. If their defense will pick up as we take offensive positions, we will send our big man to a position in which their little man will have to cover him or we may start a forward at a guard position if they cover by position so that a guard will have to guard our forward. If our opponents have a big and slow man who is not capable of covering the post, we will assign our offense so that this particular man will have to over our post man. Most teams have one player who is exceptionally good at guarding the post. Offensively, we have two men who are capable of playing the offensive post. If our opponents have a player who is exceptionally good in clearing the backboard, we maneuver him away from the basket.

As for team defense, if our opponents use a falling (sagging) defense, they will have two or three men who will do the greater part of the falling and protecting the middle of the court. We maneuver to get our best long shots covered by these boys who are falling.

LESSONS FROM THIS LEGEND...

In our screen type of play, we try to screen the man who is slow to react and to get out of a screen. To be sure that a defensive man has a hard time covering us individually, we develop in a boy the ability to do two things well. First, in the boy who is capable of shooting over the screen, we develop him so that he is capable of breaking very fast. Second, in the boy who has the ability to be an elusive dribbler so that the defensive man must play him loose or carefully, we teach him to make a very quick shot over. Men playing our post have the ability to go either to the right or the left, and when forced to come out on the floor, can hit enough to be a threat.

With this means of offense, our boys have the ability to run five different offensive maneuvers. This is a screen offense, because in our early days of coaching, we did not have boys with the ability to maneuver themselves loose for shots, so we had to devise some plan to get them open. This has a good effect on the defensive man. He must watch the opponent he is guarding and know whether he is going to be caught in a screen.

There are two distinct screens that basketball people use. One is a three-foot standing screen and the other is the moving screen. The rule book clearly states that you

can move toward the basket between the opponent and your teammate. Different sections of the country call these particular screens differently. The coaches themselves, rather than the officials, caused the interpretation of the rules involving screens to change. In one of our most important games last winter, every time we gained possession of the ball, the opponent's coach would tell the officials to watch our frontline screen. After several times, I asked him if it was that bad.

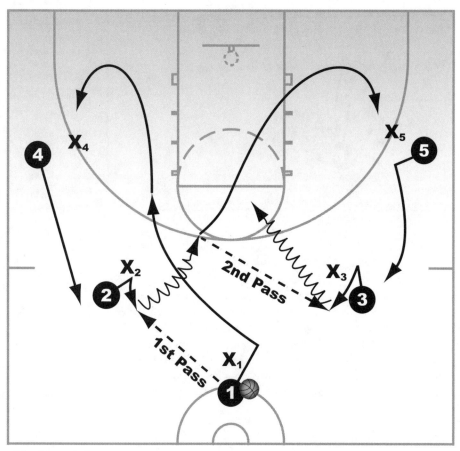

Shelton 1.0

In **Diagram 1.0**, the player doing the screening will not come close enough to cause contact. The dribbler coming around will cause the screen. The screener is moving toward the basket. At times, the defensive man will jump quickly in the path of the screener, but still we try to change our direction quickly enough to avoid contact.

Diagram 1.0 illustrates our fundamental weave offense in which O1 will pass to O2, go over toward the defensive man, and break toward the basket. If O2 moves off, dribbling during the time that O2's opponent is caught in the screen, then O2 will dribble on into the basket. If there is no play, O2 will dribble across and pass to O3, who will then dribble across and pass to O4, who then passes to O5. In turn, O5 crosses and passes to O1, who will then cross and pass to O2, which brings us back to our original set-up. The continuation of the play works into a figure eight. The screens themselves cause the defensive man to hesitate more than make contact on the play. We run this as a medium-slow weave or a very fast weave. You see that our boys have the ability to dribble and read the defensive material, as well as the ability to cover different positions on the court, rather than a frontline or baseline position. Also, they need to have the ability to cover on both the right and the left side of the court.

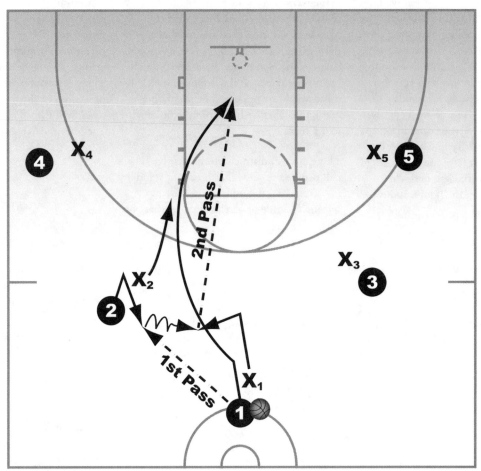

Shelton 1.1

Diagram 1.1 (Switch). Against a defense that will change men, the pass is a little longer, and if the screen is to the left, the screener will break fast and turn very quickly to take a return pass from O2 over his right shoulder. O2 will dribble across quickly to draw the defensive man of O1 out to cover him, being careful to stop his dribble in time to pass to O1 who is breaking toward the basket. We will run the play against the defensive man of our opponents who is slow to change.

In **Diagram 1.1,** we have opponents who switch or change men when two offensive men cross. O1 will pass to O2 and come towards O2. O2 will switch and take X1. O1 will false screen and break toward the basket, before X2 will be able to cover him. If the first play does not work, they will continue on as in **Diagram 1.0.**

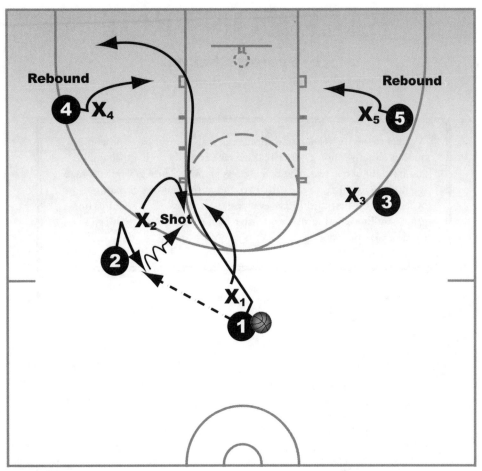

Shelton 1.2

Diagram 1.2 (Sagging). Against a defense that will sag and slip through, we make no attempt to screen, but give room for O2 to shoot. O2 passes and comes over to screen. O2 sags to slip through, and takes a step with his left foot and shoots a one-handed shot as his right foot comes forward. Our three men out on the court will line up closer to the basket, and our boys that are the best shots will do the shooting against this type of defense. O4 and O5 are in position to follow the shot.

SOURCE

Shelton, Everett F. (1943). Offense versus Defense. *Converse Basketball Yearbook.*

LESSONS FROM THIS LEGEND...

DRILLS FOR BALL CONTROL

By Everett Shelton

We here at the University of Wyoming are ball-control pattern people, but our pattern is not so strict that we take away the individual ability and freedom of a player. The defense sets all our offensive plays and here is a drill we use often in the early part and at the end of our season. I believe it is the best drill I have ever seen to improve sight reaction under game conditions and to teach offensive men to react in reference to what the defensive man does.

Shelton 2.0

In **Diagram 2.0**, O1 dribbles to the middle of the court and reverses. O2 cuts past O1. In this drill, X2 goes over the top and attempts to stay with O2.

- If X2 is trailing O2, the ball should be handed off from O1 to O2.

- If X2 is only a half-step from O2, O1 should execute a drop pass as O2 goes by.

- If X2 is even with O2, O1 waits and makes a delayed pass as O2 cuts toward the basket.

- O1's ability to read O2's defender will determine which pass is utilized.

LESSONS FROM THIS LEGEND...

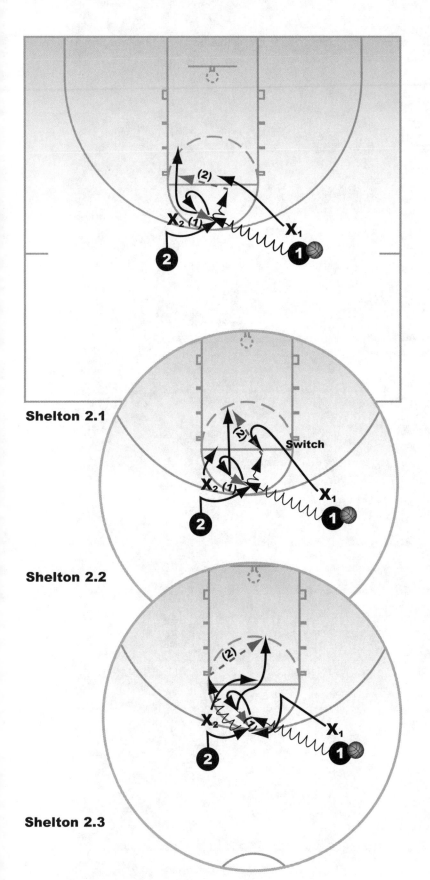

Shelton 2.1

Shelton 2.2

Shelton 2.3

In **Diagram 2.1**, O1 dribbles to the middle of the court and reverses. X1 backs up and gives X2 space to slide through. the purpose of this drill is to try and pivot one defender out of the play.

- If X2 goes behind, O2 looks for an open perimeter shot.
- If X2 slides to the right of O1, O2 drives to his left. O1 pivots (facing the ball) and breaks away, making it impossible for X1 to cover both players.
- If X2 slides to the left of O1, O2 drives to his right. After working on this, O2 should be able to immediately read the defender.
- If X1 stays with O1, O2 is clear to break to the basket.
- If X1 switches, O2 will pass to O1.
- If X1 plays between O1 and O2, O2 should take one dribble and shoot the jump shot.

In **Diagram 2.2**, the defensive players, X1 and X2, switch defensive responsibilities. We will do two things against a defensive switch. As O2 breaks by O1, O2 stops quickly and passes to O1, as he pivots and cuts toward the basket. It is important that O1 pivots and breaks toward the basket before X2 can pick him up.

If X1 is aggressive and switches in front of O2, O2 should stop and go back (see **Diagram 2.3**). O1 should pivot and force X1 out of the play. This forces X2 to cover two players. If he covers O2, O2 should pass to O1, who is breaking to the basket. If X2 covers O1, O2 will have a drive to the basket.

These are the best drills I know to develop quickness of reaction, driving, and good passing under game conditions.

Source

Shelton, Everett F. (1956) Drills for Ball Control. *Seal-O-San Basketball Coaches Digest.*

257

LEGACY OF
Fred Taylor

- Respected as a coach of the highest integrity.

- Believed the most significant qualities of a human being were loyalty, character, and self-sacrifice.

- Led Ohio State to the NCAA Finals three consecutive years (1960, 1961, and 1962) and won the NCAA title in 1960.

- Directed Ohio State to five consecutive Big Ten championships between 1960 and 1964.

- Masterfully designed his offense and defense around the talents of his players.

- Set an example that a coach can be a fierce competitor and still be a gentleman.

FRED TAYLOR

"We feel that the game of basketball is basically one of execution of the fundamentals."
— *Fred Taylor*

BIOGRAPHY

Born: December 23, 1924 in Zanesville, OH

Died: January 6, 2002

Inducted into the Naismith Basketball Hall of Fame in 1986

Fred Taylor was the head basketball coach at Ohio State from 1959 through 1976 and compiled a 297-158 won-lost record. During Taylor's tenure, the Buckeyes won the 1960 NCAA championship, finished second in 1961 and 1962, and finished third in 1968. Taylor led Ohio State to a 14-4 record in five NCAA tournaments. The Buckeyes won five consecutive Big Ten titles from 1960-1964. Taylor was named UPI and USBWA National Coach of the Year in 1961 and 1962. Taylor coached Hall of Famers Jerry Lucas, John Havlicek, and Bob Knight. He served as president of the NABC in 1972 and was an assistant coach on the 1979 USA team that won the Gold Medal at the Pan American games. Taylor served on the U.S. Olympic Basketball Committee from 1964-1972.

Fred Taylor...

Even though he had twice been cut from his high school team in Zanesville, Ohio, Fred Taylor went on to become a two-sport standout at Ohio State University. Taylor was the starting center on the Buckeye's 1950 Big Ten championship squad that finished third in the NCAA tournament. He was also a star on the baseball diamond and was Ohio State's first baseball All-American. Taylor signed a professional baseball contract with the Washington Senators and played parts of three seasons in the major leagues. During the winter months, Taylor came back to Columbus and coached Ohio State's freshmen team.

After spending five years as the Buckeye's freshmen coach, Taylor was named head basketball coach at Ohio State in 1958. The thirty-three year old coach wasted little time implementing new ideas into the Buckeye basketball program. The night Taylor was hired, he brought several friends to St. John's Arena, and they painted an "O" in the center of the basketball court. Taylor stated, "I thought, for crying out loud, it's Ohio State, and we ought to have an "O" in the center of the basketball floor. They've got something in the center of the football field, so why couldn't we have something in basketball. All I did was paint a gray "O" and outline it in black, and then I eventually got the red on the sidelines and baselines. This was something they didn't want at all. It took three or four years to get that done. (Hunter, 1981, p. 187)

During his last year as freshmen coach, Taylor helped recruit the legendary class of Jerry Lucas, John Havlicek, Mel Nowell, Gary Gearhart, and Bob Knight. Taylor knew this recruiting class had the potential to be great. At that time, freshmen were not permitted to play on the varsity. Taylor decided to expedite the progress of his fabulous freshmen by having them practice against the varsity almost every night. He even installed an offense to take advantage of Lucas' abilities. "We put in the whole kit and caboodle," Taylor admitted later. "The boys learned the offense just the way we were going to play it with Lucas in 1960." In two scrimmage games, the freshman beat the varsity squad, and Lucas scored over forty points both times.

While Buckeye fans patiently waited for this heralded group to move up to the varsity, Taylor knew that he had to improve the defensive play of his team. The Buckeyes were the worst defensive team in the Big Ten, yielding

122 points in one game and more than 90 points in four others. Taylor described his team's defensive perils this way, "We didn't play any defense at all. I mean, we couldn't catch Marilyn Monroe in a telephone booth." (Jenkins, 1999, p. 189)

Taylor believed Pete Newell was the best defensive coach in the country. He watched Newell's California Golden Bears win the 1959 NCAA championship and wanted to learn more about their defensive system. Taylor asked Newell for help, and Newell graciously agreed. Taylor told Newell, "I've got a great sophomore group coming in, and I think I've really got something. I'd like you to start from the very bottom, the most basic things" (Jenkins, 1999, p. 190). Taylor spent hours with Newell learning California's defensive system. "He showed me everything," said Taylor. "He confirmed some of my ideas, and he gave me the courage to try things I was afraid were too radical." On two other occasions, Taylor sent assistant coach Jack Graf to California to watch games and ask additional questions.

When the NCAA title game arrived in 1960, it pitted Taylor's Ohio State Buckeyes against Pete Newell's University of California Golden Bears. It was a battle between the nation's top offensive and defensive teams. The Pacific Coast Conference champion, California, allowed only 49.5 points a game, while Taylor's Buckeyes led the nation in scoring with 90.5 points a game. Taylor had his team thoroughly prepared to stop the Golden Bears. He and his assistant coaches, Jack Graf and Frank Truitt, designed a game plan that shut off the passing lanes to California's All-American, 6-foot-10 inches Darrall Imhoff. As a result, Imhoff scored only eight points, and the Golden Bears connected on only twenty field goals in fifty-nine attempts. The Buckeyes made fifteen of their first sixteen shots and built an insurmountable 37-19 halftime lead. Ohio State shot a dazzling 68.4 percent from the field for the game and beat California 75-55 for the national championship. After the game, Taylor told the media, "I used many of Pete's ideas, and they paid off for us tonight."

Newell first got to know Taylor when Newell was coaching at Michigan State and Taylor was an assistant at Ohio State. Newell (2003) said, "Fred was a good friend of my assistant coach. When Fred would scout one of our games, I would invite him over to the house, and we would talk basketball for hours. After he became head coach at Ohio State, Fred and his assistant, Jack Graf, really studied our defense. I always enjoyed talking with them and did everything I could to help them. One summer I spent more time talking with Jack than I did my own team. It was ironic that our teams would meet for the NCAA title the following year. In the championship game, Ohio State used a defensive strategy that I had suggested in one of our many discussions. We had an excellent point guard who was a wonderful ballhandler, but he didn't shoot the ball too well, so Ohio State dropped off him. They did a tremendous job and beat us in the championship game. Coach Taylor gave me the credit for that defensive tactic when he talked to reporters after the game."

Bob Knight credits Fred Taylor for one of his coaching cornerstones. "Coach Taylor taught me an appreciation of basketball, as something never to be mastered but always, every day of every year, to be studied with an unflagging zeal for answers—and a duty to pass them on. Maybe as important as anything I ever learned from him was that a coach should never be afraid to ask questions of anyone he could learn from." (Knight, 2002, p.18)

"During his 18 years as the head coach at Ohio State, he took Big Ten Basketball to a level that it had never previously achieved," stated Knight. "He, far more than any single person, was responsible for the growth and development of basketball in the Big Ten into what it is today." (Weasel, 2001, p. xiv)

Taylor was a master at designing his offensive and defensive systems to fit the talents of his players. John Havlicek described Ohio State's offensive system in these words. "We never had to call a play. The offense was geared on keys and movement. We immediately developed total communication on the floor, and our basketball intellects meshed perfectly." Havlicek credited his Hall of Fame career with the Boston Celtics to Taylor's teaching. "I don't think I would have gotten anywhere without his tutelage," Havlicek said. "My career was based on what I learned from Fred Taylor. He shaped me tremendously."

Hall of Famer Jerry Lucas remembered Taylor's organization and preparation. "He stressed fundamentals, and we worked very hard on them," said Lucas. "He left no stone unturned. I'd give him an A+ on what he did with me individually and with our team. He's one of the great coaches in my estimation." (Hunter, 1981, p. 190)

Lucas went on to stardom with the New York Knicks and was selected as one of the "Top 100 Players in the NBA." He remembered Taylor not only as a great coach, but also as a great man. "His values and character are qualities that are sadly missing in sports today, perhaps gone forever," Lucas said. (Weasel, 2001)

Bill Hosket, an All-American player under Taylor, said, "My best memories at Ohio State are the practices. It was such a time of learning from him and development for me. To say he's had an impact on my life is quite an understatement. It was never about winning with him. He was one of the fiercest competitors you'd ever want to meet, but he kept the game in perfect perspective, and he knew college basketball was about learning more than sets and out-of-bounds plays. He used the game to get us ready for everything after basketball." (Weasel, 2001)

Fred Taylor was a selfless servant for the game of basketball. His legacy is the faces and names of the players who ever wore an Ohio State uniform. It is the young men he molded into outstanding citizens, who learned that one's contribution to society would live on, long after the final horn had sounded.

SOURCE

Hunter, Bob. (1981). *Buckeye Basketball*. Huntsville, AL: Strode Publishers.

Jenkins, Bruce. (1999). *A Good Man: The Pete Newell Story*. Berkeley, CA: Frog LTD.

Knight, Bob and Bob Hammel. (2002). *Knight: My Story*. New York: Thomas Dunne Books.

Newell, Pete. Interview by Ralph Pim, September 5, 2003.

Weasel, Joe. (2001) *Higher Court: The Lost College Basketball Legacy of Fred Taylor*. Columbus: The Opening Tip.

LESSONS FROM THIS LEGEND...

OHIO STATE'S PATTERNED FRONTCOURT MOVEMENTS

By Fred Taylor

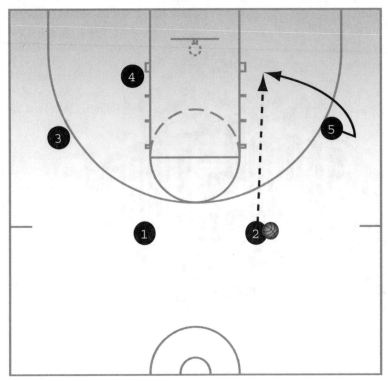

Taylor 1.0

We are a running team and have averaged 80.9 and 90.4 points per game. When assessing your team's ability to fast break, you should consider factors such as team speed, rebounding, and shooting ability. Another key factor to consider is secondary scoring opportunities after the initial fast break has been stopped. At Ohio State, we have our players positioned on the floor to go immediately into frontcourt scoring patterns.

FAST BREAK PRIORITIES

Our first priority is to break whenever we intercept a pass or get a defensive rebound. We instill confidence in our players, and they shoot with relative freedom on the break, pro-

viding we have equal numbers, or better, down the floor. We believe that a 15-foot jumper is a good percentage shot off the break.

We don't attempt to fast break after our opponent scores, because we believe this will hurt our defensive mentality. We don't want players to justify poor defense by thinking that we can fast break and get the points back.

We hope our offense will create enough movement to compound defensive problems. If there are no fast-break opportunities, our players are positioned so that we can initiate our patterned frontcourt play.

LESSONS FROM THIS LEGEND...

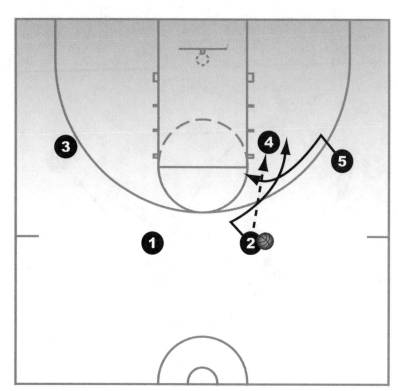

Taylor 1.1

PATTERNED FRONTCOURT MOVEMENT

Our patterned front-court play is centered around the two-man or the three-man game. We use approximately seven basic patterns, in addition to our guard clear out. We prefer a penetrating pass rather than a lateral cross-court pass to start our front-court offense. Quite often, this penetrating pass is impossible so we must rely upon our "automatics."

FRONTCOURT OPTIONS

The first option is for 05, our strongside corner man, to reverse and go baseline for a backdoor cut and possible feed. We fully realize this isn't a "bread-and-butter" maneuver, but a successful backdoor play will often give 05 more room for his play-making (see **Diagram 1.0**).

The second option is for 04, our post man, to come out to a high-post position on the side for the direct feed from the guard 02. This creates the "splitting" or "squeezing" action by 02, the strongside guard, and 05, the strongside corner man (see **Diagram 1.1**).

If the defensive pressures does not permit either of these two options, we attempt to make the cross-court pass to 03, the weak-side guard, and start our offense from that side of the floor. Should the weakside guard be contested, we attempt to run our third automatic option—the backdoor. The weakside corner, 03, breaks into the weak-side high post for a diagonal feed, and the weakside guard, 01, breaks off him for a two-man game—called the "blind pig (see **Diagram 1.2**).

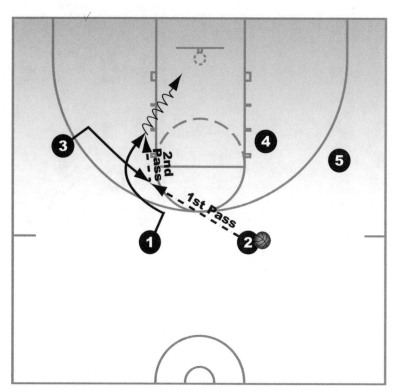

Taylor 1.2

263

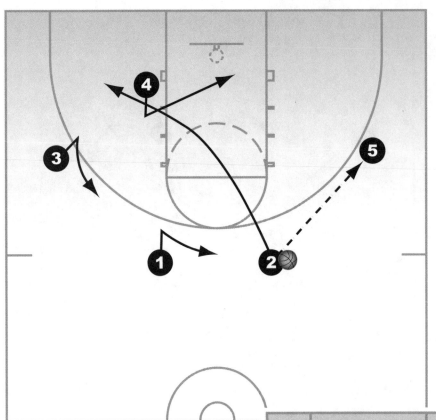

Taylor 1.3

Our guard clear-out pattern (see **Diagram 1.3**) begins with a pass from 02 to the corner man, 05. 02 goes through the lane area and establishes a weakside corner position. Quite often, it's possible for this clear-out man, 02, to screen for the post man, 04. The corner, 05, has a one-on-one situation first, and then thinks of hitting the post, 04, to start a splitting action with the weakside backcourt man, 01. We start our split, even though the post has the ball in the low position, in order to assure rebound strength.

If the post, 04, cannot maneuver in low, he must come as high as possible to receive the pass (see **Diagram 1.4**). This creates the "splitting" or "squeezing" action by 05 and 01.

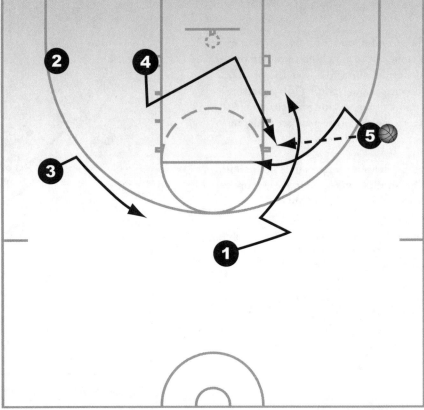

Taylor 1.4

LESSONS FROM THIS LEGEND...

Should it be impossible to hit the post, our corner, 05, drives high across the middle for a two-man game with 01, the weakside guard (see **Diagram 1.5**).

The weakside corner man, 03, fills out on top for balance and makes himself available for an outlet pass. When the ball is passed to 03, 02 breaks to the weakside high post for a diagonal feed. This creates the weakside two-man game for 02 and 03 (see **Diagram 1.6**).

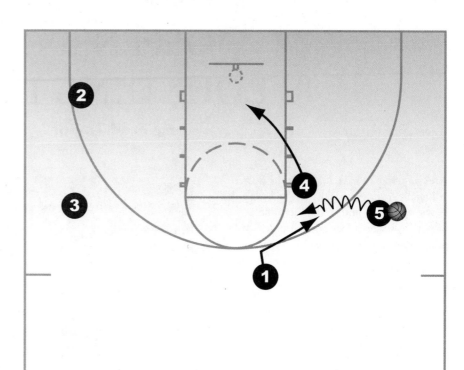

Taylor 1.5

CLOSING COMMENTS

We attempt to run our patterns to both sides of the floor, and hope that we'll be able to distribute our scoring throughout our team. We've been fortunate in having fine material—some excellent shooters, some excellent rebounders, and, most importantly, morale. Each player has dedicated himself to getting into top physical condition and has exhibited a willingness to sacrifice for the best interest of his team and school.

SOURCE

Taylor, Fred. (November 1960) Ohio State's Frontcourt Movements. *Scholastic Coach.* V30, p.7

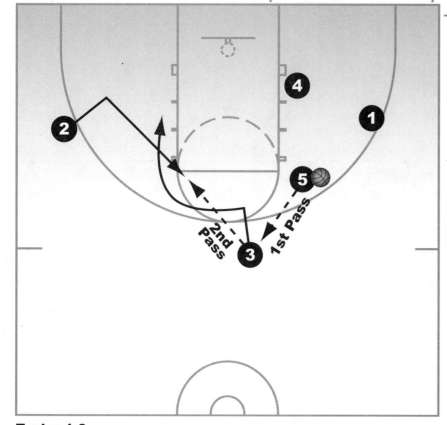

Taylor 1.6

LESSONS FROM THIS LEGEND...

OFFENSIVE
REBOUNDING DRILLS

By Fred Taylor

There's an adage in basketball that the team that literally owns the backboards will probably win the game, and, along these lines, we feel that we should spend a great deal of time with body balance, one of the basic fundamentals in rebounding. In other words, the ability to change direction in flight, the ability to land in various posture variations and still be able to go back up in the air is essential. I suppose you could call that "jumping in traffic," and because not all people are gifted along that particular line, I think we have to work on that type of thing.

Another key factor that I think we have to instill in our rebounders is the desire to make the extra effort. This requires the touch-and-go type of jumping. You've heard it said that the 2nd, 3rd, and 4th effort gets the job done, and I definitely believe it. Perimeter shooters become more confident when excellent rebounders surround them. They do not hesitate taking good shots. As a result, rebounding is an important component in our system, and we spend much of our practice time improving our rebounding. One of the teaching aids that we use to develop rebounding skills is a dome that is put over the basket and prevents the ball from going through the goal.

ONE-MAN TIPPING DRILL

This drill is used with a rebounding dome so that every shot is missed. One player tips and rebounds as many times possible in a given time period. The one-man tipping drill can also be combined with a jump shot and follow-up action.

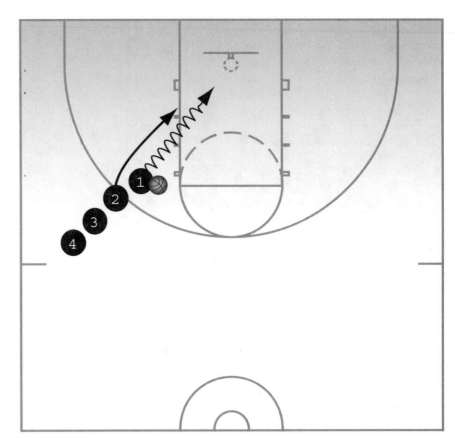

Taylor 2.0

LAY-UP WITH TRAILER DRILL

This drill is also used with a rebounding dome. 01 dribbles in and shoots a lay-up shot. 02 follows for either a tip or for a rebound and follow-up shot. Alternate from two lines or use one line (see **Diagram 2.0).**

This drill can also be used as a continuous tip drill. The dribbler puts the ball in play with the lay-up, and then successive players keep the ball alive by timing their jumps to react to the ball as it bounces or rolls off the rebounding dome. One or two lines may be used.

LESSONS FROM THIS LEGEND...

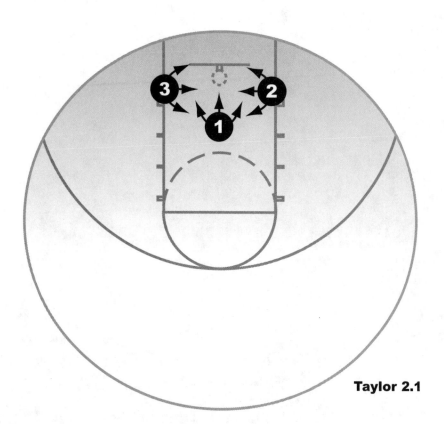

Taylor 2.1

THREE-MAN TIPPING DRILL

Three players tip and rebound the ball wherever it goes, keeping the ball in play as long as possible. When necessary, rebounders should control the ball first, before making a follow-up shot or tip (see **Diagram 2.1**).

VARIATIONS:

A coach or player begins the drill by taking shots from various positions around the key for 2-on-1 or 1-on-2 offensive/defensive rebounding.

1. TWO OFFENSIVE PLAYERS VS. ONE DEFENSIVE PLAYER

Two offensive players have the inside position and try to put as many tips or follow-up shots back up against the rebounding dome as they can, until the defensive player secures the rebound.

2. TWO DEFENSIVE PLAYERS VS ONE OFFENSIVE PLAYER

Same principle as the previous drill, except the two defensive players have the inside position, and the one offensive player must try to get as many follow-up shots as possible. The drill encourages 2nd, 3rd, and 4th efforts by both the offensive and defensive players.

SOURCE

Taylor, Fred. (1974). Rebounding Fundamentals. *Coaches' All-American "Reboundome" Drills.* Korney Board Aids: Roxton, TX

LEGACY OF
Stanley "Stan" Watts

- Led Brigham Young University to the NIT championship in 1951 and 1966.

- Recognized as a man of integrity and sportsmanship, both on and off the court.

- Taught a fast-breaking style of play, combined with relentless defensive pressure.

- Guided Brigham Young to four NIT and seven NCAA tournaments.

- Served as president of the NABC in 1969 and chairman of the U.S. Olympic Basketball Committee in 1976.

- Wrote *Developing an Offensive Attack in Basketball,* which became a classic textbook on the fast-break offense.

- Recognized as an outstanding basketball ambassador who conducted clinics in Europe, the Far East, and South Africa.

STANLEY "STAN" WATTS

"We try to be as simple as we can in our teaching so we don't overcoach. We feel strongly that our players should be well developed in fundamentals. Finally, we like to fast break—often being accused of shooting as soon as we get off the airplane."
— *Stan Watts*

BIOGRAPHY

Born: August 30, 1911 in Murray, UT

Died: April 6, 2000

Inducted into the Naismith Basketball Hall of Fame in 1986

Stanley "Stan" Watts began his coaching career in 1938 at Millard (UT) High School as a three-sport head coach. He led Millard to its first regional basketball championship. Watts moved on to Dixie Junior College, where he was athletic director and coached three sports from 1941 to 1945. His final high school stop was at Jordan (UT) High School, where he was head basketball coach from 1945 to 1947. Watts returned to his alma mater, Brigham Young University, in 1947 as baseball coach and freshman basketball coach. He was elevated to assistant basketball coach in 1949, and was chosen to be head coach in 1949. Watts served in this position for 23 years and led the Cougars to eight conference championships and 11 postseason tournament appearances. He directed Brigham Young to the NIT championship in 1951 and 1966. Watts' overall record at BYU was 372-254, and his success helped establish a national identity for the Mormon school. Watts became the seventh coach in basketball history to win 100 games in his first five years. He was highly respected for his dedication to the coaching profession. Watts served as president of the NABC, chairman of both the U.S. Olympic Basketball Committee and the NCAA Tournament Selection Committee, and was a member of the NCAA Rules Committee. Watts was enshrined into the Helms Foundation, NACDA, Utah Sports, Oklahoma City All-Sports, and the Naismith Memorial Basketball Halls of Fame.

Stanley "Stan" Watts..

Stan Watts was one of 11 children of Eugene and Gertrude Park Watts. He attended Murray (UT) High School from 1925 to 1928 and played basketball during his last two years. Following high school graduation in 1928, he struggled to continue his education. It was the time of the Great Depression, and his family, along with many in the country, struggled to make ends meet. His close-knit family helped establish his strong values that led to his success throughout life.

With the strong support of his parents, he finally was able to attend Weber Junior College (now Weber State University) in 1934. He earned his degree two years later. Stan had also been selected All-Conference in basketball both years. This opened the door to his entrance and graduation from the flagship university of his chosen Mormon religion, Brigham Young University.

At BYU, Watts won letters in football, basketball, and track. He was also selected as the school's outstanding all-around senior athlete.

Watts began his coaching career at Millard (UT) in 1938, where he spent three years coaching three sports. His coaching talents immediately shined, as he led Millard to their first-ever regional basketball championship.

From 1941 to 1945, Watts was athletic director and head coach of football, basketball, and track at Dixie Junior College in St. George, Utah. World War II prevented fielding teams two of those years. Stan's next stop was at Jordan High School in Sandy, Utah. He led Jordan to two conference championships and compiled an overall record of 32-7.

In 1947, Watts joined the athletic department at Brigham Young, where he coached baseball and freshman football and basketball. When his freshman basketball team went undefeated in 1948, Watts was named assistant basketball coach. One year later, he began a 23-year career as head basketball coach of the Cougars.

Watts brought national prominence to Brigham Young's basketball program. From 1949 to 1972, Stan compiled a 372-254 record. His teams participated in postseason play 11 times. He was only the seventh major college coach in the nation to win over 100 games in his first five seasons. In 1951, Brigham Young won the Rocky Mountain

Conference championship, and then climaxed their season with the NIT championship. His 1966 team also won the NIT, posting a 20-5 record.

After BYU joined the Western Athletic Conference in 1962, Watts' teams brought home five conference championships. One of those titles came in 1972, a few months after Watts had spent 14 hours in surgery and two months in the hospital to overcome a rare form of cancer. In 1973, Stan was selected as the Western Athletic Conference "Coach of the Decade."

Watts' teams were always well drilled in the importance of teamwork. "A sound offensive attack in basketball is like a good watch: it has fine working parts," said Watts (1959). "Unless the units work together in balance, precision, accuracy, and rhythm, the whole will not function satisfactorily. Thus in developing a winning basketball attack, you cannot afford to neglect either the part or the whole method of coaching."

"Basketball is a game of skills blended into a working unit," added Watts. "Individual skills must contribute to team versatility. When a single part becomes more important than the whole, a team cannot enjoy uninterrupted success. All five men, and the replacing substitutes, must always put team success ahead of individual success."

Coach Watts was loved and respected by his former players, not only because he molded them into outstanding teams, but also because he cared about them and treated them with respect. He made basketball fun for them and used the game to teach life lessons.

Watts maintained his keen sense of humor his entire life. At age 87, Watts was awarded the BYU Varsity Club Foundation of Excellence Award. After being assisted to the podium, Watts quipped, "That's a poor example of a fast break." Watts then described some humorous adventures he had with the team while touring South America year earlier. In one game, Watts recalled, a BYU player was dribbling downcourt, when an opposing player "pushed him out of bounds and then called a foul on him for leaving the court without permission."

During another game, BYU had called a timeout. "While the boys were over talking to me, the other team went down and scored and they counted it," laughed Watts.

In his concluding remarks to the Varsity Club, Watts said, "I had success, because I had some great young men. Without the players, the coach doesn't amount to much. In other words, of you're going to plow, you need the horses. Thank you for coming. Next time, I hope I can fast break!"

Stan Watts' teams were known as the "Running Cougars." During the 1965 and 1966 seasons, Brigham Young scored over 100 points 21 times, and at least 95 points 32 times. Watts believed speed was essential for the fast break, but the main prerequisite was good, tough rebounding.

Upon his retirement from coaching in 1972, Watts was ranked 14th among the winningest major college basketball coaches.

Source

Watts, Stan. (1959). *Developing an Offensive Attack in Basketball.* Englewood Cliffs, NJ: Prentice-Hall.

Watts, Stan. Vertical Files, Archives, Naismith Memorial Basketball Hall of Fame. Springfield, MA.

LESSONS FROM THIS LEGEND...

BRIGHAM YOUNG UNIVERSITY — FAST BREAK

By Stanley Watts

We try to be as simple as we can in our teaching and use simplicity, so that we don't over-coach the boys and give them more than they can handle, and of course in that we recognize that we have to do what the defense will let us do. We don't want to become mechanized or stereotyped to the point that we become easily defended, and so we work on the plan that we will start with organization and take opportunity as it presents itself. Because of that, we feel that we have to work a lot on individual techniques and individual abilities, so that we can drill sufficiently so that when the opportunity presents itself, our boys can capitalize on it and take advantage of it.

We feel strongly that our players should be well developed and trained in fundamentals. We feel that the house is no stronger than the foundation, There are many systems that we can operate from, but if the player can't do it individually in change-ups, setting screens, shooting, and dribbling the ball, no system will work. So, we spend a lot of time on fundamentals.

We try to get a team that can shoot well. We have been accused of shooting as soon as we get off the airplane or as soon as we come out of the dressing room, but as long as we can hit them, we don't care. We feel if we have a good ballhandling team, we are going to get good shots. Our players must also be able to use the dribble to create open passing lanes and shooting opportunities. We must also be able to play tough defense, so we are able to stop the other team. So, we spend a good deal of time in the early season on fundamentals, trying to ground players in the important phases of basketball.

We go from there and progressively teach a system wherein we can utilize the abilities of players. We start with the simple drill, like one-on-one, and try to teach them how to change direction, to change up, to pivot, and to run a man into a screen. We feel if we can do that and teach players how to play without the ball, then we are going to accomplish something on sagging defenses. Then, we teach the player how to do something with the ball. We start with a very simple drill in which we will take players and have them play one-on-one. The coach will stand at the end of the court, and when the offensive player gets free, we give him the ball and let him go to work. We then will put a post man out there and let the player learn to run his man off a screen, through angle running, angle cutting, and change ups.

We feel that we should move on to certain fundamental techniques which we think are very important. We will go on to a give-and-go opportunity, taking advantage of every mistake the defense might make. We are looking for the "swivel head," a player who turns his head to see if the ball gets in there correctly, and then we want to hit him with a give-and-go. We work on that drill with a simple two-on-two situation where we hit the side man and take off down the middle, or take off for an anticipated screen and cut off sharply to try to evade the defensive men. We work a lot on a fake and a drive off a one-and-one drill. We have always been of the opinion that we are not going to fool too many defenders with just a head fake. We utilize the head and a step fake to try to get the defense to move with us.

In the step fake, we try to have our players take a short jab about 12 or 14 inches, so if the defense steps toward us, we can come back quickly with a cross-over and long step to gain the advantage. If the defender steps back, which is generally the right defensive movement, we will come back and be available for a shot. If the defender stands there on the initial fake, we like to follow up with a second step (the step-step) and try to leave him while he is standing still. We work a lot on this, on the anticipation that we may drive the baseline if they are not playing to protect that area. Many times on a proposed run off the screen, where defenders try to overplay us, we can come back quickly and utilize the abilities of the player, because he has been taught what to do on a given situation. We also like to work our players on a fake-and-shoot situation, or a fake shot and drive, if we can get the opponents to come up on their toes or leave the floor.

We work quite a bit on what we call a drive and bait. I don't know whether you are familiar with the terminology, but I am sure you are familiar with the mechanics of it. We feel we can set the defender up, bait him, and then come back for a reverse pivot or for a reverse shot.

We also like to train our players very well in the art of jump shooting. We feel there are two places for a jump shot. One is off a dribble when we are blocked off and cannot continue; the second is off a screen. We feel in these two situations, we can utilize the jump shot much better than if we try to do it where we are matched or have a taller opponent playing against a shorter player. We like to work on jump shots, and you

LESSONS FROM THIS LEGEND...

and I know that they are tough to stop. I don't know how to stop them legally, and I am sure you don't either. That is what is raising "heck" with the game today as far as these top scorers coming in and being difficult to defend.

We like to teach our post men either to fake and wheel, or fake reverse pivot and drive when they overplay us coming out from the base line or coming across the center. We want to equip him with the tools so if he is overplayed, he can come back quickly and try to capitalize on that opportunity.

We work a lot on footwork to get open from a defensive man. With our style of attack, we initiate our offense with a pass to the wing. Teams have a tendency to overplay us. We teach our players to take their opponent into the baseline or take a step out, reverse pivot, and backdoor to the basket, looking for the bounce pass.

We feel we have to teach the players those tricks, because they are not going to get it by verbal instructions. We spend a lot of time on these moves in the early part of our practice. The first month in particular, we try to get our players to recognize and capitalize on these opportunties.

We recognize that the day of getting past a one-on-one situation and scoring is gone because of collapsing defenses. When you get past the one man, someone else is going to pick you up. We feel that if we can force a team into doing that, we can create an opening somewhere else, probably a two-on-one situation. We still work on these individual offensive techniques, with the theory that we can capitalize as soon as the defense make a mistake. We hope to make them make a mistake as we move and maneuver in angle cutting and other change-ups to gain the advantage.

We will go from that to our two-on-two drills and three-on-three drills. We like to break down our drills into actual game situations, and practice them so that we develop good habits and improve our reaction time.

We then go into our four-man drills which we use a lot in bringing the fourth man off. Then, we will go into our five-on-five in the half-court in order to work the entire program together so that we become strong as a unit.

We feel with break-down drills we not only accomplish fine offensive training, but we also provide good defensive training, because we force the defense into action. We always try to keep the pressure on the defense. We never want our players to let down. Naturally, we try to get the good inside shot first, and then if they jam us, we will try to shoot over. We hope we have the tools to do that.

We do a lot of screening on the ball and off the ball. We try to work on the theory that if we can bring men together, we can come off the screen and get an opportunity to go to the basket. We will change our attack occasionally so that we will not do the same thing all the time. Sometimes we will come up with a new type of an offense to try to upset our opponents and accomplish something they are not expecting. Consequently, we are working on an alternate system most of the year, and we will throw that in occasionally, to try to take advantage of certain situations.

We try to run our opponents into a screen, either blindly or from the side. We will mass screen; we will blind screen, and we will drive in order to get the good inside shot. We realize that with the various defenses that are now being used, it takes a tremendous amount of time to prepare. In the course of this past season, we have seen every type of defense, and we know that the time element is a very important factor. You have to spend some time on the various phases of press, semi-press, zone press, and combination and alternating defenses. The kids have to be equipped to meet various players, and they have to be equipped with the know-how to attack, or confusion arises.

We work on the theory that if the team is switching on us, we hand off and turn with the ball, so that we can see if the switch takes place. This puts us in position to bet-

ter screen the defender. We feel we have had very good success against switching defenses. We like to use trailers on switching defenses. We like to use rolls-offs and use cut-aways (false screens). We attack the press with our two guards. Against a semi-press, we like to blind screen, use a give-and-go, and change directions. We know we also have to be prepared for some tough zone defenses. So, it important to get a team ready to handle all situations.

Most of all, we like to fast break and run. We try to get the rebound pass out to the wing man, and then fill the middle as quickly as possible. We recognize that the prerequisites for the fast break are tough rebounding and a quick outlet pass..

If our fast break doesn't materialize, then we set up in our half-court offense. We cannot sacrifice one for the other, so we try to spend a lot of time on both. When we set up, we know we have to screen and drive to the basket. We have to try to get inside.

In our fast break, we bring either the farside guard or the farside outside man into the middle (see **Diagram 1.0** and **Diagram 1.1**). We want our best ball-handler in the middle. We want our three best players in the three lanes.

We like to follow up with a trailer. We never want to take our middle man in farther than the free-throw line, because we want to keep that defense spread. Most teams will throw a tandem at us, with the back man picking up the first pass and the front man covering opposite the pass. If our center man goes in farther, then he helps the defense, so we want to keep the defense spread. A lot of times, they may stop the close shot, but we are able to get a good shot at the free-throw line, which we should be able to hit.

We generally run from a single post. We have never had a big post man. The last three years our post man has been 6-foot 4-inches. He was never a good hook shooter. He was a very fine jump shooter, and he could fake and wheel very well.

LESSONS FROM THIS LEGEND...

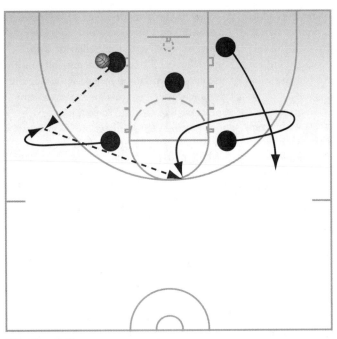

Watts 1.0

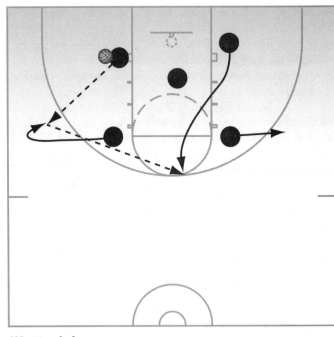

Watts 1.1

On our fast break, I would like to show you a little of what we are trying to do. We bring in the inside man or the outside man, whichever we feel is the best ballhandler. We make sure the defensive triangle is set up, and we attempt to keep the opponents out of that area. When the rebound is secured, we break the wing out as an outlet. He will buttonhook toward the ball if necessary. (see **Diagram 1.0**).

The outlet pass is thrown to the wing. After receiving the pass, the wing looks to get the ball into the middle immediately. We prefer the middle man to dribble as far as he can. We feel with that action that we can put more pressure on the defense. If the pass is being made cross court, they can generally zone you, and one man can defend two. In this situation, we feel we are going to force them to come out. If they don't come out, then we will go in as far as we can and get the close shot.

We will also bring a forward in the middle, if he is a good ballhandler (see **Diagram 1.l**). We try to have an organized fast break, so that each player knows what he is doing off the board. We want good ballhandling

as we advance. The tempo needs to decrease a little as we hit the top of the circle, so we can get organized and play under control.

Sometimes, teams, knowing we try to hit the middle with our second pass, will jam that area. We tell our side man to dribble to the middle when opponents stop the pass into the middle. We then bring the opposite man behind him. In other words, if the outlet man receives the ball, he will dribble into the middle, the normal middle man will take his side, and the opposite player, as seen in **Diagram 1.2**, will fill the other side.

We have timed the fast break with passing and dribbling. We find passing is a little faster, but we feel we can't put the pressure on as well with a pass, so we like the middle man to go with the dribble. You need to have a man in the center who can dribble well and who knows when to get rid of that ball. If the ball comes off the other side, we run the same pattern. If it comes out to the front man, we go from there, so we have about four opportunities from the fast break. We do the same thing out-of-bounds or do the same thing from a missed free

throw or a made free throw, so the pattern is always the same. Our players know who becomes the trailer and who becomes the safety. In this case, the center will become the trailer, while the man who handles the ball becomes the safety man. The safety never goes beyond the midline (see **Diagram 1.3**).

We have won a lot of ball games with the fast break. We like it, our players like to play it; our fans like to see it; and you know if you can make it go, you can bust a game wide open. We have won a lot of ball games because we have been able to go from the defensive rebound.

We recognize that teams are going to have to defense us. Some teams like to jam the board on us, putting our men in there, but we feel that if our three players are doing their job, we will make that fast break go. We hope to force them to keep two men back on defensive balance or force them to compensate in some way. Otherwise, we are not going on a fast break, and they can gang the boards and take every chance they want to with it.

LESSONS FROM THIS LEGEND...

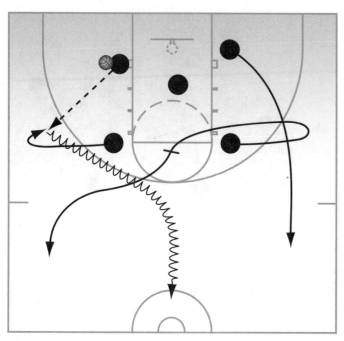

Watts 1.2

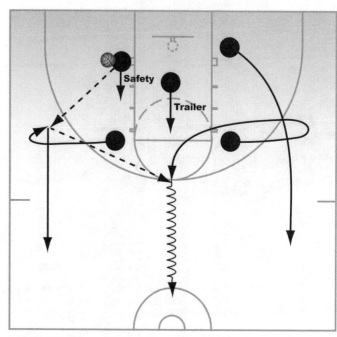

Watts 1.3

Now, in our double-post, single-post, and set offense, we use the give-and-go and other maneuvers. I will show you several of our plays that we try to run.

We put our post man opposite the ball, so we can open up the other side and give him a little room to maneuver (see **Diagram 1.4**). As I said, we had a 6-foot 4-inches player in there for the last three years, and he has done a fine job for us, considering his abilities. We try to put our two forwards at the free-throw line, where they can go either way. We want to put pressure on the defense, so they have to force us one way. We try to balance our two guards with the floor, so they can operate to either side.

We have a play we call "inside," which has a give-and-go situation on the screen for the center. This is the play that Adolph Rupp said a few years ago that BYU runs right after the "Star Spangled Banner." We want to find out what defense is being used, and this option will tell us. We have two or three variations (see **Diagram 1.5**).

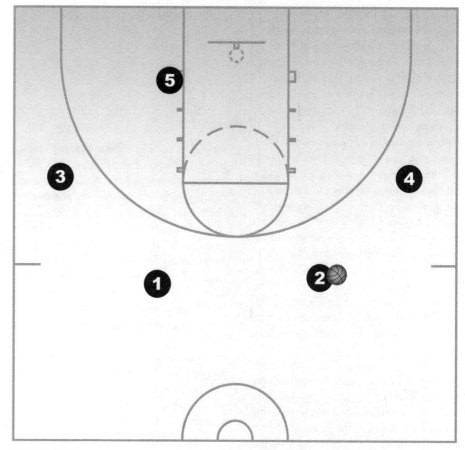

Watts 1.4

LESSONS FROM THIS LEGEND...

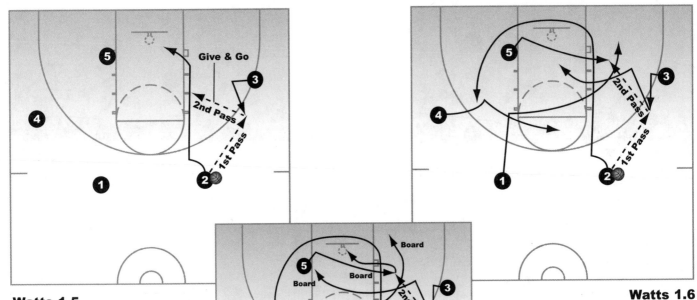

Watts 1.5

Watts 1.6

Watts 1.7

We will pass G-F, and we may either come over and screen or start to screen and run our give-and-go option. If the man is free, we hit him. If he doesn't get the ball by the time he reaches the lane, we know that he is not free, so he becomes a screener. He slows up and allows our center to start toward the baseline and come off the screen. In the meantime, this player will continue out around. This man is moving, so we try to hit the post man, coming off that cutter. As we send that man through, if we have any doubts about what defense the opponents are in, we will run him all the way through, on the theory that if they follow us, they are in man-to-man. If they don't follow, they are probably in a zone. If they try to confuse us with that, we will send the forward through on another option, trying to determine the defense (see **Diagram 1.6**).

Now, if our post man can get free, he takes the shot. If he finds he is in trouble, then we have to help him out, so we will come back with a split. We will run the passing forward off the post (the first cutter) and bring O2 to the basket as the second cutter. Generally, the passer always goes first, and we tell that passer to loosen up. We don't

want him coming off that post man tight, because as he does he takes his man in there, and we may have trouble with hand-offs. As we loosen, we tell our players to go about four feet away, so that as they come through, they set a triple screen for the second cutter. We try to get the six or eight-foot shot on the baseline. We have had excellent success with this option. We also have the give-and-go options. We have the center coming off the screen, which frees you momentarily, and then we have a split opportunity, and try to get good rebounding with the cutters. We bring these opposite men out for safety purposes, which we call defensive balance. We also attempt to get a three and one-half rebounding and one and one-half defensive balance situation. In **Diagram 1.7**, O2 and O4 become the defensive balance, and O1, O5, and O3 are responsible for rebounding. These men

are responsible for the board. O1 would continue on to get inside position, and he would wheel and get in front, and the shooter would try to get in there. We feel that as we shoot the small man in, he takes a small man with him. He should be able to work the board, and he is not giving too much size unless the switch takes place. If O1 gets inside position, the center looks to pass the ball to him.

We also like to run clear-outs. We like to bring our guards off, and we have only about five or six plays off our single post. We try to keep it simple. We believe in doing a few things well and working until we get the good shot. This year, we had some youngsters who didn't want to wait for the setup. They liked to fire the long one, and when we were hot, we were okay, but when we weren't, we were in trouble. Because we left our patterns, we got into trouble on two or three occasions. We feel that as long as we are penetrating, we can get the good shot, and we work hard for it.

As I said, we screen on the ball and off the ball. We have used this play with a lot of success, we get the shot around the keyhole, where we think our players can hit very

LESSONS FROM THIS LEGEND...

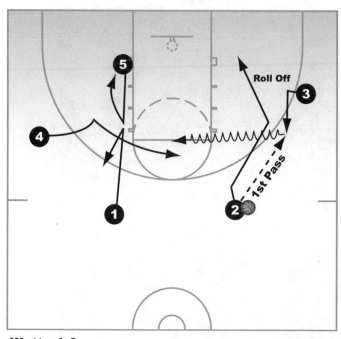

Watts 1.8

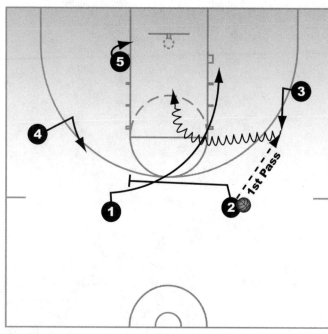

Watts 1.9

well (see **Diagram 1.8**). We start the play again with a G-F pass and set an inside screen. We always want the pass receiver to take a jab step to hold his man, so we can come off on a dribble. The screener rolls, and cuts away if a switch takes place. In the meantime, 1 and 5 are setting a double screen off the ball. If it is forced, he dribbles over to 4 and runs his man in to get the hand-off. We have felt that on a sagging defense or where the men off the ball are dropping that we can set a double screen and bring that far man, 4, off. We have never been stopped to get this shot at the keyhole. A lot of times, this inside man can take that drive all the way or if a switch takes place, he comes off the angle and pops the inside man, as he goes and he's in there for a cripple (see **Diagram 1.9**). Because we pull our center out, the defensive center will generally follow him. If he sits in the hole, then the center pops out, and he is free for a pass and shot.

We run these plays from both sides of the court. We have had fine success using this offense for small guards. A clear-out situation occurs when the G-F pass is made as illustrated in **Diagram 1.9**. Now, you will

say, "Well, how do the players differentiate plays?" We have given signals or given passes which tell the play. We will bounce pass in there. This man will start in like he is going to go, and he will set here. Then, this man dribbles in there, and this man comes off, and this man stays over there to keep the area open. We always had the threat of a drive, but if the defensive man retreated, we had the threat of a double screen where we could get a shot. A lot of teams this year tried to overplay us on this screen, beat us to the screen, and then we came back and popped down the middle for a close hand-off, and we went all the way. This shows what we are trying to do offensively; we try to take advantage of everything the defense will let us do from what we think is an organized pattern.

When we clear out our center, we will bring him to a high post if the congestion is tough defensively. We will go into a ball game with maybe three plays and try to use all options, depending on what the defense does to us.

When we attack a zone, we try to hit all our zones with a 1-3-1. We will send cut-

ters through; we will move men and the ball to try to overload the baseline or the side.

On most pressing defenses, we have two of our guards come down with the ball, and all we want to do is be concerned with getting the ball over the center line.

Basically, we again go back to the theory that we want to have our boys well versed on fundamentals and techniques, fast break if possible, and then use pattern play to operate and utilize their abilities.

SOURCE:

Watts, Stanley. (November 1959). BYU Fast Break. NABC Basketball Bulletin.

LEGACY OF
Leonard "Lenny" Wilkens

- Became the all-time winningest coach in NBA history on January 6, 1995.

- Earned a pair of Olympic gold medals as an assistant coach in 1992 and as a head coach in 1996.

- Selected as one of the 10 Greatest Coaches in NBA History and one of the 50 Greatest Players during the NBA's Golden Anniversary celebration.

- One of only three people to be elected to the Naismith Hall of Fame as both a player and a coach.

- Participated in more games as a player or coach than anyone else in NBA history.

- Quiet, fierce competitor who is recognized for his integrity and perseverance.

LEONARD "LENNY" WILKENS

"You can either allow your circumstances to be a trap and ensnare you for the rest of your life or you can use them to learn what it takes to succeed in a world where things won't always go your way."
— *Lenny Wilkens*

BIOGRAPHY

Born: October 28, 1937 in Brooklyn, N.Y.

Inducted into the Naismith Basketball Hall of Fame as a player in 1989 and as a coach in 1998.

Leonard "Lenny" Wilkens played 15 seasons in the NBA with St. Louis, Seattle, Cleveland, and Portland and is considered one of the top point guards to ever play the game. He was a nine-time NBA All-Star and was voted the Most Valuable Player in the 1971 All-Star Game. At the time of his retirement, as a player, Wilkens ranked second on the all-time assist list. He served as a player/coach for three seasons with Seattle and one with Portland. Wilkens has also coached Cleveland, Atlanta, Toronto, and New York. In 2004, he completed his 31st year as an NBA head coach. Wilkens surpassed the legendary "Red" Auerbach as the all-time winningest coach in the NBA on January 6, 1995. He has led his teams to nine 50+ win seasons, two divisional championships, and two appearances in the NBA Finals. In 1979, Wilkens directed Seattle to the NBA title. During the NBA's Golden Anniversary celebration in 1996, Lenny was selected as one of the 50 Greatest Players and one of the 10 Greatest Coaches. Wilkens has earned two Olympic gold medals—one as an assistant coach with the original 1992 Dream Team, and the other as head coach at the 1996 Olympic Games in Atlanta. He played college basketball at Providence College from 1956-1960 and was selected as the MVP in the NIT and the East-West All-Star Game in 1960. Wilkens is one of only three people to be elected to the Naismith Basketball Hall of Fame as both a player and a coach.

Leonard "Lenny" Wilkens...

Leonard "Lenny" Wilkens fought his way up from the Bedford-Stuyvesant area of New York City to the top of the NBA. He epitomized the potential of the human spirit, as he successfully met the challenges of a difficult life.

Born in Brooklyn, Wilkens, was the son of Leonard and Henrietta Wilkens. At the age of five, Wilkens' father died, making Lenny Jr. the man of the household. Wilkens (Chappell, 1999) stated, "A lot of times, people didn't think I was going to make it, but I was determined to prove them wrong. When you grow up without a dad in a tough neighborhood, you have to prove yourself all the time. I didn't mind doing that, because it was a way of life. I was going to prove to you that I was as good as you."

Responsibility at such an early age made Lenny grow up fast. "I'm not a very emotional person," Wilkens said. "I don't know if that came from having to have a lot of responsibility at a young age. I was told 'You're the man of the family now' when my father died. So, I've always been fairly serious about what I do."

The Wilkens' family was forced to go on public assistance to make ends meet. "We didn't have anything," remembered Wilkens. "It was a struggle. We didn't have new clothes like everyone else, but what we had was respect and love. My mother often told us, 'God doesn't look at your clothes. He looks at the person inside the clothes.' She said that with such conviction that, after a while, I believed it. It amazes me today at what my mother was able to go through. I never saw anyone pray as much as she did. I'm a testament that prayer works."

Henrietta became the first beacon in Lenny's life. The persevering, loving mother supported her four children on her part-time job in a candy factory and welfare. She provided direction and a strong sense of values. Henrietta believed that happiness was the result of strong faith and hard work.

Wilkens remembered his mother's dislike of laziness. "My mother didn't like anyone who was lazy," stated Wilkens (Chappell, 1999). "She wouldn't tolerate laziness among her children. I have always had a job since I was seven years old. I delivered groceries. I was a stock clerk in a store. I washed floors in this lady's house. I've tarred roofs, painted houses. I've loaded sugar trucks."

"Working at a young age gave me confidence," Wilkens (2000) said. "I knew that if I had to take care of myself, I could. I learned that the only way most people got anywhere in the world is by making their own way. You had to work. You had to understand there were going to be roadblocks, setbacks, and even heartbreaks. I'm not saying I ever liked any of those things, but I understood that they didn't have to defeat me. Some people act as if responsibility is a dirty word. But it was a big part of my life, and I grew to like it."

Another important figure in Wilkens' life was Father Thomas Mannion at Holy Rosary Church. Father Mannion became a father figure and mentor for Lenny. He got him focused on education, staying out of trouble, and developing his basketball skills at Holy Rosary gym.

"Father Mannion kept encouraging me," said Wilkens. "He was always telling me that 'the only thing that holds you back is you. You can accomplish anything you want.'

Another of Lenny's role models during his youth was baseball legend, Jackie Robinson. Robinson played for the

Brooklyn Dodgers and was the first African-American to play Major League Baseball. "I remember sitting in the bleachers as a kid and watching him play," Wilkens said. "The thing about Jackie Robinson was that he never complained about his situation. He went out there to show you he was as good as you. He was my role model. He never made excuses for himself. So, I wasn't going to."

Wilkens played only one year of basketball at Boys High School in Brooklyn, but he had acquired excellent skills on the playgrounds of New York City. "Back then, especially in the areas that I played," stated Wilkens, "if you couldn't play, they wouldn't let you on the court. When I say, couldn't play, I'm talking about making a good pass, setting a good screen, defending, and rebounding. That's the way the guys played there. It wasn't just slam-dunking and three-point shooting. We played, and we wanted to stay on the court."

Father Mannion wrote Providence College, encouraging the school's athletic director to consider Lenny for a scholarship. Providence hesitated at first, but after watching him score 36 points in a summer-league tournament game, coach Joe Mullaney offered him a scholarship.

Wilkens said, "In fairness, no one from Providence had seen me play until that summer-league game. That one game drastically changed my life."

At Providence, Wilkens led the Friars to the NIT Finals in 1960 and was named Second Team All-American by *The Sporting News*. He was also selected the Outstanding Player in New England in 1960.

During his 15-year professional career, Wilkens was a nine-time NBA All-Star and averaged 16.5 points per game, 6.7 assists, and 4.7 rebounds per game. He is considered one of the greatest point guards in NBA history.

In 2004, Wilkens finished his 31st year as an NBA coach. During his coaching career, he has become the all-time

winningest coach in NBA history. Wilkens also led the Seattle Supersonics to the NBA title in 1979. "People want to know how I've survived this long in the NBA, and I point to my faith and my family," said Wilkens (2000). "I love basketball, and there is nothing I'd rather do than coach, but basketball or beating Red Auerbach's record isn't everything to me—and I think that is healthy."

"When I was younger," Wilken's said, "I'd worry that I wouldn't live very long. Because my father died young, and I was never sure exactly why he died, in the back of my mind, it made me wonder if that would happen to me. But later, when I had a better idea of the circumstances of his death, I realized I could have a long life, and I've had an amazing life. But, I sometimes wish my father could've seen it. I stare at that picture of my father, and I see a man who wanted to raise his children the right way, a man who set out to support his family. He's a man whom I barely remember, a man who died when I was five years old, but a man who still means a lot to me today. I'd like to think I learned all the things he'd have wanted me to know. When I stare hard at his picture, I see myself."

Source

Chappell, Kevin. (1999, April). Lenny Wilkens: The Winningest Basketball Coach of All Times. *Ebony*.

Wilkens, Lenny. (2000). *Unguarded*. New York: Simon & Schuster.

Wilkens, Lenny. Vertical Files, Archives. Naismith Memorial Basketball Hall of Fame. Springfield, MA.

LESSONS FROM THIS LEGEND...

PLAYS FROM THE PROS

By Lenny Wilkens

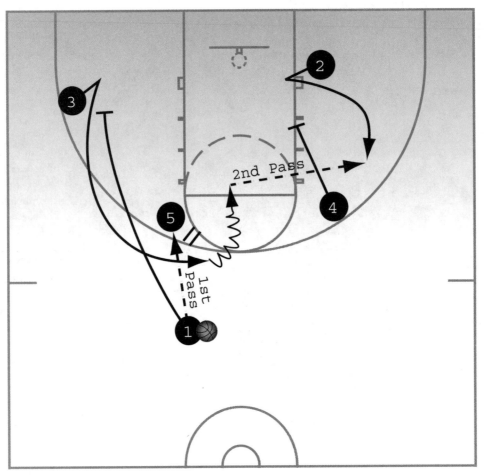

Wilkens 1.0

SPLIT POST ACTION FOR 3-MAN

Authors' Note: Coach Lenny Wilkens used this play when he coached the Atlanta Hawks and had superstar Domininque Wilkens. After Wilkens was traded, the Hawks continued to use the play for Danny Manning.

In **Diagram 1.0**, O1 passes to O5 in the high post and cuts off O5 to set a screen for O3 (Wilkens or Manning). Player O3 sets up his defender and cuts off O1. Player O5 looks to pass to O3, who is cutting off O1's screen. If the pass is denied, O3 keeps coming off O5 for a handoff. Player O4 screens down for O2 on the weakside to keep the other defenders occupied and to create a passing option for O3. Player O3 looks for a shot or drive or pass to O2.

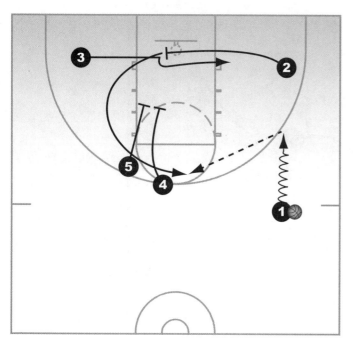

Wilkens 1.1

Wilkens 1.2

BASELINE CROSS WITH DOUBLE DOWN

Authors' Note: This play was used by Lenny Wilkens to free sharpshooter Craig Ehlo on the perimeter.

In **Diagram 1.1**, O1 dribbles to the wing as O2 (Craig Ehlo) sets a cross screen for O3. After setting the screen, O2 cuts hard to the top off a double screen by O5 and O4. O1 has the possibility of passing to O3 in the post or passing to O2 at the top of the key for a jump shot.

BASELINE CROSS WITH DOUBLE DOWN (COUNTER)

In **Diagram 1.2**, O3 fakes coming across the lane and cuts hard off O5 and O4 at the top. O1 can pass to O3 at the top for a shot, or O3 can curl the double screen. O2 follows O3 and also cuts off the O5-O4 double screen.

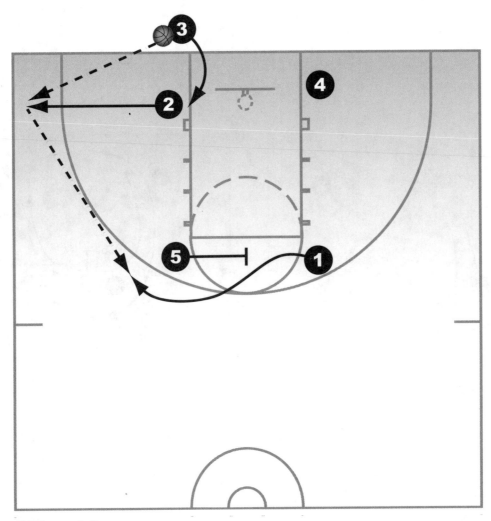

Wilkens 1.3

ATLANTA'S BASELINE TRIPLE

Authors' Note: The Baseline Triple was designed by Lenny Wilkens to free Ehlo for an open perimenter shot. Ehlo would run his defender into a series of three screens to create an open jump shot from the wing.

In **Diagram 1.3**, O3 inbounds to O2, who pops out to the corner. Player O5 screens for O1. Player O2 passes to O1, and O3 steps into the post.

In **Diagram 1.4,** O2 cuts off staggered screens by O3, O4 and O5. O1 can look for a quick post-up by O3 or pass to O2 (Ehlo) for the jump shot.

LESSONS FROM THIS LEGEND...

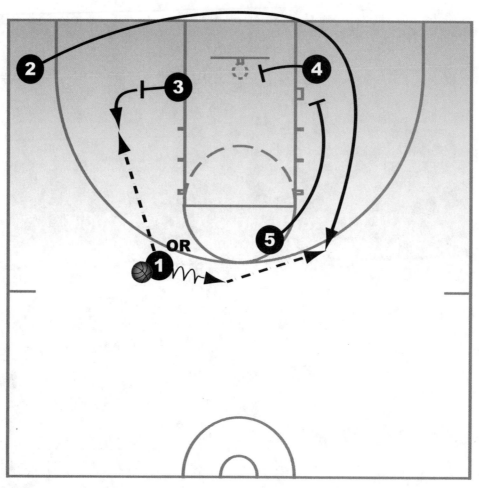

Wilkens 1.4

LIFE LESSONS:

Ehlo states that he "never heard Coach Wilkens use profanity or lose his composure in public, but he could reel off choice words and show his fiery competitiveness behind closed doors." He always told players that what went on in the locker room never left that room.

Wilkens also clearly "walked his talk" in living the value of respect. In every speaking engagement as a coach, he always mentioned and gave credit to his wife, Marilyn.

Finally, he gave tribute to his father (who died early in his life), as a strong influence in his life, teaching him the important of the father in child raising.

SOURCE:

Wilkens, Lenny. (1995). Plays from the Pros. In *Basketball Playbook*. Indianapolis: IN.

Ehlo, Craig. Interview with Jerry Krause, 2004.

LEGACY OF
John Wooden

- Led UCLA to 10 national titles, including 7 in a row.

- Philosopher-coach who developed the renowned "Pyramid of Success."

- Emphasized character development and taught life-enhancing skills.

- Inducted into the Naismith Basketball Hall of Fame as both a player and a coach.

- Selected NCAA College Basketball Coach of the Year six times (1964, 1967, 1969, 1970, 1972, 1973).

- Compiled a record of 885-203 (.813) during his 40-year coaching career.

- Led UCLA to 88 consecutive victories.

- Considered one of the finest teachers the game has ever seen.

JOHN WOODEN

"Success is peace of mind which is a direct result of self-satisfaction in knowing you did your best to become the best you are capable of becoming."
— *John Wooden*

BIOGRAPHY

Born: October 14, 1910 in Martinsville, IN

Inducted into the Naismith Memorial Basketball Hall of Fame as a player in 1960 and as a coach in 1973

The John Wooden-coached UCLA teams reached unprecedented heights that will be difficult for any team to match. The Bruins set all-time records with four perfect 30-0 seasons, 88 consecutive victories, 38 straight NCAA tournament victories, 20 conference championships, and 10 NCAA national championships, including seven in a row. Wooden is considered one of the finest teachers in the history of the game. He is one of only three people enshrined in the Naismith Memorial Basketball Hall of Fame as both a player and a coach. Wooden was a three-time All-American at Purdue University and was selected the College Player of the Year in 1932. He played for legendary Hall of Fame coach Ward "Piggy" Lambert and helped lead the Boilermakers to the 1932 National Championship. Wooden coached at Dayton (KY) H.S., South Bend (IN) Central High School, and at Indiana State University prior to his arrival at UCLA. In 2003, Wooden received two special honors. He was awarded the Presidential Medal of Honor, and UCLA named the court at Pauley Pavilion the Nell and John Wooden Court. Wooden was enshrined in the Naismith Memorial Basketball Hall of Fame as a player in 1960 and as a coach in 1973.

John Wooden...

John Wooden was a philosopher-coach, who believed our stature as a nation depended fundamentally on the strength and character of our people. He instructed his players with life-enhancing lessons. Wooden believed that athletics, when properly coached, provided an environment where individuals learned about themselves and about life. The skills he taught on the court are the same that are needed in the real world.

Wooden's remarkable success came primarily from his values and his consistency in living up to these values. He was selfless in example and was committed to helping others reach success and find inner peace.

It was Wooden's belief that participation in athletics should be a character-building experience. He emphasized to his players that they should be more concerned with their character than their reputation, and explained to them the difference between the two. Character is what you really are, while reputation is only what people say you are. A person of high character is trustworthy and honest.

Wooden believed that dishonesty was unacceptable. His father provided him with simple and direct rules for life. These were called "Two Sets of Three" and served as a compass for trying to do the right thing. The first set dealt with honesty: 1) never lie; 2) never cheat; and 3) never steal. The second set dealt with how to handle adversity: 1) don't whine; 2) don't complain; and 3) don't make excuses. Everyone encounters adversity, and people must discipline themselves to do the best that they can under the circumstances. An important key to success is how individuals respond to their perceived setbacks or disappointments. Unfortunately, many individuals blame others for their mistakes in an attempt to excuse themselves. Wooden acknowledged that he made many mistakes, but he had no failures because he did the best that he was capable of doing.

Winning was a word that Wooden rarely used. He preferred the word success, and success did not always mean scoring more points than your opponent. His emphasis was on doing your best. Wooden considered success a personal matter, because only you, as an individual, can tell if you did everything within your power to give your best effort. His focus was not on beating his opponent, but rather on developing the individuals on his team, so they grew both individually and collectively. Wooden strove for his players to attain a peace of mind that came only from giving their best effort. The goal that he believed was most important was the goal of making the most of one's ability.

EIGHT SUGGESTIONS FOR SUCCEEDING

1. Fear no opponent. Respect every opponent.
2. Remember, it's the perfection of the smallest details that make the big things happen.
3. Keep in mind that hustle makes up for many mistakes.
4. Be more interested in character than reputation.
5. Be quick, but don't hurry.
6. Understand the harder you work, the more luck you will have.
7. Know that valid self-analysis is crucial for improvement.
8. Remember that there is no substitute for hard work and careful planning. Failing to prepare is preparing to fail.

It was Coach Wooden's observations that the primary cause of unhappiness was people wanting too much materially. They overemphasized money and the material things that went with it. When it didn't come quickly or when it didn't come at all, people became discontent and unhappy. Peace of mind and inner happiness should not be dependent on material things.

NINE PROMISES THAT CAN BRING HAPPINESS

1. Promise yourself that you will talk health, happiness, and prosperity as often as possible.
2. Promise yourself to make all your friends know there is something in them that is special and that you value.
3. Promise to think only of the best, to work only for the best, and to expect only the best in yourself and others.
4. Promise to be just as enthusiastic about the success of others as you are about your own.
5. Promise yourself to be strong, so that nothing can disturb your peace of mind.

6. Promise to forget the mistakes of the past and press on to greater achievements in the future.
7. Promise to wear a cheerful appearance at all times and give every person you meet a smile.
8. Promise to give so much time to improving yourself that you have no time to criticize others.
9. Promise to be too large for worry, too noble for anger, too strong for fear, and too happy to permit trouble to press on you.

Wooden valued the principles of teaching and coaching as a sacred trust. The powerful influence of a teacher and coach must never be taken lightly. A coach helps mold character and instill productive principles. Wooden believed that coaches should be role models and provide positive examples to those with whom they come in contact. He lived and coached by his credo of industriousness and selflessness. His teams reflected his passion for hard work and teamwork. Wooden urged his players to try their hardest to improve and to make their work on that particular day a masterpiece. He explained to players that once they came to practice, they ceased to exist as an individual. They were part of a team. Every player and team manager had a role, and there were no subordinates. Wooden said, "It is remarkable how much can be accomplished when players think beyond themselves."

Wooden utilized the pedagogical principles of the whole-part method during practice sessions. He showed the desired outcome, and then divided it into teachable parts. Wooden said that he believed the laws of learning should be increased from four to eight because of the importance of repetition. His eight laws were: 1) explanation; 2) demonstration; 3) imitation; 4) repetition; 5) repetition; 6) repetition; 7) repetition; and 8) repetition. His goal was to create a correct habit that could be produced without conscious thought under great pressure. Wooden believed the best teacher was repetition of the fundamentals, performed correctly day after day, throughout the season.

When asked why he taught, Wooden responded, "There is no better place to find finer company." He warned people about taking themselves too seriously. Wooden said, "Talent is God-given, be humble; fame is man-given, be thankful; conceit is self-given, be careful."

Wooden's philosophy can be summarized in the creed given to him as he entered high school from his father:
1. Be true to yourself.
2. Help others.
3. Make each day your masterpiece.
4. Drink deeply from good books, especially the Bible.

5. Make friendship a fine art.
6. Build a shelter against a rainy day.
7. Pray for guidance, and count and give thanks for your blessings every day.

In pursuing success and living every day to its fullest, Wooden identified the following as some of his favorite maxims:
1. Happiness begins where selfishness ends.
2. Big things are accomplished only through the perfection of minor details.
3. Discipline yourself, and others won't need to.
4. Ability may get you to the top, but it takes character to keep you there.
5. If you do not have the time to do it right, when will you find the time to do it over?
6. Don't let yesterday take up too much of today.
7. It is what you learn after you know it all that counts.
8. Do not permit what you cannot do to interfere with what you can do.
9. Love is the greatest of all words in our language.
10. Never make excuses. Your friends don't need them, and your foes won't believe them.
11. The more concerned we become over the things we can't control, the less we will do with the things we can control.
12. Do not mistake activity for achievement.
13. Treat all people with dignity and respect.
14. You cannot live a perfect day without doing something for another without thought of something in return.
15. Acquire peace of mind by making the effort to become the best of which you are capable.

SOURCE

Hill, A. with J. Wooden. (2001) *Be Quick—But Don't Hurry*. New York: Simon & Schuster.

Krause, Jerry and Ralph Pim. (2002) *Coaching Basketball*. New York: McGraw-Hill.

Wooden, John. Vertical Files, Archives. Naismith Memorial Basketball Hall of Fame. Springfield, MA.

Wooden J. and S. Jamison. (1997) *Wooden: A Lifetime of Observations and Reflections On and Off the Court*. Chicago: Contemporary Books.

HIGH-POST OFFENSE

By John Wooden

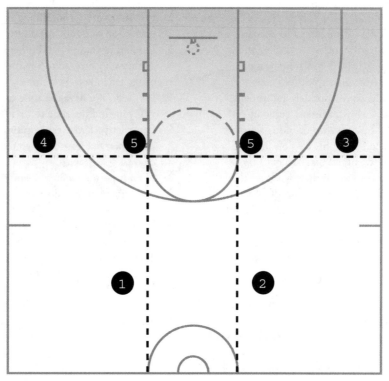

Wooden 1.0

I want shots coming from the offense, not from some individual dribbling around to get open, except in certain situations when the defense makes a mistake. I want triangle rebounding power underneath, a long rebounder, and a protector. We never pass to a player standing still, and we must attack each side of the floor equally.

BASIC ALIGNMENT

Diagram 1.0 shows the initial alignment of our high-post offense. The center, O5, starts play on either side of the foul line. We prefer that O5 start on the side of the advancing guard. The forwards, O3 and O4, start on the free-throw line extended. We would like to initiate the offense with a guard-to-guard pass.

LESSONS FROM THIS LEGEND...

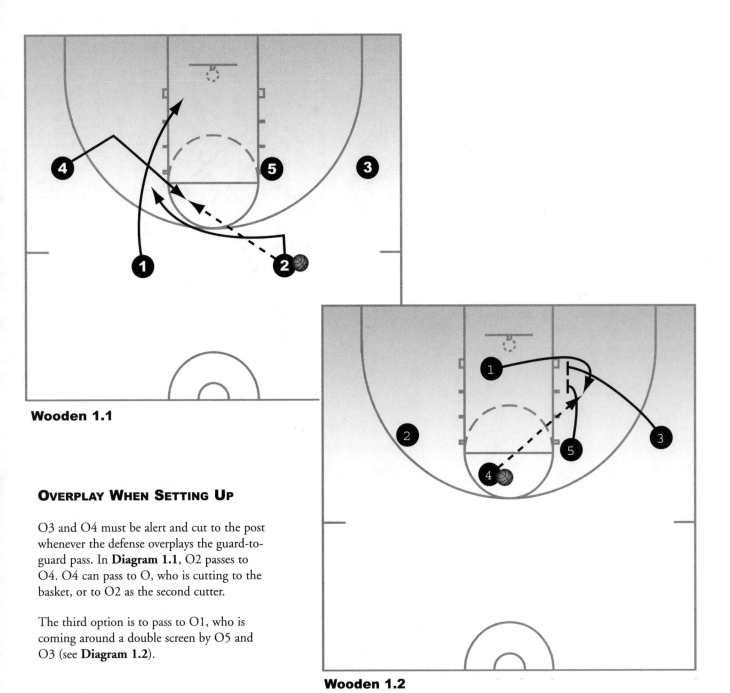

Wooden 1.1

OVERPLAY WHEN SETTING UP

O3 and O4 must be alert and cut to the post whenever the defense overplays the guard-to-guard pass. In **Diagram 1.1**, O2 passes to O4. O4 can pass to O, who is cutting to the basket, or to O2 as the second cutter.

The third option is to pass to O1, who is coming around a double screen by O5 and O3 (see **Diagram 1.2**).

Wooden 1.2

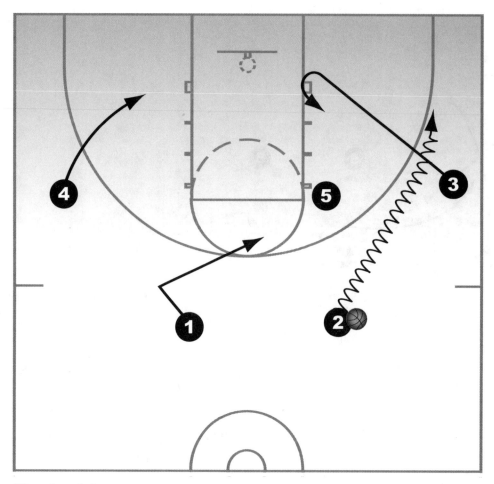

Wooden 1.3

OVERPLAY ON THE STRONG SIDE FORWARD

When O3 is being denied the pass on the wing, he accelerates to the basket on a back-door cut. If O3 does not receive the pass on the back-cut, he buttonhooks and posts up above the free-throw block (see **Diagram 1.3**).

LESSONS FROM THIS LEGEND...

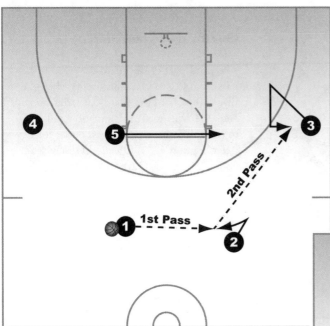

Wooden 1.4

GUARD CUT

On the guard-to-guard pass from O1 to O2, the small forward O3 makes what is called an "L" cut to get open to receive the pass. O5 moves to the high post on the ballside (see **Diagram 1.4**).

After O2 passes to O3, he cuts off of O5's screen, looking for a return pass. If O2 does not receive the pass, he will post up above the free-throw block (see **Diagram 1.5**). This is an excellent way to post up a big guard.

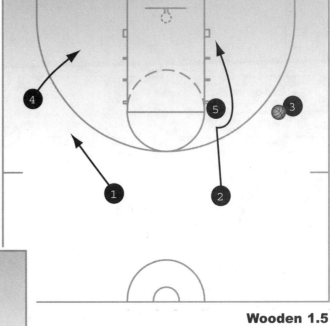

Wooden 1.5

The second-part of the guard-cut series is the pass from O3 to O5 (see **Diagram 1.6**). The first option is to pass to O4 on what we call is the "duck-in" move. If the defender is preventing this pass, O5 can also pass to O1, who then feeds O4. The next option is to pass to O2, coming off the down screen from O3. O2 must set up his defender before using the down screen.

Wooden 1.6

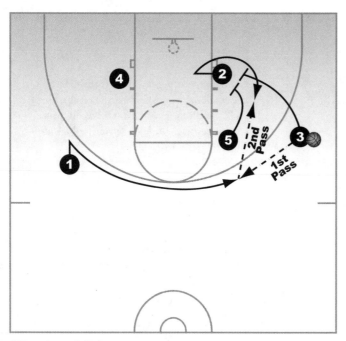

Wooden 1.7

GUARD CUT (CONTINUED)

The third-part of the guard cut series is the pass from O3 to O1. This occurs when the first two parts of the guard-cut series are covered. O1 will "read" this situation and cuts to the ball to become the pass outlet for O3 (see **Diagram 1.7**). O3 and O5 then set a double screen for O2.

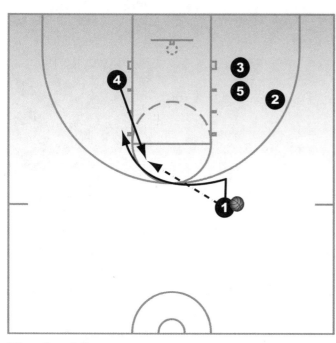

Wooden 1.8

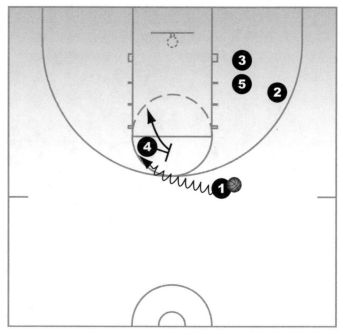

Wooden 1.9

If O2 is not open coming off the double screen, O4 cuts to the elbow. O1 passes to O4. Their side of the floor is clear and they play a two-man game (see **Diagram 1.8**).

Another option is for O1 and O4 to execute a pick-and-roll (see **Diagram 1.9**).

LESSONS FROM THIS LEGEND...

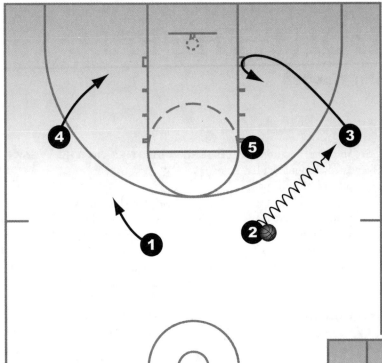

Wooden 1.10

DRIBBLE TO THE WING

When the guard-to-forward pass is denied, another way to get into the high-post offense is called dribble to the wing. O2 dribbles to the wing, and O3 goes to the block and posts up (see **Diagram 1.10**). We now have our players located in the floor positions so that we can run all the options that were described in the guard-cut series. The only difference is that O2 is at the wing, and O3 is posting up on the block.

GUARD AROUND

In this set, O2 passes to O3, follows the pass, and receives the hand-off back from O3 (see **Diagram 1.11**). O4 breaks across the lane, looking for the pass from O2. This also clears the backside for the lob play. O5 sets a screen. O3 cuts off O5's screen and looks for the lob pass from O2.

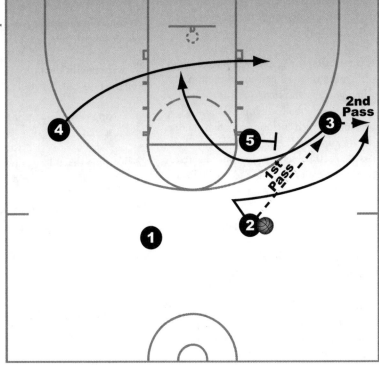

Wooden 1.11

SOURCE

Wooden, John. (1986) "High Post Offense." *MacGregor Flashback Notebook.* Volume XII. MacGregor Sporting Goods Inc..

MOVING WITHOUT THE BALL

By John Wooden

I believe that the most difficult task that I have in regard to the technical development of my players is getting individuals to work properly on offense without the ball and to play heads up, alert, off-the-ball defense in our man-to-man defensive system.

If each player on the floor had the ball an equal amount of time, no one would have the ball over 10 percent of the playing time; so what each player is doing the approximate 90 percent of the time he does not have the ball plays a vital part in the efficiency with which both the team and the individual will function.

It is true that the guards will have the ball a little more than 10 percent of the time when you are on offense, as they will usually advance the ball when possession is obtained, which makes it equally true that the forwards and center will have the ball less than 10 percent of the time. Therefore, they have even more time to operate without the ball.

FOUR MINUTES A GAME

I like to point out to my college players that most of them will have the ball considerably less than four minutes in a forty-minute game, because four minutes would be the maximum if each of the ten players would have it an equal amount of the playing time, providing some player was in possession of it at all times.

BE A COMPLETE PLAYER

At no time, do I imply that what you are able to do with the ball when it is in your possession is not important, but continually emphasize that you will not have the ball

the vast percentage of the time, and none of that time should be wasted. Too many players, who are excellent players with the ball, do very little when they do not have the ball. Therefore, they are not complete players. The offensive player without the ball has several things to do to keep him busy, and proper timing is essential for all of them.

RESPONSIBILITIES ON THE STRONGSIDE

Among the things players must do on the strongside include:

1. Screening at the proper time if the play or situation calls for it.

2. Setting defenders up in order to better use a screen.

3. Keeping defenders so busy that they will not be in position to help teammates.

4. Making defenders turn their eyes away from the ball at the proper time.

5. Setting defenders up in order to get open and provide passing opportunities for teammates at the proper time.

6. Working to get open to receive passes and be in the triple-threat position.

7. Establishing proper floor position as rebounders or as protectors when a shot is taken.

8. Seeing the floor and moving accordingly. Offensive players must be thinking constantly, and their moves will be predicated on the moves of the player who has the ball or the player who just passed the ball.

RESPONSIBILITIES ON THE WEAK-SIDE

The offensive players on the weakside do not have quite as many things to do, but the things that they must do are of vital importance. A weakside attack is of tremendous importance to the total offense. Their responsibilities include:

1. Keeping their defenders busy and preventing them from floating.

2. Setting defenders up in order to be open to receive passes in the proper position to immediately attack the defense.

WAYS TO PROMOTE OFFENSE WITHOUT THE BALL

Since it is perfectly natural and normal for players to want to score, it is perfectly natural and normal for them to subconsciously work harder when they have the ball in their possession. In order to get them to put forth the same comparative effort when they do not have the ball, we have to overcome or at least compensate for a normal subconscious reaction. This is not easy, but it is necessary to field the complete ball player and the complete team.

To help teach and promote this constant effort without the ball, it is necessary for a coach to use all of the psychology and ingenuity at his or her command. Since every player is different and every team is made up of different individuals, it does not follow that what works with one will necessarily work with another. Therefore, season after season, the coach must keep searching for the right approach to a particular player or particular team.

LESSONS FROM THIS LEGEND...

SOME IDEAS THAT I HAVE FOUND HELPFUL ARE AS FOLLOWS:

1. Constantly emphasize the previously mentioned facts to your players by word of mouth, by printed material, and by sight when viewing game movies.

2. Point out and give a lot of public credit to those who really keep working mentally and physically when they do not have the ball. Do this in your practice and follow up in your game competition.

3. Get the cooperation of your sportswriters and sportscasters, especially your own school reporters, in calling attention to these factors.

4. Be certain to indicate the preliminary movements of all those without the ball when diagramming plays of the offense. Explain the purpose of the moves of each individual.

5. Have the players diagram the offense occasionally and make certain that they show all the preliminary moves and fakes of those without the ball.

6. We do not want the players to criticize each other, but encourage them to critically analyze the play at all times and particularly watch those without the ball.

7. Run considerable offense without taking the shot so that the ball will always be brought back to the weak side and all options set up.

8. Stress constant movement without ever standing still or standing straight up. This encourages thinking and moving with a purpose.

9. Encourage your passing game by complimenting your passers at every opportunity. A fine passer will encourage players to work to get open to receive a pass, while a poor passer encourages a "what is the use" attitude.

10. The development of a proper team spirit encourages everyone to work. I like to define team spirit as an eagerness to sacrifice personal glory for the welfare of the team.

DEFINITION OF SUCCESS

Yes, basketball offense without the ball is essential for the success of the individual basketball player and for the team. I consider success to be peace of mind that can only be attained by self-satisfaction in knowing that you have done your best to become the best that you are capable of becoming. Each individual, with and without the ball, cannot achieve this in the game of basketball without total effort.

SOURCE

Wooden, John. (1973, December) Basketball Offense Without the Ball. *The Basketball Bulletin.*

LEGACY OF
Sandra "Kay" Yow

- Earned two Olympic gold medals, one as an assistant coach in 1984, and the other as head coach in 1988.

- Known for her relentless support of success, both on and off the court.

- In 2004, ranked as the fifth winningest active Division I women's coach with 653 career victories.

- Selected as the first full-time women's basketball coach in the state of North Carolina.

- Led North Carolina State to 17 appearances in the first 23 Women's NCAA Tournaments.

- Directed North Carolina State to the 1998 Final Four.

- Winningest coach in North Carolina State University history.

SANDRA "KAY" YOW

"The best thing about being a college coach is being a part of development of the person—student and athlete, striving to be a difference maker in the lives of young people."
— Kay Yow

BIOGRAPHY

Born: March 14, 1942 in Gibsonville, NC

Inducted into the Naismith Basketball Hall of Fame in 2002

Entering the 2005 season, Sandra "Kay" Yow has amassed an overall record of 653-300 in 33 years of coaching. Yow was named the second head coach in North Carolina State Women's Basketball history in 1975, and has coached all but one year of the Wolfpack's 30-years as a program. She has guided North Carolina State to nineteen, 20-win seasons and 17 NCAA Tournament appearances. Yow currently ranks as the fifth winningest active Division I women's coach. She coached the U.S. Olympic team to the gold medal in 1988. She also guided the USA National Team to gold medals in 1996 at the Goodwill Games and at the World Basketball Championships. Yow has compiled a 21-1 record in international competition and is the only coach to win gold medals in both the Olympics and the World Championships. From 1972-75, Yow led Elon College to a 57-19 record and two North Carolina state titles. She also coached at Allen Jay High School in High Point, North Carolina and Gibsonville (NC) High School. Yow has been named National Coach of the Year eight times by various organizations, including the John and Nellie Wooden Association, *USA Today*, *Sports Illustrated*, and the WBCA. Yow is one of the most admired and respected coaches in collegiate basketball and has been enshrined in six Halls of Fame—Elon College, Fellowship of Christian Athletes, North Carolina Sports Hall of Fame, Women's Sports Hall of Fame, Women's Basketball Hall of Fame, and the Naismith Memorial Basketball Hall of Fame.

Sandra "Kay" Yow...

Sandra "Kay" Yow began playing basketball as a child growing up in Gibsonville, North Carolina. "I was a kid when my father put up a hoop in our backyard, and that's where I started playing," said Yow (2002). "I went on to play on my elementary school and then junior high school teams. Growing up in North Carolina made it possible for me to play outside all year. And that's what I did from the time I could look up and see the hoop. My parents were so supportive. They taught me the value of athletics—how it built character and how it taught you to work with team members. And I just thought it was the most fun thing in the world."

The backyard games were highly competitive, as Kay's sisters and mother competed for family bragging rights. Kay's mother, Lib, finally quit playing in the games after she broke both wrists at the age of 48. Kay's younger sisters, Debbie and Susan, have made their mark in intercollegiate athletics. Debbie is the ACC's first female athletic director, and has led the Maryland Terrapins to nine NCAA national championships during her nine-year tenure. Susan, an All-American player at NC State, was one of Kay's assistant coaches in the Olympics, and is currently the head basketball coach at Providence College. During her 21 seasons as a Division I head coach, Susan has built successful basketball programs at UNC-Wilmington, Kansas State, Drake, and East Tennessee State.

Yow attended Gibsonville High School and holds the school record for the most points scored in a game with 52. She graduated in 1960, and at that time, there were no opportunities for women in intercollegiate athletics. Yow said, "I saw that there was nowhere else for me to go with basketball, so I knew my future lay in teaching." She attended East Carolina State University and majored in English. "I decided to become a high school English teacher and never thought any more about playing or coaching basketball," said Yow.

Yow's first coaching opportunity came from Allen Jay High School in High Point, North Carolina. The principal needed a basketball coach for the girls' team and contacted Yow about the opening. "I was reluctant at first because of the time commitment," remembered Yow, "but eventually he talked me into it. Those four years at Allen Jay High School made me decide that coaching was what I really wanted to do."

"Through coaching, I felt I had the opportunity to touch people physically, intellectually, emotionally, socially, and spiritually," said Yow (Nolan, 1997). "In sport, the total person is involved and you have the opportunity to help young people become outstanding athletes and help them develop as people. Teaching is a service occupation, and for me, coaching is the ultimate of teaching. You have students you can mold and implant so many qualities and characteristics, such as self-control, the setting of goals, and the developing of a plan, belief in themselves, confidence, and perseverance. I know many teachers develop a lot of those qualities, but in sports you can reach those levels more often, and because of the emotional level, catch glimpses of the truer person inside the uniform. A coach can really enjoy helping young people develop qualities that can help them succeed, not only in the classroom, but anything they do in life."

To pursue her dream in coaching, Yow went to UNC-Greensboro and got a master's degree and an undergraduate certification in physical education. While she was in her last year of graduate school, Yow coached at her alma mater, Gibsonville High School.

Yow's was named head women's basketball coach at Elon College in 1972. During her four years at Elon, Yow compiled a 57-19 record and captured two North Carolina state titles.

North Carolina State University was impressed with Yow's abilities and selected her to direct their program for the 1976 season. She is now entering her 30th year as the head coach of the Wolfpack and has led North Carolina State to a level of consistency that is nearly unmatched. Her teams have won four ACC tournament championships and five conference regular season titles. The Wolfpack's 12 ACC tournament championship appearances are more than any other league school. North Carolina State has appeared in the NCAA Tournament 17 times since the tourney's inception. Yow's record at NC State is a remarkable 596-281, and she stands as the winningest coach in Wolfpack history.

Yow has also become one of the most honored coaches in the international circles. During her career, she has worked with two United States Olympic teams and seven other U.S. select teams, including Pan American, World University, and World Championship squads. In 1988, Yow guided the U.S. Olympic Team to a gold medal. The U.S squad swept through the 24th Olympiad in Seoul, South Korea in stunning fashion, downing the Soviet Union 102-88 in the semi-finals and Yugoslavia 77-70 for the gold. Yow served as an assistant coach for the 1984 U.S. Olympic Team, which also brought home the gold medal.

But, what Yow talks about is not the medals but walking into stadiums for opening ceremonies, knowing what great fortune it was to have been born in this country and the honor of representing the United States. Yow was named head coach of the U.S. Olympic Team in 1986, but during August of 1987, her opportunity was in jeopardy when, during a routine physical, doctors discovered she had breast cancer. She had major surgery, slowly built back her strength, and brought the players to Raleigh to prepare for the 1988 Olympics. They not only held intense practices, but she had them construct a building of Popsicle sticks with one hand tied behind their backs. It forced the basketball superstars to depend on one another to get the task accomplished.

One of Yow's most renowned traits is her ability on the speaking circuit. She is a noted speaker and clinician, conducting clinics and speaking for charitable organizations around the country. Yow is a past president of the Women's Basketball Coaches Association.

In her Naismith Memorial Basketball Hall of Fame speech, Yow recognized her staff and players. In reference to their contribution, Yow stated, "You prepared, you planned, you practiced, you performed, and you persevered to make possible this moment for me."

Yow also talked about one of the first lessons she learned in coaching, and that was the importance of keeping things in perspective. As she celebrated a last-second win over an archrival for the conference tournament championship, she was "in the clouds," as the high school principal approached her. Yow was expecting words of praise, but instead, the principal reminded her to "count the towels." It was an excellent reminder that it is great to win, but never forget your responsibilities. You are always held accountable to a high standard, and it can never be forgotten during times of victory or defeat. The bywords of Kay Yow basketball programs have always been tradition, family, excellence, and success.

Yow believes the ethical conduct of coaches is essential. "A coach has to review all the potential problems," said Yow, "and come up with the answer to them before he or she is actually confronted by the difficulties. I know if I were approached by someone who asked me to cut some corners in recruiting or do something less than straightforward, I would know exactly how to respond. And what

I'm going to do must be based on my belief that you can't ever compromise ethics. People say, 'don't worry, no one will ever know about it.' Well, someone will know about it."

To make her point, Yow said, "I recently read a story about a man who was taking his two young sons to a movie, and the person in the box office told him the movie was three dollars for adults and free for any child under six years old. The father handed six dollars to the clerk, as one of his sons was three years of age and the other was seven. The clerk then said to the father that he could have gotten in for three dollars, because no one could have known his son was a seven-year old. The father answered, 'my son would have known.' That is what I mean by setting an example and doing the right thing."

Kay Yow is an exceptional human being and role model. She lives her life according to her favorite quote, "Greatness is not doing extraordinary things, but doing ordinary things extraordinarily well." She believes that success is not final and failure is not fatal. It is a lesson that she has taught well to everyone she has touched.

Source

Ingram, Sarah Sue. (2002). Leader of the Pack. *Naismith Memorial Basketball Hall of Fall Enshrinement Yearbook.*

Miller, Chennell. (2002). Championship Under Construction. *North Carolina State University Women's Basketball Media Guide.*

Nolan, Timothy. (1997, March). An "E" for Excellence and a "Kay" for Class. *Coach and Athletic Director.*

Yow, Kay. Vertical Files, Archives. Naismith Memorial Basketball Hall of Fame. Springfield, MA.

Yow, Kay. Interview with Ralph Pim, September 26, 2002.

Yow, Kay, Interview with Jerry Krause, September 2003.

LESSONS FROM THIS LEGEND...

OFFENSIVE DRILLS

By Kay Yow

TOSS-BACK DRILLS

❏ INSIDE PLAYERS

1. Rebound drill (1-2 minutes):
   - Stand on the block, facing the toss-back
   - Throw a 2-hand overhead pass into the toss-back to reflect off the backboard.
   - Grab the rebound to tap-in or take a rebound shot.

2. Outlet pass and reaction drill (1-2 minutes):
   - Shoot a layup and fire a rebound outlet into the toss-back at the wing.
   - Field the throw back, make a power move for a shot, grab the rebound, and repeat the drill.

3. Mikan and reverse Mikan drill (2-1/2 minutes each):
   - Face the basket and shoot a right handed hook layup shot.
   - Catch the rebound quickly to shoot a left-hand hook layup; repeat quickly.
   - Reverse Mikan uses a reverse layup shot.

4. Partner flare pass and roll to basket drill (1-2 minutes):
   - Shoot a layup, grab the rebound, and fire an outlet pass into the toss-back.
   - Field the throw back, moving to meet the pass, and fire a pass into the other toss-back.
   - Field the pass and use either a swing shot or a power move to the basket; continue.

5. Tapping drill (20-30 times each):
   - Tap the ball against the backboard with the right hand 20-30 times consecutively; tap the last one in for a basket.
   - Tap with the left hand 20-40 times.
   - Tap with both hands together 20-30 times

6. One-man - two ball drill (1-2 minutes.):
   - Place one ball on both blocks.
   - Player picks up on ball to shoot a layup, and then moves quickly to pick up a second ball for a layup; continue to alternate.
   - Partner rebounds and places balls on the blocks.

❏ PERIMETER PLAYERS

1. Forward continuity drill (30 seconds—one minute):
   - Shoot a layup, rebound, and pass to a toss-back at the right of the key.
   - Move to meet the pass and throw an overhead pass into the toss-back at the low post.
   - Receive a return pass on the move for a layup.

2. Intensity layups (30 seconds—one minute):
   - Stand at the top of the key, throw into the toss-back, and sprint to catch the rebound pass.
   - Shoot a layup without fumbling the pass, retrieve the rebound, and dribble quickly back to the top of the key to repeat.

3. Strongside triangle options (30 seconds—one minute):
   - Pass into a toss-back at a guard position to receive the pass on the baseline; pivot.
   - Pass into a low-post toss-back as you break toward the basket.

4. Fast break drill (30 seconds—one minute):
   - Speed dribble from mid-court to pass into a toss-back at the free-throw line.
   - Toss-back returns a bounce pass to the block.
   - Field the pass and shoot a bank shot at the block.

5. Angle passing and reaction drill (30 seconds—one minute):
   - Pass into the toss-back so that it will rebound at an angle.
   - Defensive slide to retrieve the pass, and return a pass back to the toss-back.

6. Toss back ballhandling drills (30 seconds each):
   - Behind the back passing
   - Alternate hand passing
   - Pass-dribble-pass-dribble
   - Around the body passing
   - Two-ball circle passing

LESSONS FROM THIS LEGEND...

EXPLODE DRILLS

❑ **FAKE AND DRIVE**
   1. Rocker step
   2. Cross-over step
   3. Fake and shoot
   4. Up and under
   5. Ball swoop

❑ **FAKE AND DRIVE OFF THE DRIBBLE**
   1. Cross-over dribble
   2. Change-of-pace dribble
   3. Reverse Dribble
   4. Fake-reverse dribble

SHOOTING DRILLS

❑ **FORM SHOOTING**
   1. Wall
   2. Line
   3. Basket

❑ **2 1/2-MINUTE DRILL**

❑ **ONE-MINUTE DRILL**

❑ **SPOT SHOOTING**

❑ **INDIVIDUAL MOVES**
   1. Perimeter moves:
      • Shoot off a pass around a screen or cross-court pass
      • Shoot off a dribble around a pick
      • Penetrate with fake and drive for shot
   2. Inside players:
      • Low-post shots
      • High-post shots
      • Baseline shots

FULL-COURT DRILLS

❑ **TWO-PLAYER DRILLS (FULL COURT)**
   1. Two lines with inside-line dribbling down to the corner of the free-throw line and then bounce passing to your partner for a layup
   2. Two lines chest passing down the length of court with a shot taken at corner of free-throw line
   3. Two lines bounce passing the length of the court (full-court), and the player in the outside line takes an outside shot.
   4. Two lines bounce passing the length of the court. The inside player makes the last pass to an outside player and picks up in player-to-player defense.

❑ **FAST BREAK DRILLS—THREE PLAYER DRILLS**
   1. Fast break with the middle player rebounding and passing to the outside player, who takes ball to the middle. The rebounder follows the pass and fills the lane. The dribbler takes the ball to the free-throw line at the opposite end and bounce passes to either cutter. After passing the middle man, moves to the corner of the free-throw line on the ball side.
   2. Fast break with the middle player rebounding and passing to the outlet player, who then passes to a player who is cutting to middle. The rebounder fills the fastbreak lane opposite the side she passes the ball.
   3. Three-on-two and two-on-one drill. The shooter or person turning the ball over becomes the defensive player coming back in two-on-one.

LESSONS FROM THIS LEGEND...

❑ **TEAM OFFENSIVE DRILLS**

1. Five-player drills (primary and secondary breaks):
    - 5-on-0
    - 5-on-3
    - 5-on-4
    - 5-on-5

2. Transition drills:
    - 3-on-3 line drill
    - 4-on-4 line drill
    - 5-on-5 line drill

3. Drills using screens properly:
    - We use this drill from the top, as in **Diagram 1.0,** but also from the baseline and wing position (give-and-go or pass-and-cut):
        ✓ The 1st man in line is the defensive player.
        ✓ The 2nd man in line is the offensive player.
        ✓ The offensive player becomes the next defensive player.
        ✓ The defensive player goes to the end of line.
    - Drill for setting a screen properly, using a screen properly, and screen opening to the ball properly (pass and screen away) (see **Diagram 1.1**):
        ✓ 1 passes to 3.
        ✓ 1 screens for 2.
        ✓ 2 fakes low and goes over the top.
        ✓ 1 opens to the ball and fills space.
    - Screen down (see **Diagram 1.2**):
        ✓ 2 screens for 5.
        ✓ 5 fakes inside and then pops out.
        ✓ 1 passes to 5.
        ✓ 2 opens to ball and posts inside.

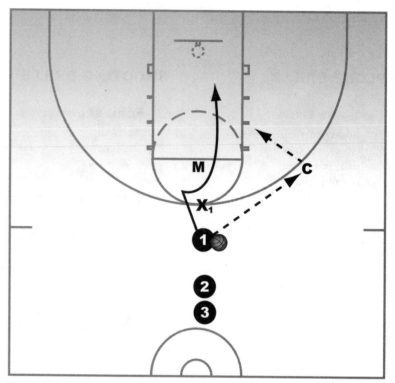

Yow 1.0

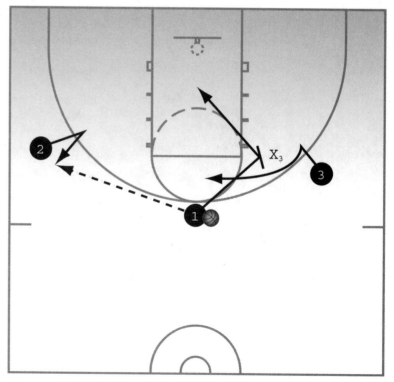

Yow 1.1

LESSONS FROM THIS LEGEND...

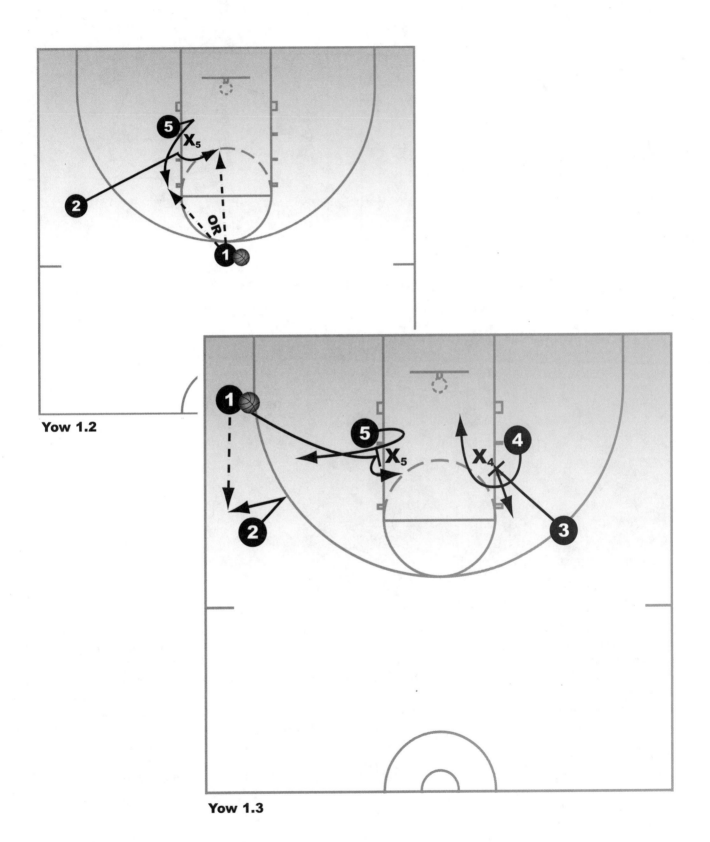

Yow 1.2

Yow 1.3

LESSONS FROM THIS LEGEND...

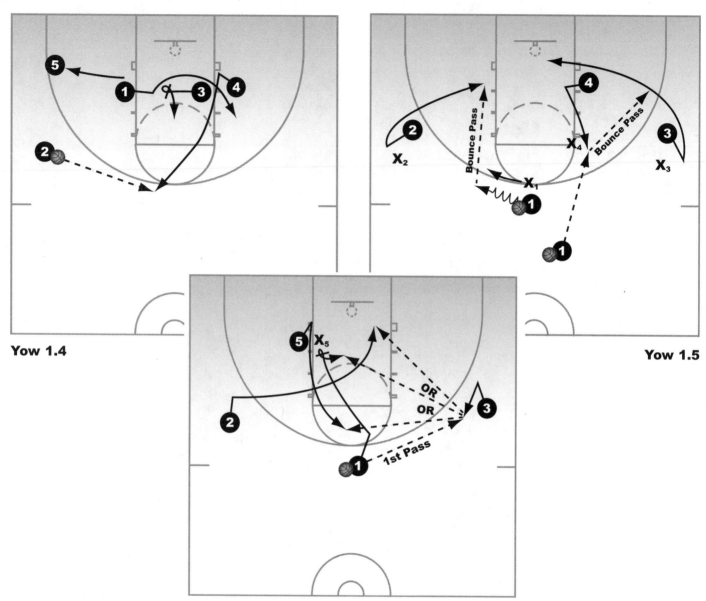

Yow 1.4

Yow 1.5

Yow 1.6

- Drill for setting two screens at once and passer reading open cutter (see **Diagrams 1.3 and 1.4**):
  - ✓ 1 passes to 2.
  - ✓ 3 screens for 4.
  - ✓ 4 fakes and cuts to the ball.
  - ✓ 2 passes to 4 and screens for 5.
  - ✓ 1 flashes across the lane.
  - ✓ 3 screens for 1 and opens to the ball.
  - ✓ 1 pops out from the screen.
  - ✓ 4 passes to the cutter (1) or screener (3).

- Backdoor cut and pass directly from the point or indirectly from the high post (see **Diagram 1.5**):
  - ✓ 2 fakes high and cuts backdoor.
  - ✓ 1 makes a backdoor pass.
  - ✓ 4 breaks up from low-to-high post.
  - ✓ 1 passes to 4 at the high post.
  - ✓ 3 fakes to receive pass from 1.
  - ✓ 4 passes to 3, going backdoor.

- Drill for timing the cut from the point-wing interchange or the cut-through the lane (see **Diagram 1.6**):
  - ✓ 1 passes to 3.
  - ✓ 1 moves to interchange with the low man the opposite ball.
  - ✓ 2 cuts off 1's back, as an interchange is being made.
  - ✓ 2 moves to the medium post if she does not receive pass for a shot.

LESSONS FROM THIS LEGEND...

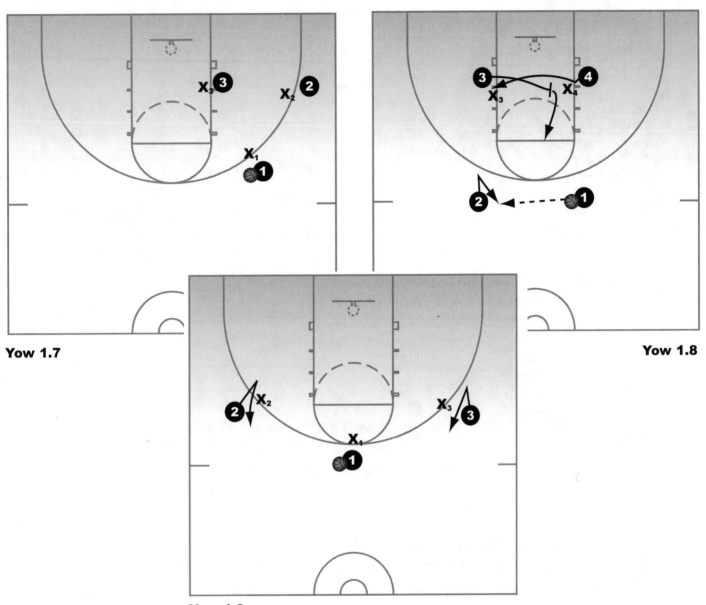

Yow 1.7

Yow 1.8

Yow 1.9

- Triangle drill (see **Diagram 1.7**):
  ✓ 1. 1, 2 and 3 work to get an inside shot, an open outside shot or a penetration shot, using explode moves or screens.
- Two-on-two inside drill (see **Diagram 1.8**):
  ✓ Four offensive players vs. two defensive players
  ✓ 1 and 2 pass the ball back and forth until they can make

a pass to one of inside players.
  ✓ The inside players screen for each other, move anywhere inside the lane (high, medium or low) to receive pass, make a move, take a shot, pass to the other post, or pass back out to the perimeter players.

- Three-on-three perimeter drill: Passer options: (see **Diagram 1.9**):

✓ Pass and screen away
✓ Pass and cut
✓ Pass and screen ball
✓ Pass and replace self
✓ Pass and receive return pass
- Balance the court with proper spacing

SOURCE

Meyer, Ray. (1979). *Flashback Notebook: Notes & Diagrams from the Greatest Basketball Clinics in the Nation.* Medalist Sports Education: Milwaukee, WI (Vol. V)

LESSONS FROM THE LEGENDS

trivia QUIZ

NAME THE NAISMITH HALL OF FAME COACH WHO...

1 Is the only American male to both play and coach in the Olympics?

Hint: He became the first coach in basketball history to win both an NCAA championship (1988) and an NBA championship (2004).

2 Was the first coach in basketball history to win the Triple Crown of coaching NIT championship in 1949, NCAA championship in 1959, and the Olympic gold medal in 1960?

Hint: He is recognized as one of the all-time greatest teachers in the game of basketball.

3 Led the movement to abolish the center jump after each basket?

Hint: He led USC to the Final Four in 1940 and coached the Trojan baseball team to the NCAA championship in 1948.

4 Was the only coach in basketball history to lead his team to both the NIT and NCAA championships in the same year? (CCNY in 1950)

Hint: He played with the Original Celtics and was nicknamed "Mr. Basketball."

5 Became the first Hall of Fame coach to win both an NBA championship and an Olympic Gold Medal?

Hint: He led the Detroit Pistons to back-to-back NBA championships in 1989 and 1990.

6 Led Tennessee A&I (now Tennessee State) to three consecutive NAIA national championships (1957, 1958, 1959)?

Hint: He became the first black coach in the ABL with the Cleveland Pipers in 1961.

7 Introduced an innovative training session on game days called the shoot-around ?

Hint: He became only the third person in basketball history to be elected to the Naismith Basketball Hall of Fame as both a player (1976) and a coach (2004).

8 Led North Carolina State to 17 of the 23 Women s NCAA Tournaments, including a Final Four appearance in 1998?

Hint: She earned two Olympic gold medals, one as an assistant coach in 1984, and the other as head coach in 1988.

9 Directed Ohio State to five consecutive Big Ten championships?

Hint: He led the Buckeyes to the NCAA national championship in 1960.

10 Coached 24 years at St. John s and led every one of his teams into postseason tournament play?

Hint: He led the New York Nets to the 1972 ABA Finals.

11 Compiled a record of 876-190 (.822) at Kentucky?

Hint: He was nicknamed the "Baron of the Bluegrass."

12 Led a national campaign in the 1940s to outlaw goaltending?

Hint: He invented the shuffle offense, a five-player continuity offense.

13 Was the only coach in basketball history to direct two different schools to the Final Four at least twice?

Hint: He led Kansas State to the 1951 NCAA Finals.

14 Became the all-time winningest coach in NBA history on January 6, 1995?

Hint: He was selected as one of the 10 Greatest Coaches in NBA History and one of the 50 Greatest Players during the NBAís Golden Anniversary celebration.

15 Led an unsuccessful campaign in 1929 to eliminate dribbling from the game?

Hint: He directed Wisconsin to the Helms Foundation national championship in 1912, 1914, and 1916.

16 Coached 29 years at Purdue and led the Boilermakers to 11 conference championships.

Hint: He pioneered the fast break in the Midwest.

17 Created the power forward position in pro basketball?

Hint: He created the NBA's first dynasty by leading the Minneapolis Lakers to four league championships in a five-year span.

18 Led UCLA to 88 consecutive victories?

Hint: He emphasized character development and developed the "Pyramid of Success."

19 Pioneered the fast break and brought national prominence to Western Kentucky University?

Hint: His trademark was a red towel that he would wave, chew, or toss along the sidelines.

20 Spent 47 years at Winston-Salem State University and was nicknamed Big House ?

Hint: He retired as the second winningest college coach in basketball history.

ANSWERS

1) Larry Brown 2) Pete Newell 3) Justin Sami Barry 4) Nat Holman 5) Chuck Daly 6) John McLendon 7) Bill Sharman 8) Sandra Kay Yow 9) Fred Taylor 10) Lou Carnesecca 11) Adolph Rupp 12) Bruce Drake 13) Jack Gardner 14) Lenny Wilkens 15) Walter Doc Meanwell 16) Ward Piggy Lambert 17) John Kundla 18) John Wooden 19) Edgar Ed Diddle 20) Clarence Big House Gaines

309

ABOUT THE AUTHORS

JERRY KRAUSE

Jerry Krause has coached and taught basketball for over forty years and is widely recognized as a master teacher and clinician. The most prolific author in the history of basketball, he has written or edited 27 coaching books and has developed over 30 instructional videos. He is the chairman of the NABC Research Committee and former chairman of the NCAA Basketball Rules Committee.

In 1998, Krause received the prestigious NABC Cliff Wells Appreciation Award for lifetime contributions to basketball. In 2002, he was honored as NABC Guardian of the Game for Advocacy—developed a rim-testing device to equate ball rebound in every gym and from rim to rim—a 20-year research project. He has been inducted into the NAIA Basketball Coaches Hall of Fame (2000) and the National Association for Sports and Physical Education Hall of Fame as a coach and physical educator (2000). Jerry Krause currently is the director of basketball operations for Gonzaga University (The Zags).

RALPH L. PIM

Ralph Pim is an assistant professor in the Department of Physical Education at the United States Military Academy at West Point. He serves as the director of instructional administration and is a basketball sport educator.

Pim has coached and taught basketball at the secondary and collegiate levels for thirty years. As a collegiate head coach, Pim built Alma (MI) College and Limestone (SC) College into highly successful programs. His Alma teams were ranked nationally for points scored and three-point field goals, and the 1989 squad recorded the school's best overall record in forty-seven years. He also coached at Central Michigan, William and Mary, Northwestern Louisiana, and Barberton (OH) High School. Barberton won the 1976 Ohio state championship and was selected the seventh best team in the country.

Pim spent ten years as the technical advisor for the Basketball Association of Wales. He implemented training programs to facilitate the development of basketball in the country of Wales and assisted with the training of their national teams.

Pim is the author of *Winning Basketball* and co-editor of *Coaching Basketball*. He has written numerous coaching articles and is a frequent contributor to the Naismith Basketball Hall of Fame Yearbook and Enshrinement Program.

Pim is a graduate of Springfield (MA) College. He earned his master's degree from The Ohio State University and his doctorate from Northwestern Louisiana State University.

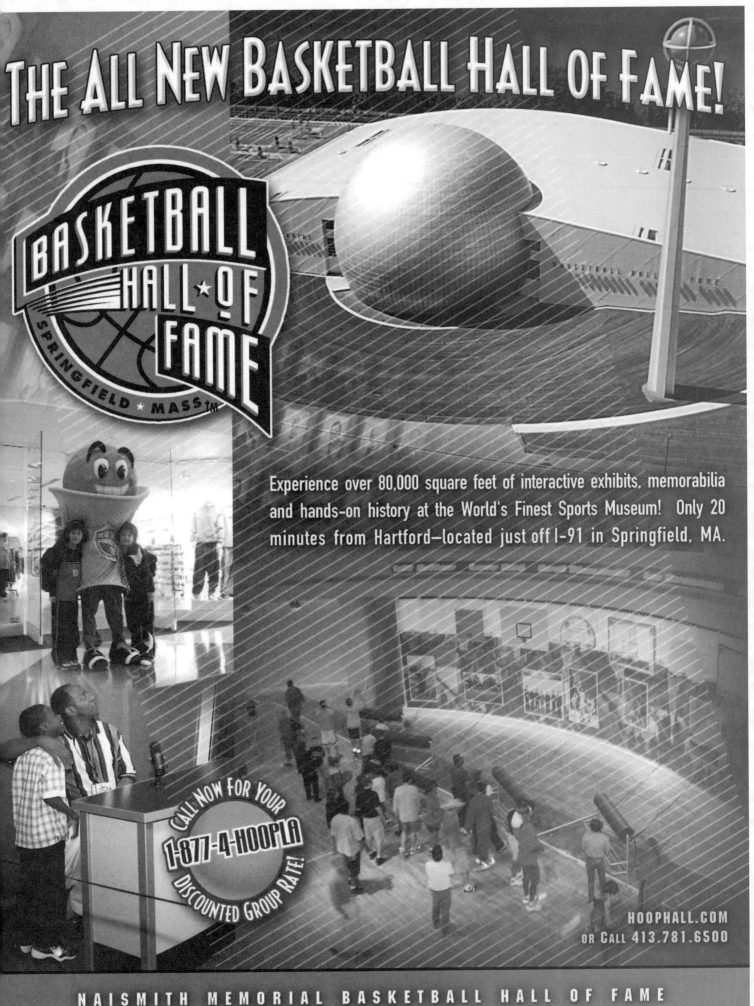